# Sports Fields:

## *A Manual for Design, Construction and Maintenance*

By Jim Puhalla,
Jeff Krans, and Mike Goatley

JOHN WILEY & SONS, INC.

*Library of Congress Cataloging-in-Publication Data:*

Puhalla, Jim.
  Sports fields: a manual for design, construction and maintenance of sports
  fields / by Jim Puhalla, Jeff Krans, and Mike Goatley.
    p.   cm.
    Includes index.
    ISBN 1-57504-070-0
    1. Athletic fields—United States—Design and construction.
  2. Athletic fields—United States—Maintenance and repair.
  3. Sports facilities—United States—Design and construction.
  4. Sports facilities—United States—Maintenance and repair.
  5. Turf management—United States.   I. Krans, Jeff.   II. Goatley, Mike.
  III. Title
  GV413.P85   1999
  786'.06'8—dc21                                              99-11902

CIP

Printed in the United States of America

10   9   8   7   6   5   4   3

# *About the Authors*

**Jim Puhalla** is the president of Sportscape International, Inc., a firm specializing in the design, construction, renovation and maintenance of sports fields and related facilities, with operations in Youngstown, Ohio and Dallas, Texas. Jim is a frequent contributor to *Sports Turf* Magazine.

Jim studied landscape architecture at Ohio State University and accounting at Youngstown State University. He has worked in the sports field industry since 1978, designing, building, or renovating hundreds of fields throughout the Northeast and in Texas. The company's reconstruction of the Boardman High School field won them a 1995 "Baseball Diamond of the Year" Award from *Sports Turf*.

**Jeff Krans** is a Professor of Agronomy at Mississippi State University in the Golf and Sports Turf Management program. He received his Ph.D. from Michigan State University in 1975, an M.S. from the University of Arizona in 1973, and his B.S. from the University of Wisconsin in 1970. He has taught and advised students in the turf management program at Mississippi State since 1976.

Jeff has conducted research in turfgrass germplasm collection and evaluation, tissue culture and cell selection techniques, and turfgrass physiology. His most recent accomplishments include the development, patenting and comercialization of turf-type bermudagrass cultivars MS-Pride, MS-Choice, MS-Express, and MS-Supreme, and the development and release of heat and disease resistant creeping bentgrass germplasm. Jeff is a member and former chairperson of the Turfgrass Science Division of the Crop Science Society of America, and seminar instructor for the Golf Course Superintendents Association of America.

A native of Springfield, Kentucky, **Mike Goatley** is a Professor of Agronomy in the Department of Plant and Soil Sciences at Mississippi State University. Mike received his Ph.D. from Virginia Tech in 1988, his M.S. from the University of Kentucky in 1986, and his B.S. from the University of Kentucky in 1983. He has taught and advised students in the Golf and Sports Turf Management program at Mississippi State since 1988.

Mike has conducted turfgrass research in the areas of plant nutrition, plant growth, regulation, and soil modification. He serves as secretary and Newsletter Editor for the Mississippi Turfgrass Association.

# *Preface*

Like so many aspects of contemporary life, our athletic and leisure pursuits are becoming increasingly influenced by economic and logistical factors. Construction and maintenance budgets are squeezed ever more tightly. The explosion in athletic opportunities for girls and women has doubled the use of some facilities, and sent planners scurrying off to build thousands of new ones. The popularity of personal injury lawsuits has forced insurance premiums higher, and led insurers to insist upon greater uniformity in the design and construction of sports facilities.

All of these factors have their impact on the construction and maintenance of sports fields. Tighter budgets mean less money for after-the-fact repairs, and greater insistence on building it right the first time. Increased pressure on the facilities means that unplayable fields create twice as many rescheduling headaches as they used to. The threat of lawsuits demands greater attention to the safety of the facility itself.

## THE PURPOSE OF THIS BOOK

This book is designed to provide a comprehensive technical reference source for those who are responsible for the design, construction, renovation, or maintenance of sports grounds. In order to address these issues, the chapters that follow will illustrate specific design elements of all popular sports facilities and explain how those elements are integrated in a successful project; explore commonly encountered sports field problems, and suggest appropriate solutions; follow the sequence of steps for construction or renovation of facilities; and provide practical guidance for continuing maintenance programs.

While soil and climate variations will sometimes create unique local challenges for those charged with building or maintaining sports facilities, the principles shared on these pages should provide a basic plan of action and a set of practical design criteria usable throughout North America and in similar geographies throughout the world. Planned and constructed according to these principles, fields will be safer and more usable, easier and cheaper to maintain, visually pleasing, and free of the kind of conditions that can impede athletic performance.

In our discussions, we will divide North America into three general growing zones: *warm season zone*, which includes the sunbelt states of the South and Southwest; the *transitional zone*, which includes Maryland, Virginia, West Virginia, Tennessee, Kentucky, and Missouri and parts of the West and Southwest (see, Figure 1.7, in Chapter 1); and the *cool season* zone, which includes the northern states. Each of these zones has its own characteristic turfgrass needs, and we will share information that is specific to each.

Of course, it must be said that there are some North American ecosystems that define special challenges. South Florida, for instance, presents the challenges of a tropical area, and so does Hawaii, which has the added complication of highly volcanic soil. The Pacific Northwest and Alaska have areas warmed by the Japan current, and other areas where even thinking about sports turf would be absurd. But, generally speaking, the vast majority of sports turf in North America falls into one of our three categories.

## THE PROPERLY EXECUTED FIELD

In approaching any sports field project, whether new construction or the renovation of an existing facility, the planner should keep in mind a number of goals for the finished field:

1. Completion within the budgetary limitation of the owner or other organization financing the work. In approaching any project in today's world, the wise planner will propose the best possible materials and methods, but be ready to suggest less expensive alternatives if necessary.
2. Accommodation within the existing topographic conditions of the site. Obviously, a sports field can't be constructed on the side of a mountain. But a field that is too flat will often prove as difficult to maintain as one that is too sloped. And, in every case, the field must be considered in the context of the local environment, to keep surrounding drainage and other topographic factors from affecting the usability of the facility.
3. The ability to deal with water. In all but the most arid parts of North America, water on the turf is the sports field manager's most common and troublesome headache. Through a combination of grading techniques and internal drainage, a good field should be able to drain away all of the water that falls on it, and be usable in the rain or soon after.
4. The playing surface should be smooth and even, to enhance the quality of the game for both players and spectators, and should be visually attractive.

In order to help the professional design and build a project that meets these goals, this manual includes the critical design criteria for each sport. However, it's important to keep in mind that these criteria are not presented as unquestionable, hard-and-fast rules that must never be broken. Rather, they are practical guidelines that can be used, in combination with local factors, to yield safe and playable sports fields.

## HOW TO USE THIS BOOK

Part I, **Principles of Sports Turf Culture**, provides the reader with information on which to base sound decisions regarding the nurture and maintenance of sports turf. This portion of the book deals with such matters as basic turfgrass and soil science, cultural practices, and stresses placed on turf during sports competition. To achieve the fullest possible value from this volume, it's advisable to begin by reading these chapters.

Part II, **Sports Fields**, provides guidance on the design, construction, renovation, and maintenance of particular types of sports fields. Each chapter combines similar facilities, based on the design and construction strategies and performance expectations of the turf. For example, Chapter 13 covers soccer, lacrosse, and field hockey fields. Field dimensions are provided at the end of each chapter.

The reader will note that this book does not include a chapter on golf courses. Although golf is played on turf, the specialized nature of golf facilities is the subject of many authoritative volumes already, and so we have elected not to deal with that topic here.

Part III, **Other Sports Surfaces**, provides guidance on other types of sports facilities for which a designer, contractor, or facilities manager might be responsible, such as volleyball courts or playground surfaces. Proper design and construction techniques can be particularly important for these facilities, which must be easily maintained in a wide range of usage and weather circumstances.

Part IV, **Quality, Evaluation and Safety of Sports Facilities,** is a review of procedures and equipment currently in use to evaluate the quality and safety of a sports field.

Part V, **Ancillary Information,** covers miscellaneous related topics, including stadium management, sand fields, turf paints and covers, and research likely to have a substantial impact on the future of sports fields.

Throughout the text, we have worked to make this book as useful as possible to those who are charged with keeping sports fields playable and beautiful, and to those students who are preparing for a career in this rewarding field. These pages share much of the latest in academic research and laboratory study of the science of sports turf, but present these latest findings in the form of practical advice for the real world. It is our fondest hope that the result of this book will be a new generation of safe, competitive, and easy-to-maintain sports facilities for people of all ages.

# *Acknowledgments*

The authors gratefully acknowledge the contributions of many academic and professional leaders whose advice and counsel have contributed to the completion of this book.

We thank Vince Paterozzi, head groundskeeper of the National Football League Baltimore Ravens; Marshall Bossard, retired head groundskeeper of the Cleveland Indians; Mike Sekula of Walker Supply Inc., for advice on the selection of materials and for comments and suggestions on the manuscript; and Hank Grover of Western Reserve Land Consultants, for reviewing the material on surveying.

We are appreciative for the advice of the following academic colleagues: Dr. Donald Waddington of The Pennsylvania State University, Andrew McNitt of The Pennsylvania State University, Dr. Coleman Ward (Professor Emeritus) of Auburn University and Dr. Ed McCoy of Ohio State University.

Thanks to James Thompson, Mukundray Patel, Victor Maddox, Wayne Philley, Dr. Don Blasingame, Dr. Pat Harris, Dr. John Byrd, Dr. Euel Coats, Dr. Paul Meints, and Dr. David Nagel, all of Mississippi State University, for providing photographs, information, and manuscript reviews. Thanks to Bart Prather of Mississippi State University and Tra Dubois of World Class Athletic Surfaces for advice on painting athletic fields.

Thanks are also in order to the management of Agro-Tech 2000 and Hunter Industries for their support of the writing of this book (and especially to Don Turner of Hunter Industries for his help in drafting Chapter 7, Irrigation).

Thanks to James Dailey Puhalla for his assistance with the development of architectural drawings used in the book. Thanks also to Henry Pearce for his editorial assistance in crafting a consistent style from copy contributed by the three authors, and for his help in organizing and managing the project.

Thanks to the many sports organizations and sanctioning bodies for sharing their specifications and field construction information, which have helped to make this volume comprehensive. These organizations are listed individually at the ends of their respective chapters. Thanks to the members of the Sports Turf Managers Association Certification Committee for reviewing the proofs of the book.

Special thanks to our colleagues at Mississippi State University, the staff of Sportscape International, Inc., and our wives and families for their patience during the writing of this book. All of these people have tolerated our preoccupation with this manuscript for the past four years.

# Contents

## Part II — Sports Fields

# Part III — Other Sports Surfaces

# Part IV – Quality, Evaluation and Safety of Sports Facilities

# Part V — Ancillary Information

# PART I

# *Principles of Sports Turf Culture*

Sports turf fields and related facilities are designed to meet two basic requirements: they must be large enough and/or the necessary shape to allow the particular sport to be played according to its recognized rules and regulations, and they must have a surface that allows the players to compete safely and at a reasonable level of competition. Because many sports turf surfaces are also used for nonsports activities (like band practice), the surface must be durable enough to withstand the stresses associated with those nonsports functions.

As any sports fan will agree, player performance depends in large part on the quality of the turf surface. But a fields manager must also keep in mind that safety, as well as performance, is dependent on turf quality. Each of these important considerations is dependent on three turf characteristics: *traction, hardness,* and *evenness.*

*Traction* is obviously critical to generating and controlling speed, making sharp changes in direction, and stopping. In addition to reducing a player's ability to avoid or (in the case of contact sports) to control collisions, poor traction can lead to muscle pulls and a variety of other common injuries.

*Hardness* can allow players to perform at maximum speed, but can also affect players' ability to cut sharply, and increase the effects of falls and tackles.

*Evenness*, along with hardness, is a major factor affecting ball response, which includes the height and direction of bounce, as well as the trueness and speed of roll. In many turf sports—and perhaps in most—predictable ball response is necessary to support the desired level of competition.

Just as good teams are created by careful attention to detail, good turf comes from practicing effective turfgrass cultural and management strategies. In the following chapters we will consider the underlying principles of turfgrass biology, selection, establishment; soil science, including fertility and fertilizers; cultivation and thatch management; irrigation and drainage; pesticide use and safety; turfgrass stresses; and even proper mowing techniques.

In the last decade of the twentieth century, one of the most popular catchphrases to sweep over the horticulture industry was "Integrated Pest Management," or "IPM." The theory behind this phrase is that, if the turf or other horticultural system is properly maintained, pests will be easily managed and represent no threat to the intended use of the system.

There is, however, a problem with the concept of IPM: it is centered around the concept of "pests," as though their management were somehow a goal of the horticultural sciences. As a more useful frame of reference for the management of sports turf and related facilities, we begin this book by proposing our own philosophy of horticultural care: "Integrated *Cultural* Management," or "ICM."

The basic difference between IPM and ICM is this: IPM focuses only on pests, but ICM considers all of the stresses that affect the turf. Turfgrass stresses can be divided into three types: *environmental* (temperature, water, light, air, etc.), *mechanical* (foot traffic, cleats, mowing, vehicles), and *pests* (weeds, insects, disease, nematodes).

This difference, while subtle, is important. By carefully managing the entire cultural system of a given sports turf facility—everything from seed selection to mowing—we create conditions which allow for vibrant, healthy, beautiful plants that resist the encroachment of pests of all kinds. ICM is the central operating philosophy on which this entire book is based. Whether reading sections of the text as a class assignment, or flipping it open to address a particular sports turf concern, the reader will find that our advice is to seek first the health of the turf and its enfolding culture, and all the rest (playability, economy, aesthetics) will be added onto it. Manage the culture correctly, and pest problems will be minimized.

# Chapter 1

# *Turfgrasses*

## 1.1  INTRODUCTION

Ironically, it may be true that it was the advent of artificial turf that has done the most to foster appreciation for sports turf as a dynamic and functional system. The sports-consuming public, and many players and coaches, welcomed the appearance of artificial turf with great joy, believing it represented the end of weather hazards and the beginning of a new era in athletic competition.

But after more than 20 years of use, the public in many cities has come to rue the installation of artificial turf. Baseball players compare playing on the material to "playing marbles in the bathtub." Major league baseball let it be known years ago that future expansion franchises would be awarded to owners committed to natural turf fields. Football fans have watched their favorite players come up groggy after landing on the artificial surface, and read the "injured reserve" list of players suffering from "turf toe," infected rug burns, and a host of other injuries.

And now the truth is revealed: turfgrass is one of the most amazing biological systems on the planet. Given a little care, it's soft but quick. It heals its own wounds. It can deal with a wide variety of environmental stresses and come back strong. On top of everything else, it has a beautiful color and, if mowed correctly, snazzy striping that makes a wonderful background for athletic achievements.

## 1.2  BIOLOGY AND IDENTIFICATION

Turfgrass biology is the study of the vital plant processes necessary for turfgrass growth and development. These processes are divided into the categories of morphology, anatomy, and physiology. Turfgrass morphology is the outward form or structure of the turfgrass plant. Turfgrass anatomy consists of the inner cell, tissue, and organ structures that combine to form the whole plant. Turfgrass physiology refers to the metabolic events and pathways that formulate the life processes of the plant. The ability of grasses to survive and persist as turf is due to their specialized morphology, anatomy, and physiology.

Turfgrass cultural practices have a great influence on grasses' ability to adapt as a turf. These cultural practices include mowing as well as seasonal renovations of the turf surface through such practices as aeration, vertical mowing, etc. An understanding of turfgrass biology and turf cultural practices allows us to predict a turfgrass response to these cultural practices, and to have a better understanding of how turf can be managed to help it tolerate injury by pests or by mechanical (competitive) or environmental stresses.

There are 11 grasses commonly used as turfgrasses. Of these 11 species, only 5 are widely used in sports turf situations: bermudagrass, Kentucky bluegrass, tall fescue, perennial ryegrass, and creeping bentgrass as shown in Table 1.1. (Two others, buffalograss and zoysiagrass, are sometimes used for sports turf, but much less frequently.)

Bermudagrass is planted and maintained alone (or as a "monostand") except when overseeded with perennial or annual ryegrass for winter play. Tall fescue, perennial ryegrass, and Kentucky bluegrass are planted and maintained as either monostands or in combination with other cultivars (as "polystands"). Creeping bentgrass is usually planted as a monostand.

The limited use of buffalograss (*Buchloe dactyloides* [Nutt.] Engelm.) and zoysiagrass (*Zoysia* spp.) results from their special characteristics. Buffalograss is a warm season grass with special adaptation to arid and cold habitats. Its limitation is poor wear tolerance, obviously a problem for sports turf. The authors recommend the grasses listed in Table 1.1 as superior choices to buffalograss for sports turf use.

Zoysiagrass, on the other hand, has the ability to adapt to cold habitats and to low-light situations such as moderate shade. One limiting factor of zoysiagrass is its slow recuperation from injury. Zoysiagrass cultivars selected for faster lateral growth rates and shade tolerance are being promoted for sports turf use for the first time in the late 1990s. Only time will tell how these grasses perform.

**Table 1.1. Characteristics of Turfgrasses Commonly Used for Sports Turf**

| Turfgrass Species | Strength as Sports Turf | Limitation as Sports Turf |
|---|---|---|
| Bermudagrass (*Cynodon* spp.) | Strong indeterminate rhizomes and stolons (excellent sod knitting), robust vegetative growth, excellent wear resistance, and good surface resiliency. | Limited to warm climatic regions of U.S., vegetative propagation only of improved types, slow establishment from seeded types. |
| Kentucky bluegrass (*Poa pratensis* L.) | Strong determinate rhizomes (excellent sod knitting), robust vegetative growth, moderate wear resistance, good surface resiliency. | Limited to cool climatic regions of U.S., slow establishment from seed. |
| Tall fescue (*Festuca arundinacea* Schreb.) | Excellent wear resistance, robust primary and vegetative growth, good surface resiliency, adapted to transition zone of U.S. | Limited to transition or warmer regions of U.S., weak determinate rhizomes (poor sod knitting). |
| Perennial ryegrass (*Lolium perenne* L.) | Excellent wear resistance, robust primary and vegetative growth, prolific tillering, rapid seedling growth. | Limited to cool regions of U.S., lacks rhizomes and stolons (very poor sod knitting). |
| Creeping bentgrass (*Agrostis stolonifera* L.) | Tolerates regular mowing at ¼", robust vegetative growth, slow seedling growth, strong stoloniferous growth habit provides recuperative potential. | Limited to cool regions of U.S., drought tolerance is poor, lacks shear strength and resistance to divoting, primary uses are for tennis, lawn bowling, croquet. |

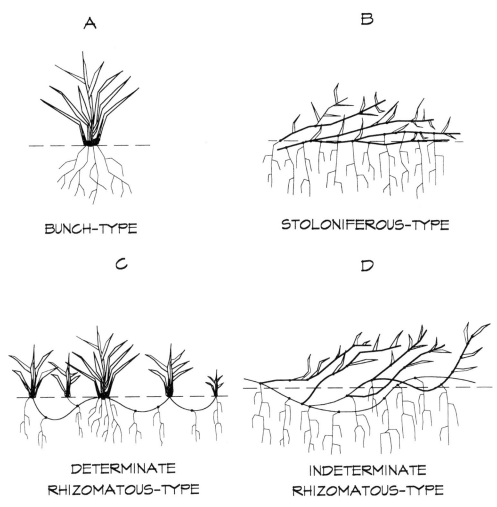

Figure 1.1. *The four morphological types of turfgrasses: (a) bunch-type, (b) stoloniferous, (c) determinate rhizomatous, and (d) indeterminate rhizomatous.*

## 1.2a Turfgrass Morphology

Turfgrass morphology is an important characteristic that allows these *grass plants* to form a dense, compact community when they are cultivated properly. The morphology of turfgrasses can be categorized into four types. These are: (a) bunch-type, (b) stoloniferous, (c) determinate rhizomatous, or (d) indeterminate rhizomatous. (See Figure 1.1 for illustrations of these four morphological types.) All morphological types are designed to keep the plant's growing points at or below the soil surface.

## 1.2b Turfgrass Anatomy

A critical aspect of turfgrass anatomy is the location of growing points (or "meristematic zones"). Localized growing points of turfgrass occur at the stem apexes or buds, leaf blade and sheath mersitems, nodes, root apexes, and root pericycle (see Figure 1.2)

Buds are the origin of all leaf (including blade and sheath meristems) and stem tissue.

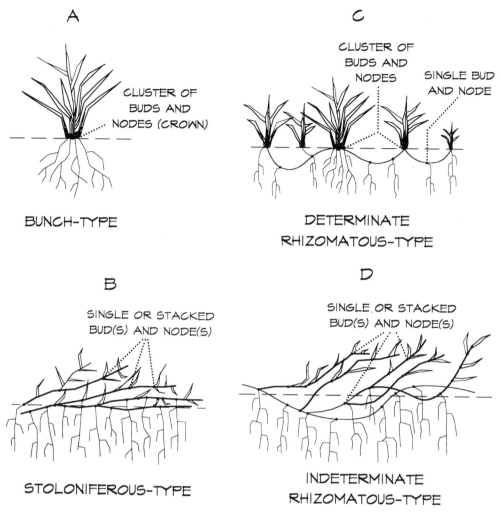

*Figure 1.2. The location of turfgrass growing points: (a) bunch-type turfgrasses, (b) stoloniferous-type turfgrasses, (c) determinate-type turfgrasses, and (d) indeterminate-type turfgrasses.*

*Apical buds* are located at the *apex* or tip of a turfgrass stem and *axillary buds* are located in the *axil* or internal fold of a leaf sheath. Blade and sheath meristems generate leaf blade and sheath structures, respectively, and the blade and sheath combine to make up the whole leaf. Turfgrasses tolerate close cutting because they are able to maintain their blade meristems close to the soil surface. Cutting too close damages the turf canopy by removing leaf tissue at or below their meristems.

Leaf shape is determined by differences in leaf anatomy among turfgrasses. Turfgrass leaves are either *rolled, folded,* or *filaform* (see Figure 1.3).

Rolled leaves have an anatomy of equally distributed and sized vascular bundles, and equally distributed zones of cells with thickened secondary cell wall transecting the turfgrass blade. Folded leaves have equally distributed but different-sized vascular bundles and different-sized zones of cells with thickened secondary cell wall transecting the turfgrass blade. Filaform leaves have equally distributed and sized vascular bundles, but

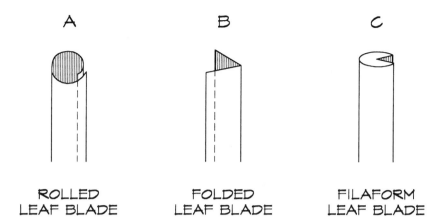

Figure 1.3. *The variation in turfgrass leaf anatomy: (a) rolled leaf, (b) folded leaf, and (c) filaform leaf.*

scattered zones of cells with thickened secondary cell walls distributed throughout the leaf.

*Nodes* are the points of attachment of the axillary stem apexes or buds, leaf blade and sheath structures (including meristems), and adventitious roots. Turfgrass nodes are part of the stem apex in turfgrasses with compressed stems; nodes can be separated by internodes in turfgrasses with elongated stems (see Figure 1.4).

Compressed stems are found on bunch-type and aboveground stems of determinate rhizomatous type turfgrasses. Elongated stems are characteristic of stoloniferous, indeterminate rhizomatous, or belowground stems (rhizomes) of determinate rhizomatous type turfgrasses. Compressed stems are usually less than ⅛ inch long and are found on perennial ryegrass, Kentucky bluegrass, and tall fescue. Elongated stems (multiple nodes with internodes) can range in size from 1 inch to 1 to 2 feet long and are characteristic of Kentucky bluegrass (rhizomes only), bermudagrass, and zoysiagrass. A collection of compressed stems located in a central core is called a node cluster or *crown*. Therefore, crowns are found only in bunch-type and aboveground stems of determinate rhizomatous species only.

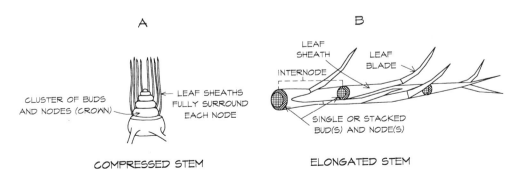

Figure 1.4. *Nodes on turfgrasses with (a) compressed stems or (b) elongated stems.*

## 1.2c   Turfgrass Physiology

Turfgrasses are divided into two groups based on their temperature requirements for optimum growth. Turfgrasses are grouped as *warm season* or *cool season* plant types. Of the five common sports turf species, bermudagrass is classified as a warm season type, and tall fescue, perennial ryegrass, Kentucky bluegrass, and creeping bentgrass are cool season types. These two groups of grasses differ in their physiology and anatomy.

Turfgrass physiology is a complex series of metabolic events. These events can be summarized as *energy capture, energy conversion*, and *energy utilization*.

*Energy capture* is the absorption by the turf of solar radiation through its canopy or leaves. To capture sufficient energy, the turf must have a minimum canopy density. Mowing defoliates the turf's canopy and if the mowing height is too low, the turf can't capture enough energy. In some situations, the canopy of the turf is sufficient to capture adequate energy, but the level of solar radiation is insufficient (e.g., shaded environments). The level of sunlight may be insufficient due to stadium design, or because of nearby trees that shade the field. Obviously, in domed stadiums, the major limitation is insufficient or filtered solar radiation. In sports turf, canopy density may become limited on baseball infields, lawn bowling greens, grass tennis courts, and other areas where close mowing heights are used (see Figure 1.5).

*Energy conversion* includes the processes of photosynthesis and respiration. In both these processes, the high energy compound *adenosine triphosphate* (ATP) is formed. If canopy density and level of sunlight are adequate, the turf can form ATP—provided all the metabolic pathways are stocked with the key substrates. These key substrates include chlorophyll, NADP, and electron transport pathway metabolites. For sports turf, adequate levels of these key substrates are maintained by supplying a proper balance of nitrogen, phosphorous, magnesium, manganese, and iron.

The conversion of carbohydrates to ATP is the *respiration* process. In this process, key substrates include nitrogen, phosphorous, copper, and zinc. Failing to maintain the proper balance or levels of these nutrients can restrict this portion of the energy conversion process (see Figure 1.6).

*Energy utilization* consists of the metabolic events that comprise the growth and development of the turfgrass plants. This component of turfgrass physiology is complex and interdependent on many diverse processes. Key substrates include nitrogen, sulfur, calcium, phosphorous, and potassium.

## 1.3   TURFGRASS SELECTION

In **warm season** areas, sports turf is generally dominated by bermudagrass cultivars. These cultivars flourish in the hot summers and mild winters, and can withstand occasional summer dryness without damage.

In the **transitional zone**, many fields include tall fescues and cold-resistant cultivars of bermudagrass developed specifically for these areas.

In **cool season** areas, Kentucky bluegrass and perennial ryegrass predominate, and a mixture of those species is probably the most popular sports turf. Both types tolerate the cold northern winters adequately, and the mixture allows for the aggressive spreading and recovery characteristic of Kentucky bluegrass, along with the stability and wear resistance of perennial ryegrass. (Figure 1.7 is a map showing the location of different turfgrass zones in the U.S. Table 1.2 shows turfgrasses which can be used in each zone.)

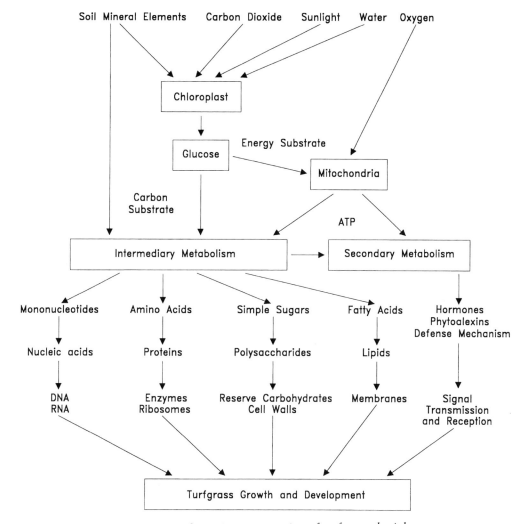

*Figure 1.5. A schematic representation of turfgrass physiology.*

## 1.3a  Warm Season

Bermudagrass (*Cynodon* spp.) is the grass of choice for most warm season sports turf surfaces. While the choices in cultivars of bermudagrasses are quite limited compared to those available for cool season turfgrasses, the growth characteristics, overall appearance, and adaptation of bermudagrass to southern climates gives southern turf managers a quality turf that will respond well to all levels of maintenance—from the high profile game field to the often neglected practice field.

There are a number of bermudagrass cultivars on the market that can be successfully used for sports turf. The standard bermudagrass cultivar for general seeding applications is "Arizona Common," which is popular because of its low cost and quick establishment. Today, however, a wide variety of improved cultivars for seeding are being brought to market. Although these cultivars normally carry a higher price per pound of seed than Arizona Common, they offer substantially higher turf density and finer leaf

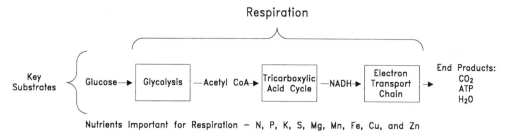

Figure 1.6. *Key substrates and nutrients that support their formation and metabolism.*

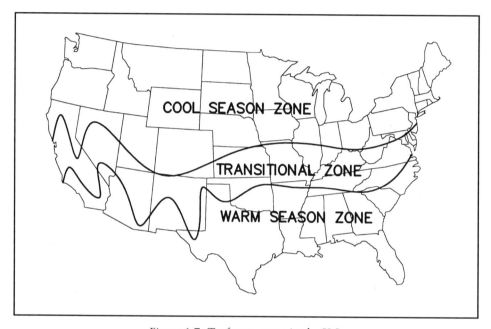

Figure 1.7. *Turfgrass zones in the U.S.*

texture. Because new and improved bermudagrass cultivars appear on the market each year, it's wise to look into the new releases before specifying bermudagrass for sports turf applications.

Although there are many high-quality bermudagrass cultivars for seeding application, the highest quality cultivars are those which must be established vegetatively by sodding, sprigging or plugging. (These grasses must be planted vegetatively because they do not produce viable seeds.) These premium cultivars offer superior density, finer leaf textures, fewer seed heads, and a tolerance for closer cutting.

These vegetatively-established bermudagrasses are commonly referred to in the industry as "hybrid bermudagrasses." However, this designation has led to some confusion when specifying grasses for athletic field establishment. By definition, a hyrid is a cross of individuals with dissimilar genetic constitution. Some seeded bermudagrasses are described as hybrids, but seeded cultivars are "intraspecific" hybrids—crosses within the same species (e.g. *Cynodon dactylon* × *C. dactylon*). Most cultivars which are only established vegetatively have originated from "interspecific" hybridization, between two species (e.g. *C. dactylon* × *C. transvaalensis*).

Table 1.2. Turfgrass Selection for Sports Fields

| Type of Grass | Type of Sport | Cool Season | Transitional Zone | Warm Season |
|---|---|---|---|---|
| Kentucky bluegrass | B, F, S | • | | |
| Perennial ryegrass | B, F, S | • | | |
| Creeping bentgrass | T, LB, C | • | • | |
| Tall fescue | B, F, S | | • | |
| Bermudagrass[a] | All | | • | • |

Code: B = Baseball
      C = Croquet
      F = Footballl
      LB = Lawn bowling
      S = Soccer
      T = Tennis

[a]Cold tolerant varieties must be used in the Transitional Zone.

It is important to understand the distinction in the hybrid bermudagrasses when developing specifications for sports turf. If a specification states only that "the field is to be planted with a hybrid bermudagrass," it can be planted with a lower quality seeded hybrid, and will meet the specifications of the bid. On the other hand, if the desire is for the field to be established with a superior cultivar of vegetatively established bermudagrass, be careful to specify a particular cultivar (or cultivars) of that type. For example,

*Figure 1.8. This group of test plots contrasts two seeded plots in the background with the foreground plot, which was vegetatively established Tifway. Note the superior density of the vegetative Tifway plot.*

Tifway™, Tifway II™, MS-Choice™, MS-Pride™, Tifsport™, and Baby™ are vegetatively established cultivars that provide superior bermudgrass turf.

A new generation of vegetatively established bermudagrasses referred to as "ultradwarfs" is now available for use on tennis, lawn bowling, and croquet playing surfaces. These bermudagrasses are fine-textured and form extremely dense turfs because they have very short internode spacing. They tolerate regular mowing at heights of ⅛″ or less, and can provide a very fast and smooth playing surface. However, the ultradwarf bermudagrasses require a very intensive management program to perform as desired.

## 1.3b  Transition Zone

For managers in the transition zone who want to plant bermudagrass, cold tolerance must be considered. Cultivars such as "Quickstand," "Midiron," "Vamont," "Tufcote," and "Midfield" are noted for their cold hardiness, but they do have slightly lower turf density and coarser leaf blades than the previously mentioned improved hybrids.

Bermudagrass has some limitations as a transitional-zone turfgrass. One of the primary ones is its dormancy period from first frost until midspring; fields that will receive heavy use in the late fall or early spring should be overseeded with perennial ryegrass to support that competition.

(Consult a local agricultural extension agent for more information on the performance of different bermudagrasses in a specific area. Most of the land-grant universities in areas where bermudagrass can be grown will have test plots of the various bermudagrasses available for the planner to examine before making a grass selection.)

Tall fescue (*Festuca arundinacea* Schreb.) can also be used for transition-zone athletic fields, particularly the newer cultivars of "turf-type" tall fescues. Tall fescue is a predominantly bunch-type cool season grass capable of producing determinate rhizomes. The "turf-type" cultivars are much finer textured and form denser turfs than the old forage-type tall fescues (e.g., KY-31, Alta, and others). Tall fescue is a very drought tolerant cool season turfgrass and will provide an acceptable playing surface in transition zone climates. However, the recommended cutting height of tall fescue is 2″ to 3″—a point that must be considered before selecting this grass for sports fields that require shorter turf, like baseball and soccer. Cutting tall fescue at heights lower than this will result in a bunchy, nonuniform turf that will not provide good footing or a smooth ball roll, and it will be subject to heavy weed pressure. The grass will also have less tolerance to temperature and moisture extremes and be more readily damaged by intense foot traffic. It's important to note that tall fescue fields need frequent overseeding to promote turf recovery after heavy use during competitive seasons; overseeding both spring and fall may be necessary on some fields.

(As the reader might have concluded from this advice on turfgrass selection for the transitional zone, this part of North America is a very difficult place to grow quality sports turf!)

## 1.3c  Cool Season

For sports turf in the cool season regions of North America, the primary choices are Kentucky bluegrass (*Poa pratensis* L.) and perennial ryegrass (*Lolium perenne* L.). Creeping bentgrass (*Agrostis stolonifera* L. syn. *A. palustris* Huds.) also finds applications for sports surfaces where very close mowing heights are required.

Kentucky bluegrass forms a dense, dark green turf with medium leaf texture and a rhizome system that spreads laterally, allowing the turf to recuperate strongly from the stresses of competition. The optimal mowing height for Kentucky bluegrass is 1½″ to 3″, with lower heights possible only for short periods, and this limitation is a concern for some sports turf applications. Kentucky bluegrass produces substantial thatch, and requires periodic core aerifying and vertical mowing.

A wide variety of Kentucky bluegrass cultivars is available for seeding, and new cultivars tolerant to closer mowing heights are being developed. In selecting a cultivar of Kentucky bluegrass, one important consideration is aggressiveness. Remember that the more aggressive cultivars also produce the most thatch.

Perennial ryegrass is a bunch-type grass with fine to medium leaf texture and a dark green color. The waxy leaf surface reflects light in a dramatic way, allowing for the striping patterns that can be achieved by mowing in specific directions. Perennial ryegrasses produce a minimal thatch layer. While perennial ryegrass has the same 1½″ to 3″ recommended mowing height as Kentucky bluegrass, perennial ryegrass will tolerate longer periods of close cutting, and will withstand heights as close as ¾″ on a high-profile field. Perennial ryegrass has excellent wear tolerance, but recovers more slowly than Kentucky bluegrass. Perennial ryegrass also germinates rapidly (in 4 to 7 days), adding to its popularity for sports fields.

Many northern fields are planted with a mixture of Kentucky bluegrass and perennial ryegrass. Their similar appearance allows uniform-looking turf, and their complementary performance characteristics combine to form an excellent field. Kentucky bluegrass offers a dark green color, aggressive growth rates, and good recuperative potential. Perennial ryegrass offers exceptional wear resistance, and tolerance for close cutting, as well as rapid seed germination and attractive striping effects. The mixture of these species also helps to protect the turf against disastrous turf loss due to pests, and environmental or mechanical stresses; the genetic diversity of the species builds protection into the turf.

For cool season football fields, a higher percentage of Kentucky bluegrass and a more aggressive cultivar of Kentucky bluegrass will contribute to a thicker thatch layer, which cushions falls better and keeps players up out of the mud in wet weather (see Chapter 5).

Creeping bentgrass is used for playing surfaces like tennis courts, golf greens, croquet courts, and lawn bowling greens, where smooth, fast playing surfaces are required. Creeping bentgrass is regularly cut as short as ¼″, and will actually deteriorate in quality if cut higher than ¾″. Creeping bentgrass is usually mowed daily or every other day, and does best where the clippings are collected. It has an attractive blue-green color and aggressive stoloniferous growth characteristics, but tolerates traffic and drought poorly and is susceptible to disease. High fertilization rates (above 1 pound of nitrogen per month) contribute to rapid thatch development, and frequent topdressing is required to promote biological thatch control and a smooth playing surface.

Several seeded cultivars of creeping bentgrass are available, with many new releases appearing each year. For many years, 'Penncross' has been the cultivar regarded as the industry standard, and it continues to be very popular for sports turf. However, several recently released cultivars offer improved heat and drought tolerance and disease resistance, and these new cultivars should be considered where creeping bentgrass is used in the South and the transition zone, as well as in the North. Even these improved cultivars must be considered to be very high maintenance turf. (Consult with state or regional turfgrass personnel for more information on what cultivars of creeping bentgrass perform best in a particular area.)

A grass that is receiving its first intensive scrutiny for use as a northern sports turf is *Poa supina* L. This grass, popular on sports fields in Europe, is stoloniferous, very wear tolerant, and much more shade tolerant than Kentucky bluegrass. It is very cold-hardy and tolerates regular mowing at ½″ to 1½″. Fertility and cultural management programs for North American use of this grass are currently being researched.

## 1.4   PLANTING TIMES AND RATES

In calculating seeding rates, pay particular attention to the information on the seed tag. Choose seed that was tested for germination no more than one year before the calendar date (and preferably much more recently than one year). Compare germination and purity percentages among choices and select those that are the highest on both accounts. A simple calculation of multiplying the purity percentage by the germination percentage will yield a pure live seed (PLS) percentage in the bag. For example, a 50 pound bag of ABC perennial ryegrass with 95% purity and 95% germination will have a PLS of approximately 90% (.95 × .95 = 90% PLS). This means that a 50 pound bag of seed contains 45 pounds of PLS (50 lb × 90% PLS = 45 lb PLS). All seeding rates should be based on pure live seed in order to ensure the turf density the field needs.

In calculating the amount of seed to apply per 1,000 square feet, divide the desired pounds per 1,000 by the percentage of PLS. For example, if 10 pounds of PLS is desired, the application rate for a cultivar with 90% PLS would be 11 pounds of seed per 1,000 square feet. (Here's the math: 10 ÷ 90% PLS = 11 pounds per 1,000.)

### 1.4a   Warm Season

On warm season fields, the ideal time to **seed** bermudagrass is from midspring to midsummer. Ideal planting conditions are when soil temperatures reach 65°F. Seeding can also be performed in mid- to late summer if good irrigation is available, but remember: the later the grass is planted, the lower the chances of achieving the desired coverage and turf density, and the greater the risk of turf loss due to cold temperature injury.

The typical seeding rate is 1 to 1½ pounds of hulled bermudagrass seed to 1000 square feet (or about 40 pounds of seed per acre). That rate should be doubled when planting unhulled bermudagrass seed. Lower seeding rates can be used if more time can be given for establishment; it's wise to plant turfgrass seed one year for play the next year, because lower seeding rates require a full year for the turf to become firmly established.

**Sprigging and plugging** can likewise be performed when soil temperatures are at least 65°F. In the southern U.S., this will typically be between April 15 and August 15, but the best results will be obtained between May 15 and July 15. Planting later in the summer will increase the risk of winter-kill.

When offering guidance on **sprigging**, most sources of information suggest a recommended rate of planting in terms of "bushels of sprigs per acre." Unfortunately, there is no established guideline to define a "bushel" of sprigs, which can vary according to how the material is handled. Some sod producers in the South define a bushel as about 2,500 sprigs, and recommend planting 400 to 500 bushels of bermudagrass sprigs per acre, sometimes as little as 200 bushels per acre, and sometimes as much as 800 bushels. As one might expect, lower rates cost less but require longer to achieve full field coverage.

When **plugging**, use 2 to 4-inch plugs spaced at 12 inches on center to achieve full coverage in two months.

**Sodding** in warm season areas can take place almost any time of year, as long as temperatures aren't expected to dip substantially below freezing for the first few days after the sod is laid and adequate rainfall or irrigation is available.

## 1.4b  Transitional Zone

In the transitional zone, use the same general planting times and rates as in the South for planting bermudagrass, both when seeding and when planting vegetatively. However, it should be noted that the optimal window for planting is somewhat smaller than for the southern U.S.

Tall fescues are best seeded in late summer, from mid-August to mid-September. Spring fescue plantings can be performed, but are generally less successful. If spring planting is necessary, the ideal time would be March or April, to allow the turf to mature as much as possible before facing the challenges of transitional zone summers.

Use 7 to 10 pounds of seed per 1,000 square feet to maintain a uniform turf and reduce the bunching effect characteristic of tall fescues.

## 1.4c  Cool Season

**Seeding** turfgrasses in cool season zones can take place just about any time the soil can be worked, since the northern grasses allow a longer window of opportunity. The optimum time, however, is usually from mid-August to mid-September. This is because the soil temperatures at that time of year are near-optimum for seed germination, there is more weed competition in the spring, and summer planting requires more water. Although October planting is sometimes performed, it's a risky practice—and the later in October, the riskier. In order to achieve good establishment before the onset of freezing temperatures, it's important that the plants progress to the three-leaf stage of development. If October and November are unusually warm, this development can take place. If not, the plants will still be in a seedling stage in cold weather, and the winter-kill (often due to desiccation) will be especially destructive.

When seeded as monostands, use 2 to 3 pounds of Kentucky bluegrass seed per 1,000 square feet or 7 to 10 pounds of perennial ryegrass seed per 1,000 square feet. If planting a mixture of 50% Kentucky bluegrass and 50% perennial ryegrass, use 4 to 6 pounds per 1,000 square feet.

The window for **sodding** in the North runs from mid-April to mid-November.

(Table 1.3 shows the planting times and rates for different species.)

## 1.5   SOIL PREPARATION

Obviously, a critical step in installing turfgrass, or any type of horticultural system, is soil preparation. The ideal soil preparation techniques apply just as much to sodding as to seeding. And, except for special soil conditions in a few areas, these techniques also apply just as well to all turfgrass zones.

The first step in preparation is to conduct soil tests to determine the nutritional status of the soil; it's foolish to go to the work and expense of installing turfgrass before knowing the condition of the soil. Send in the soil sample at least two weeks before the planned installation, and mark the package "TO BE PLANTED." That lets the staff of the testing laboratory provide their best recommendation for maximum deficiency correction.

Then when the field contours are set and final grading is complete, apply the recommended levels of lime or sulfur and mix it into the soil. If the soil is low in potassium and potash, a recommended application would be 10 pounds[1] of 0-20-20 agricultural

---

[1]Except where otherwise noted, all references to application of seed and fertilizer will be given in terms of the standard pounds per 1,000 square feet.

**Table 1.3. Planting Times and Rates for Sports Turf Species**

| | SEEDING | | |
|---|---|---|---|
| | Type of Grass | Planting Time | lb/1000 |
| Optimum Planting Time Aug 15–Sept. 15 | Kentucky bluegrass | Apr. 15–Sept. 15 | 2-3 |
| | Perennial ryegrass | Apr. 15–Sept. 30 | 7-10 |
| | 50% Ky bg 50% P rye | Apr. 15–Sept. 15 | 4-6 |
| | Creeping bentgrass | Apr. 15–Sept. 15 | 1-1½ |
| | Tall fescue | Mar. 15–Sept. 15 | 7-10 |
| Optimum Planting Time May 15–July 15 | Bermudagrass (hulled seed) | Apr. 15–Aug. 15 | 1-1½ |
| | Bermudagrass (unhulled seed) | Apr. 15–Aug. 15 | 2-3 |

| | SPRIGGING | | |
|---|---|---|---|
| Optimum Planting Time May 15–July 15 | Type of Grass | Planting Time | Sprigs/sq ft |
| | Bermudagrass | Apr. 15–Aug. 15 | 20-25 |

| | PLUGGING (2″ to 4″ diameter plugs @ 12″ o.c.) | | |
|---|---|---|---|
| Optimum Planting Time May 15–July 15 | Type of Grass | Planting Time | Sq ft sod/ 1000 sq ft |
| | Bermudagrass | Apr. 15–Aug. 15 | 110 |

| SODDING | |
|---|---|
| Type of Grass | Planting Time |
| All | Above Freezing Temperatures |

grade fertilizer mixed into the top 6 inches of soil, then 5 pounds of 18-24-12 turf grade slow-release fertilizer spread on top with the seed.

It's important to loosen the soil to a depth of at least 6 inches to let the roots of the plants develop. Probably the most common method of soil loosening is tilling, but tilling displaces soil particles, which then tend to resettle in a denser, harder form. A better method is to use an agricultural cultivator, an implement that is returning to popularity in connection with no-till farming methods. (This implement is also called a "scarifier," or an "earthcavator" in some areas.)

When preparing to install turfgrass, it's wise to keep all construction equipment off the field whenever it's wet or damp. Heavy equipment compacts wet soil so much it can inhibit the growth of roots later, and can also cause water to run off instead of penetrating to the roots of the turfgrass where it needs to be. What's more, the pore space is reduced, cutting off the flow of oxygen to the roots. The result can be conditions that promote disease and cause a very slow recuperative potential that requires extra aerating (see Chapter 4) to correct.

A common error in constructing new fields is to use a heavy roller to compact the sub-base and even the topsoil to 98% compaction, as would be typical in building a roadway. In fact, the tracks of a bulldozer used to grade the field, combined with normal rainfall, will usually provide sufficient compaction to produce a healthy field.

## 1.6 PLANTING TECHNIQUES

### 1.6a Seeding

When seeding, use a rotary or drop spreader to apply the seed evenly at the rates listed in Table 1.3. A centrifugal (rotary) spreader works well if there is little wind blowing. With centrifugal spreaders, be sure to overlap the area of spread at least 25% (e.g., a 12-foot spread means the operator should overlap 3 feet). Drop spreaders can be used at almost any time with little regard for the wind, but the operator must be careful to overlap wheel tracks in order to avoid skips. It's a good idea to apply half the seed in one direction, then apply the other half in a perpendicular direction. Just calibrate the spreader for half the rate listed and go over the area twice. Carefully rake the seed into the soil using a leaf rake, then lightly roll to improve seed-to-soil contact. Mulching allows faster germination.

### 1.6b Pregermination

Seed pregermination, sometimes called "prehydration," is a technique by which the germination time is reduced from a few days to a few hours by specially treating the seed prior to planting. One of the simplest methods used in pregermination is to put the seed in a cloth bag and soak it in a large drum of warm water for at least 12 hours. Be sure to "aerate" the seed by lifting the bag out of the water and dropping it back in several times every few hours (an air line can also be run to the drum to bubble the water). Additionally, the plant hormone gibberellic acid, or "GA," can be added to the water to further speed up germination. Most home and garden centers carry different formulations of gibberellic acid for various horticultural applications. When using a GA treatment, be sure to follow all label directions very closely; as with any chemical treatment, higher-than-recommended concentrations can actually prevent germination rather than enhance it.

If it will be spread using a drop or rotary spreader, the seed must be dried out following soaking to allow it to pass through the spreader properly. Drying is usually accomplished by pouring out the seed on a clean concrete floor or a piece of plastic. The seed will need to be stirred periodically in order to encourage drying. When the seed is dry, it is ready to spread. The drying process is not necessary if the seed will be spread by hydroseeding or by fluid drilling.

Pregerminated seed should be applied within 24 hours (sooner, if possible), to prevent desiccation.

Pregermination is not required under normal circumstances, but it is a common practice of sports turf managers who need rapid grass emergence on heavily used athletic fields.

### 1.6c Dormant Seeding

One technique sometimes used successfully in the North is "dormant seeding," the application of seed during the late fall or winter months when cold temperatures will prevent germination. Dormant seeding should not be used as the primary seeding method for a newly-seeded field; this method is best suited to overseeding by slit-seeding on an existing field. A heavy field use schedule can make dormant seeding the best alternative

*Figure 1.9. The daily freeze/thaw cycle of late winter in the North creates this cratering effect in the soil, encouraging seed:soil contact and assisting in the process of dormant seeding.*

for getting grass onto a poorly drained field that stays so wet in the spring that equipment can't be taken onto it.

The success of dormant seeding is heavily influenced by the weather of the particular winter. The ideal winter weather for dormant seeding is consistent cold to prevent premature germination, continuous snow cover to maintain a steady moisture level, and little rain to wash the seed off the soil. The worst weather would be heavy winter rain or no winter precipitation at all, which would lead to desiccation. Under any circumstances, seedling mortality is quite high with dormant seeding, so seeding rates should be increased as much as 50% or more above the normal rates.

There is one time of year when seed can be broadcast with no soil preparation as a way to thicken an existing field. In northeast Ohio, for instance, that period normally occurs around the last week of February and the first week of March. At this point in the season, the daily cycle of freezing at night and thawing in the daytime tends to create ideal conditions for seed:soil contact. To identify this window of opportunity in a specific area, watch for small "craters" in the soil in the early morning which flatten out by afternoon, helping to draw the seed into the soil (see Figure 1.9 for an illustration of these craters)

Dormant seeding has been most successful with cool season turfgrasses, because these grasses are used in climates where winter temperatures remain cold enough to inhibit germination. Dormant seeding in the South and Transitional Zone with bermudagrass or tall fescue is normally unsuccessful, because periodic warm temperatures promote seed germination, and the seedlings are killed when the mercury falls again.

*Figure 1.10. Bermudagrass sprigs, such as this one, can be successfully planted in prepared soil.*

## 1.6d  Sprigging

If sodding is cost-prohibitive, an alternative method of vegetative installation of improved bermudagrass cultivars in the South is "sprigging." A "sprig" is defined as a vegetative stem (a rhizome or a stolon) that has multiple nodes that will initiate growth when properly planted (see Figure 1.10.) This practice begins by preparing the soil as if for seeding or sodding, then planting the sprigs into the prepared soil. Sprigging is obviously more affordable than sodding, but takes several weeks longer to fully establish the turfgrass.

A typical sprigging implement is a disc-like machine that is pulled behind a tractor with vertical discs. The sprigs are randomly distributed over the soil surface and the sprigger's pans press them into the soil. Commercial planters often use a row planter for sprigging. These machines create small furrows into which the sprigs are dropped. The soil is then pressed firmly around the sprigs (see Figure 1.11.) This technique of planting the sprigs into furrowed soils improves the success of the process by increasing plant material:soil contact. If a sprigging machine or a row planter is unavailable, it is also possible to perform sprigging by simply spreading the sprigs over the prepared soil and then topdressing with ¼″ to ½″ of matching soil material.

## 1.6e  Plugging

"Plugging" turf is another viable means of planting sports turf in the South, although a much more labor-intensive one, especially for a large area. Major advantages of this technique are that no special equipment is required, and that the properly planted plugs are unlikely to dry out. Although plugs of any size can be used, the standard practice is

*Figure 1.11. This sprigging machine creates small furrows into which the sprigs are pressed for good sprig:soil contact.*

to use 4″ diameter plugs of turf planted on the field at 12″ centers; this rate will usually provide sufficient plant material to cover within two months.

Of course, closer spacing of the plugs will decrease establishment time, and smaller plugs or wider spacing will increase the time needed to cover. A standard golf-green cup cutter is an ideal tool both for cutting the plugs and for creating the holes to plant them in.

The main limitation of plugging is the labor required, so plugging tends to be most commonly used for renovating small areas.

### 1.6f  Sodding

Sod is typically supplied in one of several forms: square-cut sod is delivered in rectangular pieces. Rolled sod arrives at the site in sections 18″ wide × 6′ in length. Both of these forms are installed by hand. Big roll sod is supplied in rolls that can be 24″ or more wide and up to 40′ long, and must be installed using a machine (see Figure 1.12.)

When installing any form of sod, be careful to keep the seams tight. A common mistake is to position the sod by pulling on it. That can stretch the sod, and it will eventually shrink back to its original size, causing gaps in the turf. Take pains to water new sod liberally for the first two weeks, because letting the sod dry out too much will also contribute to shrinkage. A week or so after installation, inspect the job for any gaps that appear (even with well-installed sod, there are usually a few). Fill the gaps with matching soil and hand-seed or plug with matching turfgrass.

It's a good idea to choose a sod that has been grown on a soil that is physically and

*Figure 1.12. Big roll sod must be installed using a machine to maneuver the heavy rolls as the sod is put in place.*

chemically similar to that of the field on which the sod will be installed. That is particularly important on modified, sand-based fields. Sod that is grown on clay or organic soils and then installed on a sand-based field will not root properly and will be a constant maintenance problem, due to the layering effect of the dissimilar soils. The layering of different-textured soils results in reduced water infiltration and percolation rates. For installation on a field that has undergone complete soil modification to a sand-based soil, it's important to specify sod that has been grown in a similar sand-based material. Alternatively, the sod may be washed to remove any existing soil before installation.

Another important consideration in choosing sod is its age. Field managers are advised to choose the oldest sod available to them, because more mature sod has a more developed thatch layer, and is preferable to young sod that has netting to hold it together. This netting can be a problem on sports turf, especially for high-use football fields, where players' cleats can snag in the netting.

Some sod installation is performed by "dormant sodding"—the installation of turf in which the plants are in a dormant phase. While installing the turf during the growing season is the preferred method, it is possible to achieve successful dormant sodding. If this method is being considered, it is important to note a common mistake: failing to water adequately. Some installers wrongly conclude that the dormant sod needs no water, but dormant sod still needs water to root and establish. Although dormant sodding requires less water than sodding during the summer months, failure to water at all can desiccate the sod.

## 1.7   ESTABLISHMENT

For the purposes of our discussion, the term "establishment" refers to all steps taken to promote a viable stand of sports turf after installing turfgrass seed, sprigs, plugs, or sod.

### 1.7a   Establishing Seeded Fields

After seeding, water lightly and frequently to keep the top quarter-inch of soil moist until the seed germinates. Then begin gradually changing the watering schedule. Instead of trying to keep the top quarter-inch of soil moist all the time, begin to reduce the frequency and increase the volume of water applied at any given time. This will encourage the development of a deeper root system. Begin mowing when it's possible to observe the one-third rule,[2] cutting off the top third of the plants.

**Warm season** fields seeded with bermudagrass can be ready to use within two months after seeding if the timing is correct, and if the turf is liberally fertilized and irrigated (but longer establishment periods will result in a field with better resistance to wear). Have the soil tested for correct soil chemistry before planting, and then apply one-half pound of nitrogen per week until the turf is fully established, keeping the field moist but not saturated.

Tall fescues seeded in the **transitional zone** need at least four months before the fields can be safely used. Fields should be seeded in the late summer for use the following spring, if possible. Spring plantings should not be used until the fall, and even that interval may be too short for tall fescue turfs, especially if the summer is particularly hot and dry.

Tall fescue fields planted in the late summer should get one pound of nitrogen per month until the growing season ends. Fields planted in the spring should get one pound of nitrogen the first month, but fertilization rates should be reduced sharply—to one-half pound or less—after the first month. Overfertilization in the spring will inhibit the root growth the plants will need to survive the summer. Tall fescue that is overfertilized in the spring can also be susceptible to disease.

In **cool season** areas, perennial ryegrass and tall fescue fields take about four months to become firmly established after seeding, and it helps to apply one pound of nitrogen per month for the first four months. Kentucky bluegrass isn't firmly established for a full year, and it also needs monthly fertilization with one pound of nitrogen throughout the growing season.

### 1.7b   Establishing Sprigs and Plugs

In planting turf by sprigging or plugging, remember that planting rates have a good deal to do with how quickly the turf is fully established. It's important to remember that full establishment has not necessarily been achieved just because the entire area has grass on it. A field may be covered with grass, and still not be ready for play. Newly planted turf can easily be damaged by heavy traffic, and the limited rhizome and stolon development of immature turf will reduce the turf's recuperative potential.

Newly planted sprigs have a tendency to turn brown. Continue to water lightly and frequently, and they will soon reinitiate growth and green up again; use the same basic watering schedule that would be used with a newly seeded field. Fertilize a newly

---

[2]This is one of the most important and often-violated rules of sports turf management. Mow fields in such a way as to cut off the top third of the plants each mowing. Follow the recommended mowing heights in Chapter 6.

sprigged field at one to two pounds of nitrogen a month, and begin mowing according to the one-third rule.

After plugging, the field needs to be kept on the wet side for two weeks to allow the roots of the plugs to catch. Then water at rates typical of established turfgrass. Apply one pound of nitrogen a month for the duration of the establishment period, and observe the one-third rule for mowing.

Ideally, fields should be planted in the spring and allowed at least two months for establishment before competitive use.

## 1.7c  Establishing Sodded Fields

A newly sodded field in any zone needs to be kept on the wet side for two weeks to allow the roots to catch, then watered at rates typical of established turfgrass. The staff can start mowing as soon as the field will support tractor weight without rutting. With adequate irrigation and no more than moderate rainfall, the team should be able to use

**Table 1.4. Germination and Establishment Periods[a, b, c]**

| | **SEED** | | |
| Type of Grass | Germination Period | Establishment Period[d] | Nitrogen Requirement[e] |
| --- | --- | --- | --- |
| Kentucky bluegrass | 15–20 days | 1 year | 1 lb /month |
| Perennial ryegrass | 4–7 days | 4 months | 1 lb /month |
| 50% Ky bg 50% P rye | 4–20 days | 4 months | 1 lb /month |
| Creeping bentgrass | 15–20 days | 4 months | 1 lb /month |
| Tall fescue | 10–15 days | 4 months | 1 lb /month |
| Bermudagrass (hulled seed) | 10–15 days | 2 months | ½ lb /week |
| Bermudagrass (unhulled seed) | 15–20 days | 2 months | ½ lb /week |
| | **SPRIGS** | | |
| Type of Grass | Rooting Period | Establishment Period | Nitrogen Requirement |
| Bermudagrass | 10–14 days | 2 months | ½ lb /week |
| | **PLUGS** | | |
| Type of Grass | Rooting Period | Establishment Period | Nitrogen Requirement |
| Bermudagrass | 10–14 days | 2 months | ½ lb /week |
| | **SOD** | | |
| Type of Grass | Rooting Period | Establishment Period | Nitrogen Requirement |
| All | 10–14 days | 4–6 weeks | 1 lb /month |

[a]Watering requirements for each planting method are included in the text in this section.

[b]Observe the one-third mowing height requirement.

[c]All planting methods require some degree of renovation after using the field for practice or competition (see Renovation plus Maintenance and Management Procedures for each sport, Chapters 11–14.

[d]For seeding, sprigging, and plugging it is desirable to plant one year for play the next to allow the turf to mature as much as possible before using it for completion.

[e]During the establishment period, apply nitrogen at the listed rates until the desired turf density is achieved. Then follow the recommended fertilization rates for established turf in Chapter 3.

the field in four to six weeks. One pound of nitrogen a month for the rest of the growing season helps get the sod solidly established.

(Table 1.4 shows the germination and establishment periods for different turfgrass species.)

## 1.8    OVERSEEDING WARM SEASON FIELDS

Questions always arise concerning the positive and negative effects of overseeding on winter survival of bermudagrass fields. There is no doubt that the competition from the overseeding is a major detriment to the overall health of the bermudagrass. After spending an entire growing season trying to control other grassy weeds in the bermudagrass, overseeding essentially "reverses" normal practice—seeding millions of "weeds" into the bermudagrass turf. On the other hand, it is true that the overseeding does offer some protection for the bermudagrass on a heavily used field against physical wear and tear. For this reason, it is recommended that fields receiving heavy use throughout the fall and winter months be overseeded. Under those circumstances, if the field is *not* overseeded, it is likely to have no turf (dormant bermudagrass or otherwise) when the next season arrives.

### 1.8a    Selecting Turfgrass for Overseeding

A practice unique to southern sports turf management is overseeding bermudagrass athletic fields in early- to mid-fall with either annual ryegrass (*Lolium multiflorum* L.) or perennial ryegrass (*L. perenne* L.). Each type has its own set of characteristic strengths and weaknesses as shown in Table 1.5.

Annual ryegrasses are cheaper, they germinate and establish quickly, and they transition quickly in the spring. On the other hand, annual ryegrass tolerates wear and extreme temperatures less successfully, and is more vulnerable to disease. It also grows so fast it requires frequent mowing, and it is more likely to stain uniforms.

The selections in annual ryegrass are limited; only a few cultivars developed for pas-

## Table 1.5.  Perennial Ryegrass and Annual Ryegrass Comparisons

| Strengths | Weaknesses |
|---|---|
| **Annual Ryegrass** | |
| • economical cost | • poor wear tolerance |
| • rapid germination | • poor extreme temperature tolerance |
| • excellent seeding vigor | • disease vulnerability |
| • rapid spring transition | • may transition too quickly |
| | • rapid growth requires frequent mowing |
| | • stains sports uniforms |
| | • no sports turf-specific cultivars |
| **Perennial Ryegrass** | |
| • rapid germination | • seed is more expensive than annual ryegrass |
| • very good seeding vigor | • spring transition to Bermudagrass |
| • improved pest resistance | can be difficult |
| • good extreme temperature tolerance | |
| • excellent wear resistance | |
| • slow spring transition | |

ture use are commonly available. No improved annual ryegrass cultivars have yet been developed for turf use, so the sports turf manager will pretty much have to use whatever is available in the local market area.

Perennial ryegrass cultivars, on the other hand, provide substantially improved durability. They're more resistant to disease, insects, extreme temperatures, and wear. Like the annual cultivars, they germinate and establish quickly. Perennial ryegrasses transition more slowly in the spring, which can be an advantage for spring sports like baseball, where the remaining perennial ryegrass can help to support play. However, the transition back to bermudagrass in the spring can be somewhat difficult to manage, since the remaining perennial ryegrass will tend to compete with the bermudagrass.

Perennial ryegrass is clearly superior to annual ryegrass as a choice for overseeding athletic fields, but the lower initial cost per pound of seed still results in the use of a substantial amount of annual ryegrass. However, it's always important to distinguish between "price" and "cost." Although the *price* of annual cultivars is lower, the rapid growth rates of annual ryegrass require more frequent mowing, so some of the initial savings are quickly lost. Over a longer term, the *cost* of annual cultivars may be higher.

Today, sports turf managers have a tremendous range of choices for perennial ryegrass. There are many quality cultivars that provide excellent overseeding performance. An extension agent or state university turfgrass management research program can provide information on perennial ryegrass selections that have performed favorably in a specific area. There should be several options available, and the experts might suggest the purchase of a prepared blend of perennial ryegrass cultivars. Choosing blends of two or more cultivars broadens the genetic diversity of the turfgrass, and serves as a kind of insurance; if one grass fails due to disease or environmental extremes, then one or two other grasses in the blend may survive and thrive.

An additional option offered with some perennial ryegrass seed is pretreatment with a fungicide to prevent seedling damping-off incited by the soilborne *Pythium* fungi. This will be an added expense, but the treatment does help increase the chances of overseeding success by controlling or at least suppressing this devastating disease organism at a time when the plant is most vulnerable to damage. Perennial ryegrass seed that is "endophyte-enhanced" is also available. Unlike other fungi that can incite turf diseases, the "endophytic" fungus contained in this seed is actually desirable, producing seedlings (and ultimately turf) that has enhanced drought, insect, and heat tolerance.

A relatively new development in sports turf management is the use of *intermediate* ryegrasses (*Lolium perenne* L. × *L. multiflorum* Lam.) for winter overseeding. The first release of these grasses in the mid 1990s was accompanied by claims that the intermediate ryegrasses were cheaper alternatives to perennial ryegrass, but still provided sports turf with the desirable appearance, growth, and playing characteristics of perennial ryegrass. Only time will tell if these grasses will take a significant share of the market for overseeding.

## 1.8b  When to Overseed

The overseeding date should be scheduled far in advance. As a matter of fact, the seed for overseeding should be ordered in the spring of the year to ensure adequate availability of seed for the fall planting period. As far as planting date goes, the windows of planting opportunity for southern turf managers are: September 1 to about September 22 for the upper South; September 15 to October 8 for the mid-South; and October 1 to October 21 for the deep South (see Table 1.6, Overseeding Dates).

These windows are not absolute, but they are based upon a time when the soil tem-

Table 1.6. Overseeding Dates

| Overseeding Bermudagrass with Ryegrass | |
| --- | --- |
| Zone | Time of Year |
| Upper South | Sept. 1–Sept. 22 |
| Mid-South | Sept. 15–Oct. 8 |
| Deep South | Oct. 1–Oct. 21 |

peratures are most favorable for the germination of ryegrass—65–70°F at a 4″ depth. Overseeding can be done earlier or later than the recommended windows, depending on the situation. However, overseeding too early can result in poor establishment because of too much competition from the bermudagrass, and overseeding too late will result in poor establishment because of reduced seed germination.

## 1.8c  The Mechanics of Overseeding

A good first step in the overseeding process is to conduct a soil test, unless one has been performed within the last year. (In some cases, if a previous soil test indicated the need for substantial remediation of the soil chemistry, a second test is the only way to discover the current condition of the soil.) Apply any fertilizers recommended by the soil test, being careful not to apply excessive nitrogen that will promote further competition from the bermudagrass. For most overseeding applications, one-half pound of nitrogen is more than sufficient. A supplemental phosphorus application is recommended to promote root establishment of the perennial ryegrass seedlings.

One of the keys to successful overseeding is to ensure there will be good soil:seed contact. If any vertical mowing (verticutting) is needed, be sure it is done well in advance of overseeding in order to avoid potential winter injury to the bermudagrass base. This means verticutting several times during the summer to prepare the bermudagrass base for overseeding in the fall.

When it's time to overseed, begin by mowing the turf to its lowest recommended level (typically ¾″ for most sports turf). Then spread the seed in at least two different directions to avoid skips. After spreading, mat or drag the seed into the turf to encourage seed:soil contact. A light topdressing (⅛″ to ¼″ depth) with sand or with soil similar to the existing soil will improve seed:soil contact.

Typical perennial ryegrass overseeding rates are from 10 to 20 pounds of pure live seed per 1,000 square feet.

To optimize germination, initiate a program of light and frequent watering (a few minutes of irrigation every couple of hours or so). The goal is to ensure that the seed does not dry out, but not to keep the area saturated—a common mistake in irrigating newly seeded turfs. Maintain the irrigation program until the seed germinates, and then gradually reduce the watering frequency until finally reaching the point of applying moisture "deeply and infrequently" to encourage the development of a deep root system and a mature, well-established turf.

For the first couple of mowings, do not collect clippings, because of the chance of removing substantial amounts of seed.

## 1.8d  Winter Care

The maintenance needs of an overseeded turf will depend largely on how frequently it is used. For late fall and early spring sports, the field will have to be fertilized, mowed, and irrigated on a regular basis, according to the needs of the turf. As long as temperatures remain above freezing, the overseeded perennial ryegrass will be growing, and when the temperatures rise above 50°F the growth will accelerate. It's important to continue mowing and other maintenance functions, even during periods of low use or no use, if the turf is to be in good condition when the competitive season arrives.

Fertilization rates also depend on field use and environmental conditions. There is little benefit in applying fertilizer to turf that is not actively growing; the fertilizer is wasted, and can actually become a pollution concern. However, actively growing turf does need regularly scheduled fertilizer applications. Heavily used fields need a pound of nitrogen a month from a water-soluble fertilizer source. Lower-use fields can be maintained at about half that rate. Avoid unnecessary fertilization of overseeded ryegrasses, which can create tremendous mowing requirements and make the turf more susceptible to winter-kill and disease.

If soil testing indicates the need for phosphorus, potassium, or other nutrients, they can also be applied in the winter, but both the bermudagrass and the overseeded ryegrass can make greater use of these nutrients if they are applied at the time of overseeding, before the winter months.

Many parts of the country get enough rainfall to make supplemental irrigation unnecessary. However, if winter precipitation rates are low in the area, both overseeded and base turfs must be irrigated enough to provide for their moisture requirements. Winter desiccation of warm season turfgrasses is a vastly underappreciated contributor to winter-kill, because its effects are not visible on dormant grass. On overseeded ryegrass, wilt symptoms provide a clear indicator of moisture stress. It's important to monitor precipitation levels and provide irrigation when needed to sustain active growth. Application of one-half inch of water per week is generally sufficient to keep the overseeded ryegrass actively growing.

## 1.8e  Spring Transition

At some point, the high temperatures and lack of moisture associated with the typical weather patterns of the mid- to late spring in the South will result in significant loss of the overseeded turf, and the return to a bermudagrass field. This is actually a desirable feature of a successful overseeding event. A totally successful transition period would be one that is not noticed—the general public would not realize that one grass was dying and was being replaced by another. Of course, accomplishing such a "seamless" transition is easier said than done.

The complete transition back to bermudagrass can be best accomplished by adapting the fertility, irrigation, and mowing programs to favor the bermudagrass. This will normally involve increasing nitrogen fertility levels, reducing irrigation, and lowering mowing heights—all strategies that favor the bermudagrass.

Keep in mind that for spring baseball and soccer, the overseeding transition strategy can be just the opposite of that described above—keeping the perennial ryegrass alive until the spring season is over will result in an improved playing surface. Extending the life of the perennial ryegrass can be just as challenging as managing a successful transition back to bermudagrass. The best management strategy is to carefully supply irrigation in amounts that will maintain perennial ryegrass growth as long as possible, particularly during periods when the turfgrass is subjected to stress.

# Chapter 2

# *Soils and Soil Science*

## 2.1 INTRODUCTION

Soil is the upper layer of the earth's crust, and consists of loose, weathered, and finely ground mineral particles and organic matter that form a matrix interspersed with pores. The particles of mineral and organic matter, with their irregular size and shape, are consolidated by natural forces to form soil "aggregates," larger particles of mixed composition. The formation of these soil aggregates creates fractures or channels through the soil, and these channels are the principal source of pore space in soils. The total volume of pores in soils is referred to as soil porosity. (Figure 2.1 is a drawing of a soil matrix, illustrating mineral particles, organic matter, pore spaces, and soil aggregate.)

Soil selected and managed for sports fields is expected to perform one of two functions: serve as a **medium for turf growth,** or provide a uniform **hard surface.** The most common function, of course, is to serve as a medium in which turfgrass can grow. While specific demands placed on the soil are different for each sporting event, soil operates as a medium for turf growth by trapping nutrients and water and making them available to

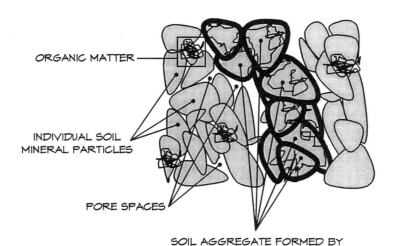

ORGANIC MATTER

INDIVIDUAL SOIL
MINERAL PARTICLES

PORE SPACES

SOIL AGGREGATE FORMED BY
THE CEMENTING TOGETHER OF SOIL
PARTICLES WITH ORGANIC MATTER RESIDUE

*Figure 2.1. Soil matrix.*

29

the roots of the plants, by providing space for air to reach the roots, and by serving as an anchor for those roots. Soil used for a hard surface, as in the "skinned area" of a baseball diamond must be uniform in texture to allow predictable ball response, solid enough to provide good footing, and loose enough at the surface to allow sliding by base runners.

## 2.2   SOIL AS A MEDIUM FOR TURFGRASS

Since the soil is expected to serve as a medium for the passage of water, nutrients, and air, the quality of a soil is judged by its ability to supply these growth requirements. High-quality turf soil has sufficient organic material to allow for the absorption and slow release of moisture and nutrients, and adequate-sized mineral particles to preserve porosity so that air can be delivered to the roots of the plants. The organic material also helps to give the soil good "stability," which for our purposes will refer to the ability of the soil to deal with mechanical stresses and moderate rainfall without collapsing into a soupy mud.

### 2.2a Plant Growth Requirements
When evaluating soil for plant growth requirements, some of most important considerations are available water, nutrients, and air.

*Water*
Although the turf relies on the soil for its supply of water, not all the water in soil can be extracted by plants. Water extracted from the soil enters the plant through its roots, and is transported throughout the plant in its vascular system. The water that can be extracted from the soil by the roots of the plants is called *available* water. Water that is present in the soil, but which cannot be taken up by the roots of the plants, is called *unavailable* or "nonextractable" water.

It's important to be aware that turfgrasses vary in their ability to extract water from soil. Therefore, water that is unavailable to one turfgrass species may be available to another species. The mechanism that holds water unavailable in the soil is the cohesion and adhesion forces of water and soil, and since different species have varying ability to overcome those forces, their ability to extract moisture varies correspondingly.

Turf uses water in a number of different ways, all equally important to the survival of the plant. Water is necessary for the plant's metabolic functions to occur. The nutrients which sustain the plant are dissolved in water and transported throughout the plant. The plant uses water to moderate its tissue temperature, and especially to counteract heat buildup due to the absorption of radiation (sunlight) by leaves and stems. Water also supplies hydrogen ions as a substrate (Hill's reaction) that combines with carbon (from $CO_2$) to form carbohydrates (in the so-called "dark reaction" of photosynthesis).

Given the variety and importance of these functions, the ability of soil to make moisture available to the roots of the plants is obviously critical to the overall turfgrass culture. Obstruction of this function may occur due to such mechanical problems as over-compaction, either by foot traffic or by excessive rolling. Heavily compacted soil can lose its porosity to the degree that it will not allow water to penetrate to the root zone of the turf plants. Soil that is too sandy will also fail to provide water, but for the opposite reason: lacking sufficient organic material, sandy soil will simply allow water to run through, beyond the reach of plant roots. (Clayey soils have good water holding capacity because of their strong attractive forces for water retention.)

**Table 2.1. Essential Turfgrass Nutrients and Functions**

Name, Symbol, Function, and Deficiency Symptom of Soil-Derived Essential
Nutrients Absorbed by Turf Roots from Soils

| Name | Symbol | Function | Deficiency Symptom |
|------|--------|----------|--------------------|
| Nitrogen | N | Constituent of amino acids, nucleic acids | Chlorosis |
| Phosphorus | P | Constituent of ATP, NADP, & nucleic acids | Red/purple coloration |
| Potassium | K | Improves environmental stress tolerance | Leaf margins brown, curled |
| Calcium | Ca | Constituent of cell walls | Deformed leaves |
| Magnesium | Mg | Constituent of chlorophyll | Chlorosis |
| Sulfur | S | Constituent of proteins | Chlorosis |
| Manganese | Mn | Cofactor for enzyme functions | Interveinal chlorosis |
| Iron | Fe | Cofactor for enzyme functions | Interveinal chlorosis |
| Boron | B | Cofactor for enzyme functions | Compressed internodes |
| Zinc | Zn | Cofactor for enzyme function | Mottled leaves |
| Copper | Cu | Cofactor for enzyme function | Leaf tip wilt |
| Molybdenum | Mo | Cofactor for enzyme function | Pale green, leaf roll |
| Chlorine | Cl | Cofactor for enzyme function | Leaf bronzing, necrosis |

## Nutrients

Nutrients are chemical elements that are used by plants as fuel, or as building materials for the growth of the plant. Nutrients occur in the soil in mineral and organic forms, and they become available after they weather or decay and become dissolved in the soil solution. The soil serves as the repository for the 13 nutrients that are required for plant growth. These 13 nutrients are listed in Table 2.1.

Of these soil-derived nutrients, six are required in large quantity by the turf and are called *macronutrients*. The macronutrients include nitrogen, phosphorus, potassium, calcium, magnesium, and sulfur. The remaining seven nutrients are required in small quantities, and are referred to as *micronutrients*. The seven micronutrients are manganese, iron, boron, zinc, copper, molybdenum, and chlorine. In addition to these 13 essential nutrients, more than 40 other nutrients are found in plants, but are not essential for their growth and reproduction.

However, a surprisingly small percentage of the weight of a plant (3% to 5%) is made up of soil-derived nutrients. The remaining 95% to 97% of the plant weight is derived from carbon dioxide in our atmosphere.

## Air

Soil aeration is the exchange of gases between the soil and the atmosphere. This process of gas exchange is driven by diffusion, which occurs when there is a difference in concentration between substances that are connected by permeable environments. In the case of soil aeration, the plant growth substances that diffuse are oxygen, carbon dioxide, and in some instances, methane or hydrogen sulfide. Oxygen diffuses from the aerial to the soil atmosphere, whereas carbon dioxide diffuses from the soil to the aerial atmosphere. The roots and rhizomes of turfgrasses consume oxygen and release carbon dioxide. This results in a higher concentration of carbon dioxide and a lower concentration of oxygen in the soil than in the aerial atmosphere.

Normally, soil pore space is sufficient to provide adequate pathways for soil aeration to occur. However, if the soil pore space becomes filled with water and that water does not drain freely from these pores, then the pathway is blocked and soil aeration will become limited. Water blocks soil aeration because gas diffusion through water is approximately 10,000 times slower than through air.

The size of the pores in a particular soil sample determines whether that soil will drain free of water due to gravity. Pore size is the result of soil particle size distribution and degree of soil aggregate formation. Large pore sizes in soils that drain freely are called *macropores*. Macropores are most commonly found in soils with a high content of large-size particles of uniform size (e.g., sand). Small pores that retain water and do not drain freely are called *micropores*. These smaller pores form in soil with uniform-sized particles and little aggregate formation. Gas diffusion is likely to be retarded in soils with micropores.

In addition to oxygen and carbon dioxide diffusion through soil pores, other gases such as methane and hydrogen sulfide diffuse as well. These gases are toxic to plants and their presence can reduce plant vigor or even cause plant mortality. This means, of course, that poor soil aeration not only limits oxygen diffusion and plant respiration, but also will cause plant injury or death due to toxic gas buildup around roots and rhizomes. (The source of toxic gases in water-saturated soils is certain types of anaerobic microbes.)

## 2.2b  Physical Properties

Soil physical properties that influence plant growth requirements are soil texture, porosity, structure, and strength.

Soil **texture** is the relative coarseness or fineness of a soil, and is determined by the relative proportions of sand, silt, and clay particles. Sand, silt, and clay are defined by their particle size diameters; grains of sand range from 2 to .05 mm; silt particles are from .05 to .002 mm in diameter; and clay particles are less than .002 mm (see Table 2.2).

There is a significant increase in surface area of the particles as soil particle size decreases. Sandy soils create macropores resulting in good soil aeration, but they fail to hold moisture in climates with limited rainfall. A soil high in silt has excellent water holding capacity, but will compact with heavy traffic. Clay soils have excellent nutrient and water holding capacity, but compact readily with only light traffic.

There are an infinite number of possible combinations of sand, silt, and clay that might make up a soil. In order to describe the texture of soil, scientists with the United States Department of Agriculture (USDA) have developed a system that divides soils into 12 groups, called "textural classes," based on percent compositions of sand, silt, and clay. These soil classification groups are called clay, sandy clay, clay loam, silty clay, silty clay loam, sandy clay loam, loam, silt loam, silt, sandy loam, loamy sand, and sand. The range of particle sizes for each class is illustrated and defined by a triangle diagram called the soil textural triangle (also conceived by USDA soil scientists), shown in Figure 2.2.

### Table 2.2. Soil Particle Sizes, Numbers, and Surface Areas

| Soil Particle | Diameter (mm) | Number of Particles Per Gram | Surface Area in One Gram (cm) |
|---|---|---|---|
| Sand | 2 to .05 | 90 to 722,000 | 11 to 227 |
| Silt | .05 to .002 | 5,776,000 | 454 |
| Clay | <.002 | 90,250,000,000 | 8,000,000 |

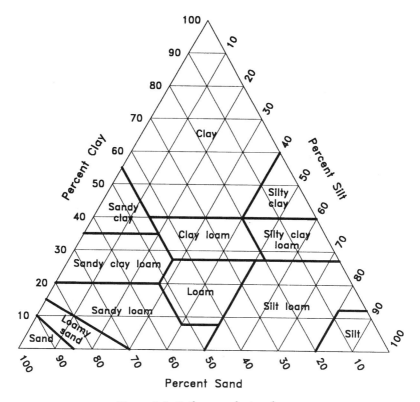

*Figure 2.2. Soil textural triangle.*

The textural class of a soil can be used to predict a wide range of soil chemical and physical properties including porosity, soil strength, cation exchange capacity, hydrology, and soil reaction. In sports turf applications, soil texture cannot be relied upon as the sole source of information for determining the suitability of a soil. Other considerations such as water percolation rate, macro- and microporosity, and soil reaction, should be individually measured, and not simply predicted on the basis of the soil texture class. However, soil texture class determination is an essential first step in evaluating a soil for sports turf use.

Soil **porosity** is the volume percentage of total pore space found in a soil. Soil porosity of 50% indicates that one-half of the soil volume consists of pores and the other half consists of solids—a suitable soil for turf growth if half of this porosity is macropores (drained free of water by gravity) and the other half is classified as micropores (not drained free of water by gravity).

Soil porosity varies with particle size; sandy soils have a low porosity, whereas a clay soil has a high soil porosity. This comparison suggests that sandy soils are poorly aerated and clay soil are well aerated based on porosity. However, experience shows that a sandy soil has greater aeration than a clayey soil, because sandy soils have a higher percentage of macropores compared to the clayey soil. It's a matter of pore size, not total pore space. The sandy soil drains free and allows aeration; the clayey soil holds water, resulting in poor soil aeration.

Soil **structure** is the combination or arrangement of soil particles into aggregates, which are clusters of particles. Aggregates are separated from adjoining aggregates by "fractures" or channels through the soil. Soil fractures between aggregates are usually large, and tend to create macropores. Soil structure becomes beneficial to plant growth when aggregate formation becomes widespread.

Aggregate formation is caused by the penetration of roots, wet and dry cycles, and freezing and thawing cycles. All of these mechanisms cluster soil particles into aggregates, which are then cemented together. Cementing together of soil aggregates is attributed to microbial gum or exudate, iron oxide, humus, and clay films. Of all the plant species that promote aggregate formation, grasses are the most effective types. Grasses are effective because their root systems are fibrous, they usually have an annual life cycle regularly depositing organic residue, and they promote microbial activity due to high root and shoot dry matter production. In soils underlying sports fields, soil aggregates are formed by grass root activity, yet the intense traffic associated with sports turf use destroys soil aggregates. The destruction of soil structure is due to compaction caused by equipment and players that breaks down the integrity of aggregates and collapses pores between adjoining aggregates.

When used in reference to soil, **strength** is the ability to resist displacement by an external force such as the cleats of athletes or the tires of equipment. Good soil strength is necessary to hold the turf firmly in the soil, and to prevent dislodgment or divoting. In the case of sports turf, good soil strength allows players to perform with minimal concern for stable footing.

The strength of a soil is determined by the forces that hold soil particles together, including textural class and moisture content. Exposed dry sand, for example, has little soil strength and provides very poor traction and sod stability. However, the same sand, if it is kept moist, has substantially better soil strength, and corresponding improvements in traction and sod stability. In contrast, a dry clay has high soil strength and provides excellent traction. But if that dry clay gets wet, it becomes slippery and provides poor traction. Obviously, in sports turf management, soil selection and moisture control are critical factors in optimizing soil strength.

In soils underlying sports fields, a clayey soil has high fertility and good water holding capacity, but also a high compaction tendency and poor natural aeration. A sandy soil has low fertility and water holding capacity, but excellent aeration and low compaction tendency. No one soil type has all the necessary plant growth requirements. Therefore, managing soil for plant growth requires consideration of compromises like blending or topdressing with different soils to achieve the optimum combination of characteristics, as well as specific cultural practices to compensate for any plant growth requirement that may be lacking in the primary soil.

## 2.2c Chemical Properties

The chemical properties of soil that directly influence plant growth are cation exchange capacity (CEC) and soil reaction (pH).

The **cation exchange capacity** refers to the soil's ability to adsorb or hold exchangeable "cations," which are positively charged atoms, some of which are essential plant nutrients. Calcium, magnesium, and potassium are examples of essential nutrients that occur in nature as cations. The adsorption force of soil that creates the exchange capacity is a negative charge associated with clay particles or organic matter residue. Clayey soils have high cation exchange capacity, whereas, silty or sandy soil types have low CEC. Soils with high clay or high CEC are considered fertile because they store plant nutrients for root extraction.

**Soil reaction** refers to the relative acidity or alkalinity of a soil and is measured in pH

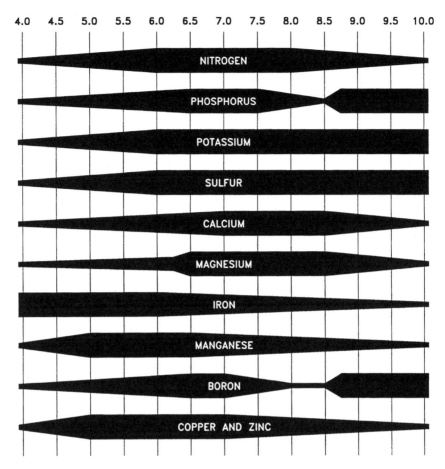

Figure 2.3. Relationship between soil pH and nutrient availability.

units. The pH scale ranges from 0 to 14; with 0 to <7 indicating an acid soil and >7 to 14 an alkaline soil. At pH of 7, the soil is said to have a "neutral pH." The normal pH range of most soils is 5.0 to 8.0. Soil pH is an important soil characteristic because it influences plant growth requirements by altering nutrient availability, soil microbial activity and composition, and solubility of toxic elements (i.e., aluminum, iron, and manganese). Figure 2.3 shows the relationship between soil pH and availability of essential nutrients.

A slightly acid pH (6 to 6.5) is desirable for most sports turf species, since nutrient availability is maximized in this range. (For information on raising and lowering soil pH, see Chapter 3, Section 3.4)

### The Importance of Soil Testing
Some turf managers conduct soil tests on their fields only when they are trying to diagnose a turf problem. Although a soil test will aid in diagnosing such problems, the soil test should be a regularly scheduled practice to predict potential problems as well as to provide a historical record of the soil's pH and nutrient status. A historical record of soil test results can then be used to compare present and past reports and to determine pH and nutrient trends.

Sometimes a turf manager will split the soil sample and send each half to a different lab. More often than not, the two labs will report different results. These different test results do not necessarily mean one lab is right and the other wrong; the variation is probably due to the labs using different soil testing methods that can give slightly different results. All soil testing methods are based on an "extraction procedure," and different extractions are used under different conditions, such as regional soil properties, plant type being grown on the soil being tested, and even the lab director's opinion on the best extraction or testing method.

A turf manager who is concerned with varying lab results, or who is just interested in better understanding soil test procedures, should contact the lab and talk to the director. The bottom line in soil testing ultimately lies in the hands of the turf manager, who is advised to try several labs and select the one that best serves his or her needs. It's important to remember that the most important thing about soil testing is to include the use of regular soil tests in the turf management program and to have testing done on a routine schedule to build a soil nutrient history. Then, when a problem arises, the manager will have a sound basis for diagnosis.

## 2.3 SOIL FOR HARD SURFACES

Soil used as a hard surface, as on the skinned areas of a baseball diamond, must provide uniform ball response, good traction, and an ability to remain playable at widely different moisture levels.

### 2.3a Properties of Soil for Hard Surfaces

When choosing soil for the skinned areas of baseball or softball fields, soil texture, porosity, strength, and surface evaporation are important soil properties to be considered.

**Soil texture** is the amount of sand, silt, and clay present in the mixture. Sandy soil as a hard surface would be preferred for increased percolation rates, but some finer textured soil (silt and clay) needs to be added to create a firm surface. Without the fines from silt and clay, the surface is too loose and sandy, like a beach. However, a surface with excessive clay is undesirable because it has the potential to dry as hard as concrete. In the sports turf industry, a wide array of soil textures are used for a hard surface. This variance is due to a number of reasons, including availability of local soil material, budget, competition level, and most common, the opinion of the field manager or coach.

**Soil porosity** decreases when fines are added, so percolation rates are very slow on a skinned area. Subsurface drain systems work poorly under these conditions because water takes too long to move through the soil to any belowground drain pipes. The only effective way to drain water from a skinned area is surface drainage.

**Soil strength** is a measure of the soil's ability to adhere or hold together when horizontal or vertical pressure is applied, and is a critical factor in traction. Clay and silt particles increase the strength of soil, whereas sand particles reduce the strength. Soil moisture levels also influence soil strength. Excessively wet soil has poor soil strength because the water acts as a lubricant, promoting the sliding of soil particles. Excessively dry soil may also have poor soil strength, due to a lack of moisture binding properties.

An effective way to change the strength of a soil is by adding conditioners such as calcined clay or calcined diatomaceous earth (the more effective choice) that alter the soil's ability to retain moisture. These materials improve soil strength in addition to aiding the soil's ability to deal with excess moisture.

**Surface evaporation,** or the ability of a soil to release moisture from the soil surface and into the air, is another important property of hard surfaces. The reason is obvious: the quicker the soil dries out, the quicker play can resume. Some soils dry more quickly than others; before choosing soil for a skinned area, take time to check on the evaporation rate of a sample. (Chapter 11, Section 11.2f describes a simple way to test soils for drying times.)

## 2.3b Playability

In measuring soil for playability, the most important consideration is the soil's ability to return to a playable condition after a heavy rain, excessive dry conditions, or heavy usage. After a heavy rain, skinned area soil should support foot traffic or tractor weight soon after the rain stops to allow dragging to take place. After prolonged dry conditions or periods of heavy usage, the surface should have a minimal tendency to become hard or dusty. A fields manager should be able to moisten and drag the field promptly. (Some soils become so hard in drought conditions that they resist water and the penetration of a nail drag.) All of these considerations are easier to achieve when conditioners are worked into the profile.

Another playability consideration is the soil's ability to resist rutting during heavy rains. The best insurance against rutting is to design the field so that surface runoff is evenly distributed throughout the entire skinned area; if all the runoff is directed through one area, rutting is very probable. Even with proper grading, some soils will wash toward the lower portions of the field. The ideal skinned area soil should hold together and resist washing out.

An example of an effective skinned area soil mix used in a moderately high rainfall area is 60% sand, 20% silt, and 20% clay. Covered baseball diamonds typically use more silt (up to 30%) and less sand. All of the granular material used in the skinned area should pass through a 3/8 inch wire screen. A minimum of 97% should pass through a Number 8 sieve, and at least 60% should pass through a Number 140 sieve. (For more on skinned area soils used for baseball diamonds, see Chapter 11, Section 11.2f, Skinned Area Soil.)

One specialized skinned surface is the baseball pitcher's mound. To withstand the special stresses placed on a mound, perhaps only clay-based soils provide the necessary soil strength. Sand and silt-based soils tend to be easily disturbed by competitive stresses, and an unacceptable portion of the soil will end up in the surrounding area. There are also clay-based soil products on the market now that are specifically designed for optimum performance on pitcher's mounds and batter's boxes.

Although many recommended soil mixes will make an ideal playing surface in most situations, a wise field manager will contact suppliers and other field managers before choosing a skinned area soil. When a soil is used successfully by a group of local managers, a new field manager can use that recommendation as a basis for his or her own facilities, and test all other soil mixes against that one. A process of gradual refinement will allow the manager to arrive at an ideal skinned area soil for the local area.

# Chapter 3

# *Fertility and Fertilizers*

## 3.1 INTRODUCTION

Anyone who has ever grown plants knows how much difference fertilizing makes. Most of the time, it's a positive difference, but many neophyte gardeners have also learned that too much fertilizer (or the wrong kind) can kill the plants. Most beginners quickly learn that the three most commonly applied nutrients are nitrogen (N), phosphorus (P), and potassium (K), but plants also need 13 other essential nutrients to grow and develop as they should. (For more on plant nutrient needs, see Chapter 2.) If any one of these elements is lacking, plant growth may be inhibited.

In this chapter, we will consider the principles of effective sports turf fertility programs—factors like optimum nutrient levels in soil and leaf tissues, and techniques for modifying soil pH to encourage the turfgrass culture. We will also suggest fertility programs designed to yield a vibrant, resilient playing surface for athletic competition.

## 3.2 NUTRIENT REQUIREMENTS

Every good fertility program begins the same way: with a soil or leaf tissue analysis. Considering the modest fee charged by most labs for these analyses, there is no better sports field investment; the information they yield is invaluable. Soil sampling continues to be the most common way to determine turf nutrient status, primarily because the procedure can be conducted quickly and cheaply. Generally, these tests are also accurate; the soil is a good indicator of what nutrients are taken up into the plant. However, it's important to remember that factors like soil moisture and temperature also influence what nutrients get into the plant.

Soil sampling is a simple process. With a soil probe or a spade, dig a sample (4″ to 6″ deep) from 10 to 15 random locations around the field, placing all the soil into a bucket. Remove any plant material from the samples and mix the soil thoroughly. Put about a pint of the soil into a soil test box (available from a county agricultural agent or commercial soil testing lab) and mail the sample to the agent or the lab. Most testing labs send back a report within two weeks.

Soil can be sampled at any time of the year, but some times are better than others, because there are times when the data can be more meaningful for the turfgrass management program. For cool season turfgrasses, a soil test in mid- to late summer helps in planning nutrient applications before the fall growing period. For warm season turfgrasses, the ideal time to sample is mid- to late winter, before the spring growing season begins. (It's worth noting that labs can be overrun with samples for row crops at certain times of the year, so test results could be slow in coming back. A one-minute call to the lab can avoid weeks of delay before the season.)

On native, clay-based soils, testing will probably be necessary only once every two to three years. On native or modified sand-based soils, soil testing should probably be done once each year since this soil type will have lower nutrient holding capacity and can experience quicker fluctuations in pH changes.

A typical soil test reports levels of phosphorus, potassium, calcium, magnesium, and zinc, as well as soil pH. Nitrogen levels are not usually reported because of the potential variability of nitrogen levels in the soil between the time the sample is taken and the time they are tested. Most reports also provide standard recommendations on how to bring the soil up to recommended nutrient and pH levels. Most testing labs can provide more detailed information for an additional charge.

Tissue testing describes exactly what nutrients are present in the leaves, and that can provide an advantage over soil test reports; the presence of acceptable levels of a nutrient in the soil does not necessarily mean it is being taken up into the plants at satisfactory levels. As with soil samples, gather leaves from multiple locations around the field. Let them air-dry before shipping or delivering them to the lab. (It's best not to use clippings following a mowing event because of potential contamination from the mower blades themselves.)

To enhance the accuracy of soil or tissue testing results, avoid sampling from noticeable "problem spots" on the field, except to diagnose the cause of the problems. (In which case, submit those samples separately, and not with the general soil sample.) Problem spots can be caused by chemical or fertilizer spills, or even by visits from neighborhood pets.

Of course, it makes no sense to take samples immediately after fertilizing; a few fertilizer pellets in the soil or a little residue on the leaves can alter test results too much to allow a meaningful representation of the nutrient status of the field.

Table 3.1 shows the levels of macro- and micronutrients that would typically be classified "low" to "very high" on a soil test. These values can vary somewhat depending on the turfgrass, the soil type, and the laboratory analytical procedures used on a particular test. For that reason, the information in this chart should be considered as less valuable than the report that might be received based on a specific soil sample. (These values provided by LESCO, Inc.)

According to research studies by Ohio State University, it's important for available phosphorus to be between 80 and 120 pounds per acre and available potassium between 300 and 500 pounds per acre. (Note that these recommended values are slightly higher than the values recommended by LESCO, Inc. in Table 3.1.)

As indicated in Table 3.2, turfgrasses have a fairly constant ratio of nitrogen, phosphorus, and potassium in the plant tissues—generally about 4% N : .5% P : 2% K by weight. The consistency of these ratios is reflected in the use of fertilizers with similar ratios to maintain N, P, and K levels in the turf. Excesses or deficiencies of some nutrients (particularly nitrogen) will lead to excesses or deficiencies of other nutrients, so it's important to keep the fertility program properly balanced to optimize turfgrass growth. It's important to remember that each of the 16 essential nutrients is required for optimal plant growth; the significant loss of even a single nutrient can weaken the overall turfgrass culture.

Table 3.1. Soil Test Designations for Levels of Macro– and Micronutrrients in Turfgrass Soils

| Nutrient | Existing Pounds Per Acre | Soil Test Designation |
|---|---|---|
| Phosphorus | < 18 | Low |
| | 18 – 30 | Medium |
| | 31 – 120 | High |
| | > 120 | Very High |
| Potassium | < 90 | Low |
| | 90 – 160 | Medium |
| | 161 – 320 | High |
| | > 320 | Very High |
| Calcium | < 500 | Low |
| Magnesium | < 40 | Low |
| Sulfur | < 15 | Low |
| | 15 – 50 | Medium |
| | > 50 | High |
| Boron | < 0.5 | Low |
| | 0.5 – 1.5 | Medium |
| | > 1.5 | High |
| Copper | < 0.5 | Low |
| | 0.5 – 5 | Medium |
| | > 5 | High |
| Iron | < 15 | Low |
| | 15 – 120 | Medium |
| | > 120 | High |
| Manganese | < 10 | Low |
| | 10 – 50 | Medium |
| | > 50 | High |
| Zinc | < 2 | Low |
| | 2 – 5 | Medium |
| | > 5 | High |

Table 3.2. General Tissue Sufficiency Ranges for Bermudagrass and Perennial Ryegrass Sports Turf[a]

| Nutrient | Bermudagrass | | | Perennial Ryegrass | | |
|---|---|---|---|---|---|---|
| | Low | Medium | High | Low | Medium | High |
| | Percentage | | | | | |
| N | 2.50–2.99 | 3.00–5.00 | >5.00 | 4.00–4.49 | 4.50–5.00 | >5.00 |
| P | 0.12–0.14 | 0.15–0.50 | >0.50 | 0.30–0.34 | 0.35–0.40 | >0.40 |
| K | 0.70–0.99 | 1.00–4.00 | >4.00 | 0.70–1.99 | 2.00–2.50 | >2.50 |
| Ca | 0.30–0.49 | 0.50–1.00 | >1.00 | 0.20–0.24 | 0.25–0.30 | >0.30 |
| Mg | 0.10–0.12 | 0.13–0.50 | >0.50 | 0.13–0.15 | 0.16–0.20 | >0.20 |
| S | 0.12–0.14 | 0.15–0.50 | >0.50 | 0.22–0.26 | 0.27–0.32 | >0.32 |
| | Parts Per Million | | | | | |
| B | 4–5 | 6–30 | >30 | <9 | 9–17 | >17 |
| Cu | 3–4 | 5–50 | >50 | 4–5 | 6–7 | >7 |
| Fe | 40–49 | 50–350 | >350 | <40 | 40–60 | >60 |
| Mn | 16–24 | 25–300 | >300 | <2 | 2–10 | >10 |

[a]Values from Jones, J.B. Jr., B. Wolf, and H.A. Mills. Plant Analysis Handbook. Micro–Macro Publishing, Inc., Athens, GA, 1991.

## 3.3 NUTRIENT UPTAKE

Plants gain nutrients in two ways. The most common is through root absorption of the nutrient from the "soil solution." (As the name indicates, a certain amount of soil moisture must be available for root absorption to occur.) The other method of nutrient uptake is direct foliar absorption through stomates and cracks in the leaf cuticle (the waxy coating found on the surface of leaves). This type of uptake is associated with a foliar spray application of a fertilizer.

In the case of root absorption, the driving force for initial entry into the plant is the "transpiration stream," or the cycling of water from the soil through the plant, and out through the stomates. The force that drives transpiration is the difference in "soil water potential" (typically relatively high) and "atmospheric water potential" (comparatively lower). A limited amount of nutrients can enter the plant's internal transportation system (the xylem) without the expenditure of any energy by the plant, but the uptake of nutrients in any substantial amounts requires the plant to expend some energy. This energy to support nutrient uptake by the root is made available by the process of respiration (the conversion of stored carbohydrates to chemical energy in the presence of oxygen). For this reason, the plant must be healthy and actively growing to take up nutrients.

"Foliar feeding" is the practice of introducing nutrients through the leaves. Application levels are typically less than those used for soil-applied granular applications. With either application method, care must be taken to prevent "foliar burn" by the fertilizer source. Many water soluble fertilizers, whether applied in granular or liquid forms, can desiccate leaf tissues because of their high salt content. A general rule of thumb for preventing foliar burn is to irrigate the turf thoroughly after fertilizer applications, although there are obvious exceptions to this philosophy like foliar feeding with reduced nutrient levels. Carefully following label directions will maximize the fertilizer's performance and prevent this problem.

## 3.4 SOIL REACTION

One of the most important pieces of information gained from a soil test is the "**soil reaction**," most commonly referred to as the **pH.** (For more on the pH scale and its effects on nutrient availability, see Figure 2.3 in Chapter 2.) A slightly acidic pH (ideally 6.0 to 6.5) maximizes nutrient availability, and should be the target range for turfgrass culture.

To raise soil pH, a "liming agent" is applied. There are a number of commonly-used liming materials, some slow to react and others that rapidly change soil pH. (Commonly-used liming sources are listed in Table 3.3.)

For established turfgrasses it is common to choose slower-acting materials, since they have limited potential for foliar burn. These materials require weeks or months to achieve their full effect on soil pH, but those effects are relatively long-lived. The faster-acting liming materials have a fast and drastic effect on pH, but the effects are short in duration and the materials have a very high potential for foliar burn due to leaf desiccation. It's worth noting that the rapid effect of the hydrated or oxide materials makes them good choices for modifying soil pH *before* establishing turf on a field.

The ideal time to apply lime is with aerification; that helps to move the liming material into the soil, where it must be to raise pH. Also, cooler temperatures (less that 50° F) reduce the potential for foliar burn. Since standard lime sources need a few months to have their full effect on pH, large-scale lime applications on warm-season turfgrasses are typically performed during the winter dormancy period, and the same practice is equally

Table 3.3. Common Lime Sources for Raising Soil pH on Athletic Fields[a]

| Liming Material | Chemical Formula | Initial Release Rate | Length of Residual Effect | Potential to Burn Turf |
|---|---|---|---|---|
| Calcium carbonate | $CaCO_3$ | slow | long | low |
| Magnesium carbonate | $MgCO_3$ | slow | long | low |
| Dolomitic limestone | $MgCO_3 * CaCo_3$ | slow | long | low |
| Hydrated lime | $Ca(OH_2) * Mg(OH_2)$ | medium | short | high |
| Calcium oxide | $CaO$ | fast | short | high |
| Quicklime | $CaO * MgO$ | fast | short | high |

[a]Adapted from Beard, J.B., *How To Have a Beautiful Lawn*, 4th ed., Beard Books, College Station, TX, 1988.

effective for cool season turfgrasses as well. Avoid applying powdered forms of lime on hot, humid days when the potential for foliar burn is high.

How much liming material is required for a typical field? Only a soil test can provide authoritative guidance, because of the specific recommendations it provides. However, Table 3.4 provides a general idea of how much of the most common liming sources is required to adjust a soil pH to the desirable 6.5 level.

It's worth noting that the required amounts of liming material become progressively higher as the soil type changes from sand to clay. This is because of the higher cation exchange capacity (CEC) of the clay soil and its tendency to resist chemical changes. (For more information on cation exchange capacity, see Chapter 2, Section 2c.) Even when higher levels of liming material are called for, it is unwise to apply more than 40 pounds of material per 1,000 square feet in a single application. More than 40 pounds increases foliar burn potential, although higher levels can be used during the turf's dormancy periods. During active growth periods, make multiple applications (spring and fall) with rainfall or irrigation between them to deliver the total amount of lime needed to correct the pH.

To lower the pH of the soil, the most common practice is to apply sulfur-based compounds, particularly elemental sulfur. There is high foliar burn potential with applications of elemental sulfur, so rates should be kept to no more than 7 pounds per 1,000 square feet per application. When greater amounts are needed, these applications should also be split between spring and fall.

As discussed in Section 3.5 of this chapter, many nitrogen materials also have the effect of lowering pH with regular usage. These fertilizers (particularly water soluble sources such as ammonium sulfate, urea, and ammonium nitrate) can be used to gradually lower the pH over time.

It's impossible for the testing lab to predict precisely how much sulfur will be needed to reduce the pH of the soil, so a yearly soil test is recommended. Soil sometimes con-

Table 3.4. Approximate Quantities of Finely Ground $CaCO_3$ (pounds/1,000 sq ft) to Raise a 6-inch Rootzone to a pH of 6.5 Prior to Planting[a]

| Original Soil pH | Sand and Loamy Sand | Loam | Clay Loam and Clay |
|---|---|---|---|
| 5.5 | 15–30 | 45–75 | 90–100 |
| 4.5 | 30–50 | 80–130 | 150–190 |

[a]Adapted from Beard, J.B., *How To Have a Beautiful Lawn*, 4th ed., Beard Books, College Station, TX, 1988.

tains inactive lime which does not show up in routine laboratory testing, but which is activated when sulfur is applied, and counteracts the sulfur. A wise fields manager is constantly checking and fine-tuning his or her sulfur application, since the process always includes an element of "trial and error."

## 3.5 FERTILIZER ANALYSIS

There are literally dozens of fertilizer sources available, in a wide variety of nutrient combinations and release rates. Fertilizer labels are required by law to include certain specified information, of which one of the most important features is the **fertilizer analysis**. The analysis represents the percentages by weight of nitrogen (N), phosphate ($P_2O_5$) and potash ($K_2O$) in the fertilizer.

It is important to reemphasize that the last two numbers of the analysis do not represent the percent by weight of phosphorus (P) and potassium (K)—a common misconception. To find the actual percentages of the elemental forms of P and K, multiply the phosphate percentage by 0.44 to calculate the phosphorus number, and multiply the potash percentage by 0.83 to determine the potassium percentage. For example, let's use the following imaginary fertilizer materials (Figure 3.1 and 3.2) to work through some examples of fertilizer analysis and calculation of what is actually contained in the package.

From the information given on this label, we can determine the following:

1. The ratio of nutrients in this fertilizer is 4 parts nitrogen (N):1 part phosphate ($P_2O_5$):2 parts potash ($K_2O$). This source will deliver a ratio of nutrients that is typically observed in turfgrasses.
2. In this bag, 75% of the nitrogen is water insoluble nitrogen (WIN) 12% ÷ 16% = 75%.
3. Fifty pounds net weight times 0.16 N = 8 pounds of total N within the bag. Of this amount, 50 pounds × 0.12 = 6 pounds of the N is water insoluble nitrogen (WIN). Only 2 pounds of the N in the bag is readily available to the plant.
4. Fifty pounds × 0.04 phosphate ($P_2O_5$) = 2 pounds of total $P_2O_5$ in the bag. In terms of the amount of elemental phosphorus, 2 pounds of $P_2O_5$ × 0.44 = 0.88 pounds of P in the bag.
5. Fifty pounds × 0.08 potash ($K_2O$) = 4 pounds of total $K_2O$ in the bag. In terms of the amout of elemental potassium (K), 4 pounds K × 0.83 = 3.32 pounds of K in the bag.

---

## Jeff, Jim, and Mike's
## Sports Turf Special Granular Fertilizer
# <u>16-4-8</u>

|  | Percent |
|---|---|
| Total Nitrogen*...................................................................................... | 16 |
| Total Phosphate....................................................................................... | 4 |
| Total Potash. ........................................................................................... | 8 |

*12% water insoluble nitrogen (WIN)
Net Weight: 50 lb

---

*Figure 3.1. Sample granular fertilizer label.*

Jeff, Jim, and Mike's
Sports Turf Liquid Iron
**16-0-0**

Percent

Total Nitrogen...........................................................................................16
Total Phosphate..........................................................................................0
Total Potash. .............................................................................................0
Total Iron ...................................................................................................6

Total Volume: 2.5 gallons      Weight per gallon: 11.8 lb

Figure 3.2. Sample liquid fertilizer label.

From the information given on this label, we can determine the following:

1. The ratio of nutrients in this fertilizer is 1 part nitrogen (N):0 parts phosphate $(P_2O_5)$:0 parts potash $(K_2O)$.
2. The net weight must be calculated since it is often not provided on the label. [2.5 gallons $\times$ 11.8 pounds per gallon = 29.5 pounds net weight. 29.5 pounds net weight $\times$ 0.16 (percentage of nitrogen) = 4.72 pounds of total N within this jug.]
3. The iron (Fe) content is 29.5 pounds $\times$ 0.06 Fe = 1.77 pounds of total Fe in the jug.

Most fertilizers include fairly high percentages of filler, which has little or no nutrient value, but helps to maintain the consistency of the material or improve spreading characteristics. However it's important to be aware of the amounts of actual nutrients in the bag to achieve the best value for the budget dollar. For instance, consider the following two products:

**15-5-10 at a cost of $4.00/40 lb bag   vs.   24-4-8 at a cost of $5.00/40 lb bag**

The first instinct is to go with the cheapest price per bag; the 15-5-10 has a cost of $0.10 per pound of fertilizer. The 24-4-8 has a cost of $0.125 per pound of fertilizer. But the cost per pound of fertilizer is less important than the cost per pound of nutrient.

For instance, let's compare these products as sources of nitrogen. Assuming that the products are comparable (i.e., both water soluble materials; complete sources, etc.). The 15-5-10 fertilizer contains 40 pounds $\times$ 0.15 = 6 pounds of N and the 24-4-8 contains 40 pounds $\times$ 0.24 = 9.6 pounds of N. The cost per pound of N for the 15-5-10 fertilizer is $4.00 $\div$ 6 lb N = $0.67 per pound of N, while for the 24-4-8, the cost per pound is $5.00 $\div$ 9.6 pounds N = $0.52 per pound of N. Based on the cost per pound of nutrient, the manager would actually save $0.15 per pound of nitrogen by choosing the 24-4-8. This difference won't be critical for a single application on a small area, but can represent a dramatic price difference for multiple applications over large areas of turf.

## 3.6 FERTILIZER SOURCES

Turfgrass fertilizer sources are broadly classified into two categories: readily or slowly available. Readily available fertilizers have high water solubility and slowly available sources have significant amounts of water insoluble nutrients. Within the slow release sources, there is a wide variety of "controlled release" fertilizers with varying degrees of water solubility.

### 3.6a Water Soluble Fertilizers

The readily available, water soluble fertilizers are the least expensive per pound of nutrient, and provide rapid turf growth response and greenup, particularly in regard to nitrogen responses. However, they are also more subject to leaching loss through the soil and are more likely to cause foliar burn. Due to the ready availability of the nutrients, they require more frequent applications at low use levels to perform as desired.

Examples of readily available, water soluble nitrogen (WSN) sources are ammonium nitrate (34-0-0), urea (45-0-0), and ammonium sulfate (18-0-0). These sources are often considered to be "agricultural grade" fertilizers because they often have not been sized or screened for product uniformity as many turf specialty products are. However, they ultimately supply the same nutrients that specialty fertilizer products do as well.

There are two easily obtained water-soluble potassium sources available from most fertilizer distributors: muriate of potash (0-0-60) and sulfate of potash (0-0-50). Sulfate of potash is typically more expensive, but has less foliar burn potential. Potassium nitrate (13-0-44) is also a very popular water soluble fertilizer that delivers both nitrogen and potassium and this source has been popular to use for sports turf purposes when only a small amount of N is desirable.

As for phosphorus sources, agricultural-grade superphosphate (0-20-0) or triple superphosphate (0-48-0) are the most common materials that deliver just phosphate. There also are two common ammonium-phosphate sources known as MAP (monoammonium phosphate, 12-61-0) and DAP (diammonium phosphate, 18-46-0) that deliver both N and P.

There are also many water soluble complete fertilizers (sources containing N, $P_2O_5$, and $K_2O$) that are premixed. Products like 10-10-10 or 13-13-13, available at most farmer's cooperatives or lawn and garden centers, are examples of agricultural-grade, water-soluble fertilizers that can fit nicely into sports turf fertility programs. The only substantial limitation of agricultural fertilizers is their larger, more irregular-sized granules, which can cause problems in equipment calibration and uniform product application. The larger particles can clog the openings of some spreaders. Before investing in agricultural grade fertilizers, check with the supplier to determine whether the product will work with the specific equipment being used.

### 3.6b Controlled Release Fertilizers

In turning our attention to controlled release products, we will generally focus on nitrogen sources, since that is the nutrient most often formulated for controlled release. These products have a wide range of release rates, but it is most common for a product to be considered a "slow release" fertilizer if at least 35% of the nitrogen is water insoluble (WIN). Controlled release products are more expensive per pound of nutrient, and the turfgrass growth and greenup responses are comparatively slower than for water soluble sources. On the other hand, the controlled release means less leaching of the nutrients, very little foliar burn potential and fewer required applications since application rates are typically two to three times the normal application rates for water soluble materials.

Some of the most popular controlled release (WIN) sources are:

### Natural Organics (e.g., Milorganite,™ Ringer,™ Harmony,™ and Others)

These products have very low nutrient analysis, and they contain small concentrations of micronutrients. These materials will gradually increase or at least maintain organic matter levels in sand-based soils. Some contain beneficial microorganisms, while others are promoted as enhancing soil microbial activity. All of these products require soil microbial activity to release nutrients, meaning that soil temperature, moisture, and pH must be conducive to microbial activity. They are relatively expensive per pound of nutrient.

### Synthetic Organics [e.g., Isobutyraldehyde Diurea (IBDU), Ureaformaldehyde (UF)]

Slow release characteristics have been built into the chemical structure of these products. IBDU's nitrogen-release rate is dependent on particle size, soil moisture, and soil temperature. The analysis of IBDU is 31-0-0. UF (38-0-0) provides extremely slow N release that is dependent on microbial activity just as the natural organics. IBDU use has been fairly widespread on sports turf, while UF has generally seen limited use due to its cost and extremely slow response.

Another group of synthetic organics, known as "methylene ureas" (MU), also have applications in sports field management. These materials are similar in composition to UF, but have shorter carbon chain lengths, resulting in higher percentages of water soluble nitrogen. They are expensive per pound of nutrient, but provide a fairly rapid nitrogen response while still maintaining many of the slow release characteristics.

### Coated Fertilizers

Coating the fertilizer granules with a differentially permeable barrier allows water to slowly move through the coating, dissolving the enclosed fertilizer pellet. The fertilizer solution is then slowly released into the soil and the nutrient is available for plant uptake. The earliest technology in coating fertilizers was with a spray application of molten sulfur combined with a chemical binding agent, a technique that is still common today. The resulting sulfur coated products are fairly inexpensive and they provide controlled nutrient release if the integrity of the sulfur coating is not disrupted by handling or application methods.

The latest in coating technology involves the spray application of a thin polymer coating, either alone or in combination with sulfur coating. These fertilizer sources are somewhat expensive, but provide very predictable, controlled nutrient release. The nutrient release rate for coated fertilizers is primarily dependent on adequate soil moisture and temperature.

There are also numerous formulations of controlled release fertilizer products which contain $P_2O_5$ and $K_2O$ sources that have been coated with sulfur or polymer. It's important to avoid paying a lot of extra money for a controlled-release fertilizer source that is high in phosphate percentage, because phosphorus is inherently "controlled release." This effect is due to its "rapid immobilization" in the soil; as soon as it is applied, much of it becomes unavailable because it chemically bonds with other nutrients in the soil. On the other hand, potassium is highly mobile in the soil and coated formulations of $K_2O$ are very beneficial in improving nutrient retention in the soil, particularly on sand-based fields.

## 3.7 APPLICATION RATES AND FREQUENCIES

It is important to keep in mind that the best fertility programs are flexible. The manager should never become "locked in" to a fertility program, because the uses and needs of a particular field may change two or three times during a growing season. When this occurs, take time to reassess fertility and maintenance practices in light of the new demands being placed on the turf.

At the end of this section are sample fertilization programs for sports fields, developed according to the nutritional needs of the various grasses, their maintenance requirements, the nutrient availability from the fertilizer source, and whether or not the soil is high in percent clay, silt, or sand. Separate programs are described for native soils and sand-based soils. These programs indicate recommended levels of water soluble or mostly water insoluble nutrient sources.

It is beyond the scope of this book to provide specific programs for every climatic region in this country. While bermudagrass is an obvious grass selection for sports fields in areas like Miami, San Diego, or Phoenix, there are lots of bermudagrass fields in places like St. Louis, Louisville, and Baltimore—cities that are not typically associated with mild winters and, therefore, with warm season turfgrasses. The growing seasons for these fields can differ by as much as four to five months, and fertility programs must obviously address these differences. The longer the growing season, the greater the need for fertilization. This fact should be kept in mind when considering the programs presented in this chapter; they should be modified to fit the particular needs of a particular field and climate.

A key point in developing a fertility program is to remember that nutrient uptake occurs only when a plant is actively growing; applications of water soluble fertilizers are basically worthless if the turf is dormant. However, the key word here is "dormant," and dormancy can occur in the heat of summer just as it can during the dead of winter. On warm season grasses, we think of the primary growing season as occurring from late spring through early fall. On cool season turfgrasses, this period is typically split into late summer through early winter, and then from late winter to late spring. Since these are the times the grasses are most actively growing, these are the times when fertilizer should be applied.

It's also important to be aware that the fact that foliar growth has *slowed* does not mean that fertilizer applications at that time cannot be beneficial. On the contrary, one of the most beneficial fertilizer application periods on cool season turfgrasses is during mid- to late fall, when leaf production slows but root growth and the storage of carbohydrates within roots and stems are increasing.

Since the "big three" nutrients of nitrogen, phosphorus, and potassium are required in the highest amounts, it is a common practice at the first spring application of fertilizer to use a complete fertilizer source containing these nutrients. Phosphorus and potassium applications are often unnecessary on soils high in clay and/or silt, particularly if clippings are always returned, or if the soil has been fertilized with phosphorus and potassium during the last growing season. However, sandy soils tend to be more deficient in these nutrients and the use of a complete fertilizer as a "jump-start" for the grass in the spring can be very effective. For the rest of the growing season, soil or tissue analyses provide the most accurate way of determining if nutrient levels are adequate.

Since potassium is very critical to enhancing stress tolerance, it has become a popular strategy by many sports turf managers to apply nitrogen and potassium at 1:1 ratios, particularly on sand-based fields where potassium leaching can be a problem. (This strategy is probably not necessary on a field high in silt or clay.) Some of the programs

Table 3.5. Fertility Programs for Bermudagrass Sports Turfs Grown on Native Clay or Silt-Based Soils Utilizing Water Soluble Nitrogen (WSN) or Water Insoluble Nitrogen (WIN) Sources

| WSN (lb/1000 sq ft) | | WIN (lb/1000 sq ft)[c] | |
|---|---|---|---|
| Date | Rates | Date | Rates |
| May 1–15[a] | 0.5-1 | May 1–15[a] | 2 |
| June 1–15 | 1 | July 1–15 | 2 |
| July 1–15 | 1 | Sept. 1–15 | 2 |
| Aug. 1–15 | 1 | Oct. 1–15 | 2 lb K |
| Sept. 1–15 | 1 | Total N | 6 |
| Oct. 1–15 | 0.5-1 + 1-2 lb K | If overseeded w/ryegrass, continue fertility program[d] | |
| Total N | 5-6 | Nov. 1–15[b] | 1 |
| If overseeded w/ryegrass, continue fertility program | | Feb. 1–15 | 1 |
| | | Apr. 1–15 | 1 |
| Date | Rates | Total N/year | 9 |
| Nov. 1–15[b] | 0.5-1 | | |
| Dec. 1–15 | 0-0.5 | | |
| Feb. 1–15 | 0-0.5 | | |
| Mar. 1–15 | 0-0.5 | | |
| Apr. 1–15 | 0.5-1 | | |
| Total N/year | 6-9.5 | | |

[a]Initiate program 14 days after spring greenup. Use a 4-1-2 ratio fertilizer in lieu of soil or tissue tests.
[b]Initiate applications 30 days after overseeding.
[c]Based on N sources containing more than 35% WIN. Use the higher rates as % WIN increases.
[d]Do not use natural organic or UF WIN sources. If more rapid growth response is required because of field use, substitute the WSN program for overseeded turf.

listed in this book include a recommendation for potassium application, since its benefits are so great.

The suggested fertility programs in Tables 3.5 through 3.9 are designed to promote aggressive turf growth resulting in fields with high density, superior color and appearance, enhanced wear tolerance, and excellent recuperation potential from mechanical stress. These management programs are to be applied in combination with regular mowing at cutting heights typically ranging from ¾ to 2 inches (and for some situations, even lower cutting heights, depending on field use and the grass selected).

Selecting one of these management programs means a commitment to having the best field possible. Regularly scheduled mowing is a must, as well as relatively low cutting heights. If Kentucky bluegrass, creeping bentgrass, or bermudagrass are used on the field, regular verticutting will be required for thatch control.

The sports field manager has many choices of fertilizer products for these programs. Be sure to look beyond the cost of the fertilizer and fully consider how that material will fit the needs of the complete fertilization program. It is unlikely that one fertilizer source can provide everything needed for a season-long fertilization program, so mix and match to meet the needs of the facility.

**Table 3.6. Fertility Programs for Bermudagrass Sports Turfs Grown on Sand–Based or Modified Soils Utilizing Water Soluble Nitrogen (WSN) or Water Insoluble Nitrogen (WIN) Sources**

| WSN (lb/1000 sq ft) | | WIN (lb/1000 sq ft)c | |
| --- | --- | --- | --- |
| Date | Rates | Date | Rates |
| May 1–15[a] | 1 | May 1–15[a] | 2 |
| June 1–15 | 1–1.5 | July 1–15 | 2 |
| July 1–15 | 1–1.5 | Sept. 1–15 | 2 |
| Aug. 1–15 | 1–1.5 | Oct. 1–15 | 2 lb K |
| Sept. 1–15 | 1 | Total N | 6 |
| Oct. 1–15 | 1 +<br>1–2 lb K | | |
| | | **If overseeded w/ryegrass,<br>continue fertility program[d]** | |
| Total N | 6–7.5 | Date | Rates |
| | | Nov. 1–15[b] | 1 |
| **If overseeded w/ryegrass,<br>continue fertility program** | | Feb. 1–15 | 1 |
| | | Mar. 1–15 | 1 |
| Date | Rates | Apr. 1–15 | 1 |
| Nov. 1–15[b] | 0.5–1 | Total N/year | 10 |
| Dec. 1–15 | 0–0.5 | | |
| Jan. 1–15 | 0–0.5 | | |
| Feb. 1–15 | 0–0.5 | | |
| Mar. 1–15 | 0.5–1 | | |
| Apr. 1–15 | 0.5–1 | | |
| Total N/year | 7.5-12 | | |

[a]Initiate program 14 days after spring green up. Use a 4-1-2 ratio fertilizer in lieu of soil or tissue tests.
[b]Initiate applications 30 days after overseeding.
[c]Based on N sources containing more than 35% WIN. Use the higher rates as % WIN increases.
[d]Do not use natural organic or UF WIN sources. If more rapid growth response is required because of field use, substitute the WSN program for overseeded turf.

**Table 3.7. Fertility Program for Tall Fescue Sports Fields Utilizing Water Soluble Nitrogen (WSN) Sources**

| WSN (lb/1000 sq ft) | |
| --- | --- |
| Date | Rates |
| May 1–15[a] | 1 |
| Sept. 1–15 | 1–1.5 |
| Nov. 1–15[b] | 1–1.5 |
| Total N | 3–4 |

[a]Initiate program after 20–30% spring green up.
[b]Final application made prior to soil freezing.

Table 3.8. Fertility Programs for Kentucky Bluegrass, Perennial Ryegrass, or Creeping Bentgrass Sports Turfs Grown on Predominantly Clay or Silt-Based Soils Utilizing Water Soluble Nitrogen (WSN) or Water Insoluble Nitrogen (WIN) Sources

| WSN (lb/1000 sq ft) | |
|---|---|
| Date | Rates |
| May 1–15[a] | 0.5–1 |
| June 1–15[b] | 0.5–1 |
| Aug. 15–31 | 1 |
| Nov. 1–15[c] | 1–1.5 |
| Total N | 3–4.5 |

| WIN (lb/1000 sq ft)[d] | |
|---|---|
| Date | Rates |
| May 1–15[a] | 1–1.5 |
| Aug. 1–15 | 1–2 |
| Nov. 1–15[c] | 1–1.5 |
| Total N | 3–5 |

[a]Initiate program after 20–30% spring greenup.
[b]June application recommended primarily for high–use fields.
[c]Final application made after last mowing while grass is still green.
[d]Based on N sources containing more than 35% WIN. Use the higher rates as % WIN increases.

Table 3.9. Fertility Programs for Kentucky Bluegrass, Perennial Ryegrass, or Creeping Bentgrass Sports Turfs Grown on Sand–Based Soils Utilizing Water Soluble Nitrogen (WSN) or Water Insoluble Nitrogen (WIN) Sources

| WSN (lb/1000 sq ft) | |
|---|---|
| Date | Rates |
| May 1–15[a] | 0.5–1 |
| June 1–15 | 0.5–1 |
| Aug. 1–15 | 1 |
| Oct. 1–15 | 1–1.5 |
| Nov. 1–15[b] | 1–1.5 |
| Total N | 4–6 |

| WIN (lb/1000 sq ft)[c] | |
|---|---|
| Date | Rates |
| May 1–15[a] | 1.5–2 |
| Aug. 1–15 | 1–2 |
| Nov. 1–15[b] | 1.5–2 |
| Total N | 4–6 |

[a]Initiate program after 20–30% spring greenup.
[b]Final application made after last mowing while grass is still green.
[c]Based on N sources containing more than 35% WIN. Use the higher rates as % WIN increases.

## 3.8 MICRONUTRIENTS

In regard to micronutrients required for plant growth, only sand-based fields will typically require regularly scheduled applications, because of the low nutrient-holding (CEC) capacity of that type of soil. Soils high in clay and/or silt will rarely need applications of the other nutrients as long as soil pH is maintained at the appropriate level and clippings are returned.

Soil and tissue testing should be used as the guide to maintaining sufficiency levels of the remaining nutrients necessary for plant growth. Unnecessary applications of micronutrients should be avoided, because these can result in phytotoxicity to the turf. At the very least, they are a waste of money.

One exception is a micronutrient of great importance to sports field managers, and one that is applied quite often: iron (Fe). Foliar applied iron results in a rapid greenup of turf without a flush of shoot growth, a very desirable response throughout much of the growing season. Liquid iron sources are also commonly tank-mixed with many pesticides to mask the yellowing the pesticide might cause. Iron is immobile within the plant, so as the turf is mowed, the effects of the iron are removed. An iron application to most sports fields that are mowed once or twice a week will provide some greening response for about 10 to 14 days (less if the turf is mowed more often).

Since iron is a micronutrient, application rates are typically presented on the label in terms of pounds per acre, in contrast to nitrogen levels, which are commonly expressed in pounds per 1000 square feet. As many turf managers know, liquid iron can dramatically enhance the quality and (especially) the appearance of sports fields.

If other micronutrients are recommended by soil or tissue testing, there are many micronutrient packages available. Some of the most popular and easiest to apply micronutrient fertilizers are formulated as "chelates." Chelate is a German word that means "claw," and the concept in the formulation of the fertilizer is that the particular micronutrient is bound in a carbon-atom ring, thus preventing the micronutrient from becoming rapidly bound into plant-unavailable forms in the soil through chemical reactions. This improves uptake efficiency of the nutrient and results in a more rapid plant response. The chelated sources are slightly more expensive, but are usually worth the extra money because of the immediate response to the nutrient application.

# Chapter 4

# *Aeration*

## 4.1 INTRODUCTION

Aeration is the process of disturbing the soil in a controlled fashion in order to relieve compaction and allow air, water, and nutrients to penetrate into the soil.

Soil compaction can be defined as the compression of the topsoil, primarily due to foot or vehicular traffic. This compression can be a particular problem on sports turf, because of the excessive amounts of foot traffic that result from its use as a playing surface, and because that traffic is largely concentrated in certain areas of the field. Compaction ultimately becomes detrimental to turfgrass growth for two primary reasons: turf root systems can't get the oxygen they need, and the compacted soil becomes a physical barrier to root penetration. To restore its capacity as the ideal growing medium for turf plants, soil on sports fields needs to be aerated from time to time.

## 4.2 AERATING FOR OPTIMUM TURF RESPONSES

When timing an aeration event, be sure that the grass is actively growing so that it will recuperate quickly. Despite its long-term benefits, aeration causes some stress on the turf. In most soils and conditions, full recovery from core aeration (the most disruptive type) takes about 15 days.

On heavily used **warm season** fields, two core aeration events would be appropriate, one of them in mid- to late spring (after the turf has completely emerged from winter dormancy) and the other in mid- to late summer. On fields that are used less, aerating once a year, in late spring, is sufficient. For warm season turfgrass, it's important to allow adequate recovery time following any late-season aeration before the onset of winter weather, which could cause cold injury.

For heavily used **cool season** fields, core aerate twice a year, once in May and once in September. Lightly used fields can be aerated once, in either of those two months. An alternative practice available to cool-season fields managers can actually turn the cold weather into a tool for combating compaction. Core aerate right before winter and leave the holes exposed. Cool season turfgrasses are unlikely to be injured by the cold, and the freezing and thawing of water in the holes will fracture the soil even more deeply than usual, and will provide improved relief from compaction.

If lime or fertilizer applications are needed, coordinate them with planned aeration events to help get the materials directly into the soil.

In the past, there were questions about the wisdom of performing core aeration following preemergent herbicide applications, and particularly about whether or not the herbicide barrier is broken by aeration. Recent information indicates that the herbicide activity is probably not greatly altered, especially if the cores are returned. Still, it is a good idea to aerate before a preemergent herbicide application if possible.

Multiple passes (in different directions) are often required at each aeration event, depending on the spacing of tines and the severity of compaction. A reasonable goal would be 12 to 16 holes per square foot of turf.

Returning the cores can be performed by mat-dragging the field after aerating, or by vertical mowing. Core return is a good idea on most fields, because it represents a form of topdressing using the soil native to the field.

## 4.3  AERATION EQUIPMENT

A wide variety of aeration equipment is available for sports turf, each type with its own strengths and weaknesses.

### 4.3a  Hollow Tine (Core) Aeration

The most common type of aeration is hollow tine core aeration, regarded by many turf managers as one of the most useful practices in the maintenance of a quality sports field. In fact, heavily used sports fields that do not get regular core aeration usually have very little turf. The beneficial effects on the soil physical properties of hollow tine aeration cannot be equaled by any other type of cultivation equipment. Core aeration provides the longest-term benefits in improving soil aeration, water infiltration, and percolation rates. The ultimate result is healthier root systems.

There are, however, two problems of core aeration which must be addressed: surface disruption and handling of the removed cores. Core aeration events must be scheduled around the most important sporting events, especially for sports such as baseball and field hockey, where true roll of the ball is critical. Core aeration holes (and the cores, if they are not removed) can create unsatisfactory playing conditions; the unbroken cores can affect footing of players and disrupt the roll of a ball, and the holes can catch players' cleats.

To shorten the recovery time following hollow tine aeration, fertilize and irrigate in amounts that promote vigorous plant growth.

There are numerous depths and diameters of tines available for core aeration. Generally, the tine diameters on most standard machines range from ¼ inch to ¾ inch in diameter, and the lengths (depth of coring action) are typically 3–6 inches. The deep tine units now available for core aeration can remove up to 1 inch diameter cores to depths of 12 inches. For most sports field aeration needs, standard units do the job effectively, but each turf manager must match the needs of the particular field with the types of equipment available. Fields with profound compaction problems or fields with standing surface water can benefit from deep tine aeration, which provides limited, but immediate, improvement in field drainage due to the holes it creates. The process can be particularly helpful on fields that were heavily compacted by rolling when they were constructed.

Deep tine aerating can be especially helpful in combination with topdressing with sand. The sand is dragged into the holes created by the aerating process, and creates a sand-filled channel that facilitates the movement of air, water, and nutrients deep into the soil. This process assists the growth of deeper roots that substantially improve the health and durability of the turfgrass culture.

*Figure 4.1. This core (or "hollow tine") aerator is designed to remove deep cores, 10" to 12" below the surface. This type of equipment both fights compaction and improves drainage on many fields. (Photo courtesy of James Thompson, Mississippi State University.)*

### 4.3b Solid Tine Aeration

Most of the principles of hollow tine core aeration should also be followed for solid tine aeration, which creates a hole but does not remove a core. Solid tines are usually selected because of the limited surface disruption they cause, but there are other important differences in the effects of solid tines on the soil. Solid tine aeration is also commonly called "shatter core" aeration. The solid tines cause a "quaking" action in the soil that can be used to fracture subsurface compaction zones. (Different types of equipment require different amounts of moisture in the soil; it's a good idea to check with the equipment distributor to determine the ideal moisture levels for the aerator to be used.)

It's important to realize that solid tine aeration alone is not a complete aeration program. As a matter of fact, the repeated use of solid tines over the years can actually *create* a compaction zone (called a cultivation pan) in the soil, particularly if the same diameter and depth tines are used. A good practice is to incorporate solid tine aeration into the overall cultivation program and use it when the field needs some short-term benefits in water infiltration and percolation with minimal surface disruption.

#### Vibration/Quaking

As previously mentioned, solid tine aeration is sometimes referred to as "quaking" or "shatter core" aeration, because of the lifting action on the top of the soil profile applied by the tines of the aerator. There are other vibration units, typically PTO-driven, which penetrate fairly shallowly, but which can still be very effective for light soil cultivation in

*Figure 4.2. This sample soil profile shows a sand channel created through the soil by aerating and topdressing. Deep roots can be seen in the sand channel at the bottom of the sample.*

areas with obstacles like tree roots that can damage traditional hollow or solid tines. These vibration units can be particularly useful in seedbed preparation.

### 4.3c Deep Tine Aeration

There are numerous machines on the market that are designed to penetrate much deeper into the soil than traditional aeration units. These machines may have either hollow or solid tines with diameters ranging from ½ to 1 inch and penetration depths from 8 to 12 inches. This equipment can be especially helpful in aerating the deeply compacted middle sections of a football field, or the areas around the goals of soccer fields. Deep tine aeration can also allow water to drain through the soil on fields that were heavily compacted by rolling when they were constructed.

*Figure 4.3. This solid tine aerator with quaking action aggressively relieves compaction, but does not remove the grass plants from the soil. It should be used when the soil is dry; used on moist soil, such devices can actually cause compaction.*

At present, most athletic field sites do not own deep tine units, and the service is usually performed by a custom applicator. However, prices for these units continue to drop, and since deep tine aeration can result in immediate improvements in field aeration and drainage, the turf manager should consider the addition of a deep tine aerator to the equipment inventory of their facility.

### 4.3d Deep Drilling

Another type of cultivation which is increasing in popularity, particularly on high profile sports fields, is deep drill aeration. The process is just what it sounds like—metal bits (typically 12″ long by 1″ in diameter) are drilled into the soil in an action similar to that of a fence posthole digger. Drill aeration is a very effective way of creating a deep channel through the soil, and the soil that is removed is not in the form of intact cores, but rather is granular material that can easily be dragged over the soil surface and back into the holes.

Another option is what the industry terms "drill and fill" operations. This type of equipment can deliver a soil amendment (such as sand or a mixture of sand and conditioner) directly into the holes as they are drilled. This creates a more permanent drainage channel through the soil profile. Research continues to explore the most beneficial uses of "drill and fill" applications.

The disadvantages of deep drilling in general are the slower operating speeds of the

*Figure 4.4. Deeply penetrating solid tines such as these help to fight the most compacted areas of a field, and can also be helpful in correcting drainage problems created by overcompaction of subsoil during the construction of a facility.*

*Figure 4.5. Deep drilling aerators remove soil to a consistent depth, and in a granular form which can be dragged back into the soil instead of being removed as intact cores.*

*Figure 4.6. Water-injection aerators use a thin jet of high-pressure water to loosen the soil to depths up to 15" without substantial surface disruption. Prototype air-injection systems are now being developed as well.*

machines and the cost of the equipment (or contract service). Even more than deep tine aeration, deep drilling is typically a contract service from an outside provider.

### 4.3e   Water-Injection Aeration
A relatively new device that provides many of the benefits of solid tine aeration with virtually no surface disruption is the high-pressure, water-injection aerator. This equipment uses self-contained pumps that generate microstreams of water at very high pressure. These microstreams can penetrate the soil to a depth of up to 15 inches, and they create a hole that's so small most people walking across the turf will not realize aeration has taken place. Roots grow freely into the small channels created by injection aerating, and the limited surface disruption means the device can be used right up until game day. The design is currently being refined to allow for the injection of pesticides and wetting agents right along with the stream of water. Like the solid tine aerator, this device cannot replace the core aerator, but the injection aerator may in time come to play an important role in sports turf maintenance. In the future, also look for a machine that will perform "air injection"; prototype machines are being tested now.

### 4.3f   Spiking and Slicing
Spiking and slicing involve the penetration of solid metal blades into the soil. The immediate results are channels that allow water and air to reach the root system. Spiking and slicing can also be used to sever the lateral stems of bermudagrass, Kentucky bluegrass,

*Figure 4.7. Spiking equipment allows water and air to reach the turfgrass roots and encourages lateral growth of some varieties. Because they cause minimal surface disruption, spikers can be used during the season.*

*Figure 4.8. Slicers have an effect similar to that of spikers, and can be successfully used to enhance the overseeding process by encouraging seed:soil contact.*

*Figure 4.9. Topdressing helps to level the surface of a field, and can be used to amend heavy, clay-based soils. (Photo courtesy of James Thompson.)*

and creeping bentgrass, in order to encourage lateral growth. Slicers and spikers also work well when used to accelerate drying of persistently wet soils. The benefits of spiking or slicing are generally considered to be more short-term in duration as compared to hollow tine cultivation.

Blades are available in a wide variety of sizes, and larger blades cause different amounts of surface disruption. If small blades are used so that surface disruption is minimal, the procedure can be done frequently with less concern about affecting surface playability.

(Slicing equipment is also helpful in overseeding existing turf. Slicers create grooves in the soil that give seeds a place to germinate. This practice is usually called "slit-seeding.")

## 4.4    TOPDRESSING

Topdressing is the addition of sand or soil to the surface of the turf. This process can be used as a form of remediation for certain soil problems. Topdressing can help to level an uneven playing surface and core aeration followed by topdressing with sand can also gradually amend a heavy, clay-based soil. It can enhance the soil for better drainage and rooting, help to control thatch, and even assist seeding operations. Topdressing is also a biological-control alternative in thatch control, since it returns to the thatch layer the microorganisms that are needed to promote the decomposition of the thatch.

## 4.4a  Topdressing Procedures

When topdressing, apply frequent thin layers (usually ¹⁄₁₆″ to ⅜″) of uniform depths. Uneven layers can restrict the flow of water and nutrients into and through the soil. Mow the turf to a relatively short height before topdressing, to allow the material to easily reach the surface of the soil.

If the condition of a field can be improved by topdressing with sand instead of returning the cores, aeration provides a logical time to do that. However, it's important to account for the amount of topdressing material that will be required to fill all the holes created by the aeration process.

For instance, topdressing with a ¼″ layer of sand on a football field that has been aerated with standard ¾″ by 3″ hollow tine aerating equipment (with 3″ tine spacing) will typically require about 100 tons of sand.

Once the topdressing material has been spread on the surface of the field, drag or brush the field to push the sand into the aeration holes. When applying topdressing material, consider taking the opportunity to level the field. A tractor with a level bar attachment can level uneven surfaces and improve playability.

## 4.4b  Topdressing Material

The material used for topdressing should be physically and chemically very similar to the existing soil unless the intent is to modify the soil texture. It's important to correctly plan for the amount of material needed. Topdressing a field to a depth of ⅜″ takes 1.5 cubic yards for every 1,000 square feet.

Topdressing can also be used to amend field soil. To gradually amend heavy soils (soils having a large percentage of silt and clay) use a uniform sand with most of the particle sizes in the coarse range (between 0.5 to 2.0 mm). Fine to medium sands (between 0.1 to 0.5 mm) are better for "soil-less" root-zone mixes than for topdressing soil fields.

To enhance the quality of an existing heavy soil field, start with an aggressive core aeration. After core aerating, leave the cores so they will be mixed into the sand during the topdressing and dragging operation. (The coarse sand needs some fine soil to make it more compatible with the existing soil.) It should be noted that consistent topdressing with sand slowly converts the native soil field to one with a high sand content, so the wise manager makes sure that an adequate supply of material with the right particle size is available.

Some sports field operations have now begun to use topdressing material that includes a conditioner like calcined diatomaceous earth or calcined clay in combination with coarse sand to increase water retention. (See Section 8.3c for further discussion.)

On amended sand fields, the authors recommend that topdressing be done with sand that matches that used in the field's construction to prevent the kind of layering that can block drainage.

# Chapter 5

# *Thatch*

## 5.1 INTRODUCTION

In the first four chapters of this book we have considered turfgrasses appropriate for sports turf and soil as a medium for turfgrass culture. Now we turn our attention to a third element in sports turf: the thatch layer.

The negative effects of thatch are well documented in dozens, if not hundreds, of books and articles. However, under some circumstances thatch can play a positive role in *sports turf management,* and this positive role has been given very little attention. For some sports (and especially for football), an appropriate thatch layer can be the difference between a playable field and a mud bog. For other sports (like tennis or lawn bowling), any thatch at all is unacceptable.

In this chapter we will consider the negative effects of thatch and ways to prevent or reduce its accumulation, as well as the positive effects of thatch for specific sports. We will also review the cultural practices necessary to enhance the health of the turf while maintaining a desired thatch layer. A healthy, vigorous turf surface is our primary objective. However, in some situations, a managed thatch layer can add just enough cushion to enhance the durability of the turf surface and keep a field playable under extreme conditions.

## 5.2 DEFINITION OF THATCH

Thatch is an intermingled layer of living and dead grass stems, roots, and other organic matter that is found between the soil surface and the grass blades. (Contrary to popular belief, turf clippings contribute very little to thatch accumulation.) Thatch development signals an imbalance between the amount of organic material produced by the plant and its rate of decomposition. The growth rates and growth habits of turfgrasses, as well as the maintenance a particular field receives, are major factors in thatch development. Table 5.1 lists the thatching tendency of the most popular grasses used for sports turf.

As a general rule, any turfgrass species that spreads by runners, either aboveground (stolons) or belowground (rhizomes), is likely to produce thatch. Bermudagrass and zoysiagrass (both have stolons and rhizomes), creeping bentgrass (stolons), and Kentucky bluegrass (rhizomes) are all heavy thatch producers. These grasses respond well to aggressive fertilization, and under such maintenance develop moderate to heavy thatch. Buffalograss (stolons) and creeping red fescue (rhizomes) can also develop thatch, but development is usually very limited, since these grasses do not respond well to aggressive fertilization and mowing. Bunch-type species, such as tall fescue and perennial ryegrass,

**Table 5.1. Thatching Tendencies of Common Sports Turfgrasses**

| Thatching Tendency | Turfgrass |
| --- | --- |
| Moderate to heavy | Bermudagrass |
| | Zoysiagrass |
| | Creeping bentgrass |
| | Kentucky bluegrass |
| Low to moderate | Buffalograss |
| | Creeping red fescue |
| Low (or nonthatching) | Tall fescue |
| | Perennial ryegrass |

do not produce much thatch unless maintained under extremely high N fertility programs.

"**Thatch Management**" usually refers to the processes involved in removing thatch or preventing its development in the first place. But for sports turf, we should include one more meaning: the cultural practice of developing and maintaining a thatch layer of a desired thickness. That thickness could vary from no thatch at all (for lawn bowling or croquet) to 1″ of thatch (particularly for football fields), depending on the turfgrass variety and the sport being played on a particular field.

## 5.3   ADVANTAGES AND DISADVANTAGES OF THATCH IN SPORTS TURF

Numerous research projects have found that thatch can become a problem when its thickness exceeds ½″. But for most sports, a thin, uniform thatch layer can improve turf quality.

### 5.3a   Advantages

A limited amount of thatch (up to ½″ depth for most situations) adds resiliency to the turf, increases wear tolerance, and increases impact absorption. These benefits of thatch are especially important in contact sports where players frequently impact the field surface, and on fields such as football and soccer, where some sections of the playing area receive a disproportionate level of traffic.

In football, for instance, the ripping action of cleats eventually causes bare spots. As the season progresses, these bare spots become larger, and by season's end, the middle of the field is completely bare. When that happens, any game that is played during a rain will be a "mud bowl." Kentucky bluegrass football fields that have accumulated up to 1″ of thatch can provide extended field playability throughout the season. This strategy was employed by Vince Paterozzi in managing the football field at Cleveland's Municipal Stadium (see Fig. 5.1). The center of the field had to periodically be resodded due to excessive wear, and the specifications for the new Kentucky bluegrass sod required at least a 1″ thatch depth.

This strategy can similarly work well for any sport in which field managers have to regularly reestablish high traffic areas, as long as the manager recognizes the problems associated with the daily management of turf with such a thatch layer. These areas typically include the middle and sideline areas of football fields and the goal areas of soccer,

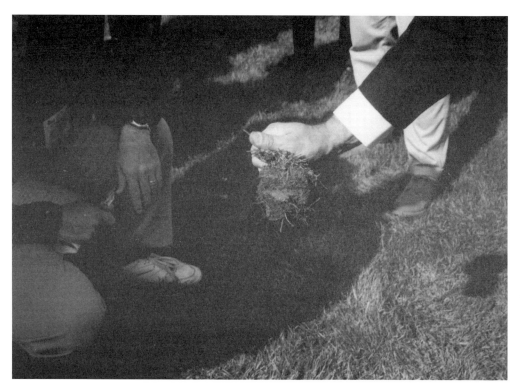

*Figure 5.1. This is a sample of a heavy thatch layer at the former Cleveland Stadium, where native clay soil could easily cause the field to turn to mud during rainy conditions. Kentucky bluegrass sod with an established thatch layer was used to support play.*

lacrosse, and field hockey fields. (It may be hard to find sod that has the desired thatch thickness; Kentucky bluegrass takes about 2 full years to develop ½″ of thatch and bermudagrass grass takes 1½ years. If regular regrassing is needed for high traffic areas, the turf manager is advised to request a sod with the desired thatch thickness at least a year in advance of the planned installation, so the sod farm can have it available when needed.)

Increased attention to watering and mowing will be required, as well as careful monitoring of potential pest problems. These thatch levels are not designed to benefit the health of the turf, but rather to enhance field playability during adverse conditions.

A limited thatch layer (less than or equal to ½″ depth) can benefit the playability of fields for sports such as baseball, soccer, lacrosse, and field hockey. As a rule of thumb, for any sport where players wear cleated footwear and make sudden turns that can rip the turf from the soil, thatch can be beneficial.

Other sports that can benefit from a limited thatch layer include the throwing events of track and field competition, especially the discus and shot put. Thatch can reduce the surface damage from the impact of the "missiles," thus reducing the depth of holes that can become trip hazards when the field is used for other sports. Even if all damage cannot be prevented, the amount of repair work will be lessened. For instance, in the 1996 Olympic venues in Atlanta, poorly performing turf was replaced with a thatched zoysiagrass to provide the needed cushion and enhance resistance to the wear and tear of the throwing events in track and field competition.

## 5.3b  Disadvantages

Although managed thatch provides benefits for most sports, excessive thatch is a disadvantage for all sports turf. Excessive thatch harbors potentially destructive turf insects and disease organisms, limits root penetration into the soil, and in some instances, creates a hydrophobic turf where water cannot infiltrate into the soil below the thatch. Heavily thatched turf also affects the performance of the field by modifying ball response, including trueness of roll and bounce. In the sports of baseball, softball, and tennis, for instance, ball response is critical to the performance of the players and the level at which the game is played.

Another disadvantage of excessive thatch is associated with seed establishment. In seeding, success is dependent on the seed reaching the soil and once germination occurs, roots of the seed must be able to penetrate the soil. Excessive thatch can prevent this establishment process.

## 5.4   HOW THATCH DEVELOPS

Thatch develops when a turfgrass produces surface organic matter at a rate faster than the organic matter can decompose. Any factor that influences the rate of organic matter production and/or decomposition also influences the thatch layer status. Thatch accumulation and decomposition occur simultaneously as part of the total turf ecosystem. If the balance between accumulation and decomposition is swayed one way or the other, the thickness of the thatch layer will be affected. Factors that influence thatch layer status include (but are not limited to): grass species, N fertilization rate and source, soil pH, mowing height, pesticide applications, soil type, and in some grasses, means of clipping disposal.

The breakdown of thatch occurs primarily by the activity of soilborne microbes and earthworms. Anything that enhances the activity of these creatures accelerates thatch decomposition. Therefore, maintaining an appropriate pH (typically, 6.5 is desirable), good soil aeration, and adequate amounts of soil moisture will reduce thatch accumulation. Also remember that many pesticides also have serious consequences in the control of nontarget organisms (beneficial fungi, earthworms, etc.) that contribute to thatch breakdown.

Increased N fertilization accelerates the growth rate of turf and often results in an increase in thatch accumulation. However, increased N fertilization does not always lead to increased thatch accumulation because such fertilization may also increase the rate of thatch-decomposition. With N fertilization, not only is the growth of the grass increased, but also the composition and concentration of thatch-decomposing bacteria and fungi can be increased. The increase in thatch decomposition with added N is most closely associated with the thatch's carbon:nitrogen ratio. Added N can create an optimal carbon:nitrogen ratio, thereby optimizing the rate of decomposition.

Sources of fertilizer also influence the thatch layer status. Some natural organic fertilizers have been shown to improve the composition and concentration of thatch-decomposing microbes by improving the overall health of the soil. Certain synthetic inorganic fertilizers not only provide essential plant nutrients, but also alter the soil environment. Some factors, such as pH, can adversely or beneficially affect the composition and concentration of thatch-decomposing microbes. Because of the varied effects of fertilizer on the thatch status, the field manager is advised to closely monitor the accumulation of thatch on each particular field.

Regular mowing helps reduce thatch accumulation by returning relatively small pieces of leaf clippings, which can be rapidly decomposed. If clippings are not to be collected, mulching mowers produce less thatch than other mowers, since the grass blades are mulched finer and therefore decompose faster. Mowing height can also affect the thatch status, depending on grass species and mowing schedules. With some bermudagrass cultivars, a low mowing height increases the accumulation of thatch. With other species, the reverse may be true; in the case of Kentucky bluegrass, cutting higher produces more thatch. In some species, like bermudagrass and zoysiagrass, clippings may contain high levels of silica or cork and contribute to excessive organic matter in the thatch layer. Depending on the circumstances and field status, clippings might be removed to avoid excessive thatch accumulation or left on the turf to help build a beneficial managed thatch layer.

Pesticides have varied effects on the thatch status. Some pesticides increase thatch levels by adversely affecting the composition and concentration of thatch-decomposing microbes. In other situations, a pesticide may slow the rate of turfgrass growth without having an adverse effect on microbes, and may therefore restrict the accumulation of thatch. The wide array of available pesticides, and the fact that these pesticides are used in various combinations, make it impossible to predict or generalize their effect on thatch accumulation.

Soil types also affect thatch formation. Turf being grown on heavy-textured soil (containing high levels of silt and clay) usually develops thatch faster than the same turf on sandy soil. This is because sandy soil has better aeration and drainage characteristics.

## 5.5    MAINTAINING A MANAGED THATCH LAYER

As we have seen, there are many factors that affect the thatch status of a turf ecosystem, and these factors are varied and difficult to predict. However, since there are clear benefits to having a managed thatch layer on most types of sports fields, careful management can be well worth the effort. In fact, where the field is a high profile school, college, or professional facility, managing a thatch layer not only is possible, but also could spell the difference between a game played on mud, and one played on acceptable or outstanding turf.

The most direct means of creating an appropriate thatch layer is to specify sod with the correct amount of thatch. However, for budgetary reasons, sodding may not be an option. In these cases, creating a managed thatch layer must be achieved by manipulating cultural practices and monitoring the thatch status. Although not a possibility in all situations, choosing the turf species is one way of gaining some control over creating a managed thatch layer. We have already discussed thatch accumulation characteristics of warm season and cool season cultivars. In transition zone areas, the planner must choose between bermudagrass and a cool season turfgrass. Bermudagrass is a better choice if thatch accumulation is a high priority. However, if the field location is clearly out of the zone of adaptation of bermudagrass (too far north), then a cool season variety must be chosen. Among the cool season choices, Kentucky bluegrass is a higher thatch-producing species than perennial ryegrass or tall fescue. This feature, along with the rhizomatous nature of Kentucky bluegrass and its resulting good sod strength, suggests the use of this species in a cool season sports turf.

Creating a suitable managed thatch layer is also assisted by appropriate cultural practices. Topdressing with sand helps to firm the thatch layer and integrate the thatch with the turf and the soil. The resulting thatch-sand mat is more beneficial than a loose thatch layer that causes shallow rooting and hydrophobic conditions. Core aeration also pro-

*Figure 5.2. Topdressing with sand adds density to the thatch layer, providing more uniform roll of a ball across the surface and better footing for the athletes.*

motes thatch decomposition, but like topdressing, this practice helps to firm the remaining thatch layer, providing a better surface for player performance.

## 5.6   REDUCING EXCESSIVE THATCH BUILDUP

### 5.6a   Mechanical Thatch Control

One of the most common methods of thatch control is vertical mowing (sometimes called "dethatching"). As the name indicates, the blades of the mower cut vertically into the turf canopy, severing lateral stems and removing some of the thatch that develops on the surface of the soil. It should be noted that vertical mowing does not substantially improve soil aeration, although it does have other benefits such as controlling the grain of the turf, thickening the grass by severing lateral stems, and preparing the turf for overseeding. (See Chapter 1, Section 1.8, for further discussion on winter overseeding of dormant bermudagrass).

Vertical mowing units are available both as riding and walk-behind units, and there are also special blades which can be installed on mowers to allow them to perform vertical mowing.

Timing a vertical mowing event requires a period of recuperation similar to that of core aeration. The tearing action of the blades can seriously disrupt the surface of the turf, so avoid vertical mowing prior to anticipated periods of environmental stress. For warm season turfgrasses, the best time for vertical mowing is late spring to early summer, when the grass is most actively growing. For cool season grasses, the optimal regimen is to conduct vertical mowing in the spring, and then again in late summer or early

*Figure 5.3. A vertical mower assists the dethatching process, severing lateral stems and removing some of the thatch from the soil surface. (Photo courtesy of James Thompson, Mississippi State University.)*

fall. Scheduling the events in these periods takes advantage of the recuperative potential of turfgrass during active growth.

The aggressive growth habit of bermudagrass, zoysiagrass, Kentucky bluegrass, and creeping bentgrass cause them to be heavy thatch producers, particularly if an aggressive fertility and irrigation program is followed. This can result in the need to dethatch the turf *as often as* once per growing season in many situations. To determine whether dethatching is needed, examine the thatch layer by removing a core with a soil sampler or even a pocket knife. If the thatch significantly exceeds ½″ in depth, dethatching is generally recommended. It's important to remove all debris that is brought to the surface by the vertical mowing operation, because leaving it on the turf will hasten thatch buildup again. (Note that the debris from bermudagrass fields contains some viable sprigs, which can serve as vegetative planting material for use on prepared seed beds.) Be sure to apply sufficient amounts of fertilizer and water after the vertical mowing operation in order to promote rapid turf recovery.

A thatch layer thicker than 2″ may require the use of a sod cutter to remove the sod (and thatch layer) in its entirety, so thatch control is critical before that thickness is reached.

## 5.6b  Topdressing

Some studies show that topdressing alone can reduce thatch; other studies show that topdressing in combination with other cultural practices such as core aerating and verticutting is a better strategy for reducing thatch. Topdressing is the best means of biological thatch control since it returns microbes to the thatch layer for decomposition. The frequency will vary depending on the turfgrass variety, the management program, and the schedule for field use.

Also, some studies show that one or two topdressings a year will reduce thatch, while others suggest four per year. When there is no clear consensus, the best advice is for the manager to use trial and error to determine the ideal strategy for the field in question.

## 5.6c Biological Controls

Horticultural technology has now developed **biological** methods of thatch control, based largely on the use of live microorganisms to break down the thatch layer. According to the manufacturers, these products work by adding the microorganisms in numbers sufficient to decompose the thatch faster than it develops.

At this writing, the authors have seen no independent research to confirm that these products work as intended.

## 5.7 CONCLUSION

Excessive thatch has always been an issue in turfgrass management, and nearly all of the research on thatch has been aimed at reducing or preventing thatch accumulation. Obviously, in the case of sports fields that would benefit from the presence of a minimum thatch layer (especially football fields), additional research needs to be performed on techniques for maintaining thatch under the extreme stresses applied by the cleats of players.

There are many studies aimed at producing quality turf, and most sports turf research is aimed at using different soil amendments to add stability to the soil, especially for football fields. We know what soil properties produce the best root systems and the cultural practices necessary to achieve dense turfgrass. However, we are leaving out an important part of turf management for certain sports; that part that comes between the grass blades and the soil: the thatch layer. A managed thatch layer can provide an important way of protecting sports fields from the most "turf disruptive sports."

## REFERENCES

*Turfgrass, Agronomy, Number 32.* Edited by D.V. Waddington, R.N. Carrow, and R.C. Shearman. 1992. American Society of Agronomy, Inc.; Crop Science Society of America, Inc.; and Soil Science Society of America, Inc., Madison, WI.

Beard, J.B. *Turfgrass: Science and Culture.* Prentice-Hall, Englewood Cliffs, NJ, 1973.

# Chapter 6

# *Mowing*

## 6.1 INTRODUCTION

Mowing is one of the most important of all turf management processes. When it's done right, mowing can help to regulate moisture in the turf, control pests, and recycle nutrients. Unfortunately, it's also a process that is often conducted with little or no thought about the impact of mowing practices—and poor management of this operation can almost ensure sickly, unattractive turf. In this chapter, we will review some of the principles of proper mowing, and we will share four of the most important rules for doing this job as part of a thoughtful program in Integrated Cultural Management.

### Rule Number 1

Always mow with a sharp blade. A sharp blade cuts each plant cleanly, and clean cutting minimizes the impact of the mowing process on the health of the turf. A dull blade pulls and shreds the blades of the plants, and that makes the turf vulnerable to disease by exposing more surface area of the plant to invading microorganisms. The most visible effect of mowing with a dull blade is a whitish cast (or sheen) on the new-mown grass. Sharpening the blades on a regular basis is absolutely essential to achieve a quality cut. For some facilities, this may mean sharpening rotary blades every week, or perhaps developing a program where the blades are sharpened based on the number of hours of operation of the equipment—for example, after every 40 hours of operation. (Reel mowers also need periodic adjustment of the reel to the bed knife to ensure a clean cut.)

### Rule Number 2

"The One-Third Rule." Cut off no more than ⅓ of the grass blade at a single mowing. Cutting off more than ⅓ of the blades erodes the health of the plants, and it also leaves an unacceptable layer of clippings on the turf. Of course, following this rule on a field that's being maintained at lower heights means more frequent mowing. For example, when cutting at 2″, the grass will need to be mowed when it reaches 3″. The grass is allowed to grow 1″ between each cutting. This could be every 3 or 4 days. But, when cutting at 1″,  and following the ⅓ rule, the staff will need to cut the grass when it reaches 1½″. The grass can be allowed to grow only ½″ before being cut again, so mowing every 2–3 days may be necessary.

*Figure 6.1. Mowing with dull blades will cause the blade ends to be shredded, increasing their vulnerability to disease.*

### Rule Number 3

When using a rotary mower, always use the highest recommended blade speed. Rapidly moving blades cut the plants more cleanly and evenly, and distribute clippings in a more uniform layer.

### Rule Number 4

Do not exceed the manufacturer's recommended ground speed with any type of mower. Speeding across the field gets the job done faster, but results in tearing of grass blades and uneven mowing.

   In addition to these four rules, it's also important to avoid mowing when the soil of the field surface is saturated; the mower wheels will cause ruts that can affect footing and ball response.

## 6.2   TYPES OF MOWERS

Most mowers are gasoline or diesel powered units, but there is now an effort by equipment manufacturers to produce high quality units powered electrically or by solar radiation (in response to energy requirements and noise ordinances). Classified by cutting action, the three types of mowers used on sports turf are rotary, reel, and flail.

### 6.2a   Rotary Mowers

Rotary mowers are the most affordable way to cut grass, and the choices in mowers vary from the 3-horsepower 21″ mowers most of us use at home, to gang mower units with

*Figure 6.2. This field was mowed when the soil was wet, causing visible ruts in the playing surface.*

an overall width greater than 15 feet. Rotary mowers cut by sheer impact of a spinning blade hitting a leaf blade; strictly speaking, the action is not a true cut, but rather more of a tearing action. Sharp blades and high blade speed make for a cleaner, higher quality tear. Operating rotaries around people, animals, buildings, or cars requires great care, because debris can be discharged at high speed along with turf clippings, and can cause serious injury. Any time a rotary mower must be operated around people, it's absolutely essential to use a shield to direct and control discharge. Under these circumstances, it's wise to consider purchasing either a self-contained, mulching mower or a rear-discharge mower.

### 6.2b  Reel Mowers

Reel units provide the highest quality cut available, and the most acceptable cut at mowing heights of less than 2″. These mowers have the cutting action like a pair of scissors, shearing the grass between one blade on the spinning reel and a "bedknife" at the base of the cutting unit. Consequently, they cut more cleanly than any other type of mower. Reel mowers have varying numbers of blades in the reel.

For turf that will be mowed at a lower height, a reel with more blades is to be preferred. Manufacturers recommend that for turf maintained above 1″, a five blade reel is sufficient. For mowing heights between ½″ and 1″, six blade reels should be used, and for heights of less that ½″, seven or eight blades are recommended.[1]

---

[1] "The Cutting Edge on Reel Mowers Versus Rotary Mowers," *SportsTURF,* February 1998, p. 14.

*Figure 6.3. This type of front-end rotary mower is one of the most common machines used for mowing sports fields around North America. This type of mower is appropriate where cutting heights will be above 2". (Photo courtesy of D. Nagel, Mississippi State University.)*

On a reel mower, the height of cut is adjusted by raising or lowering a roller that changes the height of the bedknife. Properly adjusted, this type of mower provides the closest cutting heights possible, making it the mower of choice for the highest profile turf. However, reel mowers are also by far the most expensive mowers to purchase and to maintain. Special equipment is needed to maintain both the reels and bedknives, and adjusting the mower properly takes a good deal of patience and experience.

## 6.2c  Flail Mowers

Flail mowers have seen a resurgence in popularity in sports field management in the 1990s, primarily because of product improvements leading to better mower performance and improved turf quality. Flail mowers have pivoting blades or "flails" that spin at high speed around a horizontal axle, and cut with a tearing action similar to rotary mowers. The flails "give" when they hit debris or raised spots in the turf, thus reducing the chances of a blade breaking upon impact. The mowing deck is self-contained and discharge of debris is much less than with rotary mowers, so these mowers are popular choices when mowing must be done when others might be in the area. Flail mowers are also the mowers of choice for areas surrounding the sports field itself, where there might be debris such as small stones, tree roots and branches, and spectator litter.

## 6.3  TURF RESPONSE

All kinds of biochemical processes are set into motion in a turf plant when mowing clips its leaves. First of all, the plant has to seal the wound that is created by the cutting action

*Figure 6.4. This view of a reel mower shows the blades, roller and bed knife characteristic of this equipment. (Photo courtesy of D. Nagel, Mississippi State University.)*

of the blade. Then a series of reactions take place to assist in the recovery of the plant, centered around mobilization of stored food reserves to aid in the production of new leaves and stems. Research has shown that regular mowing at the proper heights and frequencies actually encourages a thick, dense turf. Mowing according to the ⅓ rule leaves enough of each plant in place to support the necessary metabolic processes, and encourages the development of lateral stems. However, improper mowing results in turfgrass that is hard-pressed to survive the stress of environmental extremes or pests.

## 6.4   HEIGHT AND FREQUENCY

There is no single "ideal" mowing height for turfgrass. Choice of mowing height is influenced by the type of grass, the climate of the area, the time of year, even the speed and style of play of the team that will use the field. The chart in Table 6.1 represents guidelines for mowing various turfgrasses in spring, summer, and fall, and following these recommendations will provide optimum turf quality. The grass can be cut shorter than recommended by the chart, but may require more frequent mowing to observe the ⅓ rule and may stress the turf during adverse environmental conditions. Closer-cut fields may require more water, more frequent fertilization, and more help in contending with weeds and disease problems. Cutting too high creates a shock to the grass when it's time to lower the height for games.

Like all processes involved in maintaining turfgrass, proper mowing requires planning. The maintenance staff must be committed to a regular mowing program, including a planned frequency, in order to produce a quality field. The recommended frequency is

**Table 6.1. Recommended Seasonal Mowing Heights**

| Type of Grass | Lowest to Highest | Spring | Summer | Fall | Winter[a] |
|---|---|---|---|---|---|
| Kentucky bluegrass | 1½–3″ | 1½–2″ | 3″ | 1½–2″ | |
| Perennial ryegrass | 1½–3″ | 1½–2″ | 3″ | 1½–2″ | |
| Tall fescue | 1½–3″ | 1½–2″ | 3″ | 1½–3″ | |
| Bermudagrass | ¾–2″ | ¾–1″ | ¾–1″ | 1–2″ | 1–2″ |
| Creeping Bentgrass[b] | ⅛–¼″ | ⅛–³⁄₁₆″ | ³⁄₁₆–¼″ | ⅛–³⁄₁₆″ | |
| Bermudagrass[b] | ⅛–¼″ | ³⁄₁₆–¼″ | ⅛–³⁄₁₆″ | ⅛–¼″ | ⅛–¼″ |

[a]Overseeded bermudagrass.
[b]Recommendations for tennis, lawn bowling, and croquet.
Note: A reel mower should be used for cutting heights less than 2″.

based, not on the number of days since the last mowing, but rather on the ⅓ rule. With the rapid plant growth during the growing season, the turf might have to be mowed as much as 2 or 3 times per week for football, baseball, and soccer fields. For the close-cut turf of tennis, lawn bowling, and croquet, the turf may have to be mowed daily.

During the competitive season the cutting height should be based upon a number of factors: the capabilities of available mowing equipment, the amount of play on the field, and the desires of the coaches and players. These are ranked in no particular order, because for each situation, considerations specific to those circumstances would determine the basis for the cutting height.

For example, if the field is heavily used (as a practice field would be), then it is advantageous to the turf to use the high end of the cutting height range as a buffer in order to reduce the wear and tear on the turf. Lower cut turf may not provide enough biomass to sustain heavy foot traffic for long periods of time.

For lower use fields (such as game fields), cutting heights can be selected on the basis of the desires of the coaches or players that regularly use the field. If a baseball coach, for instance, has a team that lacks footspeed on defense, he might want the grass to be cut higher in order to slow ground balls so that the players have a better chance of getting to them. Conversely, if a football coach has a very quick backfield, then a faster, shorter-cut turf might be an advantage to the team. The cutting height of the turf can be a very important component of the entirely legal "home field advantage."

Less frequent mowing may be performed during the off-season, but it's still important to keep the turf mowed on a regular basis. Mowing heights could be raised by ½″ to 1½″ during the off-season to reduce frequency of cut. However, a turf that is neglected for several months at a time cannot be brought to peak playing conditions by one or two low-height mowings just before the season starts. Reducing mowing heights to game-competition heights must begin at least 4 to 6 weeks in advance of the first game. It's important to remember that reduced off-season mowing requirements do not mean that mowing is not required during the off-season.

## 6.5   PATTERN

The sports public has come to regard striping the turf as one of the hallmarks of a good field. It's possible to create all sorts of attractive patterns on the turf; striping the field is limited only by the supervisor's imagination and the available staff time, especially if a reel mower is available. Cutting the turf in different directions bends the leaves in oppo-

*Figure 6.5. The attractive striping pattern on this Kentucky bluegrass football field was created by using a roller behind a rotary mower, and mowing alternating five-yard sections in opposite directions.*

site directions, causing the leaves to reflect light differently, resulting in the appearance of dark and light green areas. The darker stripes represent areas mowed toward the viewer, who is looking into the turf and seeing a shadow from the blades; lighter turf was mowed away from the viewer, who is seeing the reflection of light from the flat leaf surface.

Turfgrass species differ in their response to striping. Perennial ryegrass has a high striping ability, whereas bermudagrass has low potential to stripe. To overcome the poor striping nature of bermudagrass, many sports turf managers apply foliar iron applications every 5 yards across the field. Done properly, this results in the visually appealing dark and light green stripes.

While striping the turf does not affect playability, the appearance of a neatly kept field does tend to encourage pride in those that maintain the field, as well as among players, who enjoy playing on a such a "professional-looking" field. From a public relations standpoint, this pride is also engendered among boosters, school officials, and others in the community whose support is essential to the long-term success of the fields maintenance program.

## 6.6  CLIPPING REMOVAL

With regular mowing, clipping removal is not usually necessary, except where the closeness of the cut and the turf's playability can be affected by the clippings. Clippings actually don't contribute significantly to the formation of thatch; rather, they act as slow release fertilizer for the turf. So it makes sense to leave clippings on the turf whenever

*Figure 6.6. This bermudagrass field shows almost the same appearance achieved by applying iron to alternating sections. Using a roller on bermudagrass does not create as much contrast between sections.*

possible. However, if mowing results in an excess of clippings that are undesirable, there are bucket or bag type collectors available for most mowers. There is also a variety of commercial sweepers, ranging from very affordable models with ground-driven brushes that can collect clippings from a few thousand square feet to PTO-driven units that can clean up several acres at a time.

## 6.7   EQUIPMENT AND SAFETY

We have already mentioned the precautions that must be taken in mowing around people or animals. Choose equipment carefully and keep all shields and guards in place—don't yield to the temptation to remove them to ease clipping discharge! Small rocks, sticks, and other debris can be discharged at high speeds if not blocked by a guard.

Ensure that all employees review the manufacturer's safety information before operating the mower—many equipment makers now provide videos in addition to printed manuals. (If a mower does not come with such information, there are several available training videos which will provide it.) Also, make it a point to insist that the staff use proper eye and ear protection and footwear, and that all safety procedures be followed to the letter.

## 6.8   CHEMICAL GROWTH REGULATORS

The practice of applying chemical plant growth regulators (PGRs) for suppressing foliar growth and/or seedhead formation of turfgrasses is not new. However, recent years have

**Table 6.2. Some Examples of Plant Growth Regulators Used in Turfgrass Maintenance**

| Decade Released | Trade Name | Chemical Name |
|---|---|---|
| 1970s | Embark | Mefluidide |
| 1980s | Cutless | Flurprimidol |
|  | Limit | Amidochlor |
|  | Shortstop | EPTC |
|  | Scotts TGR | Paclobutrazol |
| 1990s | Primo | Trinexapac-ethyl |

seen renewed interest in PGRs for turfgrass, based on new chemistry research and new products only now being brought to market. A brief summary of the PGRs that have been used in fine turf maintenance is presented in Table 6.2.

Plant growth regulators are assigned to one of three classes, depending on their mode of action. Class A PGRs interfere with the production of the plant hormones called *gibberellins*, which influence cell elongation, photoperiod response, and chilling tolerance. These products are useful on intensively managed turf areas, usually result in relatively little phytotoxicity, and provide short periods of growth suppression activity (typically 3 to 4 weeks). An example of this class of compounds is Primo™.

Class B PGRs interfere with gibberellin biosynthesis, but at earlier stages in the production pathway. They generally provide longer periods of growth regulation (typically 5 to 6 weeks), but there is also greater risk of phytotoxicity on higher maintenance turf. Two examples of Class B materials are Cutless™ and Scott's TGR™.

Class C compounds are mitotic (cell division) inhibitors; they arrest new growth for a limited time period (3 to 4 weeks). These products are noted for outstanding seedhead suppression, but can cause significant turfgrass discoloration. Common Class C PGRs are Embark™ and Limit™.

PGRs fit many sports field management programs because of their potential for reducing mowing requirements and associated maintenance, and for their ability to improve surface quality. However, in selecting PGRs it's important to be aware of the strengths and limitations of each particular product. Some PGRs provide only seedhead or foliar suppression, while others are capable of both. Next, be aware of how the product gets into the plant. This will indicate whether irrigation or rainfall is necessary or even desirable following chemical application. These factors for four popular PGRs used in sports turf maintenance are presented in Table 6.3.

The growth regulating effect of these and other PGRs can vary from site to site, based on the particular variety of turfgrass, the maintenance level of the turf, the chemical use

**Table 6.3. Uptake Site and Suppression Type for Four Popular Turfgrass PGRs**

| Chemical | Site of Uptake | PGR Activity | |
|---|---|---|---|
|  |  | Seedhead | Foliar |
| Primo | foliar | no | yes |
| Scotts TGR | root | yes | yes |
| Cutless | root | yes | no |
| Embark | foliar | yes | yes |

rate, and the degree of turf discoloration that is or is not acceptable in each situation. When used properly, a PGR such as Primo will provide at least a 50% reduction in clipping production over a 3- to 4-week period, and minimal turf discoloration. Over time, the Primo treatment will actually result in a darker green turf.

A PGR such as Embark also reduces foliar growth for similar time periods, but its real strength is in seedhead suppression. There is more initial concern with phytotoxicity from Embark applications, but it will also provide a dark green color response over time.

PGRs must be treated with the same respect afforded any other chemical agent, and that includes closely following label instructions. *Never* apply PGRs to grasses that are under stress—this increases the risk of turfgrass phytotoxicity; wastes time, money, and manpower; and falls into the "environmentally irresponsible" category.

Within one week, the response to PGRs becomes quite obvious. Following an application of a product like Primo, for instance, turfgrasses will have a thicker, darker green canopy that requires less frequent mowing. However, PGRs can also have other important applications in sports turf management, as well, including:

- Conversion programs. PGRs have been successfully used to slow the growth of one turfgrass and allow for better establishment of another when overseeding one turfgrass into another one.
- Accommodation to rain. These products can help the manager maintain control of the mowing program during inclement weather.
- Improved turf quality and playability. Some PGRs can reduce mowing without sacrificing the turf's ability to recuperate from divoting or other damage. Part of the improvement in quality comes from the tightening and thickening effects mentioned above, and some of it is due to the color response. For instance, common bermudagrass sports turfs treated with Primo take on many characteristics of the higher quality, vegetatively established bermudagrasses. The recuperative or grow-in rates of treated bermudagrasses have been shown to be equal to untreated bermudagrasses, eliminating much of the concern that growth regulation was so complete the turf did not recuperate quickly after damage.
- Ease of mowing. There are the obvious benefits in treating difficult-to-mow areas, or in edging baselines and fenced areas.
- Preliminary research is showing promising results indicating some PGRs may improve the cold tolerance of turfgrasses, promote rooting, improve water use efficiency, and make for tighter-knit sods that are more resistant to wear.

Use of a PGR has its drawbacks. The cost of the product itself may be a problem for limited budgets. (However, with the potential benefits listed above, a wise manager will carefully consider whether the cost of the product is not offset by potential savings in staff time.) There may be a higher incidence of some diseases on PGR-treated turf.

Furthermore, when using a PGR, the staff must commit to a complete program with the product. This is because of what has been called the "coiled spring" effect, a phenomenon that follows almost any PGR application. Much of the lateral and upward growth potential of the plant is held in check following PGR treatment, as a spring is compressed. When the PGR treatment wears off—when the compression is removed—the plant growth (and the spring) is quickly released. Tremendous surges in growth typically occur after the effects of the PGR diminish, and the manager must account for this rebound in planning the mowing program for the facility.

# Chapter 7

# *Irrigation*

## 7.1   INTRODUCTION

Sports turf managers are constantly concerned about how their fields look and whether or not the field is safe. A safe, green field is the goal of any sports turf manager, and proper irrigation is one of the key elements in reaching that goal.

In this chapter, we will consider the role of irrigation in the Integrated Cultural Management of a sports turf facility. As we review the subject of irrigation, it is important that we distinguish between "irrigation" as a general process and "installed irrigation systems" as one way to accomplish that process. A field can be irrigated in a number of ways; an installed irrigation system is one. We will briefly discuss some of the other irrigation methods in wide use in North America, but the bulk of our discussion will focus on installed irrigation systems, which are by far the most efficient and effective in promoting healthy turfgrass.

## 7.2   IRRIGATION AND TURFGRASS CULTURE

Strong, healthy turf will hold up better under the stress of sporting events, and adequate irrigation is critical to promoting that healthy turfgrass culture. Proper irrigation promotes deep and healthy roots, and helps the turf recover quickly from the damage inflicted by competition. Poorly irrigated sports fields may fail to recover from any substantial damage, and may become unplayable before the end of a season.

A healthy, properly watered turf will have fewer weeds and insects, reducing the need for fertilizer and pesticide applications. These reduced applications mean lower maintenance costs. Healthy turfgrass culture can have other cost advantages as well, including reduced water usage. When all of the potential savings are tabulated, it becomes increasingly apparent that a properly designed, installed, and maintained irrigation system, combined with a well thought-out watering schedule, can both reduce operating costs and contribute to a healthy turf. Even more important, well-irrigated turf promotes player safety because it's softer and more uniform. Greener, more visually appealing fields also enhance school spirit and team pride—both among the players and among the team that maintains the facility.

## 7.3   GENERAL PRINCIPLES OF TURFGRASS IRRIGATION

Among sports turf managers, the principle of "deep and infrequent" watering remains the norm. While this practice is generally an effective tactic, the physical soil properties

*Figure 7.1. Installed irrigation systems provide the most effective combination of uniform watering and operating efficiency. (Photo courtesy of Hunter Industries)*

must also be considered in planning any watering program. Obviously, a clay soil will not accept as much water as a sandy soil, and will require lighter, more frequent irrigation. Consideration must also be given to scheduled field usage; a heavy irrigation event a few hours before a game can result in slippery and even dangerous playing conditions.

Most turfgrasses, including overseeded bermudagrass, need as much as 1″ to 1½″ of water per week during the growing season to support turf growth. This could come either from rainfall or from supplemental irrigation. If the turf is not receiving enough water it will "tell" an attentive manager when it needs water. Signs like leaf rolling and wilting, sustained footprinting (failure of the turf to spring back quickly after foot or vehicular traffic), and a change in turf color to a blue-green color are all characteristic of desiccation—excessive dryness.

The best **time** to irrigate turf is in the early morning hours, just prior to or just after sunrise. Early morning irrigation does not interfere with play in most situations, and serves to minimize the period of leaf surface wetness. Reducing the time the turf leaves stay wet is an effective way to reduce disease incidence. Early morning irrigation also tends to get more water into the soil for plant use, since evaporation rates at that time of day are minimal. Also, wind disruption of the irrigation pattern are of less concern in the early morning hours. Finally, early morning irrigation usually allows for adequate field drying before competition or practice, so play can proceed without a slippery surface.

## 7.4 PORTABLE IRRIGATION SYSTEMS

Portable irrigation systems are those which move around the field, either transported by the staff or moving under their own power. Although these systems are used on many sports fields, they cannot be considered as efficient as installed systems.

## 7.4a   Traveling Irrigators

This system consists of a rotating sprinkler attached to a hose, propelling itself along a wire. The sprinkler winds itself along the wire using water pressure to drive an internal winch mechanism. When the traveling irrigator reaches the end of the wire, it turns itself off. The wire then needs to be reset to a new location and the sprinkler moved to the new line.

Traveling irrigators require a considerable amount of labor to continually move the setup, and must be actively supervised to ensure uniform and adequate irrigation. Watering is usually restricted to the daytime hours, since traveling equipment is vulnerable to vandalism (or even theft) if left out at night or unattended.

## 7.4b   Quick Coupler Systems

These systems are comprised of a series of underground pipes with quick couplers (sometimes called "quick connects") permanently installed flush with the ground. (City water systems usually provide all the water pressure required to operate the system, but where pressure is low, booster pumps may be used.) The valves on these systems are constructed so that a special connecting device, known as a "quick coupler key," must be utilized to turn them on. Hoses or sprinklers can then be attached directly to the system.

To operate the system, the key (or the direct-connection sprinkler head) is inserted into the valve and given a half turn *to the right*. (This is different than most valves, and one of the weaknesses of the quick-connect system; many valves have been damaged by being forced in the "normal" direction.) Turning the valve to the right opens it, and locks it into position.

Like traveling irrigators, quick coupler systems have many disadvantages. In order to irrigate an area, hoses must be dragged around the field or sprinklers must be moved from valve to valve in a timely manner. Often, the staff allows the sprinklers to stay on for irregular amounts of time, so coverage is not uniform. To reduce the time and effort of watering, there is a tendency to operate too many sprinklers at once. This causes a drop in pressure, and the sprinklers will fail to throw the desired distance, resulting in uneven watering.

Portable systems are cheaper to install than automatic systems. But because of their disadvantages, portable systems are viable alternatives only where budget limitations prohibit the installation of automatic irrigation.

(It should be noted that portable systems being installed today must have the same type of backflow prevention device required for installed systems. See Section 7.5a for more on backflow prevention.)

## 7.4c   Rain Guns

A rain gun is a huge impact-type sprinkler (placed above the grade), which is used to irrigate a large turf area. These devices are most commonly used in agricultural applications, but some sports field managers use them in their irrigation programs. Rain guns can be installed in two ways. The first is to permanently install the device in a fence or other barrier off the field of play. (This type of installation is commonly used for polo fields, where irrigation equipment must be kept away from the playing surface for the protection of the horses.) When irrigation is required, these permanently installed guns are simply turned on to water the turf. While this kind of permanent installation is convenient to use, it also exposes the rain gun to vandalism or theft, and also creates an appearance that many people find unappealing.

The second way to use rain guns is to run a permanent supply line to a point off the field of play, and to install a connection at that point. The rain gun, mounted on a cart or stand, is then moved into position and connected to the supply line when irrigation is necessary. This method does not expose the equipment to vandalism, but it does require a substantial amount of labor to operate.

Rain gun irrigation has several drawbacks. First of all, the application of water is typically uneven, with some areas heavily watered and others receiving very little irrigation. (Hand watering will usually be required to ensure adequate irrigation.) Also, the initial installation costs of these systems can be high, because a large pump station is usually required to supply water to a rain gun. The high flow rate of these guns also requires the installation of a large-diameter pipe. Several rain guns are usually required to water a field, further adding to the setup costs of such a system.

## 7.5   INSTALLED IRRIGATION SYSTEMS

The popularity of installed irrigation systems is growing rapidly. The price of installing an irrigation system is decreasing, while the reliability of operation is increasing. Automatic systems save maintenance labor costs when compared to portable systems, and the even distribution (and the resulting savings) of water is improved with well designed and maintained systems.

*Figure 7.2. Automatic irrigation system pop-up rotor heads like this one have a thick rubber cover, a small exposed surface, and the ability to provide uniform watering. (Photo courtesy of Hunter Industries)*

## 7.5a Design

As with the design of the field itself, proper design of the irrigation system is the critical step; a poorly designed system cannot be made to work properly by remedial steps later. The system design should be driven by player safety, as well as the need for dependability, efficiency, and easy maintenance.

It may be tempting to employ the services of a volunteer designer for an irrigation project, but an experienced sports field irrigation designer or consultant can usually allow the field manager to save both time and money in the long run. Designing an effective system requires knowledge of pipe hydraulics, zoning techniques, head spacing, wire sizing, and the efficiency, features, and reliability of various manufacturers' rotary sprinklers, valves, and controllers. The cost to repair a single error in any of these areas can easily be higher than the fee charged by an experienced designer.

In planning a system, the designer will give a great deal of consideration to choosing the most appropriate products, since each sports field project has its own specific product and budget requirements. Placement of the heads and valves will also be a major consideration, and the designer will place the heads so they are not in heavy traffic areas and the valves so they are well off the field of play.

### Pipe

The pipe running from the irrigation system's point of connection (POC) into the service line to the zone control valves is called the "continuous pressure main line," or simply the "main line." It is a common practice to use solvent-welded PVC pipe at a depth of 18 inches below the surface for pipe sizes up to 4 inches, and 24 inches below the surface for pipes larger than 4 inches. Gasketed pipe is sometimes specified and should be placed deeper; 36 inches under the surface for pipes larger than 4 inches is usually considered reasonable. However, higher system pressures may lead the designer to specify deeper installation to hold the pipe securely in place.

The nonpressure pipes which connect the control valves to the sprinkler heads are referred to as "lateral lines." These lines can be installed at a depth of 12 inches, which is standard for the industry.

The backfill surrounding the pipe should be rock-free and compacted to the same degree as the neighboring soil. The rock-free backfill will help to prevent pipe breakage, and the consistent compaction will prevent ruts in the turf that are caused by the uneven settling of the soil over the pipe trench.

Poured-in-place concrete "thrust blocks" are sometimes specified where pipe connections must be especially solid. For instance, thrust blocks are typically specified at all changes in direction on all gasketed pipe, for main line pipes over 2″ in diameter, and on long runs when the system will have higher than normal pressure.

Specifying the proper pipe sizes helps to maintain the correct water velocity and to minimize friction losses throughout the system. Water flowing through pipes experiences considerable drag or friction from the pipe itself; when the velocity of the water increases, the pressure loss from friction increases. If the pipe used for the system is too small, the operating pressure will be much lower for the heads at the end of the zone than for the heads closest to the valve serving that zone. There should be no more than a 10% variation in pressure among all heads on a zone.

Some of the sports field irrigation system designs in this book show a looped main line. This helps to maintain about the same pressure from one zone to another. The reduced pressure loss experienced when the water is flowing from two directions in a looped main line helps to achieve a relatively balanced pressure throughout the main line

*Figure 7.3. Thrust blocks at points where the pipe changes direction will keep the system from shifting, and prevent leaks at the joints.*

at a reduced cost. Achieving the same balanced pressure with a single-connection main line would require a larger pipe than is necessary with the looped system. The smaller pipe size saves money while reducing the pressure loss to the furthest valve.

PVC pipe is also commonly used as sleeves for the irrigation system's pipes and wires where they pass under walkways, driveways, and roads. A good rule of thumb for sleeve sizing is two times the size of the pipe being sleeved.

### Sprinklers, Nozzles, and Swing Joints
The sprinkler head consists of three major components: the main body of the device, the nozzles through which water flows out of the body, and the swing joint at the bottom of the body which maintains the sprinkler's connection to the lateral lines.

*Figure 7.4. A properly installed sprinkler head will be flush with the finish grade of the turf. (Photo courtesy of Hunter Industries)*

Sprinkler heads have been gradually downsized over the years, primarily for safety purposes. Newer heads have a small surface diameter and a protective thick rubber cover which makes them a very safe alternative to the older-style sprinklers. Additionally, many of the newer heads have a strong spring for positive retraction so the head will not endanger the players by staying in the up position after the watering is completed. Many of today's safer heads also have a heavy-duty body cap to stand up to the large equipment now being used in routine maintenance. Most newer gear-driven rotary sprinkler heads should be installed right at the finish grade of the turf.

Irrigation experts recommend a rotary sprinkler with a large nozzle selection. The nozzle is chosen to fine-tune the flow of water out of the system. The experienced irrigation system designer will use correct nozzle sizes to obtain "matched precipitation." (The precipitation rate for sprinkler systems is the rate, expressed in inches per hour, at which water is applied over the surface of the turf. "Matched precipitation" means the entire field is receiving about the same amount of water.)

Swing joints can be fabricated on-site by the installers of the system, or can be manu-

*Figure 7.5. Manufactured Double Swing Joint Detail. A double swing joint allows the system to absorb the weight of mowers and other pieces of equipment without damage to the system.*

factured parts provided by the supplier. A three-elbow double swing joint will perform efficiently if fabricated correctly. Manufactured double swing joints with O-ring seals cut down on installation time and are often more dependable. Correctly installed, a double-swing joint provides flexibility and resists breakage when large mowers or other heavy equipment roll over the sprinkler. Figure 7.5 shows a manufactured swing joint.

### Valves

In an irrigation system, there are two basic types of valves: shutoff valves and sprinkler valves. Shutoff valves ("gate valves" or "ball valves") are used in a continuous pressure main line to temporarily turn the water off to the entire system or a section of the system. Sprinkler valves (manual or automatic) are used to deliver the water from the continuous pressure main line to the sprinklers. In the discussion of sprinkler systems, when the term 'valve' is used alone, it usually refers to an automatic control valve.

*Gate valves* have a wheel-type handle, and several turns of the handle are required to turn on or off the flow of water. Gate valves are most commonly used on main line pipes with high water pressure or high water flow. Because several turns are required, they are easier to turn off and the potential for damage caused by water hammer is reduced. Gate valves have a brass-to-brass seat, which means that they may eventually lose their secure seal. For this reason, gate valves are not recommended for frequent use.

*Ball valves* have a single arm or lever that requires one-quarter turn to turn on or off. This single action is convenient, but caution should be used and the valve should not be turned on or off too quickly, because damage to the system from water hammer could result. Ball valves have resilient seats which maintain their ability to seal longer than brass-to-brass seats, making ball valves a better choice than gate valves where frequent use is expected.

Among sprinkler valves, *manual control valves* are not as common as they once were. The manually controlled sprinkler system requires an operator to time the irrigation of each zone, and to turn valves on and off at the proper time. The operator must be present the entire time the system is operating. Obviously, this type of system does not have the convenience of the automatic system.

*Automatic control valves* are used in conjunction with automatic controllers or timers, and are a much more convenient way to deliver water to the turf. Because these valves can be more precisely controlled, an automatic system allows the sports turf manager to efficiently schedule the delivery of the right amount of water to each zone.

There are many types of automatic control valves. On systems not connected directly to city water systems, choose a valve with an inexpensive self-cleaning filtering mechanism. Because of the possibility of higher surge pressure in a sports field system, it is recommended that the valve be able to withstand pressures up to 200 PSI. A pressure regulator can be installed at the beginning of the system, but with the long main line and the potential for high friction loss, it is generally better to have an automatic control valve with a built-in pressure regulator to control the pressure right at the valve.

Placement of the valves should be planned with maintenance and safety in mind. Automatic control valves are generally installed in groups, or manifolds, and placed underground in a plastic or concrete valve box (if the valves will be near the field of play, use plastic). The manifolds should be built with plenty of room between valves. The distance between valves is dependent on the size of the valve box; for most standard size boxes, two or three 1″ valves can be installed in a valve box, while valves larger than 1″ are usually installed one valve per box.

### Controller

The controller (or "timer") is the part of an automatic sprinkler system that determines when a valve will turn on and how long the valve will operate. The controller sends a low voltage signal through buried wires to the automatic control valve, which then opens for a predetermined amount of time, allowing water to flow to the sprinklers. When the predetermined watering time is completed, the controller turns off the valve.

A controller should be chosen for its wide range of programming capabilities as well as other convenience features. A "nonvolatile memory" means the controller will not lose the program due to power outages or surges. Surge protection will protect the controller from serious damage due to nearby lightning strikes or power surges.

Controllers should be placed in an easily accessible location, in a lockable room or waterproof enclosure. In considering the controller, it is important to remember that some systems require a pump to maintain adequate water pressure. Be sure the controller chosen for this type of system includes a pump start feature. If a pump is needed, the two pieces of equipment are typically placed in the same enclosure. However, the controller should use a separate electrical circuit to reduce the possibility of damage to the controller due to power surges.

As with any electrical equipment, to prevent injury from high voltage electrical shock, it's essential to specify that a proper ground wire be installed to the controller. Consult local codes for the grounding requirements in a specific area.

### Wires

In an automatic sprinkler system, low voltage direct burial wire is used to carry the signal from the controller to the automatic control valves. The most frequently used wire for commercial applications is single strand, heavy gauge direct burial copper wire. A lighter gauge wire can be used when installing valves close to the controller, but heavier gauge wire is necessary for longer distances, and may be necessary even for short distances on higher pressure systems. An irrigation designer or the supplier can specify the necessary wire size when the system is being designed.

The authors recommend that the wire be buried in the same trench as the main line, taped to the underside of the pipe. This will help to protect the wire, and make it easier to locate. Furthermore, a wire taped to the pipe can serve as a tracer wire to locate the main line should it become necessary to do so.

Wherever control wire will be exposed, it should be installed in a protective conduit. Waterproof wire connectors should be used to connect the solenoid wires to the low voltage irrigation wire. Where permitted by local code, wire nuts can be used for connections not exposed to moisture.

### Backflow Prevention

In order to protect the potable (drinking) water supply from contamination, most states and municipalities require the installation of *backflow prevention* devices on all plumbing systems that are connected to the public water supply. (These devices prevent water in the system from flowing backward into the supply lines.) In planning or installing a sports field irrigation system, consult with the local water company to determine the backflow devices required and their proper installation.

## 7.5b   Construction and Reconstruction

Like the designer, an irrigation system installer must be concerned with safety, ease of maintenance, and system longevity. A properly designed system using all of the best products available could still represent a squandered investment if the system is improperly installed. It's important to stress to installers that the designer must be notified of any necessary field changes, so that he or she can verify that the proposed changes will not affect system performance.

Begin the installation process by laying out the system according to the plans. Use small flags for sprinkler placement and marking spray paint or powered gypsum to indicate pipe locations. Dig the required trenches and begin laying the pipe, working out from the POC to the system supply line, then to the valves and finally to the heads. For ease of handling, lay out the control wire in the trench when installing the main line, so the wire can be taped under the pipe.

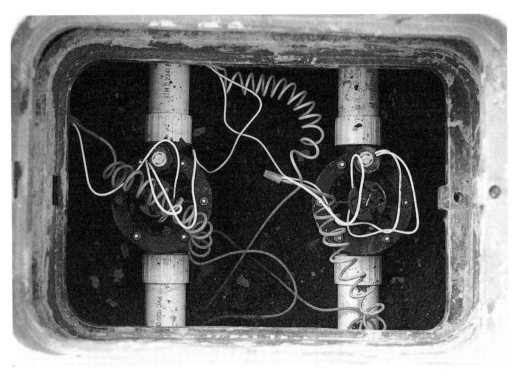

*Figure 7.6. At valve boxes, looping the control wire will provide more convenience when servicing the valves, and will also help to protect the solenoid against lightning strikes.*

Provide an expansion loop of wire at each change of direction to reduce the chance of stretching or breaking the wire. For systems that will employ thrust blocks at points where the piping changes direction, make sure that the wire does not get tangled up with the thrust block.

At each valve, make a coil by wrapping two or three feet of wire around a piece of 1 inch diameter pipe prior to connecting it to valves. This will serve two purposes: in areas susceptible to lightning strikes, static and surges from nearby strikes can be released at this coiled area, helping to protect the solenoid; and when performing maintenance on the valve, removing the bonnet or solenoid is easier with the coiled wire.

Take care to install the sprinkler heads at the correct depth according to the manufacturer's specifications. This will protect players as well as the system itself. It's also important to install the specified nozzles so that the system will perform as it was designed to perform.

When installing the valve boxes, lay a brick base under the edges of each box to reduce settling. Set the box in place, then install a 2- to 4-inch layer of gravel in the box under the valve to provide for drainage. To further reduce the amount of dirt that infiltrates the valve box, add filter cloth below the gravel and around the box. The top of the valve box should be installed at turf finish grade. Before going on to the next box, make sure that shutoff valves and control valves will clear the box lid when the valves are in both the fully closed and fully open position.

If a pressure test is required, backfill the center of the pipe, leaving the fittings exposed so that they can be checked for leakage. This sequence, called "center loading," will keep the pipe in place while it is under pressure.

It's much easier to make repairs and adjustments before backfilling the entire system. If the system will include thrust blocks, install those before turning on the system. Make sure the top of the blocks will be safely below the surface, where it will not be damaged by aeration equipment or vehicle traffic later.

After the pressure test is complete, finish backfilling the trenches and compact the soil to the same degree as the neighboring soil. When setting heads to grade, check for proper height, because the heads (along with the soil around them) may settle during the compaction process.

### As-Built Drawings and Controller Charts

Because some minor variances are sometimes made during the installation process, it has become customary for the installer to prepare an "as-built drawing." This is a drawing showing the actual installed location of all gate valves, valves, sprinkler heads, pipe (including sleeves), and wire runs. Accurate as-builts are very important, because they allow the maintenance staff to locate a pipe or wire without having to dig up large areas of the field.

Gate valves, pipe, and wire runs should be located on the drawing with measurements to two permanent reference points. At a minimum, record exact measurements for pipe and wire at each change of direction, along with their exact depth at these locations. As-built drawings should be updated frequently during the system installation.

"Controller charts" show valves and the zones that they cover, and they can also be vital to later maintenance efforts. For quick reference, mark the drawing with a different colored highlighter for each zone, and number the area on the drawing to correspond to the station number on the controller.

## 7.5c  Renovation

Before considering the subject of irrigation system renovation, it's important to establish that renovation can be useful only when the existing system was properly designed in the first place—so that when the system was in good working order, it distributed water evenly over the entire area. If the system never worked right, complete reconstruction will probably be necessary. The wrong size pipe may have been used. Too few zones may have been installed. There may not be enough pressure to operate all the heads in a zone. (This problem can be corrected easily by adding a booster pump.)

For our purposes, we'll consider irrigation system renovation to consist mainly of replacing parts that have worn out due to normal usage.

Renovation of a properly installed and maintained automatic irrigation system may be necessary every 7 to 10 years. Sprinkler heads are the parts most commonly in need of replacement, since these items are in constant mechanical operation and are subjected to possible damage by the activity on the field. Control valves can easily be rebuilt without removing the valve from the system. The valve's diaphragm and solenoid are the valve's only moving parts, and therefore the only ones that may need replacing. (Pipe and wire rarely need to be replaced, since they have no moving parts.)

When replacing heads, dig down a few inches past the swing joint so the new head can be accurately adjusted for height. When heads are being replaced, it may be wise to replace the swing joints while they are easily accessible.

Replacing valves in systems fabricated from PVC pipe, is much easier with a "slip fix." A slip fix is a PVC telescoping repair part, designed to replace a section of the existing pipe. Remove a section of the pipe near the existing valve, then remove the old valve and replace it with a new one. The slip fix replaces the section of pipe that was removed. Retract the slip fix and remove enough of the existing pipe to allow the slip fix to fit into the space. Extend the telescoping portion of the slip fix over the existing pipe. Check alignment and then solvent weld (glue) the slip-fix in place.

(A slip-fix is also useful for replacing a cracked or broken pipe. In such a case, simply adapt the procedure described above.)

When planning a renovation project, consider the possibility of improving the system. Older heads and valves can be replaced with the newer models that provide better performance. A good working manual system can also be upgraded to an automatic system by changing the manual control valves to automatic control valves. A controller (timer) must be installed and connected by wire to each valve to allow automatic operation.

## 7.5d   Inspection and Maintenance of Irrigation Systems

As with every aspect of sports field maintenance, the importance of regularly scheduled irrigation inspections cannot be overstated. Preventive maintenance saves money and improves the health and appearance of the turf. Small problems can be spotted and corrected long before they turn into big, costly problems. On the other hand, failure to perform regular maintenance can mean that a component may need to be replaced unnecessarily, or that the entire system may need renovation before the end of its normal life cycle.

Once a week, look at the overall appearance of the turf, and test the system by manually running the controller through its cycle. These two quick checks will indicate whether the system is working correctly, or whether further testing is necessary.

When appraising the general appearance of the turf, look for stress areas that indicate poor irrigation coverage. The beginnings of "donuts," dry areas around the heads, can mean there is a pressure problem, that someone has misadjusted the radius adjustment screw, or that the wrong nozzle has been installed.

Before manually activating the controller, check to see if it's keeping the correct time of day. If not, the controller may have received a power surge, or a power outage may have disrupted its programming. No display, or a default display may suggest a blown fuse caused by faulty wiring, wire connectors, or valve solenoid.

As the controller activates and deactivates each valve, check for proper opening and closing. Slow or fast opening or closing valves can usually be adjusted with the valve's flow control, but this can sometimes indicate a problem, such as high or low pressure or a torn diaphragm, and may suggest the need for further investigation.

As the different zones come on, look carefully at the spray. If the water droplets seem too large, the system may be operating at low pressure. If the droplets are too small, or if there is excessive mist, the pressure may be too high. Many times, especially if the system previously worked fine, these conditions can be corrected by adjusting the flow control at the valve.

Rotary heads which are not rotating obviously require service. Many times a nonrotating sprinkler means a dirty filter, and can be disassembled and cleaned out quickly and easily. The staff should be instructed to resist the temptation to lubricate sticking heads. Although it may temporarily improve rotation, lubrication will eventually attract dirt and make the problem worse in the long run.

Make sure the heads are at the proper height, that they are adjusted correctly, and that they are set perpendicular to the turf.

During regular inspections, remember to look for signs of broken risers beneath the sprinklers. Sometimes these signs are obvious; a broken riser will unleash water to create huge geysers. Sometimes the signs are not so obvious; a cracked riser may allow water to boil up around the sprinkler but may not be readily visible. Watch for excessively wet or unusually dry areas.

While looking for broken risers and misadjustments, inspect the sprinkler for flow-by. A worn wiper seal can allow water to flow out of the sprinkler onto adjacent paved or turf areas, wasting water, damaging turf, and worst of all, causing unsafe conditions. (A wiper seal is located between the cap and the sprinkler's riser.) A very small amount of water emitting past the wiper seal while the system is running is usually acceptable, but a leaking sprinkler head must be repaired or replaced.

It is very important that broken or poorly performing sprinkler heads be replaced as soon as possible. When a specific sprinkler is not operating correctly, the performance of all of the other heads on the zone is affected. For instance, water flowing unchecked past a wiper seal will cause a loss in pressure to all heads on a zone. Because the pressure in that zone has dropped, the other sprinklers will not adequately irrigate the area.

If water is seeping past the wiper seal long after the system has turned off, the valve needs attention. A seeping valve could mean that debris is caught between the diaphragm and the valve seat, or that the diaphragm is beginning to tear. Replacing the diaphragm is a simple, fast, and inexpensive procedure. But if the torn diaphragm is not replaced, the slow seeping will waste a great deal of water, and could eventually lead to a zone that is stuck on. If that happens at an inappropriate time, the turf could suffer severe damage.

Regularly scheduled irrigation checks will save time and money if they are performed on a consistent basis. A poorly maintained irrigation system will affect the health of the turfgrass culture and the appearance of the turf. A well maintained system will help to produce a healthy, visually appealing field which holds up well under the stress of sports events and contributes to safe, competitive play.

### Winterization of a Sprinkler System

Winterization of the sprinkler system is the blowing out or draining of water to prevent its freezing within the system and breaking pipes or components. Winterization is performed in areas of the country which are subject to prolonged freezing.

If the irrigation system is drained by gravity, the process of winterization is simple. Such a system has drains at the low points and when the water is turned off and the drains are opened, all water drains out of the system. In this type of system, it is critical to have an accurate "as-built" drawing in order to easily locate each drain valve.

More commonly, systems are winterized through a process of "blowing out" the pipes and components. With this method, there is less possibility of leaving water trapped in low areas of the piping. Replacing pipe which has cracked due to trapped and frozen water can be very costly.

A portable air compressor which can produce a high volume of air at lower pressures is used to blow out an irrigation system. Systems consisting of pipe that is three inches or less in diameter can be blown out with a 125 CFM (cubic feet per minute) at 50 PSI air compressor. Systems with pipe that is four inches in diameter or larger may require a compressor capable of producing 250 CFM or more. In no case should the air pressure exceed 80 PSI.

It is highly recommended that blowing out a sports turf irrigation system be performed by someone with experience in winterizing large systems. This is a dangerous procedure and the components can be damaged if the winterization is done incorrectly.

*Spring Start-up*

Spring start-up after a winterization also must be done carefully. Open the last valve in the system, or the valve closest to the center of a looped main line. Slowly open the isolation valve to allow the water to seep into the system. It is important to be patient during this process, so the water entering the system will not fill the pipe too rapidly and cause damage to the irrigation system due to "water hammer."

When the main line is fully charged with water, open the next-to-last valve, leaving the previous valve open. When water is flowing out of the second zone, turn off the first zone and proceed to the next valve. Continue this process with each valve in turn, until all valves in the system have been recharged.

## 7.5e  Distribution Uniformity (DU) Testing

If the irrigation system is currently in operation and field renovations are being considered, the system's "distribution uniformity" (the evenness with which water is distributed over the field) should be checked. Distribution uniformity (DU) is calculated by dividing the amount of water falling on the least watered part of a zone by the average amount of water falling on all the zones. An excellent DU percentage for rotors is 75% to 85%, while a good DU is 65% to 70%.

Once a system's DU is known, an informed decision can be made about whether to repair or completely replace a system (or, if the DU falls within acceptable range, simply to leave the system alone).

In order to determine distribution uniformity, a **catchment test** of the turf grass area should be performed. This is a fairly easy test to perform and often can uncover fixable problems, even when a system appears to be functioning correctly.

The first step in conducting a catchment test is to determine existing site conditions. Draw a sketch of the field, with measurements, showing head locations. Write down all significant information, including the type of heads used and their condition. Perform an actual head-by-head inspection to determine their condition, model number, and the nozzle type. While walking the field, look for signs of poor irrigation coverage, such as brown or bare spots.

Using a soil probe, take a few soil samples from different areas around the field to determine soil type and root depth. This information will be helpful later in writing an irrigation schedule for the system.

Next, turn on one zone at a time and perform a visual inspection. Adjust the radius and the arc of water flow from each head, and align all heads to be perpendicular to the turf for maximum coverage. While adjusting the heads, watch for heavy leaking at the riser seal, and for failure to rotate properly.

Clean any clogged nozzles, and be sure the filters are free of debris. Check for correct pressure, and for "donuts" of brown grass around the heads.

Using a rotor pitot tube (a device for testing the operating pressure at the head—see Figure 7.7) and pressure gauge, check the pressure and pressure variation at the rotor's nozzle. (Be sure to write down these pressure readings.) Variations of more than 20% from the highest pressure reading to the lowest within one zone may indicate a problem with the system, and the need for further inspection by an irrigation expert with a background in irrigation hydraulics. Frequently, pressure can be increased or decreased simply by adjusting the flow control on the valve for the zone.

Check the station start times and run times in the controller to see if there is a station with a longer run time than the others. This could indicate a problem with that particular valve or the rotors in that zone; the additional run time may be keeping the grass

*Figure 7.7. A pitot tube is used to check the operating pressure at a given head in the irrigation system. (Photo courtesy of Hunter Industries)*

green and hiding the problem. Check the run times overall. Are dry spots causing longer run times? In most areas, turf will require about 1″ to 1½″ of water per week in the hottest months. (See Section 7.5f for information on scheduling irrigation run times.) Calculate precipitation rates based on manufacturer's published performance information and determine if the run times are close to where they should be.

---

**Example:** The stations have a run time of 40 minutes, and the stations are programmed with two start times every day but Friday, Saturday, and Sunday.

**Answer:** 40 minutes x 2 start times per day x 4 days  or  40 x 2 x 4  =  320 minutes of run time. Then, 320 ÷ 60 minutes in an hour =  5.3 hours of run time per week.

A rotor with an approximate precipitation rate of .44 inches per hour would be putting down 2.3 inches of water per week (5.3 hours x .44 inches per hour  or  5.3 x .44  = 2.3 inches per week).

A rotor with an approximate precipitation rate of .85 inches per hour would be putting down 4-½ inches of water per week (5.3 hours x .85 inches per hour  or  5.3 x .85  =  4.5 inches per week).

---

If the turf is evenly green in both examples above, the first rotor system was probably just in need of a tune-up, while the second system, which is putting down over 4 inches

*Figure 7.8. Catchment test collectors, like these, allow for easy collection and measuring of irrigation distribution over the field area. (Photo courtesy of Hunter Industries)*

of water per week, indicates there may be a problem that is being covered up with over-watering. The turf is being kept healthy, but at the cost of sharply increased water usage.

If problems are discovered in this inspection, make corrections and adjustments before proceeding. Once all adjustments, nozzle, and head corrections have been made, and it has been established that the system is operating at the sprinkler manufacturer's recommended pressure, the catchment test itself can be performed.

Check the amount of water being applied to the field, one zone at a time, using small catch cans. All of the cans or other collectors should be the same size and shape, and should be placed at about the same height above the turf. Place several catch cans throughout the zone being tested, marking the location of the cans on the sketch. A catchment test should not be conducted when the wind will cause a distortion in the spray pattern. (Figure 7.8 shows the results from a typical catchment test.)

Turn on the zone, and allow it to run for 10 to 30 minutes, or until the cans have collected, on the average, at least two- to three-tenths of an inch of measurable water, or until the rotors have made at least five rotations. Write down how long each zone was allowed to run. Measure the amount of water in each can, and log the results on the sketch next to each can location. Note which zone is affecting the can's volume, and do not empty the catch can between tests if that can is collecting water from more than one zone. Repeat the test for each zone.

To determine the zone's distribution uniformity, list the catch can results from highest to lowest. Add up the lowest 25% of the numbers and divide by the number of cans in the lowest 25% to get the average reading in the lower quartile. Divide this number by the average of all of the catch cans on that zone. Multiply the result by 100 to obtain the percentage. The formula is:

$$DU\% = \frac{\text{Average reading in the lowest quartile}}{\text{Average reading overall}} \times 100$$

Using this formula, it is possible to calculate the DU for a zone, or for the entire system. As we said earlier, a DU of 75% to 85% is excellent, while good distribution is 65% to 70%.

## 7.5f   Scheduling Water Usage

Ultimately, the goal of the turfgrass manager is to apply only the amount of water needed, and to apply that water only when it is needed. Plants have an effective root zone (RZ), and water in the soil below that root zone is unusable by the plants. The effective root zone for turfgrass is about six inches to a foot deep.

A basic truth of plant irrigation is this: irrigation is not meant to water the plants; rather, it is meant to refill the reservoir from which those plants will draw the water they need. If the reservoir gets too "empty," the plants begin to wilt. When they are deprived of water for too long, a "permanent wilting point" is reached, and permanent plant damage occurs.

If the reservoir is allowed to get "too full," the soil may reach "field capacity" at levels below the plant's effective root zone, and water would go unused. Field capacity is the upper limit of storable water in a layer of soil after the water has drained through.

It might seem that a slow and constant supply of water would be the best way to fulfill the watering requirement. However, in most circumstances, daily watering is wasteful. Water evaporates quite rapidly from the top few inches of soil; the rate of evaporation can reach as much as 50% per day. The deeper the moisture level in the soil, the lower the daily evaporation rate.

It becomes important, then, to manage the amount of water in the root zone to maximize application efficiency (EA). When scheduling irrigation, the turf manager's job is to provide enough water, at the proper times to keep the moisture level at the root zone between the permanent wilting point, and the field capacity. This level of moisture is referred to as "available water holding capacity" (AWHC), and is the water that can be used by the plants. Generally, AWHC is expressed as "inches of water available per foot of soil," or inches/foot.

In order to properly manage the AWHC level and program the controller with the correct watering schedule, the turf manager needs a few pieces of information:

- The amount of water needed for the turf to be healthy.
- The acceptable level of depletion of the AWHC.
- The precipitation rate of the irrigation system, in inches per hour.
- The efficiency of the irrigation system.

With this information and some simple math, the turf manager will have the tools to properly schedule the application of water to the turf area.

### *Amount of Water Needed*

The amount of water needed by a plant is the sum of the amount lost through the evaporation of moisture at the soil's surface and the transpiration of water through the plant. The daily evapotranspiration (ET) rate for a specific area may be available from the local extension agent or weather service, or can be determined using the approximate daily values in Table 7.1.

**Table 7.1. Potential Evapotranspiration Rates for Various Climates[a]**

| Climate Type[b] | Daily Loss (in inches) |
|---|---|
| Cool humid | 0.10–0.15 |
| Cool dry | 0.15–0.20 |
| Warm humid | 0.15–0.20 |
| Warm dry | 0.20–0.25 |
| Hot humid | 0.20–0.30 |
| Hot dry | 0.30–0.40 |

[a]These evapotranspiration (ET) rates are approximate. Actual ET rates may be obtained from an extension agent. If the rate is expressed as a monthly figure, divide the number by 30 for the average daily rate.

[b]"Cool" applies to areas with average high temperatures in midsummer of under 70°F. "Warm" refers to midsummer highs between 70°F and 90°F. "Hot" indicates midsummer averages over 90°F. Areas in which the average relative humidity is over 50% in midsummer qualify as "Humid," while under 50% is considered "Dry."

**Table 7.2. Crop Coefficient ($K_C$) for Sports Turf and Other Common Plants**

| Vegetation Type | Coefficient |
|---|---|
| Mature trees | 0.80 |
| Shrubs (taller than 4 ft.) | 0.70 |
| Shrubs (shorter than 4 ft.) | 1.00 |
| Warm season turf | 0.50–0.70 |
| Cool season turf | 0.60–0.80 |

Different plants have specific watering requirements. The "crop coefficient" allows for the expression of this variation in moisture needs. Table 7.2 provides a guide of the crop coefficients for sports turf as compared to other common plants.

*Available Water Holding Capacity (AWHC) Depletion*
It is best to irrigate as infrequently as possible because of the high evaporation rate at the surface of the soil. Deeper, less frequent watering gets more water to the root zone. However, to avoid damage to the turf due to AWHC falling to a permanent wilting point, the turf manager must schedule irrigation run time before all of the AWHC is depleted. The acceptable level of depletion, called "Management Allowable Depletion" (MAD), can vary by soil type, compaction, root depth, and the stress tolerance of the plant. In most applications, a MAD of 50% of the AWHC will sustain healthy turf. Table 7.3 provides an AWHC guideline for a few soil textural classes.

*Precipitation Rate*
The "precipitation rate" (PR) for an individual sprinkler or an entire sprinkler system is the depth of water applied in a given area, expressed in inches per hour. The precipitation rate of a *sprinkler* is determined by multiplying the gallons per minute output of *that sprinkler* by a conversion factor of 96.25 (which converts cubic inches of water to inches per square foot per hour), and then dividing by the area the sprinkler covers. The precipitation rate of an *irrigation system* is found by multiplying the total gallons per minute of the *system* by 96.25 and dividing by the total area the system covers.

$$PR = \frac{GPM\ applied \times 96.25}{Area\ covered}$$

(Gallons per minute can be approximated using the manufacturer's published nozzle data.)

To calculate the precipitation rate on a particular field, use the measurements taken during an irrigation catchment test (see Section 7.5e). Add the total (in inches) of all catch cans and divide by the number of catch cans. Then divide that number by the run time of the test (in minutes), and multiply by 60 minutes to obtain inches applied per hour. This is the average precipitation rate for the field.

$$\text{Average field PR} = \frac{\text{Total inches in all catch cans}}{\text{Number of catch cans}} \div \text{Run time} \times 60$$

### Application Efficiency

Application efficiency (EA) is a measure of how much of the applied water is available for use in the effective root zone. It is also an indication of how well the system was designed and installed, and how well it has been maintained. Application efficiency is determined by dividing the amount of water in the root zone by the amount of water applied.

A perfect irrigation system where all of the water sprayed out goes directly and evenly to the turf's root zone is unachievable. In fact, while it is feasible to achieve an application efficiency (EA) rating as high as 80%, an irrigation system with an efficiency rating of 70% is considered very good. Irrigation water can be lost through excessive evaporation (watering during the heat of the day), wind drift, incorrect adjustments, improper designs, high pressure, low pressure, runoff, percolation past the effective root zone, or through the use of the wrong size nozzles or other equipment.

There are several steps and calculations needed to determine irrigation system EA. While these calculations can be very accurate, because of the effects of wind, temperature, humidity, water pressure, soil type, and root depth, EA remains an informed estimate. For general purposes, a manager can expect to achieve an EA of 60% to 80%.

### Calculating the Irrigation Run Time

We now have all of the information necessary to schedule the application of water. The following is a recap of the values that are used in the scheduling equation:

RZ     Root Zone is the effective depth, in feet, of the roots (0.5′ to 1.0′ for turf).
ET     Evaporation of soil surface water plus transpiration of water through the plant (Table 7.1).
$K_C$     Crop coefficient is the specific water requirement of the plant (Table 7.2).
AWHC   Available Water Holding Capacity is the moisture level in the soil (expressed in inches per foot) which is above the plant's permanent wilting point, and below the soil's field capacity (Table 7.3).

#### Table 7.3. AWHC for Various Soil Textures

| Soil Texture | Inches of Available Water per Foot of Soil |
|---|---|
| Sandy soils | 0.50–1.00 |
| Loamy soils | 1.00–1.75 |
| Clay soils | 1.75–2.5 |

**MAD**  Management Allowable Depletion of water from the AWHC. (In most applications, a MAD of 50% will sustain healthy turf.)

**PR**   Precipitation Rate is the depth of water per unit of time. (Multiply the total gallons per minute of the *system* by 96.25 and divide by the total area the system covers.)

**EA**   Application Efficiency is a measure of the overall efficiency of the sprinkler system (60% to 80%).

The frequency (F), or "how often to irrigate the turf," is calculated using the following formula:

$$F = \frac{AWHC \times RZ \times MAD}{ET \times K_c}$$

The amount of run time (RT) is calculated:

$$RT = \frac{60 \times F \times ET \times K_c}{PR \times EA}$$

---

**Example:**  A valve is irrigating warm season turf which is growing in a sandy loam. The average precipitation rate is 0.49 inches/hour. The system is located in San Marcos, CA, where the daily moisture loss (ET) to be replenished is 0.20 inches. The system application efficiency is approximately 65%.

**Answer:**

**Watering Frequency**

$$F = \frac{1.0'' \times 0.75' \times 50\%}{0.20 \times 0.70} = \frac{1.0 \times 0.75 \times 0.50}{0.20 \times 0.70} = \frac{0.375}{0.14} = 2.68$$

The answer is a 2- or 3-day watering interval. The turf manager may decide to use a 3-day interval (water on Day #1, wait Day #2 and Day #3, and then begin the watering interval again on the next day), and monitor the turf's condition.

**Run Time per Frequency**

$$RT = \frac{60 \times 3 \times 0.20 \times 0.70}{0.49 \times 65\%} = \frac{180 \times 0.14}{0.49 \times 0.65} = \frac{25.2}{.319} = 79$$

Water 79 minutes each watering.

---

Soil texture will provide a general idea of the rate at which water can be absorbed without runoff. Many times, the precipitation rate and run time will be more than the soil intake rate. As the soil reservoir is refilled and reaches field capacity, the additional, or free water is pulled through the soil by gravity and capillary action. If the

Table 7.4. Soil Intake Rates for Various Soil Textures

| Soil Texture | Soil Intake Rate (inches per hour) |
|---|---|
| Sandy soils | 0.50–1.00 |
| Loamy soils | 0.25–0.50 |
| Clay soils | 0.10–0.25 |

water is applied faster than the intake rate, the water will run off and be wasted, and may cause damage to the turf.

In order to determine if the watering run time must be cycled into multiple run times, look at the precipitation rate and compare it to the rate in Table 7.4.

In the previous example, the precipitation rate was calculated as 0.49 inches per hour. Comparing that to the soil intake chart, the reader can see that one cycle may or may not soak into the sandy loam before runoff, and the turf area in this example should be monitored. If runoff is evident, the 79 minutes should be broken into two 40-minute applications on the same day.

Reprogram the controller at least seasonally to the appropriate run times. Consider performing a catchment test on a periodic basis to reevaluate the system's efficiency.

Proper irrigation technique is important in developing a deep root system. Replenishing the AWHC with frequent light watering is the worst possible way to water turf. This method never allows the soil profile to be wetted to any depth, encouraging shallow root growth and leading to turf that is easily damaged and dependent on frequent watering.

The best method of producing turf with a deep root system is through cyclical watering as described in this chapter. Deeply rooted turf is less susceptible to damage from stress due to high midsummer temperatures and evaporation rates. Sports turf which is deeply rooted will be less vulnerable to damage by players, and will recover faster from the demands of the playing season.

## BIBLIOGRAPHY

Burt, C. M. *Soil, Plant and Water Relationships.* California Polytechnic State University, San Luis Obispo, CA, 1992.

*Handbook of Technical Irrigation Information.* Hunter Industries Incorporated, San Marcos, CA, 1996.

*Irrigation Hydraulics.* Hunter Industries Incorporated, San Marcos, CA, 1997.

*Precipitation Rates and Sprinkler Irrigation.* Hunter Industries Incorporated, San Marcos, CA, 1996.

Irrigation Training and Research Center. *Landscape Water Management - Principles,* Version 1.01. Polytechnic State University, San Luis Obispo, CA, 1992.

Keeson, L. *The Complete Irrigation Workbook.* G.I.E. Inc., Publishers, Cleveland, OH, 1995.

# Chapter 8

# *Drainage*

## 8.1  INTRODUCTION

Ask turf managers what single improvement would contribute most to the quality of their fields, and one answer would come back more than any other: "drainage." Just about every fields manager has had to deal with rainout headaches, but the problems go even further. Some fields hold so much water in the spring that the staff can't get on them to mow; the equipment causes ruts, and then the manager has two problems to deal with.

In fact, some sports turf professionals have come to refer to the whole business of sports fields as "the drainage game."

In this chapter we'll consider some common problems that cause fields to drain improperly, and offer some suggestions for avoiding these downfalls through proper planning and installation. We'll also look at a number of ways to improve drainage, including correcting contours, installing drain systems, and even soil modification to improve infiltration and percolation.

## 8.2  SURFACE DRAINAGE

### 8.2a  Designing for New Construction

Let's start with what is probably the most basic rule of drainage: whether designing a single field or a multifield complex, keep in mind that each field should be designed and constructed as an individual drainage unit. No field—not even one with an excellent installed drain system—can be expected to perform acceptably with water running onto it from an adjacent field or from the surrounding terrain. If the natural contours of the land will direct runoff toward the field, plan to install interceptor drains to isolate it. In laying out fields, make sure to leave enough room outside (and between) the playing areas for cuts and fills, catch basins and swales.

Generally, field designs for surface drainage fall into one of two categories: a *crowned field* sloped to the sides or a *flat field* sloped to one side or to one end. The typical percentage of slope for a sports field runs between 1% and 1.75%. When relying on surface drainage alone, and not installing a drain system, use a slope at the higher end of the range. Soccer fields are often designed using a lower percentage of slope, and installed drain systems are usually needed.

### *Crowned Fields*

Probably the most common type of football field is a crowned field with level sidelines, and this design normally can be expected to shed water fairly successfully. However, with the growing popularity of soccer in North America, many schools and other facilities now use one field for both football and soccer games. On these dual-use fields, level sidelines can be a problem; the soccer sidelines (or "touchlines") usually extend beyond the football sidelines. Unless there is consistent slope through the sideline area—which tends to get badly torn up by foot traffic at the football field bench area—the outer edges of the soccer field can become a quagmire.

On baseball and softball fields, the pitcher's mound should be the high point of the field. A good skinned area contour design is crowned behind second base, with runoff directed toward the foul lines. This design helps to avoid standing water at the infield arc, which is a common problem when a skinned area is meant to drain into the outfield.

Under most circumstances, installed drain systems are not effective for the skinned area because water percolates through the sand/silt/clay soil very slowly. Positive surface drainage is the only way to ensure a playable field in wet weather. Many baseball field designers are uncertain about how to contour the skinned area, and as a result, many diamonds are too flat. Skinned area surface drainage is so critical that proper runoff can be prevented just by allowing too much soil to build up in the grass edge.

(Chapter 11 includes detailed contour designs, including illustrations, for the infield, skinned area, and outfield of a baseball diamond. Each is a separate drainage unit, but all three must be designed to work together as an integrated system.)

### Flat Fields

Flat fields tend to be built that way because of the character of the surrounding terrain. If it's impractical or too costly to build a crowned facility, the flat, sloped design can work very well. Two factors must be kept in mind. Most flat fields need an installed drain system, at least in the lower half of the field, to prevent that area from becoming too wet. Also, make sure that field records show that it's a flat sloped field. Otherwise, ten years down the road some well-meaning person might try to "recrown" the field, causing a real mess. (We have seen this happen on football fields.)

### Catch Basins

Catch basins are a common drainage structure used for sports fields, and they can be used in two ways. They can aid in surface drainage where the surrounding terrain stops the movement of water, and they can serve as "junction boxes" of installed drain systems allowing the manager to monitor its effectiveness. With any sports field, place the catch basins well outside the field of play and use a small grid on top.

One common drain system design (often used with a crowned football or soccer field with a level 400-meter running track around it) uses a number of catch basins around the field, with swales from basin-to-basin to assist surface runoff. This approach has two drawbacks: it creates an awkward appearance of hills and valleys along the field edge, and the swales tend to stay wet for extended periods during rainy conditions. (For this reason, the trackside sand drains, described below, are a better option.)

### 8.2b   Reconstructing Field Contours

Reconstructing a field is the ideal opportunity to improve surface drainage. First, conduct a survey to verify how water moves through and around the field. Set new grades, then remove the sod and regrade. When making cuts, pay attention to the thickness of the soil layer; make sure not to leave two inches of topsoil in one place and ten inches in another. The parts with two inches will not drain as well as the areas with thicker topsoil. When making fills (adding soil), scarify the soil first to eliminate layering, which has the effect of slowing the movement of water through the soil.

### 8.2c Renovation

There are several modest processes that can contribute effectively to improving surface drainage of a sports field. For instance, one good way to deal with small spot drainage problems, such as mud puddles, is to apply a topdressing material and then use a level bar to smooth the surface of the field. This process eliminates the unevenness of the field and provides a better-draining surface.

Another renovation process used to improve surface drainage on a baseball field is removal of lips or mounded ridges that form in the grass edge along the skinned area. These lips or ridges can serve as "dams" to prevent surface drainage; keeping these grass edges free of built-up skinned area soil will allow surface water to run off into the grass.

For the mechanics of this process, see Chapter 11, Section 11.4, Renovation.

### 8.2d Maintenance

Many fields managers overlook the fact that careful maintenance practices can help prevent drainage problems. For instance, cutting the grass shorter during wet periods allows more sunlight to reach the soil and dries it faster.

Another maintenance practice that can help a slow-draining field is deep tine aeration, especially with vibrating or "quaking" equipment. If the field stays wet longer than it should, and the wetness is observed over large areas of the turf and not just in easily identifiable spots, the problem may be soil layering, or overcompaction of the soil (see Figure 8.1.) In those cases, deep tine aeration and quaking can disturb the layers enough to allow some improvement in playability.

Soil amendments or "conditioners" can also help in emergency situations. Calcined clay products have been used in the industry for many years, and a new generation of materials based on calcined diatomaceous earth (DE) is now on the market. These DE products, like Agro-Tech 2000's Axis™ for turfgrass areas and Play Ball™ for skinned areas, can provide the same drying power with lower application volumes. Amendments absorb some of the surface water and help firm up muddy soil.

## 8.3 INTERNAL DRAINAGE

Before we consider the matter of internal drainage, a couple of definitions are in order. Many professionals use the term "internal drainage" to indicate drains installed in the soil. But for our purposes, we will use "internal drainage" as a more general term for the downward movement of water into, through, and out of the soil profile. When we are discussing pipe drains, strip drains, and other kinds of installed drainage structures that remove water from the soil profile, we will use the phrase "installed drain systems."

Internal drainage is an important facet of the overall drainage performance of a sports field. Even where there is good surface drainage, water may remain trapped in the soil profile for days, creating less-than-ideal conditions. Under those circumstances, regrading would probably do little to help. As in any diagnostic process, determining the problem is half the battle. Once the manager knows why drainage is inadequate, he or she can develop a plan to improve it.

In this section we'll look at some basics of internal drainage, some common problems, and some methods of correction. (The material in 8.3a through 8.3c describes ways to get water into and through the soil, and Section 8.4, "Installed Drain Systems," consid-

*Figure 8.1. This soil profile shows layering of soil, which can prevent the downward movement of water through the soil and subsoil. Overcompaction can make this problem even more troublesome.*

ers how to use those structures to get water out of the soil and beyond the boundaries of the field.)

## 8.3a   Infiltration and Percolation

Infiltration is described as the downward entry of water *into* the soil, and percolation is the downward movement of water *through* the soil. These processes are components of "water permeability," the movement of water into and through the soil as measured in inches per hour.

Infiltration and percolation play an important part in the overall process of draining a sports field; the surface is kept free of water most effectively when some of the rainfall can pass downward through the soil to assist the removal by positive surface drainage. In terms of overall permeability, the most significant problem for sports fields is compaction, which prevents water from infiltrating and percolating.

Aeration can help improve infiltration and percolation. Aeration (especially deep tine core aeration) can open up the soil for better internal drainage. Aeration also allows air into the soil profile, further assisting the drying process.

In order to understand how water moves through soil, it's important to consider the characteristics of clay, which is one of the major components of soil. Microscopic clay particles tend to bond soil particles together to form larger units or "soil aggregates." The arrangement of these particles into larger units forms *soil structure*. This naturally occurring process is beneficial to the movement of water through the soil, because it creates free space through which the water can pass. (See Chapter 2 for further discussion of soil structure.)

Over time, compaction can break down the soil structure into "structureless soil" in which the soil aggregates have been broken down, and the soil particles are pressed together into impermeable layers. Among the causes of this compaction are the passage of heavy equipment over the surface of the ground, excessive tilling, and foot traffic.

### Compaction by Heavy Equipment

On some fields, heavy compaction of the sub-base prevents water from passing through the soil profile. In many cases, this problem begins with the plans and specifications, which call for a "compacted sub-base." To the excavator, these specs call for a sheepsfoot roller or vibrating roller—great for building roads and parking lots, but not for building sports fields.

The problem is that this equipment makes the sub-base so compacted that it becomes impervious to water, which passes through the topsoil but stops at the sub-base. The result is that the topsoil (which is not compacted) will become fully saturated during a heavy rain, because the sub-base won't allow the water to pass downward out of the topsoil.

Preventing this problem is very simple. Just include in the specs these instructions: "Avoid overcompaction of the sub-base" and "scarify sub-base before installing topsoil." These notes will alert the excavator to the drainage dynamics at work in the field system.

Although prevention is easy, correcting overcompaction of the sub-base after it has occurred is not. Deep tine aeration can help if the topsoil layer is not too thick, but even if the tines can reach the sub-base, aeration really just punches holes in the compacted sub-base. Complete correction of the problem requires stripping off the topsoil, scarifying the sub-soil, then reinstalling the topsoil.

### Excessive Tilling

It might seem that tilling would be a good way to loosen up the soil and encourage efficient infiltration and percolation. But the fact of the matter is that excessive tilling, which usually occurs when the soil is being prepared for planting, can reduce internal drainage. Tilling breaks down the beneficial soil structure by crushing the soil aggregates, creating smaller particles that compact into an impermeable layer.

To prevent this problem, the "no-till" method of soil preparation is usually preferable. Using equipment such as a cultivator or a scarifier to loosen the soil will allow seeding and sodding to be performed without changing the structure of the soil.

## Compaction by Foot Traffic

The constant pounding by players' feet is another cause of compaction that can lead to poor infiltration and percolation. Foot traffic actually exposes the soil to two different circumstances: cleats driving into the top layer of soil break down soil structure, and the weight of the players leads to damaging overcompaction. (And, by the way, don't forget that the band can cause even more compaction on a field than the team causes!) After years and years of play (especially in wet or muddy conditions), foot traffic causes the structure of the soil to break down.

To maximize internal drainage, field managers should give constant attention to the condition of the soil, and particularly to emerging areas of compaction. This attention can prevent the need to remove the soil and start all over again.

## 8.3b   Particle Size Distribution (Soil Texture)

Another important factor in the passage of water through the soil is particle size distribution. Soil that is made up of particles of a wide variety of sizes would be said to have a greater (or "nonuniform") distribution of particle size, whereas some washed sand could have a very narrow ("uniform") particle size distribution. The classification of particle sizes are shown in Table 8.1.

In terms of internal drainage, permeability is highest in the sand with particles from .15 to 2.00 mm. When finer sands, silt, and clay are added to that sand, the permeability may be reduced from as much as 15–20″ per hour to as little as .01″ per hour. Obviously, particle size distribution can make a huge difference in the effectiveness of internal drainage. With native clay-based topsoil, the movement of water will be slower than with sand.

Soils with few "fines" (microscopic particles of silt and clay) are the most permeable. However, coarse-textured soils have proved to be unstable for most sports fields, because it is the fines that help to bond the soil together. Stability is gained by adding fines to the mixture, but the fines also restrict permeability. For sports fields managers, the challenge is to find the percentage of fines that can be added before infiltration and percolation are slowed to the point where the turf becomes waterlogged (see Chapter 24, Sand and Sand-Based Fields.)

## 8.3c   Soil Amendments for Better Drainage

One way to increase the rate of infiltration and percolation is by adding amendments to the soil. In addition to improving drainage, these amendments can enhance the turf culture by allowing improved root penetration and resisting compaction. The effectiveness of soil amendments depends on the amount added, the properties of the host soil, and the uniformity of the soil/amendment mixing operation. Soil amendments can be classified as "organic" or "inorganic."

## Organic Amendments

The most popular organic amendments for sports field soil are peat, sawdust, and various waste or by-products, such as sewage sludge, manure, and compost. Fine textured organic amendments are better for amending coarse textured soil and coarse textured organic amendments are better for amending fine textured soil. All organic amendments are usually added at a rate of 10 to 20% by volume.

One of the most commonly used organic amendments is peat. Fibrous peats are to be preferred over sedimentary peats because sedimentary peats may contain excessive silt and clay. The most popular fibrous peat is sphagnum peat moss, which can be used with

**Table 8.1. Particle Size Distribution and Sieves of the Standard Screen Scale**

| USDA System of Classification | | Sieve No. | Sieve Opening, (Millimeters) | Approx. Opening, (inches) |
|---|---|---|---|---|
| Gravel >2mm | | 2½ | 8.00 | |
| | | 3 | 6.72 | ¼″ |
| | | 3½ | 5.66 | |
| | | 4 | 4.76 | |
| | | 5 | 4.00 | |
| | | 6 | 3.36 | ⅛″ |
| | | 7 | 2.83 | |
| | | 8 | 2.38 | |
| S A N D | Very coarse 1–2mm | 10 | 2.00 | |
| | | 12 | 1.68 | 1⁄16″ |
| | | 14 | 1.14 | |
| | | 16 | 1.19 | |
| | Coarse .5–1mm | 18 | 1.00 | |
| | | 20 | 0.84 | 1⁄32″ |
| | | 25 | 0.71 | |
| | | 30 | 0.59 | |
| | Medium .25–.5mm | 35 | 0.50 | |
| | | 40 | 0.42 | 1⁄64″ |
| | | 45 | 0.35 | |
| | | 50 | 0.30 | |
| | Fine .1–.25mm | 60 | 0.25 | |
| | | 70 | 0.21 | 1⁄128″ |
| | | 80 | 0.177 | |
| | | 100 | 0.149 | |
| | | 120 | 0.125 | |
| | | 140 | 0.105 | 1⁄256″ |
| | Very fine .05–.1mm | 170 | 0.088 | |
| | | 200 | 0.074 | |
| | | 230 | 0.062 | |
| | | 270 | 0.053 | 1⁄512″ |
| Silt .002–.05mm Clay <.002mm | | 325 | 0.044 | |

fine textured soil to increase permeability, and with coarse textured soil to help hold water in the soil profile.

Sawdust can be used effectively to amend sports field soil if it is well rotted and mixed with other compost at a rate of one to one. Avoid using fresh sawdust—the process of decay will rob the turf of much-needed nitrogen.

With the growing concern about waste hauling costs and landfill space, many municipalities have gone into the soil amendments business. These local governments are marketing organic by-products like sewage sludge and compost consisting of yard waste (grass clippings, leaves, and shrub and tree branches). In some parts of the country "mushroom compost" is available and is becoming a popular soil amendment. Mushroom compost often consists of about 80% straw and 20% peat moss.

The addition of organic amendments, like most turf management practices, has both advantages and disadvantages. Adding organic amendments to sand allows for better water retention, but may restrict permeability.

The opposite is true for a clay base soil. Adding organic amendments to native clay-based soil increases the permeability and enhances internal drainage. As we said earlier, the binding together of soil particles to form larger units is most desirable for improving permeability. In this type of soil, the organic amendments facilitate the binding process by acting as a cementing agent, helping to hold soil particles together.

However, this cementing process breaks down when players are put on the field. Compaction (from foot traffic) tends to break down the soil structure, resulting in a mushy, sticky soil that doesn't drain well. Under these circumstances, the water-holding characteristics of organic amendments become a problem. Even in shrub beds and flower beds (where there is no foot traffic), these amendments can hold so much moisture that the soil will not dry out. For these reasons, organic amendments are not recommended for amending native soil sports fields.

### Inorganic Amendments

The most popular inorganic amendments for sports turf soil are *sand* and *calcined materials* like calcined clay and calcined diatomaceous earth.

When adding *sand* to native topsoil (typically, topsoil with around 65% silt and clay), the objective is to add enough sand to the soil so that the sand particles are touching each other. The result is called "bridging." When bridging takes place, air spaces (pores) are created within the soil profile, and these pores allow air and water to pass into the soil.

In order to create bridging, the total sand content of the mixture should be at least 70%. In the case of topsoil with 35% sand and 65% silt and clay, a mixture of 1.5 parts sand and 1 part topsoil would be needed to reach more than 70% total sand content. (Here's the math: 1.5 new sand plus .35 sand already in the topsoil = 1.85 total sand ÷ 2.5 total volume of sand and topsoil = 74% sand).

This seems like a lot of sand to add. However, adding less than that may actually slow the internal drainage process. Without enough sand to achieve bridging, adding sand will not lead to a net increase in the "macropores," or pores that will drain freely due to the force of gravity.

To minimize compaction in soil amended with sand, the sand being added should be of a uniform size, with most of the particles falling into the "coarse" range (.5 mm to 1 mm). The medium and fine grade sands (.1 mm to .5 mm) are not as good for modifying native soil, because their smaller size does not lead to bridging as effectively. However, these medium and finer sands are preferred for making "soil-less" (predominantly sand-based) mixes (see Chapter 24, Sand and Sand-Based Fields).

The benefit of adding *calcined materials* to a native topsoil to improve permeability derives from the same principle described in regard to adding sand to a native soil. In order to be effective in bridging together to create macropore space, huge amounts of calcined materials would have to be added to the native soil. This would stretch the budget of all but the highest-profile facilities. Therefore, for the purpose of increasing permeability, these products are typically not recommended. (However, it should be noted that this is not the primary application of these products, which are meant to improve the water-absorbing capacity of soil, including the skinned areas of baseball diamonds.)

The most common application of calcined materials for amending native topsoil fields is to fill holes left by core aeration. In these holes, the calcined materials—like sand—can bridge in a column, providing a vertical channel for water percolation.

## 8.4   INSTALLED DRAIN SYSTEMS

So far in this chapter we have considered how water moves into and through the soil. We will now turn our attention to installed drain systems, which have the purpose of moving water *out of* the soil profile.

To understand how water moves out of the soil, let's start by looking at the exit point. As the first pore space empties into the exit point, that provides an opening for the next pore space to empty into, and so on. It's a little like people waiting in line to buy tickets at the movies; the people at the back of the line can't move forward until the people at the front of the line have gone into the theater. If another ticket window opens, the wait is cut in half. It's the same in the soil; providing more exit points decreases the time that water has to "wait in line" until openings are provided. These exit points could be into a porous sub-base, but in many cases an installed drain system is provided for that purpose.

(Compaction slows down this movement by pushing fine soil particles into the pore spaces between larger particles. Water moves only through pore spaces in the soil profile and permeability is slowed dramatically when pore space becomes reduced.)

Two factors determine the quality of an installed drain system: the effectiveness of water removal, and the "life of the system," or how long it will work. System effectiveness is dependent on sufficient number of drains, correct slope and layout, and proper installation. System life is affected by soil type and composition of the drain pipe used, because some soils will slowly infiltrate the drainage structure and eventually clog the drains (see Figure 8.2). Before installing any drain system, check with local drainage system suppliers to find out how local soil conditions affect the life of the system that will be installed, and the things that can be done to extend its life.

Various types of installed drainage systems are used to remove excess water from a localized area. Common types are pipe drains (sometimes called "tile drains") and strip drains. In designing a drain system, it's important to consider the discharge of the system. Many state and local codes regulate the discharge of these structures; simply tying the system into a sewage system may not be allowed. Check with local and state officials before installing any drainage system.

### 8.4a   Pipe Drains

The traditional type of drainage system for a sports field is the pipe drain, which is essentially a system of perforated pipe laid on beds of gravel in trenches beneath the topsoil. Pipe drains work by slowly and consistently removing water from the subsoil, and under some circumstances can help to drain away surface water if sand is used to fill the trench to the surface. (For removing surface water from a sports field, strip drains are more effective than pipe drains in part because pipe drains require such wide trenches that filling them to the surface with coarse sand or gravel would disrupt the footing on the playing area. Strip drains are discussed below.)

When constructing pipe drains using PVC perforated pipe with 2 or 3 rows of holes, place the holes so they are on the bottom. Water enters the pipe from the bottom. Water moves down through the gravel and stops at the bottom of the trench. As the water level rises, it finds its way into the pipe through the holes. If the holes are placed on top, the water level will have to rise all the way to top of the pipe before it can find an exit point. That means that water will be standing in the bottom 4″ to 5″ of the trench with

*Figure 8.2. This section of a pipe drain shows how the system has become so clogged with silt and clay that it no longer operates properly.*

nowhere to go. Eventually the water could move (through capillary action) into the soil around the trench and even work its way to the surface, causing soggy conditions.

(Corrugated perforated pipe has small holes all the way around the circumference of the pipe, and has no top or bottom.)

### Pipe Drains for Subsurface Water Removal

These drains have been used widely in agricultural (farm) drainage for lowering the water table of an area. Shallow water tables are very common in North America, and are caused by the presence of a water-impermeable layer 2′ to 5′ below the surface. This condition can cause the topsoil to become saturated with water following a heavy rain or irrigation.

The use of subsoil drain systems has been applied to sports fields with some success. However, since these systems work by removing water from the subsoil at a slow, consistent rate, they may have little effect in quickly draining the topsoil of a field. Subsoil pipe drains have the disadvantage that soil above the gravel will tend to become saturated before water begins to move into the gravel, creating a false (or "perched") water table on top of the subsoil. They also can dry out the soil immediately above the drain pipes in drought conditions.

This type of system was previously constructed of clay pipe (commonly referred to as "drain tile"), packed with coarse sand (typically 12″ to 18″) around the sides and top of the pipe, to prevent the system from filling up with silt and clay. Today's subsoil pipe drain systems use perforated pipe, and need to be backfilled with gravel around the pipe.

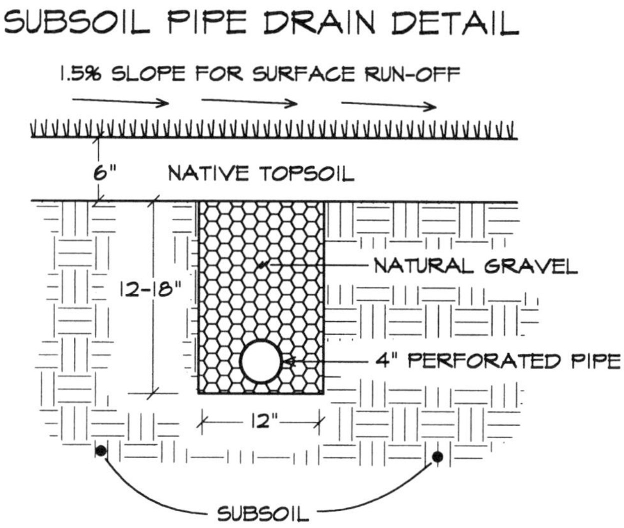

## SUBSOIL PIPE DRAIN DETAIL

Figure 8.3. Design detail for subsoil pipe drain systems. It is important to note that pipe drain systems placed under native topsoil growing media typically remove water only from the subsoil. They work more effectively to remove surface layer water if the surface layer is an amended sand medium.

The trenches in which the pipes are laid (usually 18″ to 36″ deep) are filled with gravel to a level about 6″ beneath the surface, then are filled to ground level with soil.

Sometimes this type of system is referred to as a "French drain." But, strictly speaking, a French drain is a trench filled with coarse aggregates to remove water from an area. A French drain system does not contain pipes to remove water from the trench and is not recommended for sports fields. French drains work like "dry wells," giving water somewhere to go, but when the dry well becomes completely filled, the soil around the system will become soggy.

Figure 8.3. shows the design detail of a subsoil pipe drain system.

### Interceptor Drains

These installed drain systems are designed to intercept and channel away water that might flow onto the field from the surrounding area. Although the primary function of pipe drains is to lower the water table by removing water from the subsoil, they can also be used to remove surface water in problem areas. When used in this way, pipe drain systems are called "interceptor drains."

Interceptor drains are normally pipe drains that are used in swales or in low-lying areas. They differ from the pipe drains on the field itself in that the trenches in which the pipes are laid are filled to the top with coarse sand or pea gravel to speed the removal of water (see Figure 8.4 for an interceptor drain backfilled with pea gravel). If the top 6″ of the trench is filled with sand, it could then be covered with washed sod, seeded, or left for the adjacent turf to cover over. (It is critical that the top of the trench not be covered with a layer of impermeable soil or sod.) These drains can be especially useful where the surrounding area is higher than the field itself.

Another type of interceptor drain is used to solve the problem of seepage of ground water out of a hillside. This type requires that a deep cut be made in the hillside, starting

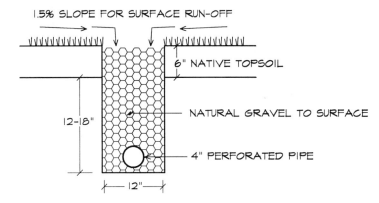

*Figure 8.4. Design detail for interceptor drain systems. Water flowing into the interceptor drain indicates its use in the bottom of a swale or low-lying area.*

above the point of the seepage, to intercept the water before it reaches the surface. Pipe is laid from the point where the water is encountered in the soil layer to an exit point where it will not compromise the playability of the field. These drains can be backfilled with topsoil, since their function is to intercept and channel away underground water, and not to remove water from the surface.

### Trackside Sand Drains

Although a system of swales and catch basins are sometimes used around the perimeter of a sports field, a better option for draining a field with a track around it is to install a trench right next to the track, sloping downward toward catch basins at the four corners. Dig a trench around the entire inside edge of the track 18" to 24" deep, then line the trench with a filter cloth. Lay a ½" bed of pea gravel in the trench, then a 4" perforated pipe. Fill with pea gravel to within 4" to 6" of the surface, top with coarse sand, and plant by seeding, sprigging, or using washed sod. The "sand drain" will serve as an open catch basin draining both field and track, and eliminating the annoying swales to catch basins. An alternative design leaves the drains open, and covers them with a metal grate to allow the free flow of water; this is a more expensive option, but a highly effective way to finish a trackside drain system. (For more on trackside drains, see Chapter 16, Track and Field Facilities.)

Figure 8.5 shows the design detail of a track drain system topped with coarse sand.

### 8.4b Strip Drains

Modern technology is also providing some new solutions to the challenge of properly draining fields. One of these new solutions is called "strip drains." These are cloth-wrapped polyethylene structures about an inch wide and 4" to 6" deep, and have the advantage that they can be installed in narrower, shallower trenches, with less labor and less disruption of the field. (Figures 8.6 and 8.7 show installation of a strip drain system.)

In a strip drain system, the sand-filled trenches at surface level drain away some of the surface water without requiring it to flow all the way across the field. In order for strip drains to remove surface water, the drains should be laid out at 45–90° to the direction

# TRACK DRAIN DETAIL

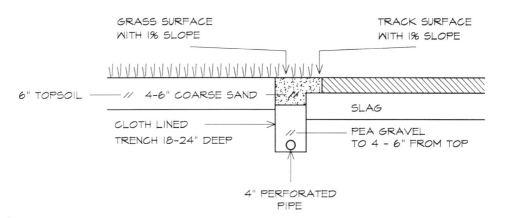

GRASS SURFACE
WITH 1% SLOPE

TRACK SURFACE
WITH 1% SLOPE

6" TOPSOIL —— // 4-6" COARSE SAND

SLAG

CLOTH LINED
TRENCH 18-24" DEEP

PEA GRAVEL
TO 4 - 6" FROM TOP

4" PERFORATED
PIPE

*Figure 8.5. Design detail for track drain systems.*

*Figure 8.6. These workers are installing a strip drain system. Note that the worker in the foreground is keeping the strip drain centered in the trench, an important step in assuring proper functioning.*

*Figure 8.7. The strip drains are connected to a collector drain to allow water to flow away from the field. Although the strip drains appear to be different colors, this is only a cosmetic matter; they are actually the same design. At lower left, a section of strip drain can be seen in side view. (Photo courtesy of Dan Zarlenga)*

of surface water runoff. The advantage of installing strip drains at a 45° angle to the direction of surface runoff is that the trench can be dug at a consistent depth following the natural downward slope. If the strip drains are installed at 90° to the direction of surface run-off, chances are good that the field surface is level in that direction, so the trench will have to be dug with a planned slope, making the job harder. Strip drains also can be used as a targeted system to attack problem areas where water tends to collect.

Strip drains are installed in the top 12″ of the soil and require only a 3″ to 4″ wide trench. The strip drain is placed in the bottom of the trench and extends halfway to the surface. The trench is then filled with coarse sand right up to surface level. The sand should be mostly coarse to very coarse and have less than 5% passing the 100 sieve screen.

Figure 8.8 shows the design detail of a strip drain system.

## 8.4c   Sand-Slit Drains

A type of drain that bears a certain resemblance to strip drains in design and function is the sand-slit drain. This system consists of narrow trenches (typically 2″ to 3″ wide and on 40″ to 80″ centers), with a thin perforated pipe at the bottom. The trenches are backfilled with sand. Perpendicular to these trenches is another set of sand-filled trenches on 13″ to 20″ centers, which help to conduct water to the perforated drain pipe. These systems can be installed with minimal disturbance to the field surface, but are usually installed by specialized firms using custom-designed equipment.

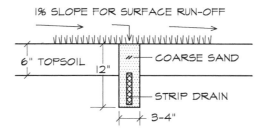

*Figure 8.8. Design detail for strip drain systems.*

### 8.4d  Common Problems of Installed Drain Systems

In an installed drain system, maybe the most common problem is a drainpipe that does not slope properly toward the outlets. Standing water in poorly-sloped pipe seeps into the soil and eventually creates a soggy surface through capillary action. A consistent downhill slope toward the outlet will keep the pipe clean by washing the fines out of the pipe.

Another common problem is the crushing of the pipe by heavy equipment. Not surprisingly, this problem is commonly encountered where the sub-base has been overcompacted. Once drain systems have been installed, heavy equipment should be kept off the field to prevent damage.

Sand-filled drain systems can slowly lose their effectiveness over time. The trench becomes covered with windblown sediment and cultivation practices like core aeration and topdressing introduce topsoil or fine sand to the coarse sand in the trenches.

The migration of fines into the drains is another chronic problem of installed drain systems. Ideally, most of the fines will be washed out of the system as they infiltrate. However, some will inevitably collect in the pipe, then attract and hold other fines and eventually clog the pipe. Chemical reactions can also occur, like the oxidation of iron compounds resulting in a rust layer that can further reduce the movement of water.

As this list of problems may indicate, installed drain systems have a finite life span, but the proper attention to detail in their design and construction can provide a reasonably effective and long-lived system.

### 8.5  OTHER DRAIN SYSTEM PRACTICES

#### Filter Cloth

This product is commonly added to an installed drain system to prevent the migration of fine particles into the pipe or to separate two layers of different soil materials. Filter cloth is available in rectangular sheets, or as "filter sock," which is supplied with the drain pipe.

It's worth noting that not all industry experts agree on the effectiveness of filter cloth; some point out that, as it prevents fines from reaching the drains, the filter cloth itself may become clogged, slowing the passage of water into the system. However, backfilling the trenches with carefully chosen and very coarse sand will tend to create an additional "filtering" structure, slowing the fines from reaching the filter cloth.

**Gravel Beds**

This is a layer of gravel placed below the topsoil and connected directly to the pipe drain system to assist in the rapid movement of water which has percolated through the soil. Although this method seems like a promising way to enhance drainage, it creates the possibility of a perched (false) water table, because the water will not move from the topsoil into the gravel layer until the topsoil is completely saturated. This can actually lead to a waterlogged playing surface in wet weather.

## 8.6   CONCLUSIONS

The secret to good field drainage is planning. Obviously, the best time to solve drainage problems is before they happen, when the field is being designed and built. On existing fields with serious drainage problems, the wise course is to identify the most serious underlying problem and to plan ways to correct it. Stopgap measures can provide a temporary fix, but unless a plan is developed for correcting the big problems, the "Band-Aid" fixes will have to be done over and over.

## REFERENCES

Tisdale, S. L. *Soil Fertility and Fertilizers (5th ed.).* Prentice-Hall, Old Tappan, NJ, 1993.
*Turfgrass, Agronomy, Number 32.* Edited by D. V. Waddington, R. N. Carrow, and R. C. Shearman. American Society of Agronomy, Inc.; Crop Science Society of America, Inc.; and Soil Science Society of America, Inc. Madison, WI, 1992.

# Chapter 9

# *Turfgrass Stresses and Remedies*

## 9.1 INTRODUCTION

One of the most important aspects of a sound program of Integrated Cultural Management (ICM) is close attention to the stresses placed on the turf by athletic competition. In fact, it would probably be reasonable to say that the primary difference between sports turf and all other kinds is that sports turf must be able to withstand additional stresses and still support play.

Every stand of turfgrass is subject to some stress. The cycle of the seasons creates times of heat and cold, too much or not enough moisture. Normal foot traffic creates compaction. Pests like insects and disease appear. Even routine practices like mowing place stress on the turfgrass. The most significant additional stress burden for sports turf is the excessive mechanical stress placed on the turf by concentrated foot traffic.

Different sports place different amounts of stress on the turf. Football, for instance, is probably the most turf-destructive sport that does not involve horses. More genteel sports like croquet and lawn bowling produce relatively little additional stress.

Chapters 1 through 8 of this book discuss the practices and procedures that are necessary to produce a strong, healthy stand of turf. While we have placed this discussion of stresses in Chapter 9, it would certainly be possible to make the case that the discussion of stresses should come first, and that cultural practices should be based on an understanding of those stresses. In any case, a meaningful understanding of sports turf stresses is absolutely essential in planning and executing an effective program of Integrated Cultural Management.

In this chapter, we will consider the various stresses to which sports turf is exposed, and, we will review some management procedures—cultural, chemical, and biological—that can help to prevent or correct the problems associated with those stresses.

## 9.2 MECHANICAL STRESSES

Having offered the viewpoint that mechanical stresses are the single greatest distinguishing challenge of sports turf, let's take a moment to look at the leading types of such stress.

### 9.2a Foot/Vehicular Traffic

#### *Foot Traffic*
Without question, the greatest mechanical stress placed on the turf on most sports fields comes from the feet of athletes. The burden of supporting sudden starts, stops, and

*Figure 9.1. This field's bench area became so compacted that only knotweed could grow in the soil. To fix the problem, the area had to be stripped, scarified, and resodded.*

sharp changes in direction is communicated directly into the turf through the cleats of the players. This mechanical action is probably more damaging to a football field than to any other type of sports field, because the center of action is always a group of large men (or relatively large boys) pushing against one another and chopping their feet into the turf. By the end of the season, many football fields have a strip of naked dirt running down the middle of the turf. While the mechanical stress on the turf is more evenly distributed on other fields, the turfgrass culture still sustains the same kinds of damage.

Foot traffic causes two distinct kinds of damage to the turf. The first is a lateral tearing motion that tends to uproot plants or rip off the blades. This type of stress can often be seen on TV replays or sports photographs, where little bits of sod come flying up as a player changes direction. It adds a lot of atmosphere to the pictures, but this kind of tearing stress rips a hole in the turfgrass culture.

Treating this type of damage requires replacement of the plants, and if possible, replacement of the soil that is ripped away. Aggressively recuperating turfgrass varieties (like bluegrass and bermudagrass) will help to minimize the damage, but topdressing and overseeding after the season is the most thorough way to restore the quality of the turf.

A second type of stress results from compaction, the downward motion that presses together the soil particles and prevents air, water, and nutrients from reaching the roots of the plants. Compaction can also become so severe that the roots of plants can no longer penetrate the soil. When this happens, the recuperative ability of the turfgrass is sharply restricted, and the ability of the turf to recover without outside help is very low (Figure 9.1).

Those who are responsible for maintaining fields at schools and universities should remember that the band can cause as much compaction as the football team. It's a matter of sheer numbers; 22 players participate in each play of the game, but there may be 200 or more members in a large marching band. The foot traffic by these musicians can substantially contribute to overcompaction. If there is any alternative location for practice, aim to minimize the use of the stadium field by the band.

Relieving overcompaction requires aeration to fracture the compacted soil layer. Solid tine aeration can be performed during the season, but core aeration will normally have to wait until afterward to prevent disruption of play. In the North, core aerating the heavily compacted portions of a football field (including the bench areas) immediately at the end of the season can provide an opportunity for the turf to recover before the growing season ends, then allow the freezing and thawing of winter to continue the process of fracturing the aerated turf. By spring, the problem should be largely relieved. If a second treatment is needed, it can be performed as soon as the field is dry enough for equipment.

### Vehicular Traffic

Another type of mechanical stress is caused by vehicular traffic. Common sense dictates two policies: keep heavy equipment off the fields at all times, and keep all equipment off wet turf. The wheels of a tractor can cause a rut in one minute that will take one year to relieve. In the meantime, a serious injury may occur. If the staff performs mowing, don't assume that they are conscious of vehicular traffic stress; take time to be actively involved in inspecting the field any time it may be too wet for mowing or other procedures. As a rule of thumb, if a "squishing" sound can be heard when walking over turf, it's too wet to mow without damage.

Vehicular traffic stress can be corrected by aerating, but usually requires filling and reseeding ruts to achieve real uniformity. It's much, much easier to prevent vehicular damage than to fix it.

## 9.2b   Mowing and Aerification Stresses

### Mowing Stresses

Next to foot traffic, the greatest mechanical stress placed on a sports field comes from improper mowing. In fact, it's possible to subject the turf to so much stress through poor mowing practices that it has little chance to withstand the demands of the competitive season. The most common type of mowing stress is probably created by mowing with dull blades. Whether the mower is a reel unit, a rotary, or a flail the importance of sharp and properly adjusted blades cannot be overemphasized. The cutting action of rotary and flail mowers tears the leaf blades in the first place; if the mower blade is dull, the cutting action shreds the leaf blades rather than tearing them cleanly. The result is a shabby-looking turf with dying leaf tips and an overall brown appearance.

But it's important to realize that the effects of dull mower blades go beyond appearances. The torn grass plants subject the turf to the increased likelihood of moisture stress, insect damage, and disease infestation. In order to repair the damage caused by dull mower blades, the turfgrass must expend precious food reserves that may be needed to prevent other, less-preventable stresses, like heat or athletic competition.

Mower blades must be inspected, sharpened, and adjusted frequently in order to get the best cut possible. Ideally, blades should be sharpened each and every mowing day!

Repeatedly mowing turf areas in the same pattern and direction also contributes to stress. It's important to set up a regularly scheduled mowing pattern that includes variations to relieve stress. For instance, move the entry and exit points around on the field. And watch areas near obstructions; when swinging around catch basins, goals, and the like, the operator can unconsciously fall into the habit of going over and over the same spot in the same direction each time, compacting and damaging the turf.

When using a rotary mower, use the highest recommended blade speed (400–600 RPM) and the lowest ground speed possible (Ideally, 3 to 5 MPH). If the blade speed is too low or the ground speed too high, the effect will be to shred the grass instead of cutting it.

Low cutting heights can also encourage weeds and disease. These problems may indicate the staff is cutting off too much of the turf. Try raising the cutting height, then gradually working back down to the desired height, cutting off not more than one-third of the turf at each mowing.

### Aeration Stresses

Another mechanical damage frequently seen on sports fields is a result of soil aeration. While necessary to promote the long-term health of the turf, aeration causes damage to the turf in the short term by disrupting the surface. If aeration is performed at the proper time of the year, when turf growth rates are at or near their maximum, the turf can recuperate rapidly. (Of course, optimum recuperation also requires proper fertility and irrigation programs to provide the plants with the nutrients and the water they need for quick recovery.)

## 9.3    ENVIRONMENTAL STRESSES

### 9.3a    Temperature

In most of North America, damage caused by extreme heat or cold is relatively rare. While turfgrass may turn yellow and then brown in the heat of the summer, this characteristic normally indicates insufficient water rather than direct response to heat. Likewise, even in the coldest parts of the winter, turfgrass root structure is usually protected from permanent damage by the layer of thatch and soil surrounding it.

However, it's important to restrict field use when frost is present on both cool season and warm season turfgrasses. Traffic on frosted turf can literally sever leaf blades due to fracturing by the ice crystals, so keep players off the fields until rising temperatures melt the frost. Melting can be accelerated with light irrigation once the temperatures have warmed to at least 36–40°F, as long as they are not expected to drop below freezing again. If the temperature *does* drop below freezing after irrigation, icing can actually make the situation worse. Another practice commonly used by sports turf managers to minimize the effect of frost is to apply a soil wetting agent; by reducing the surface tension of the water, the wetting agent minimizes the amount of moisture retained on the leaf blades. This technique is effective during the initial periods of light frost, but the damage from a killing (heavy) frost cannot be negated by a wetting agent application (Figure 9.2).

In the event of an ice storm, it's even more important to keep traffic off the turf. Even more so than frosted leaves, ice-covered blades will snap under the least pressure, resulting in distinct patterns of dead leaves everywhere a foot or a tire is placed on the turf.

(An important related concern is the risk of injury to athletes playing on a frozen field. Footing can be treacherous on frozen fields, and the impact upon bodies falling on frozen fields can result in serious injury. To prevent frozen soils, heating cables have been installed on some high-profile fields in the northern U.S. Lambeau Field in Green Bay,

*Figure 9.2. Frost damage on bermudagrass. (Photo courtesy of Don Waddington).*

Wisconsin, is a well-known example of a facility that has used underground heating cables to maintain playability in cold weather.)

Most temperature-related damage occurs because the turf is exposed to other forms of stress at the same time. We've already mentioned the combination of heat and drought conditions; heavy foot traffic during extreme heat or cold can also place the turf under special stress. However, with adequate irrigation, turfgrass can usually support play at temperatures so high that players and coaches would tend to cancel practices and games. In winter, weather cold enough to damage the turf would present a more serious hazard to players outside playing than it would to the field itself.

There are a few cultural practices that can promote turf survival during periods of extreme heat or cold. First of all, raising the cutting height is generally considered desirable to relieve some of the stress on the plant. Research has clearly shown that on warm season grasses, raising the cutting height is probably the single most important way to improve the turf's chances of surviving cold temperatures. For instance, it is common for field managers to raise the cutting heights of bermudagrass fields from 0.5 to 1 inch as winter approaches. The additional turf cover has a "blanket-like" effect, moderating soil temperatures and increasing wear tolerance if the field is to be used during the off-season.

On cool season turf, raising the mowing height during periods of high temperature stress can also improve turf performance, particularly if irrigation is available.

The second step that can be taken to improve turf survival during periods of temperature extremes is to ensure potassium fertility levels are adequate. Don't wait until the middle of a heat wave or a cold snap to apply the potassium fertilizer. The nutrient must be available to the plant as it prepares for these periods of temperature extremes.

## 9.3b    Water

Of course, the primary environmental stress faced by fields in the **warm season** zone is related to water: both drought and monsoon-like conditions are encountered. Fortunately, bermudagrass is a cosmopolitan species and is adapted to a wide variety of moisture conditions. While irrigation helps keep a bermudagrass field in top condition, the drought tolerance of these grasses is excellent and allows the turf to survive dry periods lasting for up to 20 days at a time. bermudagrass can also tolerate wet conditions for an extended period, but may not be able to survive a combination of excessive wetness and foot traffic; this problem can and should be avoided through the proper design of the drainage system, including both surface contours and installed drains.

A commonly overlooked bermudagrass stress in the South is winter desiccation. It's important to remember that dormant bermudagrass is not dead; even though temperatures are below optimum for plant growth, the turf still requires adequate moisture to survive. In areas that typically receive little winter precipitation, consider a supplemental irrigation application at least once every 2–3 weeks to ensure the turf has adequate moisture available. This is particularly critical on sand-based fields.

Despite their many strengths as a turfgrass, the ryegrasses are not noted for drought resistance or for tolerance to prolonged wet conditions. Effective drainage systems and sufficient irrigation sources will be necessary in order to ensure a high quality turf on a field overseeded with ryegrass. Fortunately, the normal winter and spring rainfall in much of the South will adequately support excellent overseeded ryegrass turf.

In **cool season** zones, climate conditions tend to be more moderate, and local levels of precipitation support turfgrass culture adequately with the addition of modest amounts of water during the summer.

## 9.3c    Light, Air, and Humidity

While light, air, and humidity represent less common environmental stresses than excesses of heat and water, each merits a moment of consideration as we survey the ways that sports turfs are placed under pressure. In the case of light and air, stress is placed on the turf by inadequate supplies. In the case of humidity, the opposite is true—excessive humidity is sometimes a cause of turfgrass stress.

By virtue of the fact that most sports fields are large, open spaces, assuring adequate sunlight to support healthy turfgrass culture is seldom a problem. However, those charged with maintaining purely recreational sports facilities at parks and camps may find that shaded volleyball courts, playgrounds, bocce courts, and the like are susceptible to substantial thinning due to inadequate sunlight. Under these circumstances, the planner may choose to overseed (or completely replace the turfgrass) with a variety specifically developed for low-light environments. The other alternative, of course, is to replace the  turf in suitable areas with a material such as wood chips, sand, or shredded rubber.

Probably the most common cause of damage from lack of light is the sloppy maintenance practice of leaving a heavy layer of clippings on the turf after mowing. Cutting too infrequently and taking off too much of the plants will result in a blanket of clippings that prevents sunlight from getting to the plants, and causes yellowed, unhealthy-looking turf (see Figure 9.3).

A more common and more frequently overlooked form of stress is inadequate passage of air into the soil. This condition is most often the result of overcompaction and under-aeration. Since plant roots require oxygen in order to carry on the process of respiration, reducing the supply of air to the roots will result in a gradually thinning turfgrass stand.

*Figure 9.3. Excessive clippings left lying on the turf will kill the plants underneath. Note the dying spot in the middle of this view.*

Environmental stress from excessive humidity typically affects the turf by retarding the normal drying process, and may create conditions ideal for infestations of disease or other pests. When relative humidity is unusually high, it's wise to check the moisture in the soil and thatch layer before watering. If the turf is already adequately irrigated, adding more water will simply aggravate an existing condition of excessive moisture.

High humidity and high temperatures can play havoc in the management of cool season turfgrasses. Turfgrasses cool themselves by the process of transpiration. However, under high humidity conditions this process of cooling by transpiration is dramatically slowed. The temperature of the plants themselves begins to increase, and there is the possibility of extensive turf loss from direct temperature kill. By itself, irrigation will not relieve this stress, and can actually make the problem worse. Fortunately, this problem is unusual for sports fields, and is a problem primarily for golf putting greens.

## 9.4    WEEDS, INSECTS, AND DISEASE

The key to successful pest management is the proper identification of the pest that is the cause of the problem. Far too often, unhealthy turf causes fields managers to jump to the same conclusion: "disease!" In a surprising number of cases, however, the real culprit turns out to be a routine problem like dull mower blades, excessive thatch layers, localized dry spots of soils, irrigation application problems, pH or fertility problems, frost damage, and so on. Dull blades on mowers cause brown, frayed leaf tips that are commonly associated with disease or insect damage. Frost damage is often misdiagnosed as a disease, particularly on warm season turfgrasses such as bermudagrass. Obviously, chemical applications for either of these problems will do no good at all. In diagnosing a problem, we must rule out as many of the cultural and environmental factors as possible, and then use all the available clues to diagnose the problem.

Once the problem is properly diagnosed, we can turn our attention to specific strategies for the control of pests. As we prepare to do so, it's important to consider a couple of the general rules with which we approach this subject.

First of all, it's important that we have a common understanding of the meaning of the term "pest." While common usage applies this term most frequently to insects, our definition is broader and more inclusive. When we speak of pests, we mean any living organism that competes with turfgrass plants for nutrients, light, water, air, and even space. Some pests even go so far as to prey upon the plants in a parasitic fashion. This broader definition thus includes pest-incited diseases, weeds, and nematodes, as well as insects.

Second, we need to be in agreement about the goal of pest control. While some pests (and especially insects like bees and fire ants) cannot be allowed to remain in sports turf, for the most part our objective must be to control, and not to totally eradicate the pest in question. A fields manager who becomes obsessive about eradicating a particular pest runs the risk of turning into Bill Murray's character in the movie *Caddyshack*—blowing up the facility to get rid of gophers. As long as pests are prevented from diminishing the quality and playability of the turf, completely wiping them out is usually not a practical goal.

One of the first and foremost methods for resisting pest infestations is to choose turfgrass varieties that have been enhanced for pest resistance. Field evaluation trials have shown that many of today's turfgrass cultivars, and particularly cool season turfgrasses, demonstrate superior insect and disease resistance characteristics, usually genetic in nature.

Evaluations of pest resistance by various cultivars are available through the USDA's National Turfgrass Evaluation Program (NTEP). For information that is more specific to the area, check with the land-grant universities, which may have participated in the evaluation of grasses for the area. Selecting a variety with improved resistance to pests that are common in the specific locale can save lots of time, money, and headaches, and sometimes can eliminate the need for pesticide application programs.

The planner can also select varieties of perennial ryegrass and tall fescue that have been "endophyte-enhanced." That means that the seeds and tissues of these grasses contain an endophyte (a fungus that actually lives in the plant) that has proved to be beneficial to the overall health of the turf. After the seed germinates and the plant matures, the endophyte continues to reside in the tissues of the plant. The fungus does not behave as a harmful parasite of the turfgrass plant, and infected plants have actually been shown to resist attack by insects or by other fungi, and also to have improved drought and temperature extreme tolerances. The improved pest resistance due to the presence of the endophyte is often well worth the few pennies extra per pound for "endophyte-enhanced" turfgrass.

Proper fertility, irrigation, and cultural management decisions can greatly reduce the incidence of pests in athletic turf. Taking care of the turf by making wise decisions in these areas of maintenance is putting into practice the concept of Integrated Cultural Management (ICM). This philosophy will reduce the need for many pesticides on athletic turf because it will help in maintaining a dense, healthy turf that will resist a lot of the pressures from weeds, insects, and diseases. However, it is nearly impossible to maintain dense turf cover on a heavily used athletic field throughout the year, and from time to time the turf succumbs to the attack of some pest.

## 9.4a  Weeds

At the risk of belaboring the obvious, let's begin with a definition—what is a weed? The answer, of course, is that a weed is any unwanted plant. Grandmother's begonias may be the pride of the county, but in the cornfield, they're weeds. Everyone is familiar with common turfgrass weeds such as dandelions, clover, and crabgrass, but some of the toughest weeds in sports field management can be other turfgrasses. For instance, the toughest weed problem the manager of a quality Tifway bermudagrass athletic field can face is another type of bermudagrass. Tall fescue or creeping bentgrass can be similar weed problems in a Kentucky bluegrass or perennial ryegrass athletic field. For this kind of weed problem, often there are no chemical control solutions, either for preemergent (PRE) or postemergent (POE) applications. (There is no selective control for bentgrass in bluegrass turf, but Lesco's TFC and Telar are both labeled for tall fescue control in Kentucky bluegrass.) Unless the plan is to replace the turf entirely, the most practical course is to shift management strategies in mowing, fertility, irrigation, etc. to favor the desirable turfgrass, or persistently overseed with a more suitable variety until the unwanted turfgrass is crowded out.

How do the weeds get there? During periods when the canopy is opened up due to heavy traffic, weed seeds begin to germinate in the soil. Weed seeds can also be windborne, moved along in running water after a rainfall or irrigation event, or carried in by equipment, human, or animal traffic on the turf. Eventually, the weeds start to compete with the turfgrass for space, light, water, and nutrients. Most weeds are easy to see when they appear, because they disrupt the uniformity of the turf; they have different growth habits, colors, shapes, and sizes than the surrounding turf plants. Mowing is an effective control mechanism for some weed species, but most turfgrass weeds have growth habits that allow them to tolerate frequent, close clipping.

### Practical Ways of Classifying Weeds

Two categories of weeds occur in turf: grass (or grass-like) weeds and broadleaf weeds. The grassy weeds are often referred to as *monocots* because they emerge from the seed with one cotyledon (seed leaf). The broadleaf weeds are often referred to as *dicots* because they emerge from the seed with two seed leaves. It is important to be able to distinguish the plants at this stage to help in planning appropriate chemical control measures.

Weeds can be further differentiated by their life cycles. *Annuals* complete a life cycle of seed germination, vegetative growth, and reproduction by seed formation within one growing season. *Biennials* require two growing seasons to complete their life cycle. *Perennial* plants can reproduce numerous times over several growing seasons; some have life spans of 2–3 years while others survive indefinitely. Relatively few turfgrass weeds are biennials, so most of the attention is focused on annuals and perennials.

### Identification of Weeds

There are numerous publications to aid in the identification of weeds, many of them produced by the extension offices of the local or regional land-grant university. Other popular identification books are listed at the end of this chapter. The state plant taxonomy department or extension weed science personnel can aid in identifying weed samples that can be shipped by mail.

However, what is most often required is simply a determination of whether the weed is a grass, grass-like, or broadleaf plant. Earlier in this chapter, we discussed the differences between monocot and dicot weeds, but this distinction is often difficult when the plants are seedlings. A few days later, as the weed develops, a clear distinction can be

*Figure 9.4. Netted veins are characteristic of most broadleaf weeds.*

*Figure 9.5. Grasses, unlike broadleaf weeds, have parallel veins on their leaves.*

made more easily, based on the leaf veins or the shape of the stem. Most broadleaf weeds have what is called "netted" veins (Figure 9.4); the veins crisscross each other numerous times. Grasses have parallel veins running the length of the leaf blade (Figure 9.5). As always, there are a few exceptions to this rule. An obvious one can be observed with plantains (*Plantago* spp.*)*, a very common perennial broadleaf weed in both cool and warm season turf, which has very distinct parallel veins on the leaf underside.

Among grass-like weeds, sedges (*Cyperus* spp.), rushes (*Juncus* spp.), and wild onion/garlic plants (*Allium* spp.) are the most common. Sedges can be identified by a characteristic triangular stem. Rushes are usually identified by a round stem and by their very wiry, upright growth habit. Wild onion and garlic are similar in appearance to the typical garden-variety onion, and they have a characteristic onion- or garlic-like smell after being mowed.

In certain situations, the presence of a particular weed can indicate that other problems exist. For instance, sedges and rushes typically occur in poorly drained or compacted soils. Goosegrass (*Eleusine indica*), knotweed (*Polygonum* sp.), spurge (*Chaemesyce* spp.), and path rush (*Juncus tenuis* Willd.) are more likely to occur on compacted soils (see Figure 9.6). A heavy population of clover (*Trifolium* sp.) usually signifies an area of low fertility (See Figure 9.7). All of these plants can be used as indicators of turf problems.

Figure 9.6. The presence of path rush (left) and knotweed (right) indicate heavily compacted soil.

Figure 9.7. Clover in the turf is a sign of low nitrogen fertility in the soil.

**Table 9.1. Common Annual Grass or Grass-Like Weeds**

| Common Name | Scientific Name | Comments and Chemical Control Strategy |
|---|---|---|
| Annual bluegrass (Figure 9.8) | *Poa annua* L. | Winter annual to short-lived perennial. Many variants of annual bluegrass exist in the U.S. Prolific seedhead producer and tolerant of close cutting heights. Poor tolerance to traffic and temperature extremes. Primary germination period in the South is late summer to early fall; in the North is early spring and late summer. Both PRE and POE control possible; PRE usually preferred. |
| Annual kyllinga, Annual sedge (Figure 9.9) | *Cyperus spp.* | Triangular stemmed, short-growing, clump-forming plants that generally prefer wet soils. POE control. |
| Crabgrass (Figure 9.10) | *Digitaria* spp. | At least 8 species of crabgrass occur in the U.S. Germination begins when soil temperatures reach 55–60°F at a 4″ depth. Will germinate throughout summer if moisture and sunlight are adequate. Dies at first frost. Thin, spiky seedhead gives plant appearance of legs of crab. Usually not a problem on thick turfgrass. Both PRE and POE control. |
| Foxtail (Figure 9.11) | *Setaria* spp. | Similar to crabgrass. Multiple species in the U.S. |
| Goosegrass (Figure 9.12) | *Eleusine indica* L. | Germinates when soil temperatures reach low-to-mid 60s. Prostrate (ground-hugging) growth habit makes it very tolerant of close cutting heights. Often difficult to control chemically if not treated early in development. Both PRE and POE control. |
| Barnyardgrass | *Echinochloa* sp. | Similar to crabgrass, can be distinguished by thicker seedhead, which resembles the head of a stalk of wheat. Prefers wet soils. |

### The Most Common Weeds in Sports Turf Management

While the lists in Table 9.1 through 9.4 are not intended to be all-inclusive, they are designed to highlight the weeds that occur most commonly on sports fields.

### Herbicides

To be consistent with our practice of making sure that we share a common understanding of basic terminology, we should consider the various terms and classifications used in discussing herbicides. This is especially important in the case of herbicides, because they are classified by many different methods.

One of the first methods of classification describes when the herbicides are applied: **preemergent** (PRE) herbicides are applied before the target weed emerges from the soil, and **postemergent** (POE) herbicides are applied after the weed has emerged.

**Preemergent** herbicides are typically applied when the particular stand of turf cannot tolerate any weeds at all—as on a grass tennis court—or when the turf has a history of heavy weed infestation (Table 9.5). Preemergent herbicides are designed to be watered

*Figure 9.8. Annual bluegrass.*

*Figure 9.9. Annual sedge.*

*Figure 9.10. Southern crabgrass.*

*Figure 9.11. Foxtail.*

*Figure 9.12. Goosegrass.*

following application, so they will pass into the soil profile, where weeds are germinating. Failure to water these herbicides into the soil within the time indicated on the label will substantially reduce their effectiveness. When properly used, PRE herbicides should cause little to no turfgrass discoloration.

**Postemergent** herbicides are applied onto the foliage of existing weeds, and they work best on weeds that are young and actively growing (Tables 9.6 and 9.7). Spraying a weed after it has initiated reproductive growth (for instance, forming seedheads), is usually a waste of time and money, and it can also be environmentally irresponsible. The effectiveness of POE herbicides is often increased by adding a *surfactant* to the solution. Surfactants are chemicals that improve the performance of the herbicide by distributing it more uniformly over the leaf surface, and ultimately increasing absorption of the material into the plant. Surfactants are typically added to the spray tank at concentrations of 0.25% or 0.5% by volume. (The amount and type of surfactant should always be confirmed by consulting the label.)

Another method of herbicide classification breaks them into those with **selective** and **nonselective** action. Many herbicides have the specific ability to control one specific weed or a group of target weeds with minimal effect on the desirable turfgrass. These herbicides are described as having **selective** action, and most herbicides used in weed control programs are of this category.

Herbicides that are classified **nonselective** kill all plant tissues that they contact (Table 9.8). These herbicides are used primarily for renovation purposes (to kill all vegetation

## Table 9.2. Common Perennial Grass or Grass-Like Weeds

| Common Name | Scientific Name | Comments and Chemical Control Strategy |
|---|---|---|
| Dallisgrass (Figure 9.13) | *Paspalum. dilatatum* Poir. | Clump-forming, warm-season grass that tolerates moderately cold temperatures. Very wide leaf blades and tall seedheads. Characteristic bulb-like stem at base of plant. Selective chemical control is possible with repeated applications. Typically POE control, but PRE possible. |
| Kikuyugrass | *Pennisetum clandestinum* L. | Particular problem in the warm, humid climates of western U.S. Very aggressive lateral growth habit due to stolons. Coarse texture. No selective chemical control alternatives. |
| Nimblewill | *Muhlenbergia* sp. | Stoloniferous, fine-textured grass with a short, jagged, membranous ligule. Resembles common bermudagrass or bentgrass, but sheaths have white edges. Thrives in shaded conditions, but will compete with both cool and warm season turfgrasses in sunny conditions. No selective chemical control available. |
| Path rush | *Juncus tenuis* Willd. | Circular stemmed, fine-textured grass-like plant typically found in compacted and/or wet soils. Similar in appearance to fine fescues. No selective chemical control alternatives available. |
| Quackgrass | *Elytrigia repens* (L.) Desv. ex B.D. Jackson | Coarse-textured, cool season grass that is similar in texture to unimproved tall fescue cultivars. Characteristic strong rhizomes, foliage has gray-green color. No selective chemical control available. |
| Nutsedges (annual, purple and yellow) Kyllinga (annual and perennial) (Figure 9.14–9.16) | *Cyperus* spp. | Of the hundreds of species of *Cyperus*, these are the most prominent in turf. Nutsedges have underground tubers that serve as reproductive and food storage organs. Perennial kyllinga is a mat-forming plant that spreads by rhizomes. Nutsedges and kyllingas can be identified by their triangular stem and pointed, sharp-edged leaves. Seedheads resemble flowers. Primarily POE control with limited PRE control available for yellow nutsedge. |
| Smutgrass | *Sporobolus. indicus* (L.) R. Br. | Coarse-textured, clump-forming, warm season grass similar in appearance to tall fescue. Erect habit. Characteristic spiky seedhead is often infested with the smut fungus. No selective chemical control alternatives available. |
| Torpedograss | *Panicum repens* L. | Coarse-textured, warm season grass with very aggressive lateral growth due to rhizomes. First set of leaves emerge opposite each other. Found primarily in warm, coastal regions of the U.S. No selective chemical control alternatives. |

Table 9.2. (Continued)

| Common Name | Scientific Name | Comments and Chemical Control Strategy |
|---|---|---|
| Velvetgrass | *Holcus lanatus* L. | Northern grassy weed with soft, pointed leaves. Sheath hairy with visible pink nerves. No selective chemical controls. |
| Wild onion/garlic (Figure 9.17) | *Allium* spp. | Grass-like plant chemically treated as broadleaf weed. Emerges in late summer to mid-fall from a bulb. Onion has a solid stem and garlic has a hollow stem. Primarily POE control. |

in a specific area), or in special situations where any vegetation at all is undesirable (such as the skinned areas of baseball fields; or at the base of fences around athletic fields).

## 9.4b   Insects

(For our purposes, references to insects in this section will include only those which actually cause damage to turf.)

Insects form a class within the phylum Arthropoda known as Insecta. They have three body parts (head, thorax, and abdomen), three sets of legs, a pair of antennae, and usually two sets of wings (see Figure 9.26). Other classes within the phylum arthropoda that can sometimes cause turf problems and are often misidentified as insects include Arach-

*Figure 9.13. Dallisgrass.*

*Figure 9.14. Yellow nutsedge.*

*Figure 9.15. Purple nutsedge.*

*Figure 9.16. Leaf blades of purple nutsedge (left) and yellow nutsedge (right).*

*Figure 9.17. Tufts of wild garlic growing among chickweed.*

## Table 9.3. Weed Families and Common Annual Broadleaf Weeds

| Common Name | Scientific Name | Comments and Chemical Control Strategy |
|---|---|---|
| **Family: Caryophyllaceae** | | |
| Common chickweed and Sticky chickweed | *Stellaria media* (L.) Cyrillo. *Cerastium glomeratum* Thuill. | Mat-forming winter annuals with very prostate growth habits. Both have opposite leaves on multiple branched stems, but sticky chickweed has densely hairy leaves. Mouse-ear chickweed (*Cerastium vulgatum* L.) is a perennial species very similar to sticky chickweed. PRE and early POE control. |
| **Family: Compositae** | | |
| Cudweeds | *Gnaphalium* spp. | Many different sizes and shapes in this family, but |
| Eclipta | *Eclipta prostrata* L. | all have similar flower shapes known as heads—for |
| Fireweed | *Erichtites hieraciifolia* (L.) Raf. ex DC. | reference, shapes similar to that of the sunflower (*Helianthus annus* L. H.). PRE and early POE |
| Fleabanes | *Erigeron* spp. | control for all. |
| Spiny sowthistle | *Sonchus asper* (L.) Hill | |
| Spurweed (Figure 9.18) | *Soliva pterosperma* (Juss.) Less. | |
| Thistles | *Carduus* spp. | |
| **Family: Cruciferae** | | |
| Shepherdspurse | *Capsella bursa-pastoris* (L.) Medic. | Flowers have four petals and occur in clusters at the ends of stems. Fruits have characteristic pods |
| Sibara | *Sibara virginica* (L.) Rollins | and shapes, and many of the leaves are typically arranged in a flattened rosette-type form. |
| Virginia pepperweed (or peppergrass) | *Lepidium Virginicum* L. | Shepherdspurse has more "jagged" leaves, pepperweed leaves have more rounded lobes. Both PRE and early POE control. |
| **Family: Euphorbiaceae** | | |
| Spurges (Figure 9.19) | *Chamaesyce* spp. | Mat-forming summer annuals with multibranched, prostrate stems that have oppositely arranged leaves. Typically found on compacted soils. Contain a characteristic white, milky sap. Both PRE and POE control. |
| **Family: Geraniaceae** | | |
| Carolina geranium | *Geranium carolinianum* L. | Semierect winter annual with deeply serrated leaves attached to the plant on long petioles. Purple to pink 5-petaled flowers. Has a tap root system which helps to distinguish it from buttercup (*Ranunculus* spp.). Both PRE and early POE control. |
| **Family: Labiatae** | | |
| Henbit (Figure 9.20) | *Lamium amplexicaule* L. | Upright growing winter annuals with characteristic greenish to purple four-sided stems. Purple flowers |
| Deadnettle | *Lamium purpureum* L | and opposite leaves. Henbit has no petioles (stems) on upper leaves, while deadnettle does. Both PRE and early POE control. |

## Table 9.3. Continued

| Common Name | Scientific Name | Comments and Chemical Control Strategy |
|---|---|---|
| **Family: Leguminosae** | | |
| Black medic | *Medicago lupulina* L. | Legumes are capable of fixing their own nitrogen, so they can compete with turf under low fertility conditions. Many, but not all legumes have trifoliate leaves. Common lespedeza is a summer annual, while the rest of the list are winter annuals. 2,4-D is only marginally successful in controlling legumes. Chemical controls usually effective only against specific varieties (check label). POE control primarily. |
| Common lespedeza | *Lespedeza striata* (Thunb.) H. & A. | |
| Hop clovers | *Trifolium* spp. | |
| Spotted burclover | *Medicago arabica* (L.) Huds. | |
| **Family: Plantaginaceae** | | |
| Bracted plantain | *Plantago aristata* Michx. | Plantains listed are winter annuals and have the characteristic parallel veins on the underside of the leaf. Knotweed has a very characteristic, prostrate growth habit, with elliptical shaped, alternating leaves on creeping stems. In the South, knotweed germinates about the same time as crabgrass; in the North, very early spring. Knotweed is a problem weed in compacted soils. Both PRE and early POE control effective. |
| Paleseed plantain | *Plantago virginica* L. | |
| **Family: Polygonaceae** | | |
| Prostrate knotweed | *Polygonum aviculare* L. | |
| **Family: Portulacaceae** | | |
| Purslanes | *Portulaca* spp. | Purslanes are prostrate-growing, mat-forming summer annuals with fleshy, thick, oblong-shaped leaves. Succulent, reddish stems. The flowers of purslanes are quite showy, so much so that some are marketed as flowering annuals by lawn and garden centers. Both PRE and early POE control. |
| **Family: Ranunculaceae** | | |
| Buttercups | *Ranunculus* spp. | Prostrate-growing, tap-rooted, winter annuals similar in appearance to *Geranium carolinianum*. Typically denoted in the spring by its bright yellow flowers. Both PRE and early POE control. |
| **Family: Scrophulariaceae** | | |
| Speedwells | *Veronica* spp. | Low-growing freely branched winter annuals. Corn speedwell has opposite leaves with hairs; purslane speedwell has smoother leaves. Corn speedwell has characteristic blue-colored flowers and purslane speedwell has white flowers. Both PRE and early POE control possible. |

nida (e.g., spiders, mites); Crustacea (e.g., crayfish); Chilopoda (e.g., centipedes); and Diplopoda (e.g., millipedes).

Insects that feed on turf can cause great concern for sports turf managers because of their rapid life cycles, voracious feeding habits on turf when present in large numbers, the ability to mate and reproduce in large numbers, and the ability to survive periods of environmental stress.

Figure 9.18. Spurweed (Photo courtesy of J. Byrd).

Figure 9.19. Prostrate spurge.

*Figure 9.20. Henbit.*

Insects undergo changes in shape or form during development by processes called complete or incomplete metamorphosis. With complete metamorphosis, the insect hatches from the egg and goes through several stages of development in what are termed the larval stages. The larvae eventually transform into adults (Figure 9.27A). Most caterpillars and worm-like insects that cause turf problems (e.g., grubworms, armyworms, cutworms) are examples of organisms that undergo complete metamorphosis. Grubworms transform into beetles upon maturity and armyworms and cutworms become moths. For these particular examples of insects that undergo complete metamorphosis, it's important to note that it is the immature forms cause turf damage, not the adult forms. Therefore, most control measures are targeted at the immature stages.

Other insects develop from eggs to adults in a process called incomplete metamorphosis (Figure 9.27B). The various stages of development after hatching are called nymphal stages. The nymphs are very much like smaller versions of the adult, typically lacking fully developed wings and being somewhat smaller in size. However, their feeding habits are almost always the same. Chinch bugs and mole crickets both develop by incomplete metamorphosis, with the nymphs often causing more turfgrass damage than the adults.

*Practical Ways of Classifying Insects*
It is often helpful to classify insects according to their feeding habits. The symptoms of the insect damage provide helpful clues in pest identification. Some insects have piercing and sucking mouthparts (e.g., chinch bugs and aphids). These insects secrete an enzyme into the leaf through their piercing mouthparts that transforms plant sap into a form they can use as a food source. The symptoms of their damage will usually be scattered

## Table 9.4. Weed Families and Common Perennial Broadleaf Weeds

| Common Name | Scientific Name | Comments and Chemical Control Strategy |
|---|---|---|
| **Family: Compositae** | | |
| Asters | *Aster* spp. | Low to tall bushy perennial that spreads by rhizomes. Produces daisy-like pink-to blue colored flowers primarily in the fall. Both PRE and early POE control effective. |
| Dandelion (Figure 9.21) | *Taraxacum officinale* L. | Deeply taprooted, stemless perennial with deep serrated leaves that point back toward the base. Leaves and flower stalks contain a milky sap. Produces airborne seeds. Both PRE and early POE control effective. |
| **Family: Leguminosae** | | |
| White clover (Figure 9.22) | *Trifolium repens* L. | Low growing perennial with creeping stems that root at the nodes. Trifoliate leaves; white flowers arranged in white heads. A common indicator of low N fertility. Compounds other than 2,4-D are required for control. Primarily POE control. |
| **Family: Oxalidaceae** | | |
| Yellow wood-sorrel | *Oxalis dillenii* Jacq. | Upright herbaceous plant with alternate, trifoliate, heart-shaped leaves and bright yellow, five-petaled flowers. Both PRE and early POE control effective. |
| **Family: Plantaginaceae** | | |
| Buckhorn plantain (Figure 9.23) | *Plantago lanceolata* L. | Plantains have a distinctive rosette of leaves with ribbed, parallel veins on the underside of the leaves. Buckhorn plantain has long, elliptical leaves while broadleaf plantain has broader, egg-shaped leaves. Both PRE and early POE control effective. |
| Broadleaf plantain | *Plantago major* L. | |
| **Family: Polygonaceae** | | |
| Curly dock (Figure 9.24) | *Rumex crispus* L. | Taprooted plant with mostly basal leaves and characteristic ruffled leaf margins. PRE and early POE control. |
| **Family: Rubiaceae** | | |
| Virginia buttonweed (Figure 9.25) | *Diodia virginiana* L. | Probably the toughest-to-control broadleaf weed in the southern U.S. Prostrate growth habit makes it tolerant of very close cutting heights. Spreading fleshy perennial with opposite elliptical shaped leaves. White flowers with four lobes. Button-like seed pods form rapidly during summer, some even belowground. No herbicide available to provide 100% control either PRE or POE. |
| **Family: Violaceae** | | |
| Violets | *Viola* spp. | A group containing both perennials and annuals, with toughest group to control being the rhizomatous perennial forms. Large, heart-shaped leaves on long stems. Typically having purple-colored leaves. Difficult to control, but some chemicals are promising in POE treatments. |

Figure 9.21. Dandelion.

Figure 9.22. White clover.

*Figure 9.23. Buckhorn plantain.*

*Figure 9.24. Curly dock.*

*Figure 9.25. Virginia buttonweed.*

chlorotic (yellow) spots on turfgrass leaves. Another group of insects feed with chewing mouthparts (e.g., armyworms, cutworms, grubworms). They physically remove plant tissues and the symptoms of their damage are easily visible.

Another way of classifying insects is according to their location when feeding on turfgrasses. This is extremely important when making pre- and postapplication decisions regarding insecticides. Some insects feed on aboveground parts such as leaves (e.g., armyworms, chinch bugs). For these insects it is desirable to leave the insecticide on the leaf surface so that the pest will consume it. Other insects feed on belowground plant parts, typically roots and stems of turfgrasses (e.g., grubworms, mole crickets). To control these insects it is necessary to apply irrigation or have rainfall after an insecticide application.

### Identification and Sampling of Insects

First of all, it is obviously imperative to determine exactly what insect is affecting the turf, and how many of them are present. If there are only a few insects present, it's possible the damage will be minimal and insecticide applications will not be necessary. However, the small number of insects and their reclusive nature in turf canopies means that a few insects today might just be the prelude to some very large numbers in the near future. To accurately determine what and how many insects are present, use the following sampling methods:

1. Remove both lids of a large can, drive the can approximately 1″ into the soil, and fill the can halfway with a solution of 1 ounce liquid detergent per 2 gallons water. The soap solution is an irritant to the insects, partially obstructing their breathing apparatus. Most of the insects will float to the top of the water for air (Figures 9.28 and 9.29).

**Table 9.5. Common Chemical Names and Trade Names of Preemergent Herbicides[a]**

| Common Chemical Name | Trade Name | Comments |
|---|---|---|
| Atrazine | Aatrex | **Use on warm season turfgrasses only,** primarily for winter broadleaf weed control in bermudagrass turf; also has activity on annual bluegrass; low cost/acre; no more than 2 applications/year; do not use around trees or ornamentals. |
| Benefin | Balan | Typically cost-competitive; good crabgrass control, weak on goosegrass. |
| Benefin + oryzalin | XL | Annual grass control; some broadleaf weeds. |
| Benefin + trifluralin | Team, others | Annual grass control; some broadleaf weeds. |
| Bensulide | Betasan | Crabgrass, annual bluegrass and many annual grass and broadleaf weeds; not strong on goosegrass. |
| DCPA | Dacthal | Same as for bensulide. |
| Dithiopyr | Dimension | Excellent annual grass control; some broadleaf weeds; has early POE activity on crabgrass until the 3–4 leaf stage. |
| Ethofumesate | Progress | Annual bluegrass control in bermudagrass and perennial ryegrass overseedings. |
| Fenarimol | Rubigan | Annual bluegrass control for overseeded warm season turf; very safe on perennial ryegrass overseedings if the label is followed closely; very expensive. |
| Isoxaben | Gallery | Excellent broadleaf weed control; no grass control. |
| Metolachlor | Pennant | Annual grass control; PRE activity on yellow nutsedge. |
| Oryzalin | Surflan | Excellent grass control along with some broadleaf weeds; has a broad label for application in ornamentals as well. |
| Oxadiazon | Ronstar | Excellent grass control along with some broadleaf weeds; safest PRE to use for weed control in vegetative establishments. |
| Oxadiazon + benefin | Regalstar | Annual grass control; some broadleaf weeds. |
| Pendimethalin | Pendulum | Excellent grass control with some broadleaf weed activity; price competitive. |
| Prodiamine | Barricade | Excellent grass control with some broadleaf weed activity; low use rates; limited mobility in the soil can be desirable when there is concern about possible off-site movement. |
| Siduron | Tupersan | Good crabgrass control; weak on goosegrass; can be applied at seeding of cool season turfgrasses; **use on cool season turfgrasses only.** |
| Simazine | Princep | Same as for atrazine above. |

[a]The trademark or proprietary products listed are only to be used as examples and their inclusion does not constitute a guarantee or warranty of the product by the authors, nor does it imply its approval to the exclusion of other suitable products. For all products listed, consult the label for a complete listing of tolerant turfgrasses and application sites and levels.

**Table 9.6. Common Chemical Names and Trade Names of Postemergent Herbicides for Broadleaf Weed Control**[a]

| Common Chemical Name | Trade Name | Comments |
|---|---|---|
| 2,4-D | many available | The standard in broadleaf weed control for many years; popular in mixtures with other broadleaf herbicides; repeat applications may be necessary; use low pressures to avoid drift onto desirable broadleaf plants; avoid use when temperatures exceed 85°F, particularly for ester formulations. |
| Dicamba | Vanquish | Excellent broadleaf herbicide; very soil-mobile, so avoid use around the base of ornamentals and trees. |
| Mecoprop | Mecomec | Good for clover control; slower-acting than 2,4-D. |
| 2,4-D + Dichloroprop 2,4-DP | Weedone DPC | Enhanced spectrum of broadleaf weed control from synergistic activity; same comments as for 2,4-D. |
| 2,4-D + Dicamba | Eight-One | Same as above. |
| 2,4-D + Mecoprop + dicamba | Trimec Classic, Three-Way | Same as above. |
| 2,4-D + Mecoprop + dicamba + MSMA | Trimec Plus | Annual grass and broadleaf weed control in bermudagrass, zoysiagrass and bluegrass. |
| Clopyralid + triclopyr | Confront | Broadleaf weed control with particular strengths in clovers and legumes. Highly leachable, so requires extra care when applied over sandy soils. |

[a]The trademark or proprietary products listed are only to be used as examples and their inclusion does not constitute a guarantee or warranty of the product by the authors, nor does it imply its approval to the exclusion of other suitable products. For all products listed, consult the label for a complete listing of tolerant turfgrasses and application sites and levels.

2. Flush the insects by applying a soapy water solution (as discussed above) onto an area of approximately 1 square yard. This is an effective way of determining what surface-feeding insects are present in the canopy.
3. Use a golf course cup cutter or a sod harvester to monitor subsurface root feeders such as grubworms. If grub damage is suspected based on poor turf performance, this is the only reliable way to confirm the nature of the problem. A standard threshold for treatment with a pesticide is accepted to be 5 grubs per square foot.
4. Watch for Mother Nature's clues that an insect is attacking the turf. A flock of birds spending a lot of time on an athletic field in midsummer is often a good indicator of a heavy population of armyworms. Burrowing damage from skunks, armadillos, and moles is a good indicator of grubworms. The damage to the turf from these burrowing animals can be worse than that caused by the insects, and typically the best way to get rid of these animals is to control the insect they are feeding on.

**Table 9.7. Common Chemical Names and Trade Names of Postemergent Herbicides for Grass and Grass-like Weeds[a]**

| Common Chemical Name | Trade Name | Comments |
|---|---|---|
| Bentazon | Basagran | Yellow nutsedge control; will not control purple nutsedge. |
| Diclofop | Illoxan | Goosegrass control in bermudagrass; **not registered in all states and for all uses; restricted use pesticide; consult label.** |
| DSMA | many available | Grass and broadleaf weed control, including Bahia grass; 2–3 repeated applications on 7–10 day intervals typically required; nutsedge control if sprayed on 30-day intervals for 3–5 growing seasons. |
| Fenoxaprop | Acclaim | Used primarily for annual grass control in cool season turfgrasses; will suppress common bermudagrass in zoysiagrass. |
| Halosulfuron methyl | Manage | Yellow and purple nutsedge control; suppression of kyllinga. |
| Imazaquin | Image | Sedge control, particularly purple nutsedge; wild onion/garlic control. |
| Metribuzin | Sencor Turf | Only used on dormant bermudagrass for winter annual broadleafs; goosegrass control in bermudagrass. |
| MSMA | many available | Same as for DSMA. |
| MSMA +metribuzin | not applicable | **For warm season turfgrasses only;** the combination is intended to improve goosegrass control in bermudagrass turf with metribuzin being applied at extremely low levels; repeat application at 7–10 days usually necessary; expect some turfgrass discoloration. |
| Pronamide | Kerb T/O | **For warm season turfgrasses only;** used primarily for annual bluegrass control in bermudagrass. |

[a]The trademark or proprietary products listed are only to be used as examples and their inclusion does not constitute a guarantee or warranty of the product by the authors, nor does it imply its approval to the exclusion of other suitable products. For all products listed, consult the label for a complete listing of tolerant turfgrasses and application sites and levels.

Some insects also leave their own "calling card" to aid in identification. Sod webworms spin a silken web over top of the hole where they live in the ground, and this web is readily seen in the summer months when there is heavy dewfall. However, don't immediately assume that webs on the turf mean there are a lot of webworms in the sod. The fungal mycelia for the disease Dollar Spot (discussed later in this chapter) can have almost identical appearances, and so can spider webs. To be sure the problem is sod

**Table 9.8. Common Chemical Names and Trade Names of Nonselective Herbicides for Weed Control and\or Renovation Uses[a]**

| Common Chemical Name | Trade Name | Comments |
|---|---|---|
| Dazomet | Basamid G | Soil fumigant used for renovation purposes. Controls most weed seeds, nematodes, and soil diseases. Incorporate granules into the soil, roll soil surface to impede fumigant escape, thoroughly wet the soil or seal with plastic. Consult label for soil temperature information regarding application and replanting timing. |
| Diquat | Reward | Contact material that provides rapid burndown. Do not mow or till for 7 days after application. Not labeled for use in all states. |
| Glufosinate methyl | Finale | Contact material that provides rapid burn-down within 2–4 days. No residual activity in the soil. |
| Glyphosate | Roundup Pro, Roundup T/O | Systemic activity results in translocation throughout the plant; very limited soil residual allows for seeding soon after application; relatively safe to handle; usually requires 7–10 days to see a visible response. |
| Methyl bromide | many available | Soil sterilant to be used for renovation purposes. Controls dormant weed seeds, vegetative structures of perennial weeds (including bermudagrass rhizomes), most forms of nematodes and fungi. Soil should be tilled to 8″ and temperatures must be at least 60°F to work as desired. Release chemical under plastic cover. Requires a 48-hour waiting period following application to plant. |
| Metham | many available | Soil fumigant used for renovation purposes that is primarily effective on dormant weed seeds. Mix with water and apply uniformly to plowed soil. Apply water after application to seal soil. Till soil 5–7 days after application. Same temperature requirement as for methyl bromide. |
| Pelargonic acid + other fatty acids | Scythe | Naturally occurring fatty acids; no soil residual; rapid degradation; contact herbicide that acts by disrupting cell membranes and gives a rapid burn-down; combinations with glyphosate have been very effective. |

[a]The trademark or proprietary products listed are only to be used as examples and their inclusion does not constitute a guarantee or warranty of the product by the authors, nor does it imply its approval to the exclusion of other suitable products. For all products listed, consult the label for a complete listing of tolerant turfgrasses and application sites and levels.

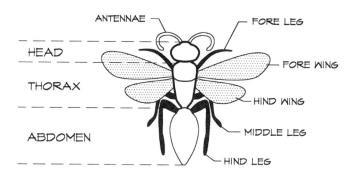

*Figure 9.26. Typical insect anatomy.*

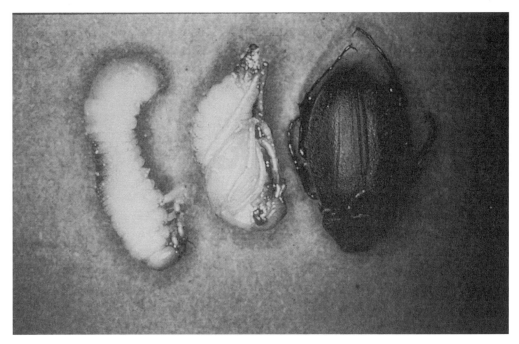

*Figure 9.27 A. Many insects undergo a developmental process known as "complete metamorphosis," in which they begin their lives as larvae, and are transformed into adults. (Photo courtesy of Pat Harris, Mississippi State University.)*

webworms, confirm that there is a hole in the ground or use the soapy water flushing method previously described. Correct diagnosis of the problem can prevent useless applications of an insecticide to control a disease or vice versa.

### Insect Control Strategies

**Chemical Control.** Once the insect has been correctly identified, and it has been determined that it is necessary to apply an insecticide, there are many pesticides to choose from. Obviously, the maintenance budget will dictate that the cost of the material be considered, but other factors are at least as important.

1. In today's world, safety must always be a predominant concern. Many insecticides affect people and other animals in ways that are similar (although milder) to the

*Figure 9.27 B. Some insects develop by "incomplete metamorphosis," hatching as nymphs, which resemble adults of the species, often smaller in size and lacking wings. (Photo courtesy of Pat Harris, Mississippi State University.)*

*Figure 9.28. A good method of checking for insect infestation is to remove the ends of a can, drive it into the soil about 1", and fill with soapy water.*

*Figure 9.29. Insects will float to the top of the soapy water, where a count can be taken to determine the severity of the infestation.*

way those chemicals act upon insects. Obviously, that means insecticides require very special attention in regard to potential nontarget effects. There is virtually no risk to humans or animals if pesticides are properly applied, but misapplication can result in serious problems for the environment and its inhabitants.

Always keep in mind the potential effects of an insecticide on the surrounding environment. Be aware that some athletes may suffer reactions to certain insecticides, and be mindful of scheduled use of the sports turf after application. Make sure that application data is properly and visibly posted. Consider whether nearby water sources could be contaminated by off-site movement of an insecticide.

Given the potential consequences of insecticide use (not to mention the cost), a wise field manager will only apply such chemicals when it is necessary to prevent or reduce significant turf damage. Before specifying an insecticide, ask whether there's another product that does the same job with less environmental impact; there's no use using an atom bomb when a flyswatter will do just as well.

2. What formulation of insecticide will work best? Does a granular or spray formulation best fit in the particular need? (See Chapter 10, Section 3.b, Choosing the Right Product.) Several granular insecticides are now utilizing a fertilizer carrier for the chemical, similar to the popular "weed and feed" products that deliver fertilizers and herbicides. Other recent developments in application technology that are proving to be highly effective and environmentally friendly include injection methods which slit-inject insecticides into the soil or apply it through high pressure liquid injection.

3. It's also important to ask whether watering will be necessary following the insecticide application; depending on the feeding habit of a problem insect, it might be. If so, be sure irrigation is available or rainfall is forecast, so the pesticide can be accu-

rately delivered to the proper location. And, just as lack of water can be a problem, too much water can also result in poor control and other off-site problems. Be careful of making insecticide applications prior to forecast thunderstorms or other rainfall events where predicted rainfall exceeds ½".

4. Remember, problem insects are not the only creatures that might be killed with an insecticide application. Small mammals and fish can be sensitive to insecticide applications and their poisoning, even if unintentional, is no longer acceptable. There is nothing that turns out a host of environmental protesters more quickly than a misapplication of a pesticide that results in a fish- or bird-kill. Don't risk a PR nightmare by failing to read labels and think through the process.

Many insecticides are particularly toxic to earthworms, a creature that is Mother Nature's tool in cultural management. Earthworms are tremendous decomposers of thatch and also improve soil porosity and aeration through their constant channeling underground. Remember the first sentence of the Hippocratic Oath every doctor takes: "First, do no harm." Make sure that killing the insect is worth killing the earthworms.

Also, don't forget that most insects are not pests. Desirable insects that are active in pollination of plants, such as honeybees, have almost been wiped out in some areas due to insecticide misapplications. Consider the relative toxicity of the insecticide to mammals, vertebrates, earthworms, and other desirable insects prior to its application. Perhaps there is a better alternative available.

**Biological Control Alternatives.** Nature provides its own series of checks and balances when it comes to insect pressures. Among the main elements in maintaining that balance are the naturally occurring enemies for any given insect. Serious insect problems typically happen where the insect has no naturally occurring enemies, or where those enemies are present in such small numbers as to have little impact. Some insects directly prey on other insects. For example, the mature and immature stages of ladybugs and many forms of ground beetles actively feed on other insects, many of which are turfgrass pests. However, it's important to note that, in many cases, it is our own chemical control programs that effectively remove natural biological controls. To return to our example, ladybugs and ground beetles are particularly sensitive to insecticides.

Many wasps and flies act as parasites of other insects. These creatures introduce their eggs into the eggs, larval, or nymphal stages of other insects. The progressing development of the immature parasite eventually results in the death of the host. In some agricultural applications, such parasites have been intentionally introduced into the environment for their pest control activity, but large-scale introductions for sports turf have not been common.

An area of biological control which has been put to use on a larger scale is using *Bacillus thuringiensis* (Bt). These bacteria are relatively easy to reproduce and increase in numbers, so they have found a place in insect control programs. *Bacillus* bacteria act as a pathogen and produce toxins that are lethal to certain insects. Other strains of *Bacillus* are available, each having slightly different uses. While *Bacillus* are somewhat effective in the control of certain insects, the results are never as spectacular as those achieved through chemical controls. Success with these pathogens requires frequent applications with the understanding that steady, effective reductions in certain targeted insect populations—rather than a sudden eradication—is the goal.

Another group of pathogens which are coming into use and bear further study are called "entomopathogenic" nematodes. These microscopic, eel-like worms attack and kill certain insect pests. Further research is being conducted in the commercial development, marketing, and application methods for these desirable nematodes.

**Cultural Strategies.** Use insect-resistant turfgrass varieties when possible. Keep thatch at a manageable level. Fertilize and water for the best recuperative potential. Mow frequently to minimize additional stresses on the turfgrass. Manage compaction through aggressive aeration.

### The Most Common Insect Pests in Sports Turf Management

While other insect problems arise from time to time, the following species represent some of the most troublesome and commonly encountered insect pests in sports turf management.

**Sod Webworms.** The adult webworm (identified in several genera including *Crambus, Parapediasia, Pediasia, Fissicrambus,* and *Herpetogramma*) is a moth, 0.5 to 0.75″ long, typically reddish-brown in color, with light streaks on the wings. Most adult webworms have very characteristic snout-like projections on their head. The larvae are typically 0.75 to 1″ in length and are gray-green to brown in color with dark spots over their body. Webworms are found in all turfgrasses used for sports turf.

One to two generations are possible per year in northern climates, while three to four generations are likely in the South, where the webworms are inactive only in the winter. The adults are short-lived and do not directly cause damage to turfgrasses. They mate and lay their eggs, and the hatch occurs typically within seven to ten days. The larvae emerge and begin feeding on the turf with chewing mouthparts that cut off leaf blades. The larvae then create a silk-lined tunnel in the soil; in this tunnel, they feed and undergo the stages of development toward adulthood. A five to six week period is typical between egg laying and adult emergence. Most species overwinter as larvae in the soil (Figures 9.30 and 9.31).

To detect the presence of webworms, watch for feeding activity by birds. Also, note the appearance of the silken webs on the turf before the dew dries in the morning. This web can be confused with the fungal mycelia of the disease Dollar Spot. Look for cut leaf blades and the presence of tunnels to confirm the infestation by webworms. Damage can be severe during periods of minimal turfgrass growth, such as drought periods, and the end of the growing season. Most feeding by the larvae takes place at night. The larvae crops off the grass blade near the soil surface; hence the turf takes on a ragged, patchy appearance.

*Control Strategies.* A number of insecticides are effective against webworms. For best results, spray in the late afternoon. Control is best if the insecticide is left on the leaf surface for insect ingestion, but some control can be achieved if the insecticide is moved into the tunnel.

Turfgrasses can often survive the attack of sod webworms if the grasses are growing aggressively. Ensure that water and adequate nutrition is available. Endophyte-enhanced cool season turfgrasses are resistant to sod webworm attack.

**Mole Crickets.** Two major species of mole crickets cause turf problems in the southeastern U.S.: the tawny (*Scapteriscus vicinus* Scudder) and southern mole crickets (*S. borelii* Giglio-Tos). Mole crickets develop through incomplete metamorphosis. The immature nymphs are smaller than the adults, but otherwise look very similar except for the lack of wings. Adults reach lengths of one inch or more. Mole crickets have very large front legs designed for digging. They thrive in all warm season turfgrasses.

The primary mole cricket species have one generation per year, except in south Florida, where the southern mole cricket usually has two generations per year. Mole crickets overwinter deep in the soil as large nymphs or adults, and become active in the spring when soil temperatures rise. Damage becomes evident as the male mole crickets

*Figure 9.30. The sod webworm can be detected by the presence of its web, here shown just to the left of a quarter.*

*Figure 9.31. The larvae of the sod webworm.*

construct their calling chambers—tunnels located right at the soil surface designed for mating with females and egg laying. Eggs are laid in May and June and egg hatch occurs in about three weeks. (Southern mole crickets typically lay eggs a few weeks later than tawny crickets.) Within four to six weeks after hatching, the nymphs are large enough to cause significant damage. The nymphs continue to grow in size and remain active until soil temperatures cool in November. At this point, the large nymphs or adults burrow deeper into the soil in order to survive cold temperatures, although activity can continue in south Florida because of the mild climate.

The tunneling activity in the spring is the first sign of activity. The tawny mole cricket feeds only on plant material, so turfgrass roots and rhizomes are obvious food sources. The southern mole cricket prefers to feed on earthworms and other insects, but will feed on plant material also. Turfgrass problems arise from the mechanical damage to the turf and the surface disruption caused by the tunneling (see Figures 9.32 and 9.33).

*Control Strategies.* Control of mole crickets frequently requires a multifaceted approach, and is much more challenging than simply seeing the damage and making a chemical application. When an infestation is suspected, map the areas of the most activity in March and April. Use a soapy water flush to gauge the number of mole crickets in problem areas. Once observations confirm that mole crickets are in fact the problem, a good rule of thumb is to chemically treat the target area three to four weeks later. This allows effective treatment for mid- to late nymphal-stage mole crickets, and also controls the recently hatched crickets. The younger the cricket is, the better the chance for successful control.

In treatment of mole crickets, the choice of insecticide is very important. Select a product that has good soil residual properties in order to effectively control nymphs in various stages of development. It's also important to moisten the soil before treating, unless recent precipitation has left good moisture in the soil.

Even with careful insecticide selection and careful application, it's unlikely that complete control of mole crickets will be achieved with a single application. Sample the treated areas about three weeks after making an application if there is evidence of more mole cricket activity, and be prepared to make follow-up insecticide applications as needed.

Biological control methods are showing promise for control of mole crickets. A commercially available entomopathogenic nematode called Vector MC® and releases of a parasitic wasp and a tachinid fly in Florida have also shown promise for the control of mole crickets. These biological controls do not provide the kind of spectacular control typical of insecticide applications, but they can significantly reduce mole cricket numbers when incorporated into a mole cricket management program that also includes other controls.

**White Grubworms.** White grubs are the larval stages of a group of insects commonly called beetles. Some of the most important turfgrass grubworms develop into green June beetles (*Cotinis nitida* L.), masked chafer beetles (*Cyclocephala* spp.), Japanese beetles (*Popillia japonica* Newman), May/June beetles (*Phyllophaga* spp.), and Black Ataenius beetles (*Ataenius spretulus* Haldeman). The adults can be identified with most any insect reference manual based on their characteristic sizes and colors. However, identification of the grubs is much more difficult, and involves distinguishing subtle differences in hair patterns on the larval abdomen.

Fortunately for the turfgrass manager, it doesn't matter much which grubworm is present; the most important determination is that the larva is indeed a grubworm. These pests are usually simple to identify by their characteristic "C" shape when at rest in the soil and their creamy white color (see Figure 9.34). Grub sizes range from about 0.2"

*Figure 9.32. Surface disruption characteristic of the mole cricket.*

*Figure 9.33. Stages in the development of the mole cricket.*

*Figure 9.34. The white grubworm can often be recognized by its characteristic "C" shape.*

in length for the final larval stage of the Black Ataenius grub to over an inch for the final stage of the May/June beetle. When causing problems, all of these grubworms will be found within the top inch of the soil surface. Grubworms will feed on all turfgrasses (Figure 9.34).

Life cycles vary among the different species of beetles. (For more specifics, consult a turfgrass insect reference manual.) Some species such as the May/June beetle may take two to three years to develop, but most species develop within one season. Larva that have overwintered at depths of four to six " in the soil become active as soil temperatures warm in the spring and the grubworm migrates to the top 1" of the turfgrass root zone in April and May. In the spring, the grubs use their chewing mouthparts to feed on turfgrass roots for a short time period before transforming into pupae from which the adults emerge in late May and June (See Figure 9.35). As adults, some of the beetles no longer feed on turfgrasses, but instead become major pests on other plants. The beetles mate during the summer months, the females deposit eggs in the soil, and the eggs begin to hatch in July and August. The young larva are tremendous feeders on turfgrass roots through the months of September and October. As cooler temperatures occur, the grubworms will migrate down into the soil for winter protection from cold temperatures.

Most grubworm damage occurs in the late summer and early fall, when turfgrasses are likely to be under increased stress due to lack of moisture. The turf will appear to wilt and brown patches will become more prevalent as the grub damage increases. The feeding activity on the roots increases the stress from hot temperatures and dry conditions. A heavily infested turf can simply be lifted from the soil like a piece of carpet, because of the removal of the roots by the grubs.

*Control Strategies.* Although grubworms can be an annoying problem, in many cases turfgrass can survive the damage caused by this pest, particularly if grub numbers are

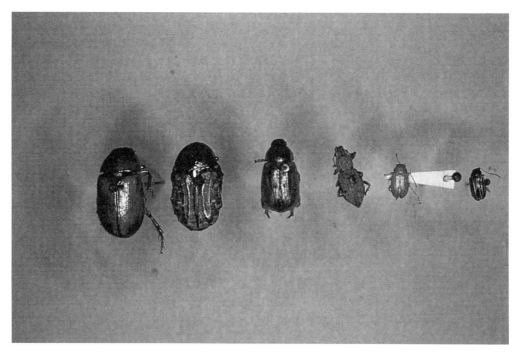

*Figure 9.35. A few of the many adult beetles that develop from grubs. Many of these beetles become pests on plants other than turf.*

small and the turf is actively growing. For this reason, white grubs do not always represent a serious problem in sports turf. Grubworms do prefer full sun areas, so sports fields represent environments that are conducive to grubs.

There are a couple of ways to effectively monitor white grub populations to help make sound decisions about insecticide applications. One effective strategy (although one that takes extra time), is to use beetle traps to monitor adult populations during early to midsummer. Researchers have shown that egg-laying by beetles occurs during a period when adult beetle counts decline for 7 consecutive days. When that decline is observed, target the insecticide application 21 days later in order to control the very small and very vulnerable larvae. (The application will typically fall somewhere between late July and mid-August.)

Insecticides are almost always more effective when applied in summer to control newly hatched grubs instead of in spring or fall applications to control older, larger grubs. Unless rainfall is expected after insecticide application, irrigation will be necessary to move the pesticide into the soil where the grubs are feeding.

To help make a decision on whether or not to apply insecticides, determine white grub numbers per square foot. If grubworm infestation is suspected, cut and lift the turf in at least a one square foot area to determine grub populations. Grub thresholds indicating the need for insecticide applications have been developed for each species, but they range from 5 to 7 grubs per square foot for the Green June Beetle to 20 to 30 grubs per square foot for the Black Turfgrass Ataenius. Obviously, this use of established thresholds to make decisions about chemical applications is an effective tactic, but it requires accurate identification of the beetle species present in a particular turf sample.

Biological control of grubs has been practiced extensively with the release of parasitic

*Figure 9.36. Chinch bugs.*

wasps, entomopathogenic nematodes, and the bacterium *Bacillus popilliae*. This bacterium induces Milky Spore disease in many of the grub species. As for any biological control method, results are not going to be as spectacular as with insecticides, and the grub-specific pathogen often has to be reintroduced to problem areas each season.

Grubs also prefer thatchy turf, so a good cultural program that limits thatch development will also help to reduce grub populations. (Thatch can also serve as an effective barrier to insecticide penetration, so it's doubly important to minimize thatch development where chemical treatment may be needed.)

**Chinch Bugs.** There are three major species of chinch bugs (*Blissus* spp.) in the United States, all with similar identification features and life cycles. Chinch bugs undergo incomplete metamorphosis as they develop into adults. They are very small in size, usually reaching adult lengths and widths of 0.04 and 0.12 inches, respectively. The adult chinch bug will have shiny white wings on a black body, an appearance that has been referred to as "angel wings." Chinch bug nymphs have more distinct colors and lack wings, but have the same general appearance as adults. Chinch bugs thrive in all turfgrasses (Figure 9.36).

Chinch bugs are capable of producing more than one generation per year, with three or more generations per year sometimes occurring in the deep South. The chinch bug overwinters as adults that emerge from leaf litter. They feed, mate, and lay eggs in the spring. Eggs are deposited directly inside the leaf sheaths of turfgrasses and the nymphs hatch within a couple of weeks, depending on the temperature.

Chinch bug damage is inflicted by the piercing and sucking mouthparts of the insect. The chinch bug inserts its mouthpart into the turfgrass, injects an enzyme to modify plant sap to a form it can better utilize, and then sucks the plant sap from the turfgrass. The processes of sap removal and enzyme injection by large numbers of chinch bugs in a serious infestation can cause turfgrass death. Sporadic patches of yellow-to-brown turf are the first symptoms of damage. Left untreated, these patches can coalesce to form much larger areas of dead turf.

*Control Strategies.* Effective control of damaging chinch bug populations is very important, especially since multiple generations can occur in one growing season. An easy way to monitor chinch bug populations is to use water flotation by the open-ended can method as described earlier (see Figures 9.28 and 9.29). Twenty or more chinch bugs per square foot usually indicate that chemical control is warranted.

When making insecticide applications to control chinch bugs, be sure to apply chemicals with different modes of action in order to reduce the possibility of pest resistance. Overuse of insecticides with similar modes of action has resulted in the development of resistance in chinch bug populations in some areas.

While some granular pesticides must be watered in to activate them, the general rule of thumb is to avoid watering-in insecticides targeted for chinch bug control, since these pests reside and feed on the surface. To effectively control chinch bugs, it's common for application to be made periodically throughout the year. However, properly timed spring treatments can be the most effective, since they reduce chinch bug populations at the start of the growing season.

Among biological controls, the use of insect-resistant and endophyte-enhanced turfgrass cultivars has proved to be an effective way to reduce chinch bug numbers. Also, naturally occuring predators and parasites such as ground beetles and the fungus *Beauvaria* spp. can substantially reduce chinch bug populations. However, it's important to remember that populations of these naturally occurring predators can themselves be significantly reduced by chemical control applications targeted at chinch bugs or other pests.

Chinch bugs require hot, dry conditions for optimum survival and reproduction, and prefer thatchy turf. To help control chinch bugs, remove thatch if it exists and avoid overfertilization that promotes thatch accumulation. If limited chinch bug damage occurs, turfgrass recovery can be promoted by light fertilization and irrigation.

**Cutworms.** At least three species of cutworms in the United States cause turfgrass damage: the black cutworm (*Agrotis ipsilon* Hufnagel), the bronzed cutworm (*Nephelodes minians* Guenée), and the variegated cutworm (*Peridroma saucia* Hubner). The adult form of the cutworm is a dull-colored moth with wing spans of 1.5″ and lengths of approximately 1″. Cutworms go through complete metamorphosis in their development. The larvae are 0.2″wide and 1.5 to 2″ long. The cutworm larvae will be noticeably hairless, coil into a C-shape when disturbed, and can be readily distinguished from grubworms because their colors will range from brown to black instead of the creamy white color characteristic for the grubworm. Cutworms live in all common turfgrasses.

Life cycles vary by species of cutworm. In the deep South, all three species remain active year-round. In the North, there can be two to four generations per year of the black and variegated cutworms, while the bronzed cutworm will have only one cycle per year. Females mate and feed at night and lay eggs on turfgrass leaf blades. The eggs hatch about a week later, and the larvae begin to feed on the turfgrass leaves as they work their way down to the soil surface. Cutworm larvae dig holes in the thatch or soil surface, remaining in the holes during the day and emerging at night to feed. In three to seven weeks the cutworms complete their development into adult moths. If weather conditions are still warm, the moths can mate, lay eggs, and repeat the cycle.

Cutworms feed on turf blades with chewing mouthparts. They characteristically clip off the turf blade at the soil surface and take it back into the hole to feed. Therefore, the damage will typically be a brown, circular, somewhat depressed area of turf that will

*Figure 9.37. Cutworm damage resembles the mark left by a golf ball. The keys on the left provide a sense of scale for the damage.*

have a hole somewhere near the center. In closely mowed turf, the damage resembles that of a golf ball mark (see Figure 9.37).

*Control Strategies.* To quantify cutworm numbers, use a soapy water flush to bring the cutworms to the surface. Five to ten larvae per square yard is considered to be the threshold for chemical applications. If cutworm populations are below this threshold, the field can probably withstand the limited damage cutworms cause, assuming the turf is adequately fertilized and irrigated. Since the cutworms feed at night, apply insecticides to the turf in the late afternoon or early evening hours. Do not water-in the pesticide, un-less it is a granular formulation and label directions indicate the need for light watering to activate the product. Follow up the insecticide application with another soapy water flush to determine what stages of larvae development are still present. If an insecticide with a short residual is used, it may be necessary to treat again.

In the area of biological controls, certain turfgrass varieties have demonstrated en-hanced cutworm resistance, and endophyte-enhanced ryegrasses and fescues also can greatly reduce cutworm problems. Contact the state or region's turfgrass research group to find out which locally-grown cultivars offer improved cutworm resistance. As a bio-logical control alternative, the *Bacillus* bacterium has been shown to be successful in controlling very young cutworm larvae if available in sufficient quantities.

**Armyworms.** Two species of armyworms feed primarily on turfgrasses: the fall army-worm (*Spodoptera frugiperda* Smith) and the yellow striped armyworm (*S. ornithogalli* Guenée); the fall armyworm is usually of greater importance as a turfgrass pest. Another prominent armyworm species, known as the common armyworm (*Pseudaletia unipuncta* Haworth), typically feeds on grain crops, although it can feed on turfgrasses if the turf is grown near a grain field. Armyworm larvae are about 1.5″ in length in their final stage, and their bodies have characteristic black striping running the entire length. Colors

*Figure 9.38. The fall armyworm can be identified by its characteristic black striping and the inverted "Y" marking on its head.*

ranges from black to olive green. The fall armyworm has an inverted Y on its head, which provides an easy identification feature (Figure 9.38). The adults are dull-colored moths, although the male moths usually are more vividly marked, with very distinct diagonal markings on the distinctly gray front wings. The moths look very much like the adult stage of the cutworm. All turfgrasses used for sports turf are host to this pest.

Fall armyworms are a constant threat to southern turfgrasses. The adult moths migrate northward during the spring and summer months and can cause problems on cool season turfgrasses later in the growing season, but in the North the fall armyworm is generally a threat to grain crops and not to turf.

There's the potential for multiple annual armyworm generations in the South, while the shorter season permits only one generation in the North. Armyworms present in the North in any given year have migrated there, because this species cannot survive northern winters. All stages of fall armyworms are present in the deep South throughout the year. In the spring, fall armyworm moths are most active at night and are attracted to light, where they usually encounter a mate. The female moths lay their eggs in grasses, trees, or shrubs, and sometimes on light-colored objects adjacent to stands of turfgrass, such as goalposts or fences surrounding athletic fields. The eggs hatch within a week in cool weather and as quickly as two days in hot weather. If the larvae cannot feed on the egg-laying site, they drop to the ground to begin feeding on turfgrasses and weeds. The larvae feed for 2–3 weeks and then burrow into the ground to pupate and transform into the adult moth, a process that typically takes 10 to 14 days.

Heavy bird-feeding activity is typically a sign of fall armyworm activity, especially since the larvae often feed on the turf during the day. As their name implies, the fall armyworms typically become significant pests from the months of July through October. The larvae feed with chewing mouthparts on all aboveground plant parts, but the most common sign of damage is of skeletonizing the leaf blade. Soapy water flushes can be used to bring larvae to the turf surface to further quantify numbers. The last two stages (instars) of larval development before pupating are voracious feeders, and can literally defoliate turfgrasses within two to three days. In large numbers, they can cause extreme damage in a very short time period.

*Control Strategies.* Almost any contact/stomach poison insecticide will work effectively on this insect. Mow the turf before application to ensure better coverage and improve contact with the armyworms. While fall armyworm larvae feed at any time of the day, they seem to be most active late in the afternoon, so target insecticide applications for late afternoon to maximize pest exposure. Do not irrigate or water-in the pesticide.

This pest typically represents more of a problem for bermudagrass sports fields than for cool season turfgrass fields. Even in the South, if bermudagrass is rapidly growing, it is unusual for fall armyworms to cause permanent damage. Given adequate fertility and irrigation, the turf can usually recuperate from the feeding damage. Among cool-season turfgrasses, bunch-type varieties suffer the most fall armyworm damage, due to the limited recuperative capacity of these grasses. Select resistant or endophyte-enhanced turfgrasses to minimize fall armyworm problems.

**Fire Ants.** One of the most problematic—and, in fact, dangerous—insect species in North America is the fire ant. The gravity of fire ant infestation in turfgrass comes from their swarming aggressiveness, which has been known to cause serious injury and even death to humans and livestock.

There are four species of fire ants in the United States, but the red imported fire ant (*Solenopsis invicta* Buren) is the most important. The fire ant is found throughout all of Florida and up the east coast to South Carolina, then across to Oklahoma and down through Texas. Fire ants are predators as well as scavengers. The fire ants develop through complete metamorphosis, having egg, larval, pupal, and adult stages. A unique feature of fire ants is that adults belong to several castes—winged queens that mate and lay eggs, winged males that mate, and wingless worker ants of various sizes. The worker ants are most typically visible in and around the colony. The ant itself is usually about ⅛ to ¼″ in size; winged adults are about twice that size. All southern turfgrasses in the described region may be host to fire ants.

Mating flights of winged adults to develop new colonies usually take place from April to June. The impregnated queen constructs a small chamber in the soil into which she lays her first eggs. New colonies are inconspicuous for several months after the queen starts to lay eggs. Eggs hatch within 10 days of laying, and the immature ants are tended by the queen until they emerge as worker ant adults in about three weeks. The worker ants then care for the queen, whose primary function at this point is to lay more eggs—up to 200 per day. The worker ants, which can eventually number up to 200,000 per colony after a few years, care for the eggs, gather food, and defend the colony from intruders. Worker ants live for 2–3 months, while queens live for 5 years or more. The colony survives periods of cold weather by moving down in the soil profile.

The obvious sign of fire ant activity is the mound of soil created by the worker ants (see Figure 9.39). This mound can be up to 24″ in diameter and 12″ in height. The mound is used as an incubation chamber for the eggs that are being laid by the queen. Any disruption of the mound leads to a swarming of worker ants to defend the territory. The ants do not directly attack turf, although the mounding of soil does disrupt the surface and can cover the surrounding turf. The main concern from fire ants is from the

*Figure 9.39. Fire ant mound on the turf.*

painful sting they can inflict. Upon stinging, the ant releases a pheromone that incites other ants to swarm and sting as well.

*Control Strategies.* The queen ants are the key to controlling fire ant colonies, and their location deep in the soil makes reaching them a difficult task; repeated chemical applications are usually required. It is important to minimize disturbance of the colony when applying a chemical. Any significant disturbance will simply trigger the worker ants to move the queen to a new location, away from the chemical application. Contact or stomach poison insecticides and poison baits will work as long as the worker ants carry the insecticide back to the colony and ultimately it is passed along to the queen. Early spring applications work best, because they control newly developed queens before they mate and lay eggs to establish new colonies.

A good chemical treatment program begins with broadcasting the granular pesticide baits in the spring, when soil temperatures are between 70 and 90° F and there is no chance of rain. The granular bait applications are most effective if applied in the midafternoon when temperatures are cooler so that the bait is not photodecomposed. Three to four weeks later, follow up with a soil drench of insecticide in 1–2 gallons of water applied directly to the mound in midmorning as the sun warms the colony. Be prepared to continue treatment programs, because eradication is almost impossible.

Recent success in fire ant control has been achieved with steam injection of fire ant mounds. Obviously, this method is environmentally responsible and the control being obtained is quite good.

Among cultural control strategies, regular, close mowing is an effective means of discouraging fire ant mounds because the constant disruption of their mound forces them to move to a site not likely to be disturbed.

**Billbugs.** Billbugs are another of the many different types of beetles which affect turfgrass. Two species of billbugs are important sports turf pests in North America: the blue-grass billbug (*Sphenophorus parvulus* Gyllenhal) and the hunting billbug (*S. venatus vestitus* Chittenden). The bluegrass billbug is most common on cool season turfs, while the hunting billbug is found usually in transition zone and southern regions. The adults are typical weevils with long, pronounced snouts. They are usually .25 to .50″ long, and are brown to gray-black in color. The larvae are cream-colored grubworms that look similar to white grubworm larvae except that they are significantly smaller and they lack the legs that grubworms have. The larve range in size from 0.05″ in recently hatched lar-vae to .35″ before pupating and becoming an adult. Billbugs can infest all turfgrasses used for sports turf.

Billbugs survive the winter as dormant adults in the soil, thatch, or leaf litter. The adults feed on suitable grasses in the spring, mate, and deposit their eggs directly into the holes of chewed grass stems. The eggs hatch within three to ten days and the larvae begin to tunnel up and down the stem. When they become too large for the turfgrass stem, they fall to the ground and begin to feed on turfgrass crowns and roots. This feed-ing occurs during the summer months, and can result in severe damage if moisture is lacking. After five to eight weeks of development, the larvae pupate, developing into adults in late summer. The adults feed on a limited basis, but primarily direct their ef-forts to seeking out areas in which to overwinter.

Billbugs have chewing mouthparts and their burrowing results in clumps of dead tis-sue that look like the disease Dollar Spot. The stems of damaged turfgrasses will snap easily, and will be filled with insect frass that resembles sawdust. Watch for large num-bers of billbugs migrating on sidewalks or driveways in the spring as temperatures begin to warm.

*Control Strategies.* Usually, the most successful insecticide applications for adult bill-bugs are made in the spring, where a good deal of insect movement is observed on side-walks and other concrete areas. The best time to treat is usually late April to mid-May, and the insecticide is most effective when left on the surface of the turf. Treat billbug lar-vae when they are small and actively feeding at the base of the turf plant in early mid-summer. Water-in insecticides aimed at the larvae.

Culturally, use insect-resistant or endophyte-enhanced cultivars of turfgrasses at the time of establishment or renovation. These varieties can substantially reduce billbug problems. Also, make sure that sufficient moisture and fertility are available to the plants, so they can recuperate from the tunneling damage of billbugs.

**Bermudagrass Mite.** Mites are not true insects; they belong to the class Arachnida and are more closely related to spiders in that they have eight legs, rather than the six char-acteristic of insects. There are several mites that will attack turfgrasses, but the bermuda-grass mite (*Eriophyes cynodoniensis* Sayed) is of the greatest importance. It is extremely small, usually only 0.005″ long as an adult. The mite develops through incomplete meta-morphosis in that the nymphs are smaller still and have only two pairs of legs rather than four. Because of their extremely small size, one rarely sees the actual mites unless they are present in mass. As the name implies, these pests live primarily in bermudagrass.

Bermudagrass mites are active during the late spring and summer. Eggs are laid in leaf sheaths as temperatures warm and the complete development process from nymph to adult only takes five to ten days. During warmer weather, numerous generations can occur and populations can increase rapidly.

The characteristic symptom of mite damage is what is referred to as "witch's broom-ing" of the turf. The grass infested by mites will have a very stunted appearance that will first be visible on scattered clumps of grass. The mites feed through piercing/sucking mouthparts which are used to inject an enzyme into the plant and to remove the plant sap as a food source. The enzyme triggers what amounts to a "plant growth regulator" effect by shortening the internodes and leaves. As mite populations increase, damage increases correspondingly, and can soon result in widespread turf death. The damage is usually most severe in hot, dry weather.

*Control Strategies.* Unless the "witch's broom" symptom is clear, mite damage can be almost identical to moisture stress. Confirm the mites by removing leaf sheaths and looking for the mites with at least a 30× magnification hand lens or microscope. For controlling mites, "miticides" do not work—but many traditional insecticides do. Diazinon and fluvalinate are labeled for bermudagrass mite control. Repeat applications are necessary for effective control.

In considering cultural controls, remember that common bermudagrass is quite susceptible to mite infestation, but many improved cultivars are somewhat resistant to bermudagrass mites. Mite damage is seldom a problem if a turf is adequately irrigated. Severe damage is usually associated with moisture stress, but even then bermudagrass can recuperate with adequate irrigation and fertility.

### Insecticides

1. **Organophosphates**: a category of insecticides that has been around since the 1950s. The water solubility of organophosphate (OP) insecticides is highly variable and this should be considered before making an application to turf. This class of insecticides is very broad spectrum in its control, and can be a problem with mammals and other vertebrate animals. The level of toxicity is another characteristic that should be considered prior to application. The examples of OPs commonly used for turf insect control are shown in Table 9.9.

2. **Carbamates**: Carbamates are broad spectrum insecticides which have substantial impact on earthworms, honeybees, and other beneficial organisms. Quite a bit of variability exists within this class regarding water solubility, persistence, and toxicity, so be sure to check the MSDS. Common examples of carbamate insecticides are shown in Table 9.10.

3. **Synthetic pyrethroids** (SP): these compounds are synthetic derivatives of the naturally occurring mild insecticidal compound pyrethrum. They tend to be less stable in the environment, and a chronic problem has been rapid photodegradation (breakdown when exposed to sunlight). However, the newest SPs are more stable in sunlight and can remain active for weeks. Synthetic pyrethroids are not so much of a threat for mammalian toxicity as they are for fish. Use rates are significantly lower than those for OPs and carbamates. Some popular examples of SPs are shown in Table 9.11.

### Table 9.9. Chemical Names and Trade Names of Common Organophosphates

| Common Chemical Name | Common Trade Name |
|---|---|
| Acephate | Orthene |
| Chlorpyrifos | Dursban |
| Diazinon | Diazinon |
| Fonofos | Crusade |
| Isazofos | Triumph |
| Isofenphos | Oftanol |
| Trichlorfor | Dylox |

### Table 9.10. Chemical Names and Trade Names of Common Carbamate Insecticides

| Common Chemical Name | Common Trade Name |
|---|---|
| Bendiocarb | Turcam |
| Carbaryl | Sevin |

**Table 9.11. Chemical Names and Trade Names of Common Synthetic Pyrethroids**

| Common Chemical Name | Common Trade Name |
| --- | --- |
| Bifenthrin | Talstar |
| Cyfluthrin | Tempo |
| Fluvalinate | Mavrik |
| Lambda-cyhalothrin | Battle, Scimitar |

**4. Chloronicotinyls:** This recently introduced class of insecticides has first reached the market as imidacloprid (trade name: Merit). This chemical is applied at low use rates and stays active in the soil for up to 4 months, making it an outstanding grubworm control chemical. It is less toxic to earthworms and other beneficial insects than other insecticides. It is common for imidacloprid to be formulated on a fertilizer carrier to apply pesticide and nutrient simultaneously.

**5. Phenylpyrazoles:** This recently introduced class has been brought to market as fipronil (trade name: Chipco Choice). Fipronil is applied at extremely low rates through slit-soil applications or liquid injections because its water solubility is so low it is hard to move it into the soil following an application. While the injection technology means it is typically more expensive to apply fipronil than many other insecticides, the excellent insecticide activity and limited potential for nontarget movement are highly desirable. Fipronil has been extremely successful in the control of mole crickets in southern turfgrasses.

**6. Insect Growth Regulators:** Halofenozide (Mach 2®) is the first release of a new group of soil insecticides that are being termed "insect growth regulators (IGRs)." This compound triggers a premature molt of the insect, resulting in its death within 1 to 3 weeks. The compound is considered very safe for the environment and, since its mode of action is so unique, it is highly unlikely that local populations will demonstrate resistance to this insecticide. Halofenozide provides excellent preventive control of grubworms and other turf caterpillars. Furthermore, its growth regulating mode of action results in early curative control of recently hatched insects.

## 9.4c  Diseases

A disease can be simply defined as a situation where the normal function of a host organism is compromised through the intervention of another organism inside or on the host. For turfgrasses, our common understanding of disease revolves around the obvious symptoms of declining turf (leaf spots, circular patches of affected turf, blighted turf, etc.), but it's important to remember that vulnerability to disease is affected by just about every cultural management practice we perform on turf.

Also, just as for humans the common cold rarely results in death, most turf diseases rarely result in the death of a significant number of turfgrass plants.

To have an outbreak of disease on turf, three elements must be present. These elements are a suitable *environment*, a virulent *pathogen*, and a susceptible *host*. (Figure 9.40 illustrates the interaction of these elements in a "Turf Disease Triangle.") Many of the most virulent pathogens that attack turfgrasses are present in the turf canopy or in the soil all the time. Others are introduced to the turfgrass culture by maintenance equipment, foot traffic, water movement, wind, and other carriers. Fortunately, these potentially virulent pathogens do not attack turf because one of the parts of the triangle is missing; the environment does not support their rapid reproduction, or the turfgrass is too healthy to be susceptible. It is only when all three factors are satisfied that a disease outbreak occurs.

As this triangular matrix suggests, turf managers can have a great deal of influence over the factors in the disease triangle. That influence begins with the selection of turfgrass varieties. Many turf cultivars are selected for their resistance or tolerance to certain

SUITABLE ENVIRONMENT

*Figure 9.40. Turf disease triangle.*

turf diseases, and it is always prudent to carefully consider the selection of cultivars if the area has a history of certain diseases.

The manager also has plenty of opportunity to manipulate the turfgrass environment, particularly in regard to irrigation timing and amounts. Many fungi, for instance, require significant periods of leaf moisture to initiate their colonization of turf. So carefully monitoring leaf moisture and precise timing of irrigation can prevent the appearance of these fungi (see Chapter 7, Section 7.2, Irrigation and Turfgrass Culture).

Conversely, we can make the environment very conducive to disease outbreaks by such practices as the use of rain-fast covers to keep playing surfaces dry. These covers create very warm, moist environments in the turf canopy, successfully completing the disease triangle. The results can include a significant disease outbreak from a particularly devastating fungus known as *Pythium* spp. (see Chapter 26, Paints and Covers).

### Factors That Incite Diseases

The factors that can incite diseases can be designated as either "biotic" (living) or "abiotic" (nonliving). Some of the most common disease-causing factors are listed in Table 9.12.

We most often associate turf diseases with **biotic** factors, although the **abiotic** practices are just as surely "causes" of disease outbreaks. Of the **biotic** group, the fungi are by far the most important and damaging disease-inciting agent.

The *fungi*, of which there are thousands of species, are typically divided into two general groups, known as "parasites" and "saprophytes." Parasites feed on other living plant tissues and saprophytes feed on decaying plant tissues. These two categories can even be further divided according to the preference of the particular fungus for specific types of living or dead plant tissues.

The terms "obligate" and "facultative" are commonly used in conjunction with parasites and saprophytes to indicate their feeding preference. An obligate parasitic fungus must have living plant tissues on which to feed; such a fungus will not feed on decaying plant debris. On the other hand, a facultative plant parasite prefers to colonize living plant tissues, but is also capable of feeding on decaying debris if this is the primary food source available.

Fortunately, most fungi fall into the categories of obligate or facultative saprophytes, meaning that colonizing living plants is either not possible or desirable for that fungus. However, the relatively small number of fungi that *do* incite turf diseases can cause spectacular damage under the right conditions, and these fungi are those that generate the most attention.

**Table 9.12. Disease-Causing Factors**

| Biotic | Abiotic |
|---|---|
| Fungi | Excessive thatch development |
| Nematodes | Mowing |
| Bacteria | Environmental conditions: |
| Viruses | temperature, moisture, wind |
| | Cultural management practices: |
| | fertility, cultivation, irrigation, |
| | pesticide applications |
| | Excessive vehicular or foot traffic |

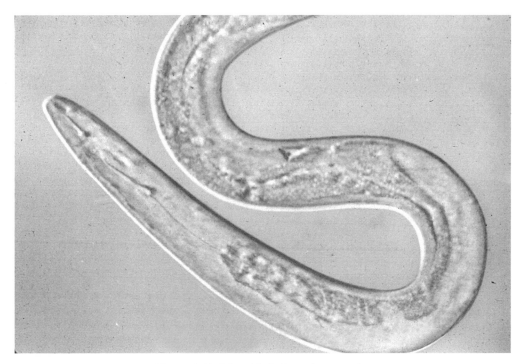

*Figure 9.41. Magnified view of nematode.*

It is important to note that most fungi actually are beneficial to turfgrass and other plants, because the fungi assist in the decomposition of organic matter. This process, which amounts to the recycling of plant tissues, makes nutrients available to the turf's root system. These beneficial fungi are just as likely to be "controlled" by fungicide applications as are the targeted variety—another reason to minimize pesticide use whenever possible.

*Nematodes* are soilborne, microscopic, worm-like animals that attack the root systems of plants (Figure 9.41). They prefer well aerated, light textured soils, so nematodes can be a particular problem in high-sand-content soils, either native or intentionally amended. Like fungi, most nematodes are actually beneficial, often feeding on harmful insects and fungi. However, certain species of nematodes are parasitic to turfgrasses and attack root systems with their piercing, sucking mouthparts.

The diagnosis of nematode damage by visual examination of the turf is extremely difficult. The overall appearance of nematode-infested turf will be patchy and moisture-stressed. Some galling (swelling) of the root system might be evident upon close inspection, but this symptom usually can be detected only by a highly trained eye. In most cases, the only sure way to diagnose a nematode problem is by sampling the soil from the problem area and having nematode counts made in a disease diagnostic laboratory.

If a nematode infestation is suspected, sample the affected areas to depths of 4″ in late spring to early summer and again in late summer to early fall. Place the soil samples in a tightly sealed plastic bag and send them by overnight courier to the laboratory as soon as possible after collection. Otherwise, the nematodes can die of temperature extremes and the assay will provide erroneous information. Many state disease diagnostic laboratories provide the nematode assay either free of charge or for modest fees. These laboratories can identify any potentially parasitic nematodes present in the sample, and can recommend treatment.

Most laboratories have established "threshold" levels for the most prevalent parasitic nematodes of that state or region. These thresholds, based on years of research in the local ecosystem, show how many nematodes must be present per unit volume of soil to cause significant damage. Many nematodes have very high threshold values—several hundred per pint of sampled soil. On the other hand, others such as the Sting nematode (*Belonoliamus* spp.) are often assigned a threshold value of one—meaning if a single specimen is found, chemical treatment is recommended.

The chemicals used to control nematodes ("nematicides") are some of the most toxic pesticides applied to turf, and they should never be used unless the threshold values have definitely been reached. Consult the local extension service agent for further information on available nematode testing services, and make it a policy to use nematicides only as a last resort.

*Bacterial and viral diseases* are of minimal concern for turfgrasses. The only viral disease that causes widespread turf problems occurs on St. Augustinegrass (*Stenotaphrum secundatum* Kuntze), and is known as "St. Augustinegrass Decline," or "SAD virus," (pathogen: Panicum mosaic virus). However, since St. Augustinegrass has limited use for sports turf, the impact of this disease is limited only to this particular species (and SAD-resistant cultivars of St. Augustinegrass are available). Bacterial wilts are extremely rare, and are not considered as major disease problems on sports turfs.

The realization that many **abiotic** factors cause disease-like symptoms is a surprise to most people, and so is the direct relationship between these abiotic or cultural factors and the onset of actual disease. The experienced turf manager, on the other hand, usually understands that these cultural factors can alter plant function in some way or another, and can weaken the plants, making them vulnerable to biotically-induced disease.

*Excessive thatch* contributes to turf disease, serving as a haven for fungi and fungal spores that incite disease, as well as exposing the turf's root system in a way that leads to desiccation during dry weather.

*Mowing*, the maintenance practice that separates turfgrasses from other plant cultures, can also incite disease. The physical process of cutting the leaf blade triggers a chain of biochemical and physiological events inside the plant in response to the gaping wound inflicted on the plant. The wound has an immediate impact on the function of the turf itself, and also serves as an entry point for fungi and insects to attack the plant. The amount of damage is increased when a dull mower blade is used.

Other factors which can expose the turf to disease are core cultivation, foot or vehicular traffic, fertility or chemical applications, and irrigation practices. All of these processes are at work in either the management or the use of sports fields, and as such they are "necessary evils." If conducted or managed properly, each of these processes will improve the overall health of sports turf culture, as well as increase our enjoyment in their use.

### Diagnosis and Identification of Diseases

**Diagnosis.** Some turfgrass diseases caused by fungi can be diagnosed by their very distinguishable leaf, stem, or root symptoms, such as spots, blighted areas, visible fungal growth, fruiting structures, etc. However, other fungal diseases and nematode damage are much more subtle in their symptoms, and their accurate diagnosis is much more difficult.

The first step in accurate diagnosis is to eliminate any of the previously mentioned abiotic factors as the cause of the symptoms. The disease diagnostic specialist at the Mississippi State University Plant Disease Laboratory has determined that, in 65% of the samples sent to his lab for suspected fungal disease, the real cause of the problem is poor soil conditions, such as improper pH, compaction, incorrect moisture levels, and so on. Only when abiotic factors have been eliminated as the cause of the symptoms should the manager look for the visible symptoms of fungus on the leaves or stems of the turf.

**Identification.** One valuable identification tool is a "Turf Disease Calendar," available through state or regional extension offices, or through most land-grant universities. This type of calendar indicates the time of year that common diseases are likely to occur in a given area, and allows the narrowing of the search for the fungal agent by eliminating diseases that do not occur during the current season. For instance, the disease dollar spot is typically classified by pathologists as a "cool-to-warm wet weather disease," and occurs from March to June and again from September to October on bermudagrass sports fields in the Southeast. Further north, on cool-season turfgrasses, the cooler summer climate will give dollar spot a longer window of occurrence during the summer.

After eliminating from consideration those diseases that do not occur in the specific climate and time of year, the manager should look for the symptoms of fungal attack on the leaves, stems, or roots of the turfgrass. These symptoms are the characteristic visible expressions by the turfgrass that it has been invaded by a fungus.

Among the most obvious symptoms produced by fungal pathogens is the web-like "mycelia" that the fungus uses to spread from plant to plant. Mycelia are usually visible in the early morning hours when dew is present on the turf. Diseases such as Dollar Spot, Pythium blight, and red thread all have characteristic mycelia that vary in color and density.

Another sign of fungal disease is the presence of "fruiting structures," which are the reproductive mechanism of the fungus. Some fungi produce elaborate fruiting structures that disseminate spores from the leaves and stems of turfgrasses. Another reproductive form is what pathologists call "**sclerotia**"—hardened masses of mycelia that serve as reproductive structures in lieu of spores; diseases such as brown patch and gray snow mold will be marked by the presence of sclerotia. The fungus that incites fairy ring typically produces a ring of mushroom fruiting structures which immediately aids in disease identification.

In the absence of visible signs of the fungus, the manager should consider the symptoms visible on the turf. There may be banding or spotting on the foliage that is typical of a certain fungus. Larger sections of turf may show distinct patches of chlorotic (yellow) turf or circular patterns that can range in diameter from a few inches to several feet. These rings are characteristic symptoms of brown patch, fairy ring, and fusarium blight, among other diseases.

Finally, a small microscope with 20–50× magnification can be very useful in the identification of the fungus based on its reproductive spores. For some diseases such as leaf rust, no microscope is needed to identify the pathogen, because the bright orange/red color of the spores is the key to identification. Other diseases, such as those caused by *Fusarium*, will have spores of characteristic shapes and sizes to aid in identification.

Obviously, identifying turfgrass diseases becomes easier after seeing them in the field on a regular basis. For the manager with less specific experience in diagnosis, identification can best be facilitated by consulting a turf pathology reference book that contains color plates of the signs and symptoms of various turf diseases, along with thorough descriptions of the likely hosts and timing of disease occurrence. This type of book is essential to making an accurate diagnosis on the basis of spore shape and size. It's very important to confirm any diagnosis through the diagnostic experts at the local cooperative extension service office.

If an outbreak of disease is threatening to kill significant areas of turf, sample a 4-inch-diameter plug of turf that spans both diseased and uninfected areas. Include 1–2″ of soil on the sample to minimize desiccation. Wrap the plug tightly in paper and, when boxing it for shipping, surround the plug with additional packing material to ensure it arrives at the lab intact. Ship the sample by overnight mail to the plant disease lab for identification. It's a good idea to include some pertinent information about the diseased turf area, either sending it along with the sample or calling the laboratory to discuss the matter. (Calling is the better option if there is the possibility of losing significant portions of grass; the immediacy of a phone call helps to indicate the importance of a rapid diagnosis.)

The diagnostician is going to want to know things such as: (1) the species and cultivar of grass, (2) the location of the problem area and the kind of soil on which the turf is grown, (3) a description of the management program to which the turf is subjected, (4) any recent chemical applications, particularly fungicides, that have been made to the turf, and (5) the circumstances under which the symptoms were first observed and the progression of the condition while it has been under observation.

This type of information is usually requested on the disease identification submission forms used by pathologists. For convenience's sake, consider having the laboratory fax this form to make sure all the information required for an informed diagnosis is provided. When such a form is not available, be prepared to supply the information in writing, to improve the accuracy of the diagnosis. (To be on the safe side, request a copy of this form from the extension service before it is needed, and keep the form on file.)

Of course, time can seem to pass very slowly while the manager is waiting for a diagnosis. What can the field manager do about a unknown disease that is progressing on the turf in the mean time? If circumstances don't permit risking additional turf loss through inaction, consider applying a broad spectrum fungicide (several examples are listed later in this chapter in Table 9.13) that will control as many fungal pathogens as possible. But be aware that certain diseases, such as Pythium blight, can kill broad swathes of turf in a matter of hours, and this fungus can be controlled only by very specific fungicides that target this particular fungus. Sometimes, there is no correct answer in attacking an ongoing disease and only experience in field identification will make the manager's future decisions easier.

### Disease Control Strategies

Following proper identification of the disease and the disease-causing agent, appropriate decisions can be made to combat the disease. There are three strategies to consider for disease control, of which chemical applications should generally be the last choice. However, as any fields manager knows, sometimes it is just plain unacceptable to have any visible signs of disease on an athletic field and preventive and/or curative chemical applications are necessary. Still, don't fall into the mentality that spraying pesticides is the only way to suppress disease. There are at least two strategies that, while not yielding immediate results in disease control, are intended as long-term strategies aimed at fortifying the turfgrass culture to encourage natural disease resistance.

**Disease Resistant Cultivars.** One of the most potent tools in controlling disease is the genetic potential of the turfgrass. Whenever turfgrass is installed, whether it be by seeding, sodding, or overseeding, consider whether there are any available cultivars with known resistance to problematic diseases. Check with suppliers for available varieties that are resistant or at least tolerant to certain diseases that are regularly encountered.

**Cultural Control.** The second method of fighting diseases is to modify cultural programs to combat the disease. Improving soil drainage, raising mowing heights, modifying irrigation and fertility strategies, and improving air circulation are just a few of the methods that can be used to control disease.

**Chemical Control Strategies.** The last resort in fighting a disease is chemical control. All too often, this alternative is used first, with the result that chemical agents are often overused and misused. However, when time does not permit the use of cultural controls or disease-resistant cultivars, chemical controls may provide the best and fastest relief.

There are two strategies in disease control with chemicals: *preventive* and *curative*.

*Preventive* chemical disease control is the application of chemical agents prior to conditions that are favorable for the disease. Most commonly, preventive control is practiced when the turf has a history of disease outbreaks, and the pressure of the competitive season makes even small amounts of disease unacceptable.

Of course, there are times when preventive methods are wise choices that actually can reduce overall fungicide use. For instance, the use of fungicide-treated seed during turf establishment is a preventive method that increases the cost per pound of seed, but more often than not pays for itself by reducing the need for later spraying.

The *curative* approach applies chemical agents to attack the disease after it has been diagnosed. It is important for the fields manager to keep a watchful eye on the disease, to avoid making a chemical application that is too late to effectively control the fungus. In comparison to preventive applications, the curative approach saves time, money, and unnecessary fungicide applications.

In areas subject to frequent outbreaks of fungus-caused disease, however, the knowledge and experience of the fields manager is an essential element of disease control. Like the practice of a skilled doctor, effective turfgrass disease treatment is as much an art as a science.

### Common Diseases in Sports Turf Management

As with weeds and insects, it is impractical in the space provided here to provide a complete description of all diseases that occur on turfgrasses. It is rather the objective here to present information on the most common diseases that occur on warm and cool season athletic turfs, and to prepare the fields manager to deal with outbreaks. Control options are discussed for each disease, and a table of chemical control alternatives can be found at the end of this section. To aid in diagnosis, the diseases are organized according to the most likely season for their occurrence.

### Winter Diseases

**Snow Mold.** Two major forms of snow mold attack cool season turfgrasses over the winter months. Pink snow mold (often called Fusarium patch) is caused by *Michrodochium nivale* (Fr.) Samuels and Hallett, and gray snow mold (also called Typhula blight) is caused by two fungi: *Typhula incarnata* Lasch ex Fr., and/or *T. ishikariensis* Imai. These diseases are unique in that they occur in temperatures that are only slightly above freezing. Part of their "competitive edge" is that they attack turfgrasses when they are either dormant or in a very slow growth period.

As their name implies, these pathogens are active primarily on turf under snow cover, and tarps or leaf litter can also provide the covered environment that invites the disease. Pink snow mold can colonize turf without snow cover, as long as there is plenty of moisture present, so its range extends further into the South. The patches of infected turf typically range in size from 3 to 8″ in diameter, although larger patches several feet in diameter are common. Snow molds produce millions of spores, allowing the fungus to spread easily by way of water and machinery. These fungi survive periods of inactivity as either spores or as hardened masses of mycelia (sclerotia) that remain in the thatch layer of the turf until conditions are again favorable for fungal development and turf infection.

*Control Strategies.* Fungicide applications are sometimes necessary, when the turf has a history of severe snow mold outbreaks. In most cases, however, the problem is not severe enough to justify the expense of broadscale chemical applications on large sports fields. On bentgrass putting greens, lawn bowling greens, or grass tennis courts, a history of severe snow mold occurrence more likely justifies making a preventive fungicide application. For these situations, chemical agents should be applied before the first major snowfall of the season. For turf with a history of truly severe outbreaks, consider further applications during winter thaws.

The nature of snow mold suggests a number of cultural control strategies. Snow mold severity can be increased by late season nitrogen fertilization, so a wise manager avoids that practice. Allowing the turf to enter the winter at excessively tall heights causes it to mat under the snowfall, providing a growing environment favorable to snow mold. For optimum cultural control of snow mold, maintain balanced fertility programs and keep the soil pH slightly acidic.

### Fall and/or Spring Diseases

**Seedling Damping Off.** Technically, seedling damping off can occur any time that grass seed is planted, but outbreaks are most common in early to midsummer for cool season turfgrasses and mid- to late spring for seeded bermudagrasses. Several fungi can incite seedling damping off, including species of the genera *Rhizoctonia, Drechslera,* and *Fusarium.* The *Pythium* species are probably of the most concern. Seedling turfgrasses are extremely vulnerable to disease, and soilborne pathogens are just one of the many dangers they must elude in order to successfully establish.

*Control Strategies.* To prevent damping off, take care to plant seed for each species during periods when the climate is most favorable for successful establishment. To combat this devastating disease during seedling establishment, consider using seed that has been pretreated with a *Pythium*-specific fungicide, and make sure an appropriate fungicide is on hand to respond to any signs of disease development as the seedlings establish.

For cultural management of the disease, make sure that the irrigation regime for newly seeded grasses calls for light and frequent watering to prevent seed desiccation and to minimize soil saturation, which can promote water-loving fungi. Gradually change the irrigation strategy to "deeply and infrequently" as the turf stand establishes. To reduce matting, be sure to mow the turf as needed; allowing it to grow excessively high is not a benefit.

**Dollar Spot.** This is one of the most common diseases of sports turf. The causal agent is *Sclerotinia homoeocarpa* F.T. Bennett. This fungus does not produce spores, so its spread is accomplished primarily by the movement of mycelium and infected turfgrass leaves, making mowing equipment a primary carrier. This disease is favored by cool nights, warm days, and heavy amounts of dew. Anything that can be done to speed the rate of turf drying reduces the incidence of dollar spot.

The symptoms on turf that is cut at 1.5 to 3″ tall are characteristic hourglass-shaped bands, usually with a light tan center surrounded by dark brown-purple bands. On closer cut turf, the initial symptoms are small areas of blighted leaves that are about the

*Figure 9.42. Dollar spot can be identified by the characteristic areas of blight about the size of a silver dollar. The other common symptom is web-like mycelia in the morning.*

size of a silver dollar—hence the name dollar spot (Figure 9.42). A web-like fungal mycelia will often be visible early in the morning when dew is still present. This disease is not usually a major concern on bermudagrasses, but turf damage can be quite severe if left unchecked on cool season grasses.

*Control Strategies.* Several chemical control options are available for dollar spot, but resistance has developed in some parts of the country because of repetitive spraying of the same chemical agents or of products with a similar mode of action. In controlling dollar spot, be sure to alternate fungicides to prevent the development of resistance.

Dollar spot is more prevalent in low fertility situations and the disease incidence can often be reduced by maintaining a higher and more balanced fertility program. Other cultural controls include early morning irrigation to shorten periods of leaf wetness, and mowing early in the morning to speed up the drying process.

**Melting Out (*Helminthosporium* Leaf Spot).** Many people recognize this common turfgrass disease by the formerly recognized genus of the pathogen, *Helminthosporium*. However, the fungi that cause melting out are now divided into several species that make up the genera *Drechslera* or *Bipolaris*. This disease occurs on all sports turfs, and most species prefer the cool nights and warm days of fall and spring months. However, there are also species that do most of their damage in the summer; this disease can occur almost any time of year, if conditions are favorable to the fungi.

The initial stage in the development of melting out is the leaf spot phase, when characteristic dark purple lesions appear on the turf foliage. As the disease progresses and the tissues are killed, the centers of these spots change to a light tan color. When large areas

*Figure 9.43. Helminthosporium leaf spot causes large areas of melting out (crown blight).*

are infected, the turf takes on a red-brown cast. The leaf spot phase on turfgrasses looks bad, but at this stage the turf is not being killed, and the disease can usually be treated successfully with chemical agents.

The second phase occurs when the fungus moves into the stems of the turfgrasses and begins to kill the crowns (growing points). At this point the leaf-spot phase has progressed into a "crown blight" and the melting out stage of the disease has begun. Turf loss can be severe and quick if the disease reaches this stage (Figures 9.43 and 9.44).

*Control Strategies.* The disease can be best managed culturally by selecting resistant cultivars. Particularly for cool season turfgrasses, a substantial investment in plant selection and breeding work has led to varieties with good melting out resistance. Other cultural controls include raising mowing heights to avoid removing any more of the damaged leaf area than necessary, so that enough remains to support the necessary metabolic processes and avoiding heavy spring applications of water-soluble N fertilizers. Aeration can also help in controlling the disease by combating compaction, which is one of the conditions that promotes disease.

Cultural practices are particularly important for the control of melting out. This pathogen can produce millions of spores throughout the growing season, so it is likely that inoculum for melting out will always be present in many soils. It's up to the turfgrass manager to choose the best cultivars available and to modify the environment in a manner that suppresses the disease.

**Red Thread/Pink Patch.** These two diseases occur on all sports turfs, but are more common on cool season grasses than on warm season varieties. For many years it was thought that these diseases were caused by the same fungus, but now the real causal agents have been identified as *Laetisaria fuciformis* (McAlpine) Burdsall for red thread and it is *Liminomyces roseipellis* Stalpers and Loerakker for pink patch.

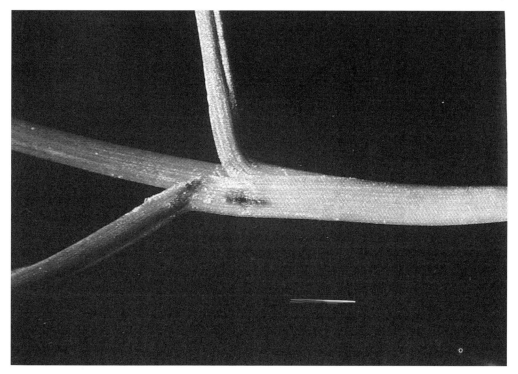

*Figure 9.44. Once the leaf spot reaches the stems of the turfgrass, damage can be quick and severe.*

These diseases occur in the spring, and in late summer or early fall as temperatures cool. The symptoms of both diseases are pinkish-red colored threads of mycelium that attack the turfgrass in patches that range from one inch to two feet in diameter. The color of the fungus is easily distinguishable during the early morning hours when dew is present. The easily visible threads of the fungus are a survival feature; during periods of unfavorable growth, they dry up and fall into the turf canopy, where the fungus remains inactive until conditions are again conducive for disease development. Pink patch almost always occurs with red thread, but red thread can occur alone, and is capable of attacking a wider range of grass hosts.

*Control Strategies.* These two diseases are most typically a problem of underfertilized turfs. Maintaining fertility levels with a balanced N-P-K program is critical to the suppression of red thread and pink patch. If the diseases do occur in well-fertilized turf, control can be achieved with any of a number of commercially available fungicides.

**Spring Dead Spot.** This disease, a major concern on bermudagrass, takes its name from the fact that patches of dead turf appear as the turf emerges from winter dormancy (Figure 9.45). These patches range from 4 to 10″ in diameter the first year, and may grow to several feet in diameter if left unchecked for several years.

Spring dead spot (SDS) is incited by a complex of soilborne fungi, and pathologists continue to identify suspected pathogens each year. The pathogens apparently attack the turfgrass root system, and the resulting stress on the turf during the winter months results in its death. Not surprisingly, long, very cold winters are responsible for higher incidences of spring dead spot damage than mild winters. Diseased areas are usually covered again as the grass creeps back laterally from rhizomes and stolons, but the problems

*Figure 9.45. Spring dead spot appears as the turf is emerging from winter dormancy.*

will most likely occur again the next winter in the same location unless steps are taken to control the disease.

*Control Strategies.* If this disease has become a problem, map the problem areas and target them with appropriate fungicide treatments in the fall—approximately 30 days before the first killing frost. Springtime fungicide applications are useless in controlling the dead spot fungi.

To minimize SDS, keep potassium levels high, minimize late season nitrogen applications in areas subject to outbreaks, keep thatch at acceptable levels, and minimize soil compaction. Encourage spring regrowth by maintaining adequate nitrogen fertility to promote lateral bermudagrass spread.

It is common for turf managers to transplant healthy bermudagrass plugs into the diseased area as the bermudagrass emerges from dormancy. In using this technique, it is important to discard the plugs taken from the diseased area; replacing healthy plugs with the diseased ones essentially transplants the fungus to new areas of the field.

### Summer Diseases

**Bermudagrass Decline.** Damage from this disease has increased rapidly in recent years. Fortunately, most of the bermudagrass decline problems have occurred on turf cut at heights of less than ½". The disease is caused by the soilborne *Gaummanomyces graminis* (Sacc.) Arx and Olivier var. *graminis*, the same fungus that incites take-all patch on creeping bentgrass. This pathogen causes a root decline in bermudagrass, and the symptoms are similar to those of nematode damage: irregular patches that thin out and appear to be suffering from moisture stress. Like nematode damage, bermudagrass decline is extremely difficult to diagnose, and a pathologist's diagnosis is usually required.

*Control Strategies.* Little is known about chemical control of bermudagrass decline and researchers have had little success with fungicide control to date. The best ways to combat bermudagrass decline are cultural: maintain adequate P and K levels in the soil to promote root growth and maintain a mowing height well above ½″ (the most successful single tactic for bermudagrass decline). This tactic works very effectively on taller-cut athletic fields, but is obviously of limited value on turfs that require close cutting for the best playability.

**Brown Patch (Rhizoctonia Blight).** The primary causal agent of brown patch is *Rhizoctonia solani* Kuhn, but *R. zeae* Voorhees and *R. oryzae* Ryker and Gooch are also known to incite brown patch-type symptoms on warm season turfgrasses. *R. solani* can behave as either a parasite or a saprophyte and is widely distributed throughout agricultural soils (Figure 9.46).

The common symptoms of brown patch usually begin as small circular patches ranging from a few inches to several feet in diameter. During active periods of fungal growth, a "halo-like" ring (also called a "smoke-ring") is often visible, particularly on closer cut turf, but don't wait for the halo to confirm brown patch because it may not occur. The leaf lesions associated with brown patch are a medium shade of brown, and are not always as distinctly banded as the lesions of dollar spot on taller cut turf. Brown patch usually blights the leaves from the tip down, giving the turf its characteristic brown color.

Brown patch occurs on different grasses at different times of year: on bermudagrass and zoysiagrass it is typically a spring/fall disease, while on cool season turf, it is most

*Figure 9.46. Brown patch (rhizoctonia blight) on Tifway bermudagrass.*

common during the summer months. The disease is most active under high humidity conditions when daytime temperatures are above 85°F and nighttime temperatures remain above 70°F. However, *R. solani* is active at cooler temperatures, and can strike warm season turfgrasses during cooler periods, when the grass is not rapidly growing.

The brown patch fungus does not produce spores, but instead spreads itself by mycelium from plant to plant. It survives stress periods by forming sclerotia that remain in the thatch layer.

*Control Strategies.* Brown patch rarely kills warm season turfgrasses, although it can result in poor turf appearance for several days due to the presence of the rings. If the turf is showing obvious signs of recovery within the ringed area where it has previously been infected, then the turf is going to recover without chemical treatment. On cool season turfs, the concern with potential turf loss is much greater, since the warm, humid conditions that favor fungal development are not favorable growing conditions for these grasses. If the grass is weakened by environmental or cultural management stresses it will be very susceptible to severe damage from *R. solani* and will probably need to be treated with an appropriate fungicide.

To reduce the incidence of the disease, reduce tissue succulence by minimizing water-soluble N applications during periods of disease activity. Fall applications on cool season turf are less likely to trigger brown patch than spring applications. Also, try to minimize leaf wetness periods in order to reduce the spread of the mycelium from plant to plant. Since the *R. solani* does not produce spores, it is not likely to spread rapidly. However, eradicating the fungus is essentially impossible, since it can either parasitize living plant tissues or subsist on decaying organic matter in the soil.

**Pythium Blight (Cottony Blight).** Although Pythium blight is included here under the heading of summer diseases, it must be understood that there are numerous species of the *Pythium* genus that can attack turfgrasses during cool weather, as well as in summer's heat. The species of *Pythium* that trigger Pythium blight are usually considered leaf colonizers, but other forms of *Pythium* typically attack the crown and root systems. The most severe form of Pythium blight typically occurs in hot weather on established creeping bentgrass and perennial ryegrass from the transition zone northward, and on tall fescue and bermudagrass from the transition zone southward. (Note that the transition zone contains all four turfgrasses that are susceptible to Pythium blight.)

Hot, wet conditions can trigger an outbreak of Pythium blight severe enough to kill large areas of turf in a matter of hours. To anticipate the onset of this disease, carefully watch both temperature and humidity. A rule of thumb for anticipating Pythium blight in the North is to monitor nighttime temperatures and relative humidity. If the predicted nighttime temperatures and relative humidity readings total 150 or more, the potential for an outbreak is particularly high.

The *Pythium* fungi are soilborne, but they flourish where water is plentiful. As a matter of fact, the disease is often said to be caused by "water mold" because the *Pythium* fungi thrive in standing water. These fungi are extremely mobile in water, and it is common to see damage where drainage is poor.

The "cottony blight" name of this disease comes from the thick, cotton-like web of mycelia on the turf foliage when the dew is still present. The *Pythium* mycelia have a much thicker mass than those of dollar spot, but the best way to distinguish the relatively slow-moving dollar spot fungus from the *Pythium* fungus is to check the integrity of the turf blades in the infected area when they are wet. The dollar spot infected leaves will remain intact and show the characteristic banding described above, while the Pythium blight infected leaves will be turned into a greasy, water-soaked mass with no distinguishable lesions on the turf blades (Figure 9.47). Upon drying, the Pythium blight areas will have a copper to golden color on the blighted foliage.

*Control Strategies.* Pythium blight is not going to be a major problem every growing season on athletic turf, but when it does occur one must be ready to respond rapidly due to the quick-kill potential of the disease. Most popular broad-spectrum fungicides have no effect on these fungi, so *Pythium*-specific fungicides should be kept on hand or should be readily available if needed. Avoid applying the same chemical agents on a repetitive basis, because fungicide-resistant *Pythium* biotypes have developed in areas where the same product has been applied regularly for Pythium blight control.

Cultural management to reduce the incidence of Pythium blight generally centers around minimizing excessive moisture, particular during the nighttime hours. Reducing the succulence of the turfgrass by minimizing nitrogen levels will also help reduce outbreaks of the disease.

Placing impermeable tarps over athletic fields when there is a threat of rain can substantially increase the chances of Pythium blight, because both the temperature and the relative humidity escalate rapidly under the tarp. This creates an almost perfect environment for the disease, particularly on a sensitive species such as perennial ryegrass. If tarps must remain in place for a day or more at a time, it is often wise to treat the turf with a *Pythium*-specific fungicide before installing the tarps. In the South, Pythium blight has even been observed following the application of tarps to protect an overseeded field from an ice storm in early February. Even with the unusually cold temperatures, the heat and humidity trapped under the tarp for several days were sufficient to trigger Pythium blight on the ryegrass turf.

**Fairy Ring.** There are over 50 species of fungi that can cause fairy ring and the disease can occur on any turfgrass. These fungi are soilborne saprophytes that live on organic matter. As the fungal mycelia spread outward in a ring through the upper soil profile, the fungus decomposes organic matter and releases nitrogen and other nutrients. This can cause a positive nitrogen growth response by the turf, resulting in a dark ring of turf. In the ring area, mushroom-like fruiting bodies can emerge, but they are not always present. The rings may be as small as a few inches in diameter, or as large as many feet across, as the fungus typically moves out through the soil season after season (Figure 9.48).

The fungal mat can effectively seal off the upper soil profile, especially during dry periods. This hydrophobic condition results in turf that suffers from drought stress and soil that is very difficult to wet. The once-dark green ring changes color and becomes brown when this occurs. Some pathologists have suggested that the fairy ring fungi also secrete a toxin that further inhibits turf growth.

*Control Strategies.* The chemical control options for fairy ring are very limited and most attempts are futile. The only way to effectively control fairy ring is to physically remove the soil from the ring area, starting 12″ outside the visibly affected area and removing soil to a 12″ depth, then installing fungus-free soil, and reestablishing the turf. Most field managers try to live with fairy ring, and fortunately on taller mowed turf it is usually not going to be a major problem. Masking the green ring with nitrogen or iron fertilizer applications is an effective way to manage fairy ring. In combating the wetting difficulty, solid tine aeration can improve moisture penetration, and some improvement in soil wetting has been achieved by including a soil wetting agent with the aeration treatment.

**Necrotic Ring Spot.** This root disease, which occurs primarily on Kentucky bluegrass, is caused by *Leptosphaeria korrae* Walker & Smith. The fungus actually attacks the turf in the spring and fall, but the stress on the plant usually is not evident until summer heat

Figure 9.47. *Pythium blight can be detected during the morning hours by the characteristic mycelia, which resemble a cotton ball. By afternoon, these structures have turned into a greasy, water-soaked mass. (Photo courtesy of D. Blasingame.)*

Figure 9.48. *Fairy ring creates a large dark-colored circle in the turf with mushroom-like fruiting bodies. This condition gradually moves outward from the center of the circle.*

and drought conditions develop. Necrotic ring spot (NRS) is often confused with summer patch, but the patches of NRS-blighted turf are usually more than 1 foot in diameter, while summer patch usually causes smaller areas of dead turf. NRS also results in a characteristic "frog-eye" pattern.

*Control strategies.* Natural organic fertilizers made from animal wastes have been shown to be helpful in combating necrotic ring spot. Spring applications of fenarimol (Rubigan®) have also been reported to reduce NRS activity. If this disease has been a problem in the past, be aware of the possibility that it is likely to occur again.

**Summer Patch.** Like necrotic ring spot, summer patch is most often a concern on Kentucky bluegrass. The causal agent is *Magnaporthe poae* Landschoot & Jackson. Initially, the patches look much like dollar spot, but they rapidly increase in size and can have the "frog-eye" pattern characteristic of NRS (but the patches are typically smaller than those caused by necrotic ring spot). The fungus begins to attack the root system in the spring and the damage becomes most pronounced during hot and dry summer weather.

*Control strategies.* The use of acidifying fertilizers (such as sulfur-based materials) to lower or maintain acid soil pH and raising mowing heights above 2″ have both been shown to help combat summer patch. Soil drenches with fungicides such as propiconazole (Banner®), fenarimol (Rubigan®), and triadimefon (Bayleton®) have also been successfully used, particularly on areas where the disease has a history of occurring.

**Fusarium Blight.** This is a troublesome summer patch disease on all cool season turfgrasses, but Kentucky bluegrass and creeping bentgrass are the most susceptible. The fungal causal agent is *Fusarium culmorum* (W.G. Smith) Sacc. The fungus attacks leaves, roots, crowns, and stems, and there are no initial symptoms that aid an untrained eye in accurately diagnosing the disease. In advanced stages, the turf can have a "frog-eye" pattern of living grass surrounded by blighted foliage. However, accurate diagnosis requires examination by a turf pathologist, since there are several diseases with which Fusarium blight can be confused.

(It's worth noting that some turf pathologists no longer believe there actually *is* a disease called Fusarium blight; they assert that reported outbreaks are either necrotic ring spot or summer patch.)

*Control strategies.* Fusarium blight is likely to occur during periods of hot, dry weather. It is typical for the disease to be most pronounced in areas where air and soil temperatures are elevated, such as next to bleachers, the running track, parking lots, etc. Irrigate the turf during the early morning hours to minimize leaf wetness duration and maintain sufficient soil moisture to promote active growth. Avoid heavy spring N applications and keep thatch levels to 0.5″ depths or less. Even with the use of all these cultural control strategies, it's likely that an appropriate fungicide will have to be applied to achieve effective disease control.

**Gray Leaf Spot.** Gray leaf spot has traditionally been regarded as a problem only for St. Augustinegrass in shaded areas in the deep South. However, this disease has greatly increased in severity on perennial ryegrass and tall fescue within the last few years. The causal agent is *Pyricularia grisea* (Cooke) Sacc. Gray leaf spot occurs in late summer following periods of high heat and humidity. The disease blights ryegrass and fescue turf leaves, beginning as leaf lesions that are gray-brown in color and oblong in shape. This fungus produces tremendous numbers of spores that can help to spread the infection as they are carried around by equipment and traffic.

*Control Strategies.* Research is being conducted to determine if there are perennial ryegrass and tall fescue cultivars with improved resistance to gray leaf spot, but as of this writing there are no firm recommendations available yet. The manager can avoid water-soluble nitrogen applications and minimize leaf wetness periods to suppress the disease.

*Figure 9.49. Rust pustules on the blades of Kentucky bluegrass. (Photo courtesy of D. Blasingame.)*

While not yet considered a major disease affecting sports turfs, the increasingly severe outbreaks of gray leaf spot in the mid-Atlantic states bears watching until the prevalence of the disease can be determined.

**Rust.** There are many rust fungi that attack turfgrasses, and the disease they cause is easy to identify because of the bright red or orange pustules of spores that cover the leaves of the turf. Just walking across the spore-covered turf in an affected area will leave shoes and pants a bright red/orange color as well. Usually, the greatest concern with rusts is the obvious color change associated with affected turf (Figure 9.49).

Leaf rust normally occurs during extended cloudy periods in late summer and early fall. Leaf rusts usually do not actually kill the turf, but problems can arise when the overcast conditions persist, resulting in a high incidence of disease. The rust fruiting structures containing spores are thrust through the leaf surface, placing the turf at extreme risk of desiccation, especially if weather conditions are warm and sunny.

*Control Strategies.* Fungicide treatments usually are not necessary in controlling rust. When mowing rust-infected turf, increase the cutting height and mowing frequency to reduce spore populations.

**Slime Mold.** A disease that looks terrible but is usually quite harmless to turfgrasses is slime mold. There are several species of saprophytic fungi that can cause slime mold on any sports turf. These fungi never actually infect the turfgrasses, but they elevate themselves onto the surface of turfgrass leaves during cloudy summer days in order to disperse their spores. The characteristic symptom of this fungus is the presence of fruiting structures that resemble cigarette ashes on the turf surface (Figure 9.50). The only real

*Figure 9.50. Slime mold resembles cigarette ashes on the blades of the grass.*

threat to turf health posed by slime mold fungi is that they temporarily block the sunlight needed for photosynthesis.

*Control Strategies.* No chemical controls are warranted. Slime mold is best controlled simply by mowing, dragging, or irrigating the turf to remove the fruiting structures from the leaf surface.

### Fungicides

Fungicides can be divided into two classes, based on how they protect the plant. Some materials are effective only as **contact** sources; they protect only that part of the plant that is actually covered with the fungicide, and they are active only on the surface of the turf. Examples of contact fungicides are chloroneb, chlorothalonil, ethazole, mancozeb, maneb, quintozene, and thiram. **Penetrant** fungicides are absorbed into the plant, but their modes of action vary widely. Localized penetrants move into the leaf tissues and remain near the point of entry. Examples of this group are iprodione, propamocarb, and vinclozolin. "Acropetal" penetrants are translocated in the xylem of the plant, so movement is upward in the water stream. Many of the most recently released fungicides are acropetal penetrants. Examples are azoxystrobin, cyproconazole, fenarimol, flutolanil, metalaxyl, myclobutanil, propiconazole, thiophanate-methyl, and triadimefon. Fosetyl-AL is the only example of a systemic fungicide that is clearly translocated both up and down within the turfgrass.

Understanding the mobility of fungicides allows the manager to make informed decisions regarding fungicide choice and expected period of disease control. Contact fungicides are typically cheaper, must thoroughly dry on leaves before irrigation or a rainfall event to maintain activity, and offer control lengths of typically 7–14 days. The length of

**Table 9.13. List of Fungicides for Disease Control on Sports Turf**

| Fungicide | | Diseases Controlled | | | | | | | | | | | | |
| Common Name | Trade Names | Brown Patch | Dollar Spot | Gray Leaf Spot | Melting Out | Pythium Blight | Rusts | Spring Dead Spot | Snow Mold | Damping Off | Red Thread/Pink Patch | Nec. Ring Spot/Summer Patch | Fusarium Blight | Bermuda-grass Decline |
| --- | --- | --- | --- | --- | --- | --- | --- | --- | --- | --- | --- | --- | --- | --- |
| Azoxystrobin | Heritage | X | | | X | X | | X | X | | X | X | X | |
| Chloroneb | Fungicide V, Termeric | X | | | | X | | | X | X | | | | |
| Chloroneb + thiophanate-methyl | Fungicide IX | X | | | | X | | | | | | | | |
| Chlorothalonil | Chlorostal FL, ECHO 90DF, Daconil 2787, Manicure Thalonil | X | X | X | X | | | | | X | X | | | |
| Chlorothalonil + fenarimol | TwoSome Flowable | X | X | X | X | | X | X | | | | X | X | |
| Chlorothalonil + thiophanate-methyl | ConSyst WDG | X | X | X | X | | | | | X | | | | |
| Cyproconazole | Sentinel | X | X | | X | | X | | X | | X | X | X | |
| Ethazole | Koban Terrazole | X | | X | | X | | | | X | | | | |
| Fenarimol | Rubigan | X | X | | | | | X | X | | X | X | X | X |
| Flutolanil | ProStar 50WP | X | X | | | | | | | | X | | | |
| Flutolanil and triadimefon | ProStar Plus | X | X | | | X | X | | | | | | | |
| Fosetyl-AL | Chipco Aliette | | | | | X | | | | X | | | | |
| Iprodione | Chipco 26019, Fungicide X | X | X | | X | | | | X | X | X | X | | |
| Mancozeb | Cleary's PROTECT T/O, Dithane, Fore | X | X | | X | X | X | | | X | | | | |
| Maneb | Maneb | X | X | | X | | X | | | X | | | | |
| Metalaxy | Pythium Control, Subdue | | X | | X | X | X | | | | | | | |
| Metalaxy + mancozeb | Pace | X | X | | X | X | X | | | | | | | |
| Myclobutanil | Eagle | X | | | | | X | X | | | | X | X | |
| Propamocarb hydrochloride | Banol | | | | | X | | | | X | | | | |
| Propiconazole | Banner | X | X | | X | | X | X | X | | X | X | X | |
| Quintozene (pcnb) | Defend, Engage, PCNB, Penstar, Revere, Terraclor, Turfcide, TURFPRO | X | X | | X | | | | X | | | | | X |
| Thiophanate-methyl | Cleary's 3336, Fungo, SysTec 1998, Systemic Fungicide | X | X | | X | | | | X | | | | | |
| Thiophanate-methyl + iprodione | Fluid Fungicide | X | X | | X | X | | | | | | X | X | |
| Thiophanate-methyl + mancozeb | Duosan | X | X | | X | | X | | | | | | | |
| Thiram | Spotrete | X | X | | | | | | | | | | | |
| Triadimefon | Bayleton, Granular Turf Fungicide, Fungicide VII | X | X | | | | X | X | | | X | X | X | X |
| Triadimefon + metalaxyl | Fluid Fungicide II | X | X | | | X | X | | | | | | | |
| Triadimefon + thiram | Fluid Fungicide III | X | X | | | | X | | | | X | X | X | |
| Vinclozolin | Curalan, Touche Flowable, Vorlan | X | X | | X | | X | | | | X | | | |

This document was compiled by Mukund V. Patel, Extention Plant Pathologist and Don J. Blasingame, Emeritus Plant Pathologist, both of Mississipi State University. The information given here is for educational purposes only. Reference to commercial products or trade names is made with the understanding that no discrimination is intended toward other products which may also be suitable, and that these products have maintained label clearance activity with contact fungicides depends on the mowing regime. Mowing removes most of the fungicide from the plant.

The penetrant fungicides offer both protective and curative activity, since they are absorbed and some are even translocated within the plant. Penetrants are typically more expensive, maintain their potency better if an unexpected rainfall event occurs after application, and offer control periods of 21–28 days. The control period for the penetrants is also affected by maintenance programs and the climate.

(These "expectations" for performance of contacts and penetrants are, of course, generalizations, and the reader should be aware that performance aspects of individual chemicals can vary considerably. To learn much more about maximizing fungicide performance, the reader is encouraged to consult H. B. Couch's *Diseases of Turfgrasses* or J.M. Vargas, Jr.'s *Management of Turfgrass Diseases*. These books include thorough discussions of factors that turf managers typically overlook when applying fungicides, but this information will be extremely important in maximizing fungicide performance.)

Table 9.13 lists the anticipated level of disease control for several fungicides and many of the diseases discussed in this chapter. Fungicide control levels for cool season turfgrasses were taken from information presented by turf pathologists such as Couch, Vargas, and P.H. Dernoeden. This table can help in making better choices in fungicides specifically targeted for the best control of a certain disease. However, the information presented is not to be interpreted as all-inclusive, and it is likely that in some situations certain chemicals not noted in this table would provide satisfactory results.

## REFERENCES

The information presented in this chapter was compiled from the following sources:

Brandenburg, R. L. and M. G. Villani, *Handbook of Turfgrass Insect Pests.* Entomological Society of America, Lanham, MD, 1995.

Couch, H. B., *Turfgrass Diseases,* 2nd ed. Krieger Publishing Company, Melbourne, FL, 1995.

Murphy, T. R., D. L. Colvin, R. Dickens, J. W. Everest, D. Hall, and L. B. McCarty, "Weeds of Southern Turfgrassess" Publication SP79, Institute of Food and Agricultural Sciences, University of Florida, Gainesville.

Potter, D. A., *Destructive Turfgrass Insects: Biology, Diagnosis, and Control.* Ann Arbor Press, Chelsea, MI, 1997.

Smiley, R. W., *Compendium of Turfgrass Diseases.* APS Press, St. Paul, MN, 1992.

Vargas, J. M., *Management of Turfgrass Diseases.* Lewis Publishers, Boca Raton, FL, 1994.

Vittum, P. J., Back to Basics—Insecticide Primer, Part Two: Chemical Classes of Turfgrass Insecticides, in *Turfgrass Trends,* 6 (I), pp. 9–17, 1997.

Watschke, T. L., P.H. Dernoeden, and D. J. Shetlar, *Managing Turfgrass Pests.* Lewis Publishers, Boca Raton, FL, 1995.

# Chapter 10

# *Wise Use of Chemicals*

## 10.1  INTRODUCTION

In the last chapter, we looked at a number of pests which commonly affect turfgrass, and talked about some of the chemical strategies used to control them. Earlier in the book, we likewise considered some of the fertilizers and other materials that are added to the soil to enhance its ability to support turfgrass culture.

When they are used carefully, chemical agents like pesticides and fertilizers provide valuable tools for promoting productive agriculture. When handled and applied according to label instructions, these chemicals pose little or no serious health or environmental hazard. On the other hand, careless use of chemical agents can lead to serious or fatal injuries to people, domestic animals, and wildlife—not to mention damage to the turf itself.

In this chapter we will review procedures by which chemical agents can be used safely in the promotion of turfgrass. However, if the reader learns only one thing from reading this chapter let it be this: **Always follow the manufacturer's label instructions as precisely as possible.** This single step is the most effective way to ensure safe and wise use of chemicals.

## 10.2  THE LABEL IS THE LAW

It's important to remember that the application guidelines given on the label have the force of law regarding that particular pesticide formulation. In other words, "The label is the law." Any use of a pesticide or other chemical agent that is different from those indicated by label guidelines is a violation of the law, and is subject to legal action by local, state, and/or federal authorities. Especially when unfamiliar with a particular product, it's wise to read the label a minimum of three times before any pesticide application. It really is that important to have a full understanding of the product and its safe uses.

The label provides specific direction for handling, application, and disposal that will help maximize the effectiveness (and minimize the hazard) of the chemical. Labels will also suggest what other products (such as fertilizers or other pesticides) can be safely mixed with sprayable formulations. Knowing this before putting two or more chemicals together can prevent disasters in pest control as well as in the spray tank!

### 10.2a  Toxicity and the MSDS

Labels will always contain a signal word that will quickly indicate the **toxicity**, or the potential hazard represented by the product. Each label will include one of three words:

"Caution," "Warning," or "Danger." These terms are meant to alert the user to the toxicity of the product and to suggested treatments and antidotes in case of accidental exposure. "Caution" designates the least toxic chemical agents, and "Danger" indicates the most toxic.

Next to the product labels themselves, Material Safety Data Sheets, or MSDSs, are the most critical documents for the wise use of chemicals. An MSDS is a federally mandated written description of the action of a particular product, with detailed instructions on cleaning up spills and treating exposure. The law requires that an MSDS be physically present whenever a hazardous product is being used or transported. Whenever staff members are using or moving any form of pesticide, be sure that the appropriate sheets are present; the potential cost of failing to comply with these requirements can be staggering.

The MSDS should be received at the same time as the product. If the sheet is missing, contact the chemical distributor or the manufacturer of the product and get this important information.

It is absolutely necessary that this information be kept in an easily accessed location and that workers using chemical agents be trained on a regular basis on the precautions and concerns regarding chemicals in the workplace. If the crew is the subject of an OSHA or EPA inspection, members will be asked to produce the MSDSs for all chemicals in use at the job site, and will usually be asked to explain the information on the sheet. If they can't tell the inspector what it all means, at least from a practical standpoint, the employer will be judged to be in violation, and may be subject to fines and other punishments.

(By the way, be aware that pesticides are not the only materials that are considered to be "hazardous chemicals." Gasoline, solvents, and many other products typically used around the shop are also classified as hazardous. Make sure *all* MSDSs are on hand.)

### Toxicity Classifications

Most chemicals commonly applied to turfgrasses have undergone a series of tests under EPA guidelines to determine their various toxicity levels. This information is contained in the MSDS that accompanies the chemical and it must be readily available for inspection and review. The $LD_{50}$ and $LC_{50}$ values represent lethal dosages (LD) or lethal concentrations (LC) of a substance that kills half of the test organisms in an acute study. Typical test organisms are laboratory mice and/or rats that are exposed to the substances through ingestion (swallowing), dermal exposure (on the skin), or inhalation. Table 10.1 illustrates the toxicity classification used on the MSDS.

From a practical standpoint, the lower the numbers in the respective toxicity classifications, the more toxic the substance (that is, it takes relatively little to kill 50% of the

Table 10.1. Toxicity Classification

| Toxicity Classification | Label Signal Word | Oral $LD_{50}$ Ratings (mg/kg body weight) | Dermal $LD_{50}$ (mg/kg body weight) | Inhalation $LC_{50}$ (mg/L of volume) |
|---|---|---|---|---|
| I | Danger | <50 | <200 | <0.05 |
| II | Warning | >50–500 | >200–2,000 | >0.05–0.5 |
| III | Caution | >500–5,000 | >2,000–5,000 | >0.5–2.0 |
| IV | Caution | >5,000 | >5,000 | >2.0 |

test population). A couple of examples of $LD_{50}$ values for commonly used pesticides will help to explain the concept. Consider that glyphosate (trade name of Roundup Pro), a commonly used nonselective herbicide, has an Acute Oral $LD_{50}$ for rats of >5,000 mg/kg, thus placing glyphosate for this category of toxicity in Classification IV and a label signal word of CAUTION (a relatively safe product). On the other hand, fenamiphos (common trade name is Nemacur) has an Acute Oral $LD_{50}$ of approximately 12 mg/kg for rats, categorizing it as a Classification I material that says DANGER-POISON on the label (a relatively toxic substance). Each MSDS contains this type of information, and it is important that all applicators be aware of these data.

The point is not to discourage the use of Nemacur, because when used and handled properly, it controls the target pest safely and effectively. However, understanding the potential danger associated with exposure to a substance helps to increase the respect with which the chemical is handled and applied. Turf scientist Dr. Bruce Augustin once gave a seminar to a group of turfgrass managers that contained one bit of information that illustrates this point very clearly. He asked the question of the audience, "How many of you have ever siphoned gas through a hose with your mouth?" Roughly 75% of the audience raised their hands. Next he asked "How many of you have ever siphoned 2,4-D in the same manner?" Not one of the hundreds of attendees raised a hand. The audience was shocked when Dr. Augustin shared the fact that gasoline has a much lower oral $LD_{50}$ value (is more toxic) than 2,4-D. This example can serve as a reminder that we must treat every chemical with respect, and that pesticides, while warranting careful attention, are far from the only chemicals that deserve serious scrutiny.

### 10.2b  Safety in Mixing and Application

Once the label instructions are fully understood, it's time to prepare the chemical agent for application. It's vitally important that mixing and handling procedures be followed carefully. It is during the mixing stage that the chemicals are exposed in their most concentrated form, and accidents at this stage can be tragic.

Start by securing the clothes and protective equipment called for by the instructions. Goggles are required for many products, because if the concentrate splashes in the eyes it could cause permanent eye damage. Some chemical agents can be handled safely only when wearing rubber gloves or other safety protection. Be on guard against any employees who are inclined to demonstrate their courage by neglecting to wear appropriate protective gear; today's foolish staff members are tomorrow's plaintiffs. Make sure everyone is dressed in appropriate apparel and using mandated protective gear.

The same is true for application; it is essential to follow the label's instructions for proper clothing and protective gear when applying any chemical agent, and that goes double for any product applied by spraying. These regulations are designed to ensure the safety of applicators. If the crew is found to be in violation of these dress requirements, fines are possible.

In applying chemical agents, it's important to be aware of the potential for drift. Spraying (or even mixing) in windy conditions can dramatically increase the likelihood of a chemical drifting away from the target area and onto potentially susceptible plants. Drift is of particular concern with broadleaf herbicides that might affect desirable ornamentals in the area of application. With certain pesticides, particularly those from the chemical group known as "esters," there is also the possibility of pesticide drift through the process of chemical volatilization (conversion from a liquid to a gas) and then condensation of the chemical onto other plant materials off-site. The chance of volatilization is much greater in hot weather.

*Figure 10.1. The maintenance staff using this sprayer fabricated a skirt to cut down wind drift during applications.*

Obviously, the wisest course is to avoid spraying any chemical agent when it's windy or when the temperature is above the recommended maximum stated on the label. If, for some reason, it's absolutely necessary to spray during windy conditions, use a "skirt" or shield on the sprayer to cut down on drift (Figure 10.1).

## 10.2c Postapplication Instructions

An important part of the label for any chemical agent—and one that has a direct bearing on the use of chemical agents by the sports turf industry—is the minimum reentry period following a chemical application. This information indicates how soon after the application humans and domestic animals can safely reenter the area, and is a critical tool in preventing unnecessary exposure to humans or pets.

If a chemical application is necessary on the turf, it's essential to make sure it will be possible to close the field until the minimum reentry period has expired, or the application may have to wait until after the season.

If a particular problem demands immediate applications of chemical agents—as when damage from a particular pest is severe and on the increase, the wisest course is to treat the problem immediately. That probably means accepting criticism from an uneducated public that doesn't understand why the game is postponed. Be sure to prominently post a notice of the chemical application and a statement regarding field use. And no matter how much the parents and coaches complain, do not yield to pressure to authorize use of a chemically treated facility until it is completely safe to do so. The temporary displeasure of the public pales in comparison to the potential hazards of improper chemical exposure. If the manager green-lights the use of a field before the stated reentry period and a chemical injury or severe allergic reaction occurs, he or she can probably expect to wind up spending a lot of time in a courtroom.

## 10.3 PLANNING AND PERFORMING APPLICATIONS

### 10.3a Identification, Scouting, and Application Thresholds

Especially in the use of chemical pesticides, proper identification of the pest is the key in making the right choice of the product to be applied. A careless job of diagnosing the infestation may lead to an expensive application of the wrong product, and achieving little or no control of the target pest.

(For descriptions of a variety of test methods that can help to identify particular insects infesting a field, as well as characteristics of other forms of turf stress, see Chapter 9, Turfgrass Stresses and Remedies.)

But even when the particular pest is identified, it's important to "scout" the field, or check the entire field to see if the pest is in evidence throughout the area. Scouting will help make a decision on whether to make a blanket application or just to spot-treat the affected area. Obviously, spot-treatments are cheaper, easier, and less environmentally risky.

The term "application threshold" refers to the point at which the severity of a pest infestation becomes great enough to warrant application of a chemical agent. Discovering some grubworms in the turf may influence some managers to order an immediate insecticide application, but the mere presence of a pest does not necessarily indicate that an application is warranted. Healthy turf will outgrow many pest problems; a good rule of thumb is to apply chemical agents to control a pest only if that pest is threatening the usefulness or the aesthetic value of the turf. If the turf is dealing with the pest, keep a watchful eye, but demonstrate some restraint. Remember that each application adds in small part to hastening the onset of pesticide-resistant organisms.

### 10.3b Choosing the Right Product

Any time that pesticide applications are made, it's wise to choose the most specific product that will control that particular pest. For instance, if purple nutsedge is the problem, don't apply a general-purpose weed killer. Instead, look for a herbicide specifically designed to control purple nutsedge. Applying a product without carefully checking the label first may waste time and money by applying the wrong agent, and may lead to a reapplication to solve the problem later.

Other factors to consider in choosing a pesticide are:

1. General use vs. restricted use pesticides. General use pesticides are available over the counter, and can be purchased by nonlicensed consumers. However, many of the most useful pesticides in sports turf management are classified as "restricted use." That means that only certified pesticide applicators or employees of a certified applicator can legally apply these products. In most states, certification as a pesticide applicator requires passing a series of tests designed to test knowledge of pests, chemicals, and the appropriate handling and application methods. Those interested in being certified should check with their state's division of plant industry or similar regulatory agency to learn how.

2. Granular vs. spray applications. A primary concern is whether or not the proper equipment (tractors, spray systems, spreaders, etc.) is available to accurately deliver chemicals in the preferred manner. Another concern is how soon after the application

players will be using the field. Granular applications need to be watered in, so that the product is washed off the leaf blades and skin contact is minimized for athletes on the field. Label instructions for many liquid products say that reentry is safe as soon as the material has dried, but most state regulations require a 24-hour reentry period after the application of any pesticide.

It's also important to check the label on liquid products to make sure the available type of spray equipment can deliver the recommended concentration of product. If the sprayer can only deliver 2 gallons per 1,000 square feet, don't buy a product that requires a minimum of 4 gallons per 1,000 square feet. As the saying goes, you have to sweat the details.

3. Formulation. An additional decision for sports turf managers is the selection of a particular formulation of pesticide or other chemical agent. For instance, one immediate concern for liquid applications is the amount of agitation needed to keep the chemical agent properly mixed, or "suspended" in the spray tank. Many mixtures require constant agitation to prevent the active agent from "settling out" of the mixture. Low volume sprayers typically have small pumps with minimum agitation. If using a low volume sprayer, check with the distributor to find out which product will stay suspended with minimal agitation. Higher volume equipment typically provides adequate agitation.

Another formulation-related question is the percentage by weight of the active ingredient (or "AI") in the chemical product being used. In most chemical products, the active ingredient makes up only a small percentage of the weight, with the rest comprised of "inert ingredients" which serve as a carrier or binding agent for the active ingredient. Of course, it is the AI that will ultimately control the pest, so it's important to know how much of it is present in the product being used.

Liquid formulations of chemical products are labeled with the AI expressed in terms of pounds per gallon. For example, a product labeled as a "3.3 EC" is an emulsifiable concentrate (more on that phrase later) which contains 3.3 pounds of active ingredient per gallon. Dry formulations have their AI expressed as a percent of product weight. For example, a "65 WP" formulation means the product is a "wettable powder" that contains 65% AI by weight.

It's important to be thoughtful when reading the labeling information or specifications for applying chemical agents. For instance, AI labeling for liquid formulations refers to the product before it is mixed or diluted, but the actual AI of the applied material will usually be much lower. And be sure to understand whether the recommended application rates for the product are expressed in pounds of product per unit area or pounds of active ingredient per unit area. Close attention to this kind of information can spell the difference between a successful chemical application and a disaster.

It's a good idea to use products that have a low "active ingredient per acre" (or "AIA"). Low AIA products are usually less toxic to humans in their concentrated forms and present less danger to the environment with reduced risk to the applicator. Low AIA products usually carry "Caution" or "Warning" designation on the label. As a rule of thumb, use a pesticide with the "Caution" signal word whenever possible.

Some chemical agents have formulations that allow application in either solid or liquid form. **Granular** formulations, on the other hand, are meant to be applied as they are purchased. These products are relatively easy to handle and deliver, are those least affected by wind during application, but are typically more expensive per pound of active ingredient. Granular formulations typically contain low percentages of active ingredients, to allow for more uniform spreading in small areas. Of course, that means the purchase of what seem like huge amounts of granular material when applying this type of product to larger areas.

*Figure 10.2. Hiring a commercial applicator to apply fertilizers and pesticides can often represent a cost-saving alternative to using the facility's staff to perform these processes.*

Many commercially available pesticides, particularly PRE herbicides, are now being added to granular fertilizer carriers. These products, marketed under the designation of "weed and feed" materials, allow the applicator to apply both fertilizers and herbicides in a single application. Weed and feed products have become very popular with home gardeners, and there are many commercial firms around the country that now offer both the materials and their custom application at very competitive prices.

(It is the intent of this book to provide the fields manager and his or her staff with the information to make the necessary chemical applications. However, with the regulatory requirements for chemical application training, and the need for special equipment, filling and cleanup areas, and storage facilities for chemicals, many managers are discovering that hiring outside contractors to make pesticide and fertilizer applications is a cost-effective alternative. See Figure 10.2).

Most other formulations are intended for application as liquids through a sprayer system. Most sprayable formulations do not form true "solutions" when mixed with water; instead, they form "suspensions." The difference is that suspension requires agitation in the spray tank to keep the material suspended and to prevent the sprayer from becoming clogged. One of the cheapest, most concentrated formulations designed to be applied as a spray is the **wettable powder** (**WP**). Wettable powders are hard to handle because of the small particle size of the powder pesticide carrier. Formulations with larger particles are called **dry flowables** (**DF**) or **dispersible granules** (**DG**). These products employ pelletized carriers of the active ingredient, and are easier to handle and mix in the tank. A popular liquid formulation for turf pesticides is the **emulsifiable concentrate** (**EC**). Emulsifiable concentrates are typically oil-based pesticide carriers that are suspended in water.

These formulations are easy to handle and are relatively inexpensive. Although they are sold in the form of a liquid, ECs also require proper spray tank agitation in order to keep the pesticide in proper suspension.

The listed examples are the most common formulations of turfgrass chemical agents, but other formulations, specifically designed to have particular performance characteristics, may be encountered occasionally.

### 10.3c  Equipment and Calibration

*Equipment.* For most facilities, budgetary constraints prevent the purchase of a large variety of application equipment. However, it's important to keep in mind that the more types of equipment on hand, the greater the manager's range of options in selecting chemical products. At the very least, every field manager and his or her staff should have access to a broadcast spreader and a sprayer.

Broadcast spreaders are available in both walk-behind and tractor-driven configurations. Walk-behind spreaders can usually deal with a single field, but facilities with multiple fields should consider tractor-driven spreaders, which will pay for themselves in reduced labor costs.

In selecting a sprayer, a key consideration is the gallons per minute of product delivered. Most equipment delivers between ½ gallon and 4 gallons per minute. Sprayers applying up to 2 gallons per minute are called "low volume" sprayers and are adequate for most sports field applications. Many weed control products can be applied at rates as low as ½ gallon per minute, but most insecticides and fungicides require a sprayer that can put out a minimum of 2 gallons per minute.

*Calibration.*  It's important that application equipment be calibrated to deliver the amount of product that's listed on the label, usually in pounds per 1,000 square feet or ounces per 1,000 square feet. (Carefully clean any piece of equipment before calibrating it, and at least daily during large applications. A dirty spreader or sprayer may deliver the product unevenly, or in amounts much different than the initial calibration would indicate. If the crew calibrates at the beginning of a large job and applies material for five days without cleaning or recalibrating, by the end of the application the operator has no idea what the actual application rate may be.)

*Granular broadcast spreaders* deliver fertilizers and pesticides by dropping the material out of the hopper onto a spinning wheel that throws the pellet away from the spreader. The advantages in using rotary spreaders are the speed with which an applicator can deliver granular chemicals over larger areas, the reduced chance of skips in chemical delivery, and their usability for virtually any grade (size) of fertilizer or pesticide. The limitations are that they sacrifice some accuracy in chemical delivery, and cannot accurately apply materials under windy conditions.

Broadcast spreaders usually have calibration knobs with numbers or letters to calibrate fairly precisely. (Many pesticide and fertilizer labels suggest settings for the more popular brands of spreader.) However, even with properly calibrated equipment, it's possible to apply too much or too little of the product. In the case of broadcast spreaders, the most important consideration must be the amount of material delivered per 1,000 square feet.

Spacing between spreader paths (equipment tracks) is probably the biggest variable. Common practice is to maintain a 40% overlap of the broadcast pattern; if the spreader is throwing a band 12 feet wide, overlap about 5 feet on the next pass to ensure uniform coverage. It is important to maintain a constant walking speed in order to be consistent in the granular material delivery.

To calibrate a broadcast spreader, follow this procedure: first, measure off an area of 5,000 square feet (50′ × 100′). Next, place 25 pounds of fertilizer in the spreader and apply the material, carefully observing an overlap of about 40% (applying material all the way to the closest wheel tracks of the last pass). After the entire area has been covered, remove the remaining fertilizer (let's imagine that 10 pounds are left in the spreader) and weigh it. Subtract the remaining amount from the original 25 pounds (25 − 10 = 15). This procedure indicates that the spreader applies 15 pounds per 5,000 square feet, or 3 pounds per 1,000 square feet.

If the test indicates that the spreader has applied too much or too little material, adjust the spreader to increase or decrease the application rate and conduct another test application. The second test will allow calibration at settings which result in very nearly the ideal rate of application.

Of course, determining the amount of material to be applied requires an accurate knowledge of the square footage of the area to be treated. Experience with the spreader will allow the operator to know whether further adjustment is needed to maintain the desired rate of application. Monitoring the rate of application is an everyday process—a spreader is never calibrated "once and for all time." Be sure to record all settings and information in an application logbook to use as a reference for future calibrations and chemical applications.

An obvious problem with this method of calibration is that it requires the delivery of material over an actual turf area, and will result in a response to the chemical application. While this method can be safely done with low analysis fertilizers, calibrating for granular pesticide formulations requires greater care. In such a case, adjust the spreader to a setting that is expected to deliver a rate of material on the low side of the desired rate. If it turns out that the spreader is delivering only half of the desired rate, make a second pass over the test area before adjusting the settings to the proper rate.

One tool now being marketed for many broadcast spreaders is a "fertilizer skirt" that fits around the spreader's whirling delivery wheel. This collection device is meant to collect all the product to be delivered without spreading it over the turf itself. With this device, calibration can be done just about anywhere without fear of turfgrass phytotoxicity or discoloration. Overall, however, the calibration method above will typically allow for more accurate settings.

*Drop spreaders* are much easier to calibrate because there are fewer variables, with the size of the openings being the most important. The drop spreader simply delivers granular material by gravity, and the larger the opening on the spreader, the more material falls through. A practical way to calibrate a drop spreader is to use the same procedure we described for a broadcast spreader. First, determine the width of the drop spreader (for the purpose of this example consider it to be 2′). Next, measure off a known length. (A minimum of 50′ is desirable. A drop spreader can be calibrated in a smaller area than a broadcast spreader, because there is no need to factor-in overlap.) Load the spreader with a preweighed quantity of material, and apply it across the calibration area (for this example that calibration area would be 100 square feet—2′ wide spreader × 50′ length). Then remove the remaining material and weigh it. Divide 1000 by the number of square feet in the calibration area to determine what factor to use in the last conversion—to pounds of material applied per 1000 square feet (as given, 1000 square feet ÷ 100 square feet = 10). For this example, multiply the amount of material applied by 10 to determine how much material would be applied per 1,000 square feet. Adjust the spreader setting appropriately and repeat the process until the spreader is calibrated to deliver the desired amount of material.

On a smaller scale, it's possible to accurately calibrate drop spreaders by catching or collecting the material that is dropped. This can be done with a pan attachment that fits under the spreader (available on some models), or by dropping the material on a piece of plastic or even a clean shop floor (followed by sweeping and picking up the product). Test applications 10′ in length are appropriate for this calibration. After collecting the material, weigh it (a small electronic scale will be needed to accurately measure the small amounts of product collected) and determine the amount delivered per 1000 square feet, as described above. This method eliminates the need to apply chemicals to turf areas where repeated calibration runs could lead to turfgrass phytotoxicity.

The limitations of drop spreaders are the smaller coverage area (typically 2 to 6 feet wide), the fact that agricultural grade fertilizers may not fit through the small spreader openings, and the need for precise delivery in order to prevent skips or overapplication of the material.

When using drop spreaders, overlap the wheels for an even distribution of particles. (Spreaders vary in the distance from the inside of the wheels to the openings for material; the operator needs to know that distance for the spreader being used, and watch carefully to match the edges of each pass.) It's also important to avoid overapplication at the edges of the field, where turns are made. Drop spreaders are best used in the morning when dew allows the operator to clearly see the spreader's tracks.

For *spray equipment,* several components of the system play a critical part in maximizing equipment performance. Sprayers feature different types of pumps (piston, centrifugal, gear, roller-vane, and diaphragm), each with its own advantages and disadvantages in terms of cost, method of operation, and performance. The fields manager can consult his or her equipment supplier or extension specialist to review the options appropriate to the particular needs of the facility.

One crucial sprayer part is the nozzle, which disperses the spray solution into droplets. For general purpose spraying, the best choice is a nozzle designated as a "flat fan." The spray pattern from this type of nozzle is intended to overlap approximately 33%, so nozzle spacing and boom height are crucial for proper spray delivery. Many chemical spray application disasters result from improper nozzle spacing or boom height, each of which can result in significant misapplication rates. Other types of nozzles (cone, hollow-cone, even-fan, etc.) are designed for applications that require various spray pressures to get chemicals into the turf canopy, or for various chemical formulations. Equipment suppliers can also provide advice on which nozzle is best suited to a particular need.

As with other components of the spraying system, proper nozzle maintenance is required to achieve optimum performance from the system. Nozzles that are clogged, mismatched or damaged will not apply the material evenly and at the proper rates.

(Sprayers also have filters to remove impurities and large particles which can clog the system. These filters should be cleaned and/or replaced periodically to maximize sprayer performance.)

Physical calibration of sprayers is most difficult because it is a multiple step process. The following is an example of one of several ways to calibrate a sprayer. Begin by measuring the width of the spray pattern and divide 1,000 by that width to determine how far the sprayer has to travel to cover 1,000 square feet. For example, if the spray pattern is 8′ wide, the applicator would have to travel 125′ to cover 1,000 square feet. (1,000′ ÷ 8′ = 125′) Next, time how long it takes to travel that distance. A speed of 3 MPH takes approximately 30 seconds to drive or walk this length. Be sure to calibrate the sprayer on terrain similar to the area where spraying will take place to ensure the most accurate spray application. After determining the throttle and gear settings to operate at the desired speed, make sure that the RPMs from the PTO setting are sufficient to properly drive the pump. Most tractors and utility vehicles will have this setting marked directly on the speedometer, or it can be found in the operator's manual. At this point in this example, calculations show that the spray system covers 1,000 square feet every 30 seconds of operation.

The next step is to determine the amount of solution the sprayer is delivering per 1,000 square feet. Do this by operating the tractor pump at the same RPM setting as used in the calibration timing run and collecting the liquid from each nozzle in buckets for the time required to cover 1,000 square feet (in our example, 30 seconds). If the nozzle output turns out to be approximately 32 ounces of liquid per nozzle, the total volume of liquid is 128 ounces of spray delivered (4 nozzles × 32 ounces = 128 ounces). This corresponds to a volume of 1 gallon per 1,000 square feet, or approximately 44 gallons per acre.

Since the purpose of calibrating equipment is to make sure the equipment is delivering the rate recommended on the label, the last step is to calculate the application rate. For this example, if the label instructions call for one ounce of product per 1,000 square feet, mix one ounce of product for every gallon of water added to the spray tank. The application rate would be the specified one ounce of material (mixed into one gallon of water) per 1,000 square feet.

It's wise to keep good notes in a record log about the sprayer information for this particular calibration. As for granular applications, don't consider these particular sprayer settings to be written in stone because equipment and applicator performances vary over time. However, having this information handy will allow more efficient calibration in the future.

Emphasize to staff members that the driving or walking speed in the chemical application must be comparable to that used in the calibration run. The amount of spray solution delivered is inversely proportional to ground speed. For instance, if ground speed is doubled, the equipment will be delivering exactly half the desired rate of chemical; if the driving speed is halved, the equipment will be delivering twice the calibrated rate. In the first case, the equipment is not delivering sufficient chemical to obtain the desired response; in the second, the overapplication may potentially damage the turf.

## 10.3d  Curative vs. Preventive Applications

Many of us have long since come to recognize the wisdom of the old adage, "an ounce of prevention is worth a pound of cure." In the case of application of chemicals, however, this proverb is not a good rule of thumb.

In sports turf maintenance, curative applications are generally preferred over preventive applications, particularly for insecticide and fungicide applications. Here's why:

First of all, an anticipated problem like a damaging pest population may not really occur, so a preventive treatment may well turn out to be a waste of money.

Second, pest resistance to pesticides is a substantial and threatening problem—and the onset of that resistance may be accelerated when more applications than necessary are made.

Third, remember that planned seeding operations (including regular overseeding or slit-seeding) may fail due to the application of some preventive pesticides like PRE herbicides, which control the grass just as they control the weeds. Weeds are almost always a problem on a sports field, a problem that is often accelerated by the fact that a heavily-used field has a more open turf canopy due to the traffic on the turf. Some sports field managers will have little tolerance of weeds on their field due to playability considerations or expectations of the players and/or other officials. These fields will require

PRE herbicides to maintain the best-looking turf. However, even these managers should adopt a philosophy to only apply the pesticide that is necessary and make use of POE cleanup applications as weeds occur later in the season.

## 10.3e  Spot vs. Blanket Applications

Spot applications are preferred over blanket applications, for obvious reasons. Why go to the time, trouble, and expense of treating the entire field if the pest is concentrated in one area, or if the damage is sparsely scattered throughout the entire field? Using the spot approach targets the real problem and reduces pesticide cost and waste. Spot applications are to blanket applications what a scalpel is to a chain saw; use the least intrusive technology.

One caution with spot applications, especially when using a hand sprayer: be sure to follow the label instructions very carefully regarding mixing and applying the chemical. For instance, the label instructions for many spot applications with handheld sprayers say "apply to point of runoff;" this means exactly what it says—saturating the area risks extensive turf damage.

## 10.3f  Timing Applications

Chemical applications should always be made at times when they will maximize control of the problem pest with minimal effect on the turfgrass. For example, there is little sense in making a late-season POE herbicide application to kill crabgrass that has already produced seed. This grass is a summer annual that will die anyway at the first heavy frost, so a fall chemical application would be both a waste of money and environmentally irresponsible. Treat the weeds with POE herbicides when the plants are young and actively growing.

Similar logic applies to the application of pesticides for the control of insects and diseases. Target pesticide applications to times of peak pest activity (as described in the previous chapter) in order to maximize control. Also, don't forget to consider whether the turfgrass might already be under stress due to heat, drought, or other growing conditions—these stresses could limit the turf's ability to recuperate from the effects of the application.

Is rainfall or irrigation following the chemical application desirable or not? For PRE herbicides, watering-in the chemical within a specified time period (provided on the label) is absolutely necessary in order for the chemical to perform as desired. The same is true for insecticides and nematicides designed to control subsurface pests. However, irrigation or rainfall following application of a POE herbicide or any insecticide designed to control aboveground insects can compromise the effectiveness of these products. Consult weather forecasts before making chemical applications.

## 10.3g  Alternating Products

Avoid repeat applications of the same chemicals (or chemicals that are in the same family) on a regular basis. This practice can increase the chances of developing a resistant biotype of weed, insect, or disease. Make a point to alternate chemicals with different modes of action in order to minimize the potential for resistance. Although various products have varying degrees of effectiveness, the range of available pesticides usually allows for adequate control using at least two or three different products to prevent the development of resistance to a single product.

## 10.4   RECORD KEEPING

No job is finished, as the saying goes, until the paperwork is done. That certainly applies to the application of chemical agents. For professional peace of mind, keep careful records of all pesticide applications. Since the 1990 U.S. Farm Bill that was enacted May 10, 1993, specified record keeping procedures have been federally mandated for all certified pesticide applicators. Within 30 days of the application of a restricted use pesticide, make a written record of the following information:

A.   The brand and product name and EPA registration number
B.   The total amount of the product applied
C.   The specific location of the application
D.   The size of the area treated
E.   The crop (for our purposes, usually "turfgrass"), commodity, stored product, or site (specific field or fields) to which the pesticide was applied
F.   The month, day, and year of the application
G.   The name and certification number of the applicator or of the applicator's certified supervisor.

Under federal law, all records must be maintained for a minimum of 2 years from the date of pesticide application.

(It's important to check state requirements for maintaining pesticide records, to determine whether there are any additional requirements not mandated under federal law.)

Questions about a planned pesticide application can be answered by a trained professional *prior to pesticide application* because there is no quicker way to damage or even kill turf than by misapplying a pesticide. The selection of pesticides and the timing of their applications can typically be answered through publications developed for each region by a university extension service. The extension personnel can also offer assistance in spreader and sprayer calibration and proper delivery of the pesticide to the turf. Many state turfgrass associations conduct workshops or seminars in sprayer and spreader calibration each year. The state turfgrass extension office can also help complete the steps required to obtain the proper license for the application of certain restricted use pesticides.

Rules and regulations governing chemical weed control vary state by state. Check with local and state officials for products approved for use, and on regulations governing their application.

# PART II

# *Sports Fields*

Chapters 11 through 14 provide a comprehensive guide to the design, construction, renovation, and maintenance of the types of sports fields commonly used in North America and around the world. Each chapter provides information on contours and orientation, techniques for constructing and renovating a field to allow for safe and competitive play, and maintenance practices required to keep the facility in optimum condition, including times of year when various maintenance processes should be conducted. At the end of each chapter, you will find information on the correct dimensions of fields and governing bodies for each sport.

Each chapter combines sports that are similar in terms of the design, construction, and maintenance strategies required for fields. Chapters are divided into five sections:

1. *Design Principles*, including surveying and layout, contour plans and specifications, drainage and irrigation systems.
2. *Construction and Reconstruction*, with grading and installation techniques for both new construction and reconstruction of problem facilities. For our purposes, reconstruction is defined as the process of tearing down (or, in the case of a field, tearing up) an existing facility and rebuilding it in a substantially improved fashion. In the case of sports turf, that includes such changes as improving the subgrade, the field contours, installed drain and irrigation systems, even the topsoil or other growing medium.
3. *Renovation* is the process of restoring a facility to sound condition after it has been damaged by use. For our purposes, renovation is here defined as the use of minor remediation techniques that should be performed annually, or at least every two to three years.
4. *Maintenance and Management Procedures*, including daily, weekly, monthly, and seasonal practices to keep the field in optimum playing condition.
5. *Field Rules and Governing Bodies*, including field dimensions, common points of confusion about fields, and the major governing bodies of North American competition in each sport. It's wise for anyone involved in the design, construction, or maintenance of a sports field to have on hand a copy of the latest rule book from the organization or organizations sanctioning competition on that field.

# Chapter 11

# *Baseball and Softball Fields*

## 11.1  INTRODUCTION

Over the past 20 years, renovation work on more than 100 baseball fields has revealed that just about every one of those fields had a number of things in common.

- First of all, almost all had a problem with standing water in the infield.
- Second, the problem of standing water was nearly always caused by poor grading.
- Third, although some of the facilities had some sort of installed drain system, the system did not work as intended.

The one thing the fields did not have in common was the way they were graded. Each field had been designed and constructed, it seemed, with a completely different set of grading standards.

Finally, the fields nearly always had in common the only practical and effective solution for their problem: regrading the field to provide for positive surface runoff of water.

Probably more than any other sport, baseball is sensitive to field conditions and especially to water. Skinned infields have a tendency to turn into little lakes at the first cloudburst, and require long delays while they dry out or the application of drying agents or other materials to try to soak up the wet spots and allow play to go on.

To successfully construct or renovate a baseball diamond requires careful attention to the subtleties of survey, layout, and grading.

## 11.2  DESIGN

In designing and laying out a baseball or softball diamond, it's important to proceed according to this sequence: (1) survey the outer boundaries of the field, making sure there is sufficient room for foul territory; (2) lay out home plate and then the bases and the pitcher's mound; (3) set out the skinned areas of the infield; then (4) the grass area of the infield, and (5) the outfield and foul territory.

### 11.2a  Survey and Layout

One of the most common errors made in the construction of sports facilities is the simple failure to survey. Professionals engaged in this field will frequently be called upon to "fix" fields which were constructed without the benefit of surveying, either because planners just thought it looked level or, as sometimes happened, because the field started

**Table 11.1. Space Requirements**

| Type of Field | Distance to Center Field Fence (ft) | Acres | Sq Ft[a] |
|---|---|---|---|
| Baseball: | | | |
|    90′ Bases | 400 | 4.5 | 195,000 |
|    80′ Bases | 315 | 2.8 | 123,000 |
|    70′ Bases | 275 | 2 | 90,000 |
|    60′ Bases | 215 | 1.5 | 64,000 |
| Softball: | | | |
|    65′ Bases | 275 | 2.4 | 105,000 |
|    60′ Bases | 200 | 1.4 | 60,000 |

[a]Numbers are rounded to the nearest 1,000 sq ft.

out as a mowed area used for practice or informal play and then evolved into a more widely used facility.

Whatever the reason, it is vitally important that any new construction or reconstruction project begin with a thorough survey of the site. Intuition and the naked eye will not provide sufficient understanding of the topography of the area; only a careful survey will accomplish that end.

Survey enough land to show how water moves through and around the area, and especially to show how it will move off the playing area. In many cases, it's necessary to survey about twice the area of the field itself.

Although many fields are simply oriented to the available space, official rule books for baseball suggest that a line drawn from the tip of home plate through the pitcher's mound and second base should point in an east-northeast direction. Such an orientation prevents the batter and catcher from looking into the sun as they stand at the plate, and positions most of the fielders in such a way that their eye-line to the batter is not directly into the setting sun.

In laying out the field, it is important to reserve space for dugouts, backstop, surrounding fence, and other peripheral elements. All too often, a failure to plan for these structures forces the builders to install them in an awkward and unsuitable fashion, which may compromise player safety and disturb a well-planned drainage scheme.

Table 11.1 suggests minimum space requirements for baseball and softball fields, with sufficient space around the playing field for fence lines, dugouts, spectator seating, and swales.

The chart in Table 11.2 displays the square footage of the skinned area and the grass area for common size baseball and softball fields, including foul territory.

## 11.2b  Design Criteria for New Construction

The highest point on the field is the pitcher's mound, and the field slopes away from the mound in all directions. The height of the pitching plate, or "rubber," is specified by the sanctioning body for each level of competition.

The infield should be higher than the rest of the field. To keep the infield playable, it's important that no water passes into the infield from the outfield or the sideline areas.

Although installed drain systems can be used successfully in some areas of the baseball diamond, these systems typically work poorly in the sand/clay soil of the skinned area. Under normal circumstances, water does not pass satisfactorily through the soil

Table 11.2. Square Footage of Skinned Area and Grass Area

| Type of Field | Distance to Center Field Fence (ft) | Skinned Area (sq ft) | Grass Area Sq Ft |
|---|---|---|---|
| Baseball: | | | |
| 90' Bases—95' arc | | | |
| w/ Grass infield | 400 | 11,550 | 120,500 |
| w/ Skinned infield | 400 | 18,300 | 113,750 |
| 80' Bases—80' arc | | | |
| w/ Grass infield | 315 | 8,400 | 74,500 |
| w/ Skinned infield | 315 | 13,650 | 69,250 |
| 70' Bases—70' arc | | | |
| w/ Grass infield | 275 | 6,800 | 53,550 |
| w/ Skinned infield | 275 | 10,700 | 49,650 |
| 60' Bases—50' arc | | | |
| w/ Grass infield | 215 | 3,850 | 39,500 |
| w/ Skinned infield | 215 | 6,700 | 36,650 |
| Softball: (Skinned infield) | | | |
| 65' Bases—65' arc | 275 | 9,300 | 61,450 |
| 60' Bases—60' arc | 200 | 8,350 | 31,500 |

and into the drain structures. Therefore, proper positive surface drainage is the only way to prevent standing water on the skinned part of the infield.

The base lines should be carefully laid out to be as level as possible.

All slopes should have a continuous even grade from contour line to contour line at about ½% for the infield and 1 to 1½% for the outfield. This degree of slope will allow for runoff of water from the playing area to catch basins or swales outside the boundary lines or to lower contours.

### Safety Issues

In designing the diamond, a number of important safety issues must be considered. One of the most obvious is the distance from the foul lines to the dugouts, grandstands, or other fixed objects. As a general rule, a minimum clearance of 25 ft is required for Little League and softball fields, with twice as much for high school baseball and above. Because players must run through this area looking upward to track foul balls, the greatest possible clear area should be allowed (see Tables 11.8 and 11.9 for recommended clearance for each level of baseball and softball).

If possible, catch basins should be located outside the fences surrounding the playing area to prevent player injury. If the presence of grandstands requires the installation of catch basins inside the fences, they should be placed as close as possible to the fence or grandstand. In these circumstances, a small grid should be used to minimize the risk of injury.

In general, there should be no obstructions in the field of play (including foul territory). The rule books for each governing authority include requirements and other guidance related to that level of play. In designing a competitive baseball field (or, for that matter, any athletic field), it's always wise to have a copy of the rule book for the organization that governs that level of play. A list of addresses for governing bodies is included at the end of this chapter.

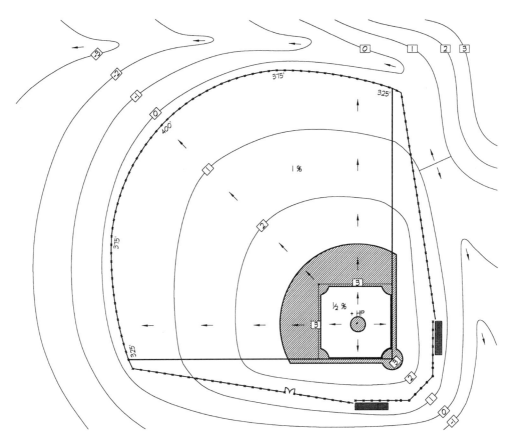

*Figure 11.1. The simplest and most common (good) field design—elevations noted in feet.*

### 11.2c  Field Designs with Preferred Contours

The following drawings illustrate three schemes for contouring the baseball field, including outside boundaries as well as infield and outfield. Note that (as we discussed above) the infield is higher than the outfield or the boundary areas.

In discussing these field contours, we will refer to three distinct areas of the baseball diamond. **The Outfield** is used here as commonly understood. **The Skinned Area** is the groomed dirt portion of the field where the infielders customarily stand during play. **The Infield** is the area enclosed by the base paths.

#### The Outfield

Figure 11.1 shows one of the simplest and most common field designs. The outfield slopes downward from the second and third base lines to the outfield fence at a rate of approximately 1%. The advantage of this design obviously lies in part in the simplicity of its contours and the ease of construction. The disadvantage is that the outfield fence is almost three feet lower than the base paths, which can give the field a rather disorienting look and feel (see Figure 11.4 for detailed skinned area and infield contours).

Grade stakes for this field can be set on a 50 foot grid pattern.

Figure 11.2 is an improved design, crowned from second base through center field to

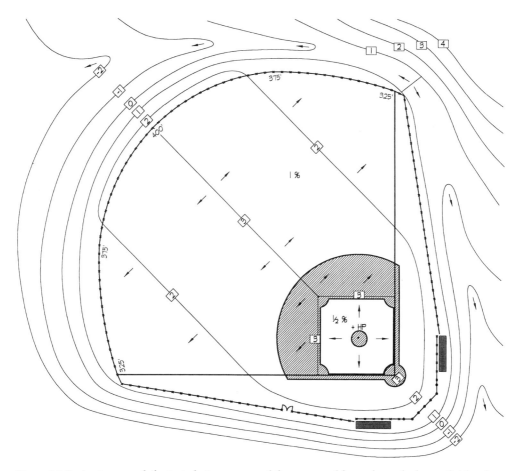

*Figure 11.2. An improved (better) design, crowned from second base through the outfield—elevations noted in feet.*

the outfield fence. The center crown directs water toward the boundaries and away from the center of the field. This design also provides a shorter path for runoff from the outfield—to the sidelines rather than all the way to the outfield fence. (The skinned area and infield detail for this design is provided in Figure 11.5.)

When surveying this field design, set the stakes on the contour lines.

Figure 11.3 shows the authors' preferred design, which includes elements from each of the first two layouts. A crown has been developed from second base about one-third of the way to the outfield fence, allowing water to run off the heart of the field toward the foul lines. In the outer half of the outfield, runoff is toward the fence. Notice that fence lines are level around the entire field.  (Skinned area and infield detail in Figure 11.5.)

When surveying this field design, grade stakes should be set on the contour lines.

### The Skinned Area

In nearly every case, a field that is chronically unplayable is in that condition because of a poorly conceived skinned area design. Field planners typically fail to give this portion

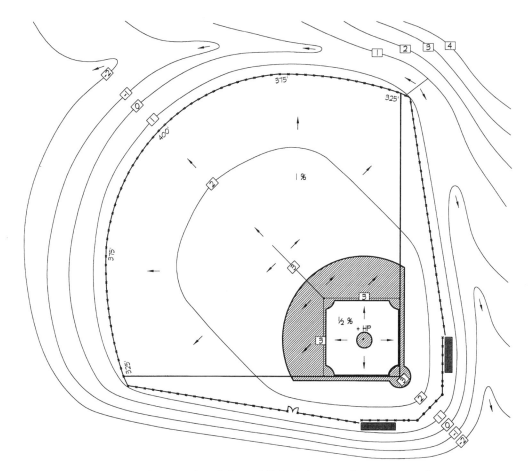

*Figure 11.3. Authors' preferred (best) full-field design—elevations noted in feet.*

of the diamond the attention it deserves; remember that, at any given moment, all but three of the defensive players are standing on the skinned area.

In laying out and surveying the skinned area, it's important to use more grade stakes than usual, due to the more gradual slope. A smaller error can have more troublesome consequences.

Figure 11.4 is a simple skinned area contour scheme (designed for use with the overall field design in Figure 11.1), with a downward slope from the second and third base lines to the outfield. Although this is a relatively simple design to construct, and one which works adequately in medium to dry climates, it has the disadvantage that infield water must run off through the circled grass edge of the boundary between the skinned area and the outfield. Because loose soil from the skinned area tends to build up in that circled edge, a natural sill or "lip" can occur at that point, preventing proper drainage and holding the water in the skinned area.

Figure 11.5 shows a crowned skinned surface (for use with the field designs in Figures 11.2 and 11.3), which channels runoff to the foul lines, rather than toward the outfield. Because of this contour, water does not have to flow through the circled grass edge to leave the infield, making it a preferred design for moderate and rainy areas.

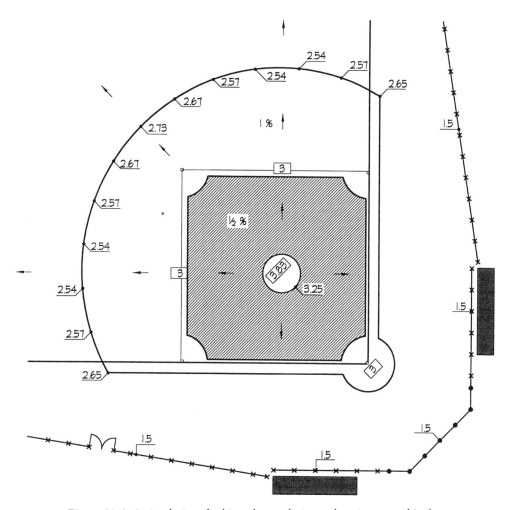

*Figure 11.4. A simple (good) skinned area design—elevations noted in feet.*

### The Infield

The pitcher's mound is the highest point of the field, with the rest of the infield sloping away in all directions toward the base paths, as shown in Figures 11.4 and 11.5.

Figure 11.6 is an alternative infield design which raises both the pitcher's mound and home plate by three inches. This change creates the illusion of a higher pitcher's mound, increasing the visual interest in the game for spectators and helping to keep the heart of the infield as dry as possible, but does not change the relative height of the pitcher and the batter. This design can be used to replace the grass infield design in Figure 11.4 or Figure 11.5 to create a field that is superior in both esthetics and performance. This design is also well suited to **softball,** since the pitcher's plate and home plate are level.

### The Pitcher's Mound

The regulation pitcher's mound is a circle 18 feet in diameter, with a flattened top area that is 5 feet wide and 34 inches from front to back. This flattened area extends 6

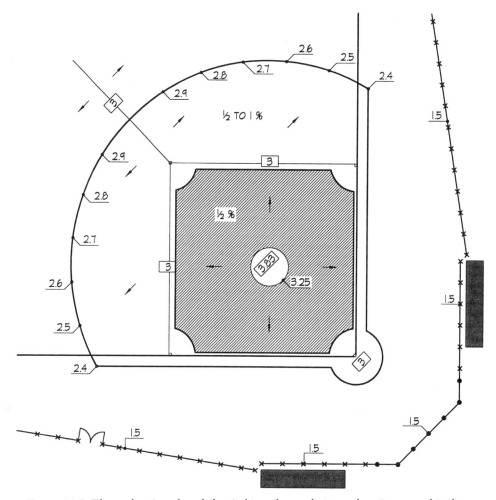

*Figure 11.5. The authors' preferred (best) skinned area design—elevations noted in feet.*

inches in front of the pitcher's plate, or rubber, and is elevated 10 inches above home plate. Beginning at the front of the flattened area, the mound is to slope toward home plate at the rate of 1 inch per foot for the first 6 feet, then gradually slope the remaining 4 inches. The center of the mound is 59 feet from the white point of home plate, and 18 inches in front of the pitcher's plate. Figure 11.7 shows the appropriate contours for a pitcher's mound, and Figure 11.22 (in Section 11.3 on field construction) is a photograph showing a tool that can simplify the task of setting or resetting the correct contours.

## 11.2d  Skinned Infields

Skinned infields (sometimes called "dirt infields") are those which have a continuous skinned playing surface all the way to the grass arc where the outfield begins. Skinned infields are recommended for softball fields, and are a requirement for some softball tournament play. Skinned infields could also work well for baseball fields, and may be preferred to grass infields, which require more maintenance and more frequent reno-

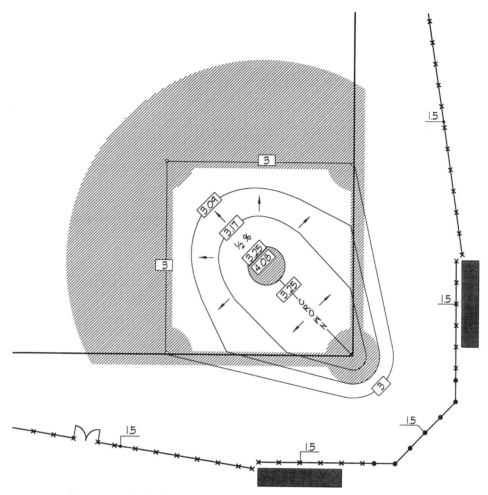

*Figure 11.6. Alternative infield design with raised mound and home plate—elevations noted in feet.*

vation. If the facility has a limited maintenance staff, the skinned infield is easier to keep playable, requiring less attention to matters such as lip buildup and removal.

A skinned infield that has grass in foul territory has greater visual appeal than a skinned infield that has a dirt surface all the way to the dugouts. This is especially true of a completely skinned regulation (90 foot bases) baseball field, which has some 25,000 square feet of skinned surface, better than half an acre. Figure 11.8 shows an example of the typical skinned infield (without grass in foul territory), and an alternative and superior design with grass in foul territory, which allows for improved appearance and playability. The grading plan is the same as shown in Figures 11.4 and 11.5. For softball, use the infield grading plan shown in Figure 11.6 to keep the pitcher's plate level with home plate.

## 11.2e  Multiple-Field Layouts

In recent years, the growing popularity of amateur sports leagues has led to the construction of hundreds of multiple-field complexes throughout North America. In designing this type of facility, several important factors should be kept in mind.

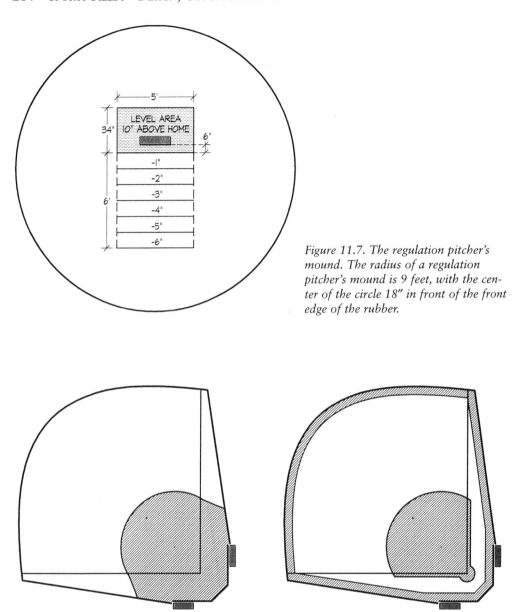

*Figure 11.7. The regulation pitcher's mound. The radius of a regulation pitcher's mound is 9 feet, with the center of the circle 18″ in front of the front edge of the rubber.*

*Figure 11.8. Skinned infields, typical design (left) and superior design (right).*

Ideally, all fields in a complex should be oriented so that a line from home plate through the pitcher's mound is pointing east-northeast. This avoids the need for either the catcher or the batter to look directly into the sun during play. However, orienting all the fields in this manner isn't the most space-efficient way to design the complex.

A common multiple-field layout for younger children is to place four home plates at the corner of a square with the outfields from the four fields sharing space. Younger players (especially Pee-Wee and Little League minor leagues) seldom hit the ball far into

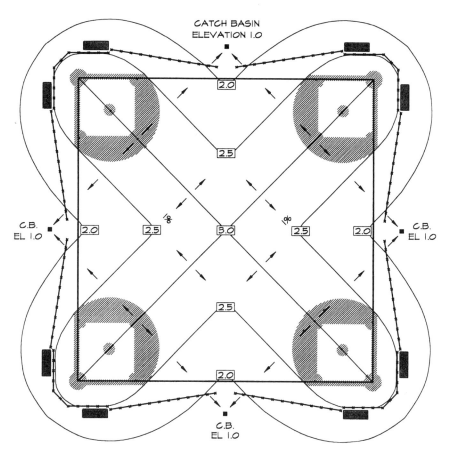

*Figure 11.9. Multiple-field layout with home plates at four corners of square—elevations noted in feet.*

the outfield, and the danger of contact among players from different games is minimal (see Figure 11.9).

Many complexes for older players are designed with home plates from four fields back-to-back (see Figure 11.10). This is a fairly efficient use of space, but can lead to a hazard when pop-ups in foul territory stray into another field. This design should be used only for experienced players, and as much space as possible should be left between the backstops. In addition, overhanging backstops should be used wherever possible, to prevent pop-ups from going backward onto the next field.

This back-to-back design is obviously a preferred method for players of Little League age and older, who need more clearance for safety's sake. However, it requires substantially more space to lay out four fields in this fashion; if the two layouts in Figures 11.9 and 11.10 show the same size fields, than the back-to-back layout would take up more space (almost twice as much).

In designing multiple-fields complexes, keep two other criteria in mind: each field should be designed to function as its own drainage system, with water draining away from the center of the complex, and within each field, the infield should not be lower than the outfield.

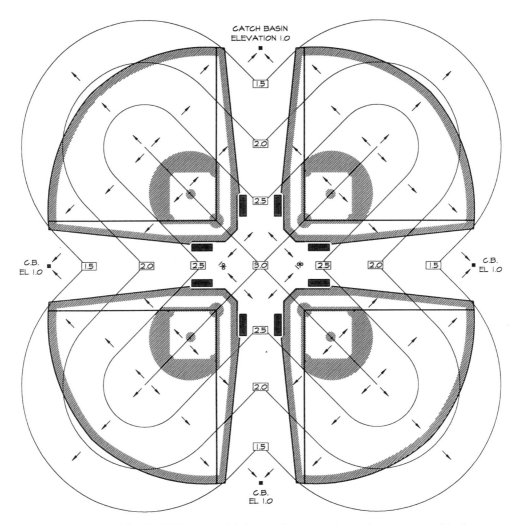

*Figure 11.10. Multiple-field layout with home plates together—elevations noted in feet.*

## 11.2f  Skinned Area Soil

### Soil Selection

A critical factor in the competitiveness of any baseball diamond is the quality of the material used to surface the skinned area. We prefer a mixture of about 60% sand, 20% silt, and 20% clay. Covered diamonds typically use more silt—as much as 30%—and less sand. Higher-budget fields will typically add calcined clay or calcined diatomaceous earth to increase permeability.

All of the soil used in the skinned area should pass through a ⅜″ wire screen. A minimum of 97% should pass through a number 8 sieve, and at least 60% should pass through a number 140 sieve.

Although particle size analysis is recommended before the installation of any skinned area soil, such analysis will not tell the planner how well the material will perform. It's a

*Figure 11.11. This easy-to-perform cup test allows for the comparison of skinned area soils. The soil that firms up fastest will become playable most quickly after a rain.*

good idea to compare two or more different soils with similar particle sizes by doing some testing of material samples. There are several ways to do this.

One way is to punch four or five eighth-inch holes in the bottom of eight-ounce plastic cups, and then fill the cups ¾ full with samples of the soil being compared. Pour in water until it reaches the top of the cup. Allow the water to drain away, and see how long it takes the various samples to become firm enough to offer some resistance when a finger is pushed into the soil. The soil that firms up faster will return to playable condition faster. (Figure 11.11 illustrates this "cup test.")

A second test is to dump a bucket of each soil on the ground, then use a hose to soak it thoroughly. Then, as in the previous case, compare the time it takes each sample to firm up.

It's also a good idea to visit the stockyard before accepting material, and to look at undisturbed piles of the material to see the size of the gravel that is present in each. Choose the soil with the smallest gravel preferably ⅛″ or smaller. (The best time to visit the stockyard is shortly after a rain, which exposes the gravel.)

### Pitcher's Mound and Batter's Box Soil

As any baseball or softball fan knows, the normal competitive stresses on the pitcher's mound typically leave that area riddled with pits and holes by the end of the game. Each pitcher scraps and kicks at the dirt to customize the surface to his or her liking, and this process goes on at least twice an inning throughout the game.

*Figure 11.12. To ensure optimal pitcher's mound or batters box performance, a clay-based soil material should be installed. Some manufacturers are now producing a material specifically designed for this purpose.*

In order to construct a mound that will be fairly solid, and will stand up well both to the weather and to the continual excavation by pitchers, we recommend the use of clay-based soils for construction of the mound. Sand and silt-based soils tend to be easily disturbed by competitive stresses. Figure 11.12 shows the installation of a clay-based pitcher's mound material.

### Skinned Area Conditioners and Drying Agents

One way to enhance the ability of the skinned area to withstand weather is through the use of conditioners designed for that purpose. Most of these products take one of two forms: calcined clay products and calcined diatomaceous earth products. Conditioners are tilled into the soil to soak up extra water during wet weather, and hold water in the soil during dry weather.

These conditioners can also be spread on wet portions of the skinned area to soak extra standing water. When used in the manner, these conditioners become "drying agents," drying out the field to allow play. There are also organic products, such as those manufactured from corncobs, which are specifically marketed as drying agents rather than conditioners. These organic products can soak up water to allow one game to be played, but should be removed before the next rain to prevent more serious problems, such as making the soil gummy and compacted. If these organic products are used as a conditioner (tilled into the soil and left), the affected portion of the skinned area may have to be completely excavated later to get rid of the gummy mess those corncob products can leave.

(To digress a moment on the subject of dealing with puddles: it's common to see people trying to get rid of puddles by *sweeping* the water out of them with a broom. This practice will certainly spread the water around and promote drying. However, unless the depression is then filled with additional soil, sweeping creates the potential for an even larger puddle the next time.)

Calcined clay and diatomaceous earth conditioners are also promoted as helping to fight compaction. Skinned areas with conditioners incorporated in the soil will loosen more easily and uniformly when a nail drag is used on the surface. Conditioners also let the skinned area support tractor weight faster than unconditioned skinned areas, so the maintenance staff can get out onto the field to drag it much faster after a rain.

One real benefit of calcined diatomaceous earth products is that they allow the maintenance staff to *rake soil out of the edge of the grass*, which is just about impossible with any other conditioner. As far as some fields managers are concerned, that quality alone makes these products worth the price, because it allows quick and easy removal of the grass-edge lip before it builds up.

Since these products absorb so much water, they also make the skinned area much less slippery. Of course, that's the main factor umpires use in deciding whether to call a game because of rain. If they see players slipping, they'll stop the game. So, once or twice a season, a conditioner should allow a field to support play when an unconditioned field would not. Of course, that also means it's a little *safer* for the players on the skinned area.

Skinned area conditioners also help with dust control during the summer, because they hold water in the soil longer. This is particularly true of the diatomaceous earth products; in most of the country, it should be possible to wet the soil thoroughly in the morning and play on it all day without having to stop and rewater. So for facilities that have games going on from morning until night, that can be a substantial benefit.

The diatomaceous earth conditioners can also be used in smaller volumes than calcined clay. Table 11.3 compares the volume and weight of various types of conditioners required for installation on a regulation baseball field to a depth of three inches.

Installing three and a half tons of diatomaceous earth conditioner, and tilling it in about three inches deep on an official size baseball field with a grass infield, takes about 40 man-hours from start to finish. Obviously, installation time is somewhat less for a smaller field, such as a Little League field.

Manufacturers' recommendations for the calcined clay products call for the skinned

**Table 11.3. Comparing Conditioners**

| Product | Conditioning a Regulation Size Skinned Area (with a Grass Infield) | | |
| | Type of Conditioner | Percent Recommended | Tons Needed to Condition Skinned Area |
|---|---|---|---|
| Terra Green | Calcined clay | 20% | 9 tons |
| Diamond Pro | Calcined clay | 25% | 18 tons |
| Turface | Calcined clay | 25% | 12 tons |
| Play Ball | Diatomaceous earth | 10% | 3.6 tons |

*Figure 11.13. The first step in installing a conditioner is to spread the material evenly over the surface of the skinned area.*

*Figure 11.14. Once the conditioner has been distributed evenly over the surface, it is tilled into the soil to the depth indicated by the manufacturer's directions.*

*Figure 11.15. After tilling, a pulverizer helps to firm up the skinned area soil.*

*Figure 11.16. A tractor with a level bar helps to fill in any low spots and provides a uniform surface for the conditioned skinned area.*

area soil to be mixed with 20 to 25% conditioner. Diatomaceous earth products require only a 10% mix, allowing a cost advantage.

Figures 11.13 through 11.16 show the installation sequence for skinned area conditioners.

## 11.2g  Turfgrass Selection

In selecting turfgrass for baseball fields, planners should consider the same general information on turf strengths and weaknesses outlined in Chapter 1. However, due to the character of the game of baseball, a smooth, fast infield which provides little resistance to the passage of grounders is usually considered ideal.

**Warm season** bermudagrass shows good overall tolerance to close cutting, making it ideal for baseball and softball installation, both in the South and in the transitional zone.

In **cool season** areas, however, turfgrass selection can be a little more complicated. In general, a highly effective method is to use a 50:50 mix of Kentucky bluegrass and perennial ryegrass, and some experts suggest using two varieties each of the Kentucky bluegrass and perennial ryegrass for genetic diversity and disease resistance.

To establish a turfgrass that will withstand cutting as short as 1″, the planner may want to consider a mixture of perennial ryegrass and a Kentucky bluegrass cultivar chosen to tolerate close cutting. This mixture provides a good combination of aggressive growth habits and ability to tolerate low cutting heights preferred by coaches and players.

## 11.2h  Installed Irrigation Systems

Since each baseball or softball field has its own dimensions, it's next to impossible to describe a "typical" irrigation plan for all fields. For instance, the distance from home plate to the outfield fence varies from field to field. The distance between the heads could vary from 47 feet to 67 feet, depending on the number of rows needed to reach the outfield fence from the infield arc, the water pressure at the field's edge, and the type of head used.

The distance between the heads could even be greater in foul territory around the infield. For example, if the width of the grass area from the base line to the dugout is 20 feet, the heads must be set no more than 20 feet apart. A field that has 50 feet of grass between the baseline and the dugout needs to have heads that are set 50 feet apart. Obviously, the type of head and the number of heads on a zone are important considerations.

The infield is the hardest area of the field on which to achieve good distribution uniformity. No matter where the heads are placed, some areas of the infield will receive more water than others, and supplemental hand-watering will be necessary. For this reason, the installation of a quick-coupler valve in the grass behind the pitcher's mound is recommended. The quick-coupler valve can also be used to hand-water the skinned area.

Figure 11.17 is an example of an installed irrigation system design for a baseball field that has 90 feet bases, a 355 feet distance to center field, and 60 feet between the baselines and the dugouts. This design requires water pressure of 75 PSI at field edge and yields a pressure of 60 PSI at the base of the sprinkler heads. Average precipitation rate for this system will be .35 inches/hour for full circle heads, .7 inches/hour for half-circle heads and .29 inches/hour for the infield. Run time for 1″ watering will be 2 hours 51 minutes for full circle heads, 1 hour 26 minutes for half-circle heads, and 3 hours 28 minutes for the infield.

Figure 11.18 shows an installed irrigation system for a softball field or a Little League baseball field (with a skinned infield). Bases are 60 feet, center field is 215 feet, and the

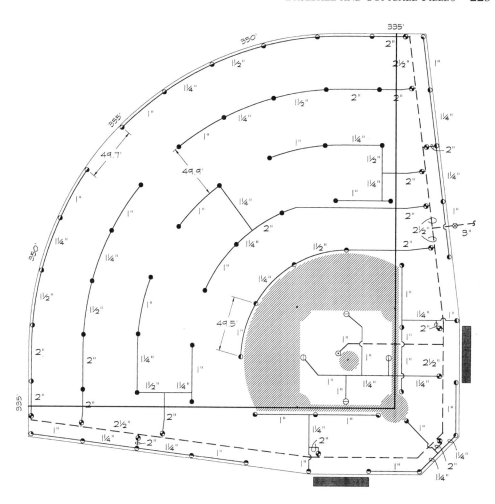

IRRIGATION LEGEND

| | DESCRIPTION | PSI | GPM | RADIUS | ARC | UNITS |
|---|---|---|---|---|---|---|
| ● | HUNTER 1-25-36S-08 FULL CIRCLE | 60 | 9.2 | 50 FT. | 360° | 25 |
| ◑ | HUNTER 1-25-ADS-10 PART CIRCLE | 60 | 12.0 | 54 FT. | 225° | 3 |
| ◕ | HUNTER 1-25-ADS-08 PART CIRCLE | 60 | 9.2 | 50 FT. | 180° | 29 |
| ◔ | HUNTER 1-25-ADS-07 PART CIRCLE | 60 | 7.5 | 48 FT. | 135° | 4 |
| ◔ | HUNTER 1-25-ADS-05 PART CIRCLE | 60 | 5.3 | 45 FT. | 90° | 2 |
| ⊖ | HUNTER 1-25-ADS-05 PART CIRCLE | 60 | 5.3 | 45 FT. | 180° | 4 |
| ◐ | 1½" HUNTER ICV 151G REMOTE CONTROL VALVE | | | | | 14 |
| ⊙ | 1" QUICK COUPLER VALVE | | | | | 1 |
| ⊗ | 3" GATE VALVE FOR MAINLINE ISOLATION | | | | | 1 |
| —— | NON-PRESSURE PIPE (PVC CLASS 160 RECOMMENDED) | | | | | |
| — — | PRESSURE PIPE (PVC CLASS 200 RECOMMENDED) | | | | | |

NOT SHOWN:
BACKFLOW PREVENTION DEVICE
(AS REQUIRED PER CODE AND/OR ORDINANCE - AND FOR SAFETY)                1

HUNTER ICC IRRIGATION CONTROLLER (14 STATIONS)
LOCATION AS NEEDED                                                     1

DESIGN PROVIDED BY HUNTER INDUSTRIES

*Figure 11.17. Regulation baseball field irrigation system (90-foot bases).*

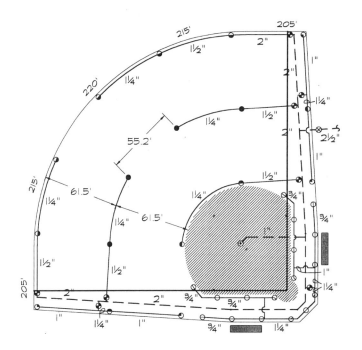

## IRRIGATION LEGEND

| | DESCRIPTION | PSI | GPM | RADIUS | ARC | UNITS |
|---|---|---|---|---|---|---|
| ● | HUNTER I-25-36S-18 FULL CIRCLE | 60 | 15.7 | 61 FT. | 360° | 4 |
| ◕ | HUNTER I-25-ADS-18 PART CIRCLE | 60 | 15.7 | 61 FT. | 180° | 9 |
| ◓ | HUNTER I-25-ADS-10 PART CIRCLE | 60 | 12.0 | 54 FT. | 90° | 4 |
| ⊕ | HUNTER PGM-06-A WITH 1.5 NOZZLE | 40 | 1.5 | 24 FT. | ADJ. | 4 |
| ⊖ | HUNTER PGM-06-A WITH 2.0 NOZZLE | 40 | 2.0 | 27 FT. | ADJ. | 13 |
| ◍ | 1½" HUNTER ICV 151G REMOTE CONTROL VALVE | | | | | 8 |
| ⊙ | 1" QUICK COUPLER VALVE | | | | | 1 |
| ⊗ | 2½" GATE VALVE FOR MAINLINE ISOLATION | | | | | 1 |

——— NON-PRESSURE PIPE (PVC CLASS 160 RECOMMENDED)

— — PRESSURE PIPE (PVC CLASS 200 RECOMMENDED)

NOT SHOWN:
BACKFLOW PREVENTION DEVICE
(AS REQUIRED PER CODE AND/OR ORDINANCE - AND FOR SAFETY)    1

HUNTER ICC IRRIGATION CONTROLLER (8 STATIONS)
LOCATION AS NEEDED    1

DESIGN PROVIDED BY HUNTER INDUSTRIES

*Figure 11.18. Softball field or Little League irrigation system (60-foot bases).*

distance from home plate to the backstop is 25 feet. For a Little League field with a grass infield, install four sprinkler heads in the infield.

This design requires water pressure of 75 PSI at field edge and yields a pressure of 60 PSI at the base of the sprinkler heads. Average precipitation rate for this system will be .43 inches/hour for full circle heads, and .82 inches/hour for half-circle heads. Run time for 1″ watering will be 2 hours 20 minutes for full circle heads, and 1 hour 13 minutes for half-circle heads.

## 11.2i   Installed Drain Systems and Catch Basins

### Installed Drain Systems

While the goal in designing a baseball diamond is to provide for positive surface drainage that will move water off the entire field without the need for installed drain systems, sometimes adequate surface drainage cannot be achieved. Under these circumstances, and where budgets allow, installed drain systems must be included. In nearly all cases, water can be moved off grass areas more quickly by internal drainage structures. (But remember that installed drain systems are not effective for skinned areas.)

Before installing drainage structures, it's vitally important to understand the local soil type and the direction of water movement on the field. In many cases, even where soils are heavy, drainage structures are installed parallel to the direction of water movement, with the goal of helping the water move in its natural direction.

However, as a wise farmer would point out, in heavy soils, good drainage structures are installed *across* the flow of water, rather than parallel to it. (In sandy soils, the planner has a good deal more flexibility in designing installed drain systems.) By laying out the drainage structure 45 to 90 degrees from the direction of movement, the planner allows the structure to intercept the water and channel it away from the area. This is especially true when installing strip drains, as discussed in Chapter 12 (12.2g). In planning installed drain systems, it's important to remember that *the purpose of an installed drain system is to minimize the distance water must travel before it begins rapid removal from the playing surface.*

So, before making a decision on the design or construction of an installed drain system, it's a good idea to try to observe the direction of water movement, either by going to the site during a rain, or performing a topographic survey. (See Chapter 8 for more information on the design and construction of installed drain systems.)

Figures 11.19 through 11.21 show installed drain system designs for use with field designs shown in this chapter. All of these designs could be constructed either with pipe drains or with strip drains. The advantage of these designs is the trench can be laid out at a consistent depth because they follow the contour, sloping downward toward the collector drain. Also, the field drains are installed at a 45 degree angle to the direction of the flow of the surface water. For strip drain systems, that means some of the runoff will be intercepted.

(The purpose of the drain lines in the skinned area is to provide a continuous flow of water from turf areas and does not mean positive surface drainage can be compromised in these areas. For completely skinned [dirt] infields, drain lines can be eliminated altogether, since they will have little or no effect on skinned area surface drainage.)

### Catch Basins

Space limitations sometimes make it impossible to design sideline contours that are sufficient to shed the necessary amount of water from the playing surface. This problem

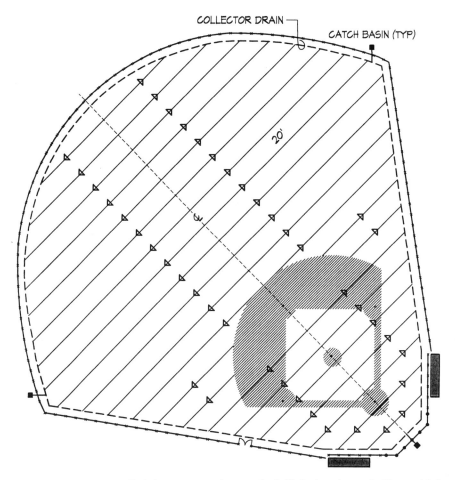

*Figure 11.19. Installed drain system for simple field design shown in Figure 11.1.*

is frequently caused by sideline grandstands or by hilly surrounding terrain. Under such circumstances, it may be necessary to install catch basins.

In planning for catch basins, select locations just outside fences, where they will be shielded from the playing area. Because of the disturbance to contours that grandstands can cause, placing the catch basin right in front of the stands can often help to drain swampy areas. (Catch basins also serve as junction boxes for installed drain systems.)

## 11.3 CONSTRUCTION AND RECONSTRUCTION

### Construction

After surveying the field and developing a grading plan, it's time to start construction. A critical first step in the construction process is to transfer the grading plan to the field, using grade stakes.

The skinned area of a baseball diamond typically has grades ranging from ¼% to 1%, while infields (either skinned or grass) should have a ½% downward slope toward the

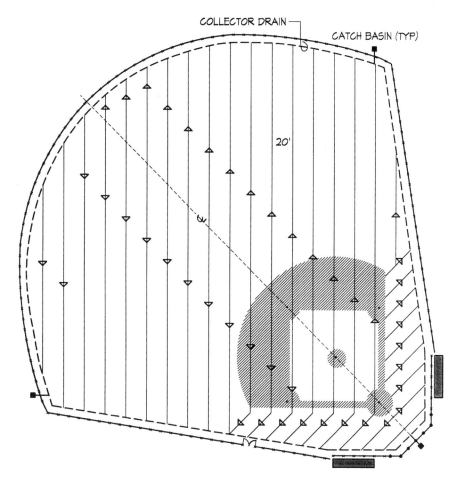

*Figure 11.20. Installed drain system for better field design shown in Figure 11.2.*

baselines. Since these are such gradual slopes, it's necessary to use as many as 50 grade stakes for these areas. Set the stakes first, then mark the proposed grade on the stakes using a marker.

In setting the grade, string lines can be used in two different ways. The first is to place the string lines on the straight edges between the grass and the skinned areas. Everything on one side of the line is topsoil, while the other side is sand/clay soil. (For these straight edges, string lines serve a dual purpose: separating the grass area from the skinned area, and setting the string at finish grade as a visible guideline for the crew.) String lines can also be used to check grade between stakes by tying the string to one stake at finish grade, then pulling tight and tying to another stake at finish grade.

Use a paint line on the field arcs. Place stakes along the arc to mark the finish grade. Remember to account for settling by pressing firmly on both sides of these lines. This can be done with foot pressure, but a tractor is even better.

Use string lines to hand-grade the entire infield by attaching a string to a stake at the base of the pitcher's mound and pulling it to another stake at the baseline. A line can also be tied to a stake at the baseline between first and second base, or between second

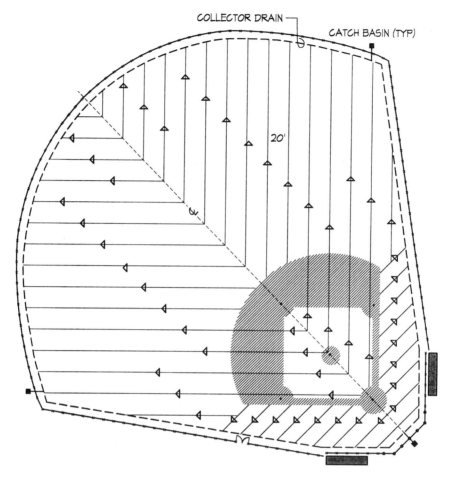

*Figure 11.21. Installed drain system for authors' preferred field design shown in Figure 11.3.*

and third, and pulling it to another stake at the arc where the skinned area meets the outfield grass.

One easy way to check the slope in front of the pitcher's plate is to make a measuring tool from a piece of 2″×4″×10′ lumber, as shown in Figure 11.22. Lay the 2×4 on top of the pitcher's plate, and stake it level on the home plate side. Mark the board 18″ in front of the pitcher's plate, and then every foot until there are six marks. Then adjust the slope until the first mark is one inch above the ground, the second mark is two inches, and so on. The rest of the mound can be sloped evenly to the bottom.

For overall field designs shown in Figures 11.2 and 11.3, set the outfield grade stakes on the contour lines. To allow the field to drain properly, it's important to have an even grade from contour line to contour line. That means grade stakes and spot elevation checks are necessary to ensure an even grade and to prevent puddling.

One common mistake is to fail to set grade stakes in foul territory around the infield to allow for continuous grades from the infield to the dugouts. These are highly used areas in the field of play, and they require special attention to make sure the players

*Figure 11.22. Simple tool for building the pitcher's mound. This simple tool can be made from a 2× 4, and used to accurately set or reset the grade for a pitcher's mound.*

using them will not be standing in water or mud. Remember that catchers will be running through these areas looking straight up for foul balls, and grabbing throws from the outfield with runners approaching the plate. Obviously, under these circumstances, good traction is essential.

It's also important to keep heavy equipment off the field whenever it's wet. Equipment on the field at these times can cause excessive compaction to the sub-base and the top-soil.

## Reconstruction

When approaching a reconstruction project, the sports field professional is well advised to consider the diamond as a whole, and only then to attempt spot solutions to observed problems like standing water. Without a clear idea of what's going on with the field and the surrounding terrain, any "Band-Aid" fixes are likely to fail.

As with new-field construction, the best first step is to survey the ground. Often a survey will instantly reveal the cause of the problems observed at the facility, and suggest solutions. Likewise, observing the behavior of water on the surface during a heavy rain can yield important insights about the field.

Analyzing the existing elevations will allow the field planner to determine whether to reconstruct the entire infield and surrounding areas, or whether edge removal will provide adequate surface drainage.

Figure 11.23 is an example of a worksheet that can be used to conduct an effective

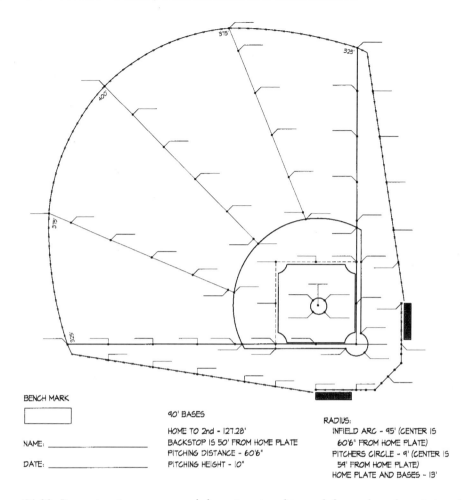

*Figure 11.23. Reconstruction survey worksheet. In using this worksheet, place the existing elevation on top of each line and the proposed elevation underneath.*

survey of an existing field. By taking an elevation reading at each of the indicated marks and filling in the appropriate values, the planner will collect more than 65 different elevations of the field surface—plenty to yield an accurate understanding of the topography of the field and how it will need to be adjusted to result in a sound diamond. It's also a good idea to survey the area outside the fence.

Before surveying, lay out the field using string lines for the straight-aways and paint lines for the arcs. Then take an elevation reading at each point indicated on the layout sheet. Notice that the points are very close together in the area where the skinned area meets the outfield grass. This is frequently a problem area, because soil from the skinned area accumulates at the grass edge.

When redesigning a skinned area, it's worthwhile to try to get water to run off toward the foul lines, as shown in Figure 11.5.

Once the planner has a clear idea of the dynamics of the diamond, planning for the reconstruction should begin with adjusting the difference in elevation between the pitcher's mound and home plate. The next step is to adjust the slope at the baselines to

*Figure 11.24 A high school field before reconstruction. This Eastern Ohio field drained so poorly that it had been all but abandoned within a few years after construction.*

allow water to run across the lines and into foul territory. Finally, refine and adjust the rest of the skinned area as discussed above, and the rest of the diamond.

It's vitally important to follow new diamond design criteria as closely as possible in performing the reconstruction. Correcting field problems may require solutions that seem at first blush excessive; we have completed reconstruction projects that began with the addition of two feet of soil on the infield to allow for the required positive surface drainage and to prevent outfield and sideline water from crossing into the skinned area and infield.

The planner will sometimes be challenged as to the need for such substantial reconstruction of the field, and the wisdom of such expenditures will be questioned. However, accurate maintenance records, as well as records of rain outs, makeup games and related inconvenience and expense, will often lend great weight to the case for a major reconstruction instead of a few small fixes (Figures 11.24 and 11.25).

## 11.4   RENOVATION

Renovation is the process of restoring a field to its original condition after it has undergone the stresses of a competitive season. Typically, these processes do not require substantial removal of turf or changes to the grade. Renovation should be deferred until after the season is over, unless the planner can count on a two to four-week period after the work to let the field settle. Remember that if a process is begun before the season and heavy rains delay completion, the field might not be playable when the season starts.

Renovation techniques include:

*Figure 11.25  The same field after reconstruction. After the field was reconstructed, including raising the infield 2 feet to allow for positive surface drainage, the field won a national 1995 Baseball Field of the Year Award, and has been consistently playable ever since. (Photo by David Grantonic).*

- **Deep Tilling** of the skinned area—especially tilling over 2″ deep.
- **Adding Soil for Drainage.** Another renovation process is adding soil to improve surface drainage. If drainage has been a problem, perform a survey to check the contours of the field, and plan to add soil to correct the grade once the season ends.
- **Lip Removal.** Every season, dragging and weather conditions like wind and rain push lots of dirt into the grass at the arc of the infield and along the baselines. That dirt forms a lip that keeps rain from draining away into the grass the way it's supposed to. This lip also becomes a hazard to players because it causes erratic bounces of the ball, and because of the possibility of tripping.

  Failure to remove this lip will allow a grass mound to form, and will then require removal of sod, lowering the grade, and resodding. Left untreated, this type of grass mound will prevent water from running off the skinned area. At some fields, the resulting standing water has been dealt with by adding more sand/clay soil, which can then turn the mounds into hills. This can make the problem worse by reversing the direction of the slope toward the infield. The result is standing water near the baselines.

  Most of the time, a useful solution to this kind of buildup is to excavate and remove sand/clay soil from the area to create the proper slope required for surface runoff. This will usually require regrading three to seven feet of the grass surrounding the skinned area (Figures 11.26 to 11.28).
- **Seeding and Sodding.** Perform reseeding or sodding operations on areas that were cut out to remove lips or hills.

*Figure 11.26. To remove the lip at the grass edge, use a standard sod cutter.*

*Figure 11.27. Once the sod has been removed, lower the grade to allow for positive surface drainage.*

*Figure 11.28. When the correct grade is established, replace the turf by seeding or sodding.*

Turf renovation work should be carried out when the turf is actively growing. Skinned area renovation can obviously be performed whenever convenient for the field staff, but it's important to remember that the skinned area requires one week to resettle for each inch deep that tilling or other processes disturb the soil.

## 11.5   MAINTENANCE AND MANAGEMENT PROCEDURES

In order to practice effective maintenance and management of a baseball or softball facility, it's important to conduct regular inspections of the field or fields. Table 11.4 shows a chart to guide inspections. Using this chart will help remind the field manager of the various factors and observations which should be included in regular examinations. Maintenance procedures should be planned on the basis of these inspections.

In order to learn as much as possible about the condition of the field as an ecosystem, take time to go beyond the superficial in making inspections. For instance, take along a soil probe and push it into the soil at various spots around the grass portions of the field to check for moisture level, compaction, and thatch buildup. Pull up a few plugs and inspect the root system, thatch, and the ends of the grass blades. Look for tearing and shredding at the ends of the blades, characteristic of the effects of dull mower blades.

Effective inspections should also be timed to observe the field in a variety of conditions. For instance, check the grass after it's mowed, to see whether the mowing is correctly taking off about ⅓ of the plant. And make a point to inspect the field during or

**Table 11.4. Sample Field Inspection Report**

# Inspection Report

### Baseball or Softball Field:[a]

Field: _____

| Grass Area | Overall Appearance | Clippings | Height of Cut | Sharpen Mower Blade | Soil Moisture | Other: Color, Density, Thatch, Compaction, Weeds, Catch Basins, Sprinkler Heads, etc. |
|---|---|---|---|---|---|---|
| Date: | | | | | | |
| Date: | | | | | | |
| Date: | | | | | | |
| Date: | | | | | | |
| Date: | | | | | | |
| Date: | | | | | | |
| Date: | | | | | | |
| Date: | | | | | | |

| Skinned Area | Proper Dragging Methods[b] | Cupped Baselines | Holes at Pitcher's Mound | Holes at Home Plate and Bases | Lip Buildup at Grass Edges | Other: Dugouts, Fences, Spectator Areas, Trash, etc. |
|---|---|---|---|---|---|---|
| Date: | | | | | | |
| Date: | | | | | | |
| Date: | | | | | | |
| Date: | | | | | | |
| Date: | | | | | | |
| Date: | | | | | | |
| Date: | | | | | | |
| Date: | | | | | | |

[a]Edging: May & Sept. Foul lines: chalk skinned areas and paint grass.

[b]Dragging: start 6″ from the grass edge and work toward the middle of the skinned area.

immediately after a sustained, heavy rain. See where water is standing on the field, and especially where it is puddling on the skinned areas. These inspections are the best source of information on which to base maintenance decisions.

## 11.5a  Skinned Area Maintenance

Because of the importance of keeping the skinned areas smooth and free of compaction, daily maintenance is required during the playing season. After the surface is

*Figure 11.29. Dragging should be conducted at low speeds, and should begin 6" from the grass edge to avoid slinging dirt into the grass.*

*Figure 11.30. The drag should be lifted before leaving the skinned area to prevent pulling soil into the grass.*

*Figure 11.31. A high-pressure water hose directed at the grass edge will blast out skinned area soil which has collected there during the season. (Photo by David Grantonic).*

moistened to allow for good surface penetration, use a nail drag to keep the soil loose. Next, a mat drag is used to break up soil clumps and level the surface. Dragging should begin six inches from the grass edge and work toward the middle of the skinned area to prevent the loss of sand/clay into the grass. If heavy rains make use of a tractor unwise, the skinned areas can be hand-raked to achieve a similar effect (Figure 11.29).

It's also important to lift the drag before leaving the skinned area, to avoid pulling soil into the grass edge, where it may block a critical surface drainage point (Figure 11.30).

Holes at the batter's box, the pitcher's mound and the bases are filled, tamped, and hand-raked each day.

Edging the grass areas should be performed at least twice a year. Before edging is performed, a high-pressure water hose should be used to remove any of the skinned-area material that has accumulated at the grass edge. Stand on the turfgrass area and direct the stream of water at the first 2″ to 4″ of turfgrass so that the loose soil is pushed out into the skinned area. Avoid directing the stream at the sand/clay soil (Figure 11.31).

At the beginning of each season, a tractor with a pulverizer attachment is used to break up the layer of compaction that forms over the winter.

### 11.5b  Warm Season Maintenance

Table 11.5 shows a sample maintenance program that can be tailored to fit the needs of any baseball or softball field in the warm season zone. This is only one example of a maintenance program that is being used successfully on a warm season baseball field. In

**Table 11.5. Warm season maintenance program**

## Sample Maintenance Schedule
(Warm Season)

| | | | |
|---|---|---|---|
| Field Name: | Sean Rochelle Field | Address: | P. O. Box 4929 |
| Type of Field: | Baseball Game Field | | Elkins, Arkansas 72727 |

| | | | |
|---|---|---|---|
| Condition: | good | Compaction: | moderate |
| Type of Grass: | Tifway bermudagrass | Drainage: | surface |
| Type of Mower: | 3 gang reel | Irrigation: | installed automatic system |
| Type of Soil: | native sandy loam | Thatch: | ¼″ to ½″ |

Soil Test:                                        Notes:        mow 3 times a week during
Year:            1997      Phosphorus: 20              active growth
pH:              6.2       Potassium:   110

| Time of Year | Fertilization | Aeration | Topdress | Overseed | ⅓ Rule Mowing Ht | 1″ Week Watering | Weed Control |
|---|---|---|---|---|---|---|---|
| May | 13-13-13 ½ lb 13-13-13 ½ lb | verticle mow late | | | ¾″ | as needed | |
| June | 34-0-0 ½ lb 13-13-13 ½ lb | core aeration | ⅛″ sand | | ¾″ | ½″ two times a week | POE grass and sedge |
| July | 34-0-0 ½ lb 13-13-13 ½ lb | solid tine areation | ⅛″ sand | | ¾″ | ½″ two times a week | POE grass and sedge |
| August | 34-0-0 ½ lb 13-13-13 ½ lb | light verticle mow before overseed | | | ¾″ | ½″ two times a week | |
| September | 13-13-13 ½ lb | | ⅛″ sand | 12 lb perennial rye | ¾″ | light frequent for overseed | |
| October | 21-2-20 1 lb N 0-0-60 1 lb K | | | 3 lb perennial rye | 1¼″ | as needed | |
| November | | | | | 1¼″ | as needed | |
| December | | | | | 1¼″ | as needed | |
| January | | | | | 1¼″ | as needed | |
| February | 21-2-20 ½ lb N 50% SRN | | | | 1¼″ | as needed | |
| March | 21-2-20 ½ lb N 50% SRN | | | | 1¼″ | as needed | |
| April | 10-24-18 1 lb N 50% SRN | | | | 1″ | as needed | |

planning a fertilization program, the field manager should consult the more detailed information found in Chapter 3, Fertility and Fertilizers.

This maintenance program is used on a baseball field that has a fall practice period, a spring season from mid-February through mid-May, and a summer season that begins in mid-June and lasts through August.

### Fertilization

The P and K levels in this typical native sandy loam soil are in the low-medium range, and the fertility program outlined here reflects the recommendations of soil tests, which called for sources high in P and K. A complete 13-13-13 fertilizer is used in split applications in May and then is alternated with ammonium nitrate from June to August. In September, ½ pound of N is applied with 13-13-13 to minimize bermudagrass growth while the overseeded perennial ryegrass is establishing. In early October, a 21-2-20 sulfur-coated source is applied at one pound of N in order to sustain overseeding growth through November. A winterizing application of one pound K, using 0-0-60, is performed in mid-October.

The fertility program resumes in the following year with applications of ½ pound of N using 21-2-20 in February and March, again designed to slowly supply the overseeded ryegrass with just enough nutrients to maintain active growth during the cooler temperature periods. An application of sulfur-coated 10-24-18 goes down in April to supply additional P and K for the transitioning bermudagrass. The frequency of complete fertilizer applications would be reduced in future years when P and K levels are brought up to recommended levels.

### Aeration and Topdressing

Vertical mowing should be performed in late May, following the completion of the spring schedule, if a significant thatch layer (greater than ½″) is present. In June, the turf can be hollow tine-tine aerated with 4″ deep, ½″ diameter tines, and then a medium-coarse textured sand is applied over the entire field at a depth of ⅛″ to smooth the surface, and the sand and cores are dragged in. This process should take place during a 10-day period when the field is not in use to give the turf a chance to recover from the stress of the operation. Solid tines (⅜″ diameter, 4″ deep) can be used in July over the entire field to provide temporary compaction relief without disrupting the playing surface. Once again, the field can be topdressed with ⅛″ of medium-coarse sand.

Vertical mowing can be performed again in August in preparation for overseeding in early September. The vertical mowing in August is not intended as a dethatching event because this practice has been shown to increase the winterkill potential of the bermudagrass. For this reason, August vertical mowing should include only one pass over the field, instead of the two or three passes performed when serious dethatching is the goal. Following overseeding, the turf is again topdressed with ⅛″ of sand to promote seed:soil contact.

### Overseeding

Overseeding is recommended for fields which are used for both fall practice and the spring season. The bermudagrass base is overseeded in mid-September with 12 pounds of pure live seed per 1,000 square feet with a blend of perennial ryegrasses. Follow this application in a few weeks with an additional 3 pounds of seed, paying particular attention to poorly established areas. After overseeding, topdress as described previously.

In planning for overseeding of a baseball diamond, remember that the infield is the critical portion of the field, and be sure to apply the full amount of seed in that area. According to Dr. Coleman Ward, retired turfgrass extension specialist from Auburn University, a workable rule of thumb is to plant the infield at the full rate and the outfield at a half-rate if budget restrictions are a concern.

Keep in mind that with rotary spreading, some drop seeding might be necessary in order to maintain precise shape or definition of areas in the boundaries. Reliance on rotary seeding often will not result in the desired straight edges.

If the field is being used only for baseball, there will be a few months during the winter when the staff is actively maintaining the turf while it is not being played on. However, this is necessary in order to have the field in optimal condition the next spring.

If the baseball season extends into the late spring and early summer months, then the overseeded ryegrass will need to receive extra attention to get it through the extreme heat and moisture stress periods during this time of year. This can be accomplished by paying careful attention to moisture status of the turf and monitoring irrigation frequencies and amounts so that they keep the overseeded ryegrass actively growing.

### Mowing

Mowing at ¾″ from May through September promotes sod strength and lateral spread. (Cutting this short requires mowing at least three times per week during periods of active growth.) The cutting height should be raised to 1¼″ from October through March to promote winter hardiness of the bermudagrass. The cutting height can then be reduced to 1″ in April, gradually working toward ¾″ by May.

### Irrigation

During periods of no rainfall, an effective irrigation strategy is for the turf to receive two irrigation events per week from June through August, each irrigation delivering approximately ½″ of water. Following overseeding in September, water lightly but frequently, keeping the top ¼″ of soil moist at all times to improve germination. Then water on an as-needed basis to maintain the perennial ryegrass through the rest of the year.

### Weed Control

An aggressive fertility program encourages a thick turfgrass canopy and reduces the need for a preemergence program. This allows a strategy of spot-treating weeds with post-emergence herbicides on an as-needed basis. The primary weeds of concern tend to be the summer annuals crabgrass and goosegrass, and a few clumps of the perennial weed dallisgrass grass may need to be treated during June and July with MSMA. Where there is a persistent problem with purple nutsedge and perennial (green) kyllinga, these weeds can be treated during the summer months with halosulfuron (Manage™).

## 11.5c  Transitional Zone Maintenance

In establishing a maintenance program for fields in the Transitional Zone, adapt the program appropriate for the type of turfgrass being used on the field. Maintain warm season species according to the warm season program, and cool season species according to the typical northern program.

## 11.5d  Cool Season Maintenance

Cool season turfgrasses run through an annual cycle of strong active growth in the spring and early summer, with dormancy in the hottest part of the year, followed by an-

**Table 11.6. Cool season maintenance program**

## Sample Maintenance Schedule
(Cool Season)

| | | | |
|---|---|---|---|
| Field Name: | Canfield High School | Address: | 100 Cardinal Dr. |
| Type of Field: | Baseball Field | | Canfield, Ohio |

| | | | |
|---|---|---|---|
| Condition: | good | Compaction: | yes—dugout, home plate, pitchers |
| Type of Grass: | blue/rye | Drainage: | installed pipe drain system |
| Type of Mower: | 60″ rotary | Irrigation: | installed automatic system |
| Type of Soil: | clay/loam | Thatch: | ½″ infield, ¼″ outfield |

| | | | | |
|---|---|---|---|---|
| Soil Test: | | | Notes: | Chickweek near outfield fence |
| Year: | 1997 | Phosphorus: 95 | | Some clover-crabgrass |
| pH: | 6.8 | Potassium:  395 | | check sprinkler head elevations |

| Time of Year | Fertilization | Aeration | Topdress | Overseed | ⅓ Rule Mowing Ht | 1″ Week Watering | Weed Control |
|---|---|---|---|---|---|---|---|
| April | 18-24-12 ½ lb N 50% SRN | | | | 2″ | | |
| May | 24-5-11 ¾ lb N 50% SRN | 12″ solid-tine areation | | | 2″ | as needed | spot treatment |
| June | | slice entire field | | | 2¼″ | deeper less frequent | |
| July | 16-0-31 ½ lb N 25% SRN | | | | 2½″ | deeply | spot treatment |
| August | | | | blue/rye touchup spots | 2½″ | deeply | |
| September | 32-5-7 1 lb N 50% SRN | core and drag | for surface leveling | sod worn areas | 2¼″ | water new sod | spot or blanket |
| October | 20-5-10 ¾ lb N 50% SRN | core and drag | | | 2″ | as needed | |
| November | 1 lb N after last mowing | core and drag | | | 2″ | | |

other strong growing season in the late summer and fall. For the cool season turfgrass manager this cycle creates a substantial maintenance challenge, since baseball extends into the hottest part of the summer. Table 11.6 shows a sample maintenance program that can be tailored for any baseball or softball facility in the cool season zone.

## Fertilization

As a general rule, cool season fields should get less than 30% of their annual nitrogen needs in the spring, with the remainder applied in the fall. Restricting N application at this time of year helps to prevent excessive shoot growth, which often comes at the expense of needed root growth. The first fertilization of the spring is a good time to apply a starter fertilizer such as 18-24-12, since the actively growing turfgrass plants will benefit from the additional P and K at this point in the year. Also, excessive N in the spring could cause a severe leaf spot problem.

During the summer, one application of ½ pound N and a full pound of K helps preserve plant health during the heat of the summer, and enhances the turf's ability to resist disease.

Applying the largest portion of the N in the fall contributes to strong root growth, and helps the turf recover from the stresses placed upon it by the competitive season. The very best time to apply N is right after the last mowing of the season, when the grass is still green. During this period, shoot growth slows, but root growth continues. The fall application of nitrogen sustains active root growth and allows for the accumulation of carbohydrates (stored food reserves) in the roots and stems. This results in an early spring greenup, and a further enhancement of the turf's ability to withstand stresses.

## Aeration

Aerating frequently, and varying the equipment, helps to make the turf stronger. In May and June, it would be a good idea to use solid tine aeration unless the cores can be removed. Leaving cores on the field at this time of the year will cause erratic ball bounces. After the season is over, core aerate as much as once a month. It's a good idea to drag the cores to break them up. Cores left unbroken could cause a bumpy surface.

## Topdressing and Slit-Seeding

Consider topdressing after the games are over for the year. Topdressing provides the benefit of helping to level the surface. First, core aerate the field. Then topdress and use a level bar to get the surface as smooth as possible.

This would also be a good time to slit-seed if the turf is not as thick as desired, or to introduce a new species into the existing turf.

## Mowing

The perennial ryegrass starts growing first in the spring, so keep the mowing height at about 2″ to let sunlight reach the Kentucky bluegrass base. When the Kentucky bluegrass starts growing in May, try to maintain the mowing height at 2″. Then, raise the height ¼″ in June to help the turf prepare for the summer's heat. In July, the grass should be higher than at any other time of year.

Begin lowering the height when temperatures drop in September. The lower height will be beneficial when it's time to topdress and level. The level bar moves much more smoothly over shorter grass.

Keep mowing at 2″ until growth has completely stopped, remembering not to remove more than ⅓ of the grass blade each cutting. If the grass is left too long over the winter, the risk of snow mold increases. However, scalping in late fall can expose the crowns of the plant during the winter, weakening the grass.

## Watering

In the spring, apply water as needed to meet the 1″ per week requirement. Gradually reduce the frequency and increase the amount, so that by summer, more water is being ap-

Table 11.7. Recommended Warning Track Dimensions

| Distance from Home Plate to Backstop[a] | Recommended Warning Track Width | |
|---|---|---|
| | Foul Territory[b] | Outfield Fence |
| 25' | 8' | 12' |
| 30' | 10' | 12' |
| 40' | 12' | 15' |
| 50' | 15' | 15' |
| 60' | 15' | 15' |

[a]The distance from the foul lines to the dugouts are the same.
[b]Includes backstop fence and foul line fence.

plied at one time and the soil is given a chance to dry. Watering lightly in the summer encourages shallow roots (and may also increase the likelihood of disease), while heavy summertime watering fosters the deeper roots that make for strong turf.

If the fall brings dry weather, keep watering to help maintain turf growth, especially if overseeding has been performed. If areas have been sodded around the baselines or the outfield arc, don't forget to water those areas deeply until the new sod is rooted.

*Weed Control*
As a general rule, a spot application of postemergent weed control should be all that's needed. Apply the treatment when the weeds and the turf are actively growing, and when there will be no activity on the field for a few days. If a blanket treatment is needed, a better time would be in the fall when the games are over, but the turf is still actively growing.

## 11.6 WARNING TRACKS

As the phrase implies, warning tracks are meant to give players a warning when they are approaching a solid structure (usually a fence) or the out-of-bounds area when no fence

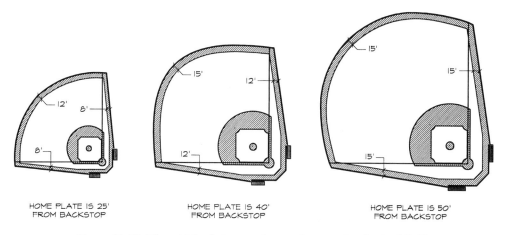

HOME PLATE IS 25'
FROM BACKSTOP

HOME PLATE IS 40'
FROM BACKSTOP

HOME PLATE IS 50'
FROM BACKSTOP

*Figure 11.32. The width of the warning track on variously sized fields.*

is used. Although many fields are constructed without warning tracks, the additional margin for safety provided by a warning track indicates the wisdom of constructing one wherever budgets permit.

### Warning Track Dimensions

There is no "standard size" warning track; rather, recommended warning track widths are based on such factors as the distance from home plate to the backstop, the distance from the foul line to the dugout, and the age and ability of players. Although warning track dimensions are not typically included in rule books, the distances from home plate to the backstop are listed. For instance, for softball fields, the rule book recommends a minimum of 25 feet and a maximum of 30 feet from home plate to the backstop. An 8 foot warning track, therefore, would tell a catcher that he or she had crossed two-thirds of the distance to the backstop. Table 11.7 shows recommended warning track widths for variously sized fields. (Also see Section 11.7b, Line and Boundary Dimensions, for field dimensions recommended by rule books.)

Figure 11.32 illustrates how appropriate warning track width is affected by field dimensions. Obviously, the field on the left has less space around the infield for a warning track than the one on the right. If the same warning track width was used on both fields, the one on the left would only have a few feet of grass in foul territory.

### Choosing Warning Track Material

Since the purpose of a warning track is meant to warn players that they are running out of room—basically a safety function—the material should be chosen with that purpose in mind. The best material is firm enough to prevent slipping and has a noticeably different texture than the turfgrass next to it, since the difference in texture is the characteristic that warns players they are approaching the end of the playing area.

Most warning tracks are constructed from a granular material with many different size aggregates that bind together when thoroughly settled. It would be next to impossible to specify a standard particle size distribution for warning tracks; most field managers use local suppliers to hold down costs, and every region has its own native materials. However, there is one recommendation that can be applied in every region: use a granular material with large aggregates that are less than $\frac{5}{16}''$, and enough small aggregates to cause the material to bind together. The best way to verify how well a particular material binds together is to visit a field where the material is already in use.

One popular material is a crushed red brick material with reddish sand and/or other materials to allow for a contrasting color warning track to enhance the field's appearance. Check with suppliers in the area to find out what similar materials are available in the local market.

### Warning Track Installation

The depth of warning track material is dependent on the budget, the type of underling soil, and whether or not a filter cloth is used between the soil and the warning track material itself. Usually three to four inches of material is sufficient to prevent weeds from being a serious problem. When a filter cloth is used, three inches is sufficient to cover the filter cloth to prevent it from surfacing. When final grade is achieved, the warning track should be level with the grass. To prevent weeds from coming through, preemergents can be applied before the warning track material is installed.

Installed subsurface drainage systems are usually not effective; since the material binds together, water drains through too slowly to allow drains to have much effect. It's more useful to make sure the final grade provides for positive surface drainage. (However, installed drains may be effective in helping to lower the water table.)

Warning tracks are sometimes installed with edging material, such as lumber, plastic, or aluminum normally used for shrub bed edging, between track and turf. This practice is not recommended, since these materials are next to impossible to keep flush with the finish grade.

For new construction, excavate the area to the desired depth and install the warning track material. Then level the area with a leveling bar or similar tractor attachment to the same level as the grass. (Remember to allow for settling, about ½″ for a 3″ deep track.) Finally, roll the area with a standard garden roller to firm up the surface.

If a warning track is being installed on an existing field, lay out the area with paint lines and sod cut the entire area. Till the area to the desired depth and remove the soil. Then, edge the grass area next to the warning track by hand, install the warning track material, level, and roll.

### Warning Track Renovation

With proper maintenance, the only renovation a warning track will need is adding more material after 3 to 5 years of use. The material may settle into the soil or the soil may migrate up into the warning track. Filter cloths help prevent this problem, but they also add to initial cost of the installation. One inch of material is usually sufficient to make the warning track look like new.

### Warning Track Maintenance

Warning tracks look best when they are edged regularly to provide a distinct contrast between the grass and the warning track. Among the tools used to edge the track are powered sidewalk edgers, string trimmers, and hand edgers. Edging should be performed at least twice a year.

The best approach to weeding warning tracks is to use three methods; preemergent herbicides, postemergent herbicides, and mechanical weeding. The best strategy for use of preemergents is to use one that is labeled for the particular weeds that are observed during the growing season. Prior to the next growing season, apply a preemergent that is labeled for those weeds. A nonselective herbicide, such as Roundup™, can be used to control weeds that have already emerged. Mechanical weeding with a hoe or by hand takes care of any random weeds that escape chemical controls.

Dragging helps to keep the warning track look like new, and should be performed at least once a month during the season. Use a nail drag to loosen the surface and then a mat drag for final smoothing. If the surface gets too hard for a nail drag to penetrate, use a pulverizer, roller, and mat drag.

## 11.7   RULES AND REGULATIONS

### 11.7a  Common Points of Confusion

Figure 11.32 illustrates some details of field layout that are frequently rendered incorrectly, either because the rule book is misinterpreted, or because the rules are observed by convention but remain unwritten.

In taking measurements from home plate, the *white* point on the plate, not the black point, is the one that is used. Foul lines pass through the outside edge of first and third base and continue to the *outside* of the foul poles, which are themselves in fair territory.

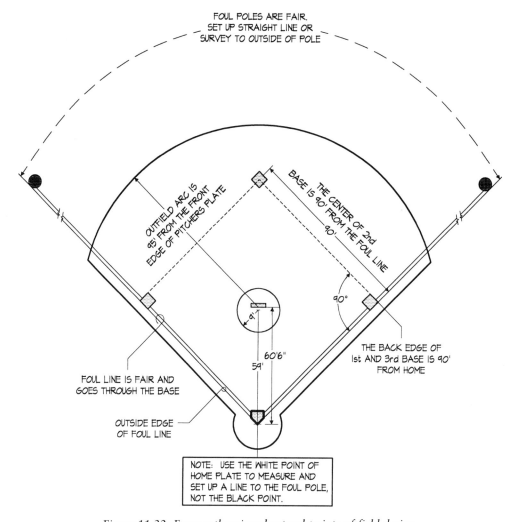

Figure 11.32. Frequently misunderstood points of field design

The *back edge* of first and third base are 90 feet from home plate, but the *center* of second base is 90 feet from the foul lines. The front of the pitcher's plate is 60 feet, 6 inches from the white point on home plate, and the center of second base is 127 feet, 3⅜" from the white point of home (Table 11.8).

The circled edge of the skinned area is 95 feet from the front edge of the pitcher's plate. In laying out a softball field, the arc of the infield does not always have its center at the pitcher's plate. Instead, it is sometimes centered on a point several feet behind the pitcher's plate. In designing a softball field, see Table 11.9 or consult the rule book for the appropriate governing or sanctioning body to determine the exact center point for the infield arc.

## 11.7b  Line and Boundary Dimensions
Tables 11.8 and 11.9 show dimensions for the most common fields.

Table 11.8. Baseball Dimensions

| Type of Field | | Required | | | Recommended | | | |
|---|---|---|---|---|---|---|---|---|
| | | Base Lines | Pitching Distance | Pitching Height | Backstop from HP[b] | Foul Lines | Center Field | Infield Arc from PP |
| **Offical Baseball Rules** | | 90' | 60½' | 10" | 60' | 325' | 400' | 95' |
| **College—NCAA Rules** | | 90' | 60½' | 10" | 60' | 330' | 400' | 95' |
| **High School—NFSHSA Rules** | | 90' | 60½' | 10" | 60' | 300' min | 350' min | 95' |
| **Pony Baseball, Inc.** | | | | | | | | |
| Shetland | 5 & 6 | 50' | 40'[a] | n/a | 20'[a] | 125'[a] | 125'[a] | 40'[a] |
| Pinto | 7 & 8 | 50' | 40'[a] | n/a | 25'[a] | 150'[a] | 150'[a] | 40'[a] |
| Mustang | 9 & 10 | 60' | 44' | 6"[a] | 25'[a] | 180'[a] | 200'[a] | 50'[a] |
| Bronco | 11 & 12 | 70' | 48' | 6" | 30' | 225' | 275' | 70'[a] |
| Pony | 13 & 14 | 80' | 54' | 8" | 40' | 265' | 315' | 80'[a] |
| Colt | 15 & 16 | 90' | 60½' | 10" | 50' | 300' | 350' | 95'[a] |
| Palomino | 17 & 18 | 90' | 60½' | 10" | 50' | 300' | 350' | 95'[a] |
| **Babe Ruth Baseball, Inc.** | | | | | | | | |
| Bambino Divison | 5 to 12 | 60' | 46' | 6" | 25'[a] | 200' min | 200' min | 50' |
| Babe Ruth League | 13 to 15 | 90' | 60½' | 10" | 60' | 250' min | 250' min | 95' |
| 16–18 League | 16 to 18 | 90' | 60½' | 10" | 60' | 300'[a] | 350'[a] | 95' |
| **Little League Baseball, Inc.** | 9 to 12 | 60' | 46' | 6" | 25' min | 205' | 215' | 50' |

[a]Authors' recommendation—not in rule book.
[b]The distance from the foul lines to the dugouts are the same.
HP = Home Plate. PP = Pitchers Plate.

**Table 11.9. Softball Dimensions**

| Type of Field | | Required | | Recommended | | |
|---|---|---|---|---|---|---|
| | | Base Lines | Pitching Distance | Home Run Fence Min. | Max. | Infield Arc from 46' PP |
| **College - NCAA Rules** | | 60' | 43' | 190' foul 200' center | 225' | 60' from 43' PP |
| **High School - NFSHSA Rules** | | | | | | |
| Fast Pitch w/ 12" ball | | | | | | |
| Female | | 60' | 40' | 185' | 235' | 60' |
| Male | | 60' | 46' | 185' | 235' | 60' |
| Slow Pitch | | | | | | |
| Female w/ 12" ball | | 60' | 46' | 250' | 275' | 60' |
| Female w/ 11" ball | | 65' | 50' | 250' | 275' | 65'a |
| Male w/12" ball | | 65' | 46' | 275' | 300' | 65'a |
| **Amateur Softball Assoc.** | | | | | | |
| All (Fast & Slow Pitch) | 10-under | 55' | 35' | 150' | 175' | 55' |
| Fast Pitch | | | | | | |
| Girls | 12-under | 60' | 35' | 175' | 200' | 60' |
| Boys | 12-under | 60' | 40' | 175' | 200' | 60' |
| Girls | 14-under | 60' | 40' | 175' | 200' | 60' |
| Boys | 14-under | 60' | 46' | 175' | 200' | 60' |
| Girls | 15 to 19 | 60' | 40' | 200' | 225' | 60' |
| Boys | 15 to 19 | 60' | 46' | 200' | 225' | 60' |
| Women | Adult | 60' | 40' | 200' | 225' | 60' |
| Men | Adult | 60' | 46' | 225' | 250' | 60' |
| Slow Pitch | | | | | | |
| Girls & Boys | 12-under | 60' | 40' | 175' | 200' | 60' |
| Girls | 13 to 19 | 65' | 46' | 225' | 250' | 65' |
| Boys | 13 & 14 | 65' | 46' | 250' | 275' | 65' |
| Boys | 15 to 19 | 65' | 46' | 275' | 300' | 65' |
| Women | Adult | 65' | 46' | 250' | 250' | 65' |
| Men | Adult | 65' | 46' | 275' | 300' | 65' |
| Slow Pitch w/ 16" ball | | | | | | |
| Women | Adult | 55' | 38' | 200' | 200' | 55' |
| Men | Adult | 55' | 38' | 250' | 250' | 55' |

aAuthors' recommendation—not in rule book.

PP = Pitchers' Plate

Notes:

1. Pitcher's plate is level with home plate.
2. The distance from home plate to the backstop is a minimum of 25' and a maximum of 30'. The distance from the foul lines to the dugouts are the same.
3. A skinned infield is recommended and for some tournament play it's a requirement.

## 11.7c Governing and Sanctioning Bodies

Among the most important governing bodies for North American baseball and softball are the following:

Official Baseball Rules are published and distributed by:
**Sporting News**
P.O. Box 11229
Des Moines, Iowa   50340
(800) 825-8508

These rules are followed by Professional Baseball, National Baseball Congress, Stan Musial, American Legion, Connie Mack, Babe Ruth, Mickey Mantle, Sandy Koufax, and others. For fields used for competition sanctioned by these organizations, contact the sanctioning body for up-to-date rules.

*College Baseball and Softball:*
The National Collegiate Athletic Association
6201 College Boulevard
Overland Park, Kansas   66211
(913) 339-1906

*High School Baseball and Softball:*
National Federation of State High School Associations
11724 Plaza Circle, Box 20626
Kansas City, Missouri   64195
(816) 464-5400

*Pony League Baseball:*
Pony Baseball, Inc.
P.O. Box 225
Washington, Pennsylvania   15301-0225
(412) 225-1060

*Babe Ruth Baseball:*
Babe Ruth League, Inc.
1770 Brunswick Pike, P.O. Box 5000
Trenton, New Jersey   08638
(609) 695-1434

*Little League Baseball:*
Little League Baseball, Inc.
P.O. Box 3485
Williamsport, Pennsylvania   17701
(717) 326-1921

*Softball:*
Amateur Softball Association of America
2801 North East 50th Street
Oklahoma City, Oklahoma   73111
(405) 424-5266

# Chapter 12

# *Football and Rugby Fields*

## 12.1 INTRODUCTION

While North American football fields have much in common with the fields used for soccer, field hockey, and lacrosse, the interaction between the players and turf in football is substantially different than in any of those sports, and it is probably true that only rugby subjects the turf to similar stresses.

First of all, while sports like soccer and lacrosse require turf that will allow for the smooth and consistent passage of a ball across the surface of the ground, football is different. In football, the turf represents only a platform for the movement of human bodies; the rolling of a ball across the turf is a rare event—and a generally undesirable one. (Of course, the turf also plays another role in football: that of a landing surface for falling bodies.)

Two other aspects of the sports of football and its cousin, rugby, merit some consideration when managing a turf surface on which games can be played. Although speed is certainly a cherished trait for football and rugby players, so is sheer bulk. Along the line of scrimmage, huge men and boys exert enormous forces on each other—and on the turf beneath them. Their cleats rip and tear at the grass as they struggle for advantage. And since these big players nearly always line up in the middle third of the field, that portion of the turf is reduced to bare dirt by season's end in all but the most carefully—maintained facilities.

Finally, the traditional season for football runs from the so-called "dog days" of summer into the month of November. For some teams, including many colleges and universities, the most important games of the season, including matchups against traditional arch-rivals, take place after the growing season has ended in much of the country.

All things considered, probably only the odd combination of turf and skinned surfaces in baseball presents as much of a sports turf management challenge as does a football field.

Before we consider the football field as a venue for competition, it's worth taking a moment to raise one related point. These fields are often used as a rehearsal site for a school's marching band, which can place as much stress on the turf as the football team itself. Some school bands have 300 or more members, and this amount of traffic can lead to substantial over-compaction of the soil and mechanical stress on the turfgrass. Wherever possible, the field manager should urge that a separate field be provided for marching band rehearsals.

## 12.2   DESIGN

### 12.2a   Survey and Layout

The basic design process for a football field is obviously simpler than that encountered in baseball; the field is a rectangle, either 120 yards long (in the United States), or 160 yards long (in Canada). Field widths vary somewhat, but the official size for American high school, college, and professional football is 160 feet, and Canadian fields are 195 feet (65 yards) wide. In thinly-populated areas of the West and Southwest, many high schools play six and eight-man football, with the standard field size of 100 yards long (80 yard playing area plus two 10-yard end zones) and 40 yards wide.

The majority of football fields are laid out along a north-south axis, and crowned longitudinally down the center of the field, to promote surface drainage toward the sidelines and away from the part of the field subject to the greatest mechanical stresses. However, there are many fields in use which are flat and sloped to one side so that the entire playing field drains in a single direction. If the topography of the area lends itself better to a flat field sloped in one direction, such a field can be perfectly serviceable. A problem with this type of field is that someone may get the idea of "increasing the crown" on a field to improve drainage, not realizing that there is no crown there in the first place. Under these circumstances, raising the center of the field has the same effect as building a dam down the middle of the field. By restricting the flow of water, crowning an uncrowned field can turn the uphill half of the playing surface into a swamp.

### 12.2b   Design Criteria for New Construction

The degree of slope should be from 1% to 1.75%. Fields sloped at the low end of this range may also need installed drain systems to speed up the movement of water.

Another equally basic question which must be addressed before designing a football field is the way it will be used. Because of the stresses placed on the turf by football competition, nearly all teams maintain separate practice and game (or "stadium") fields. Game fields must be designed to be durable enough to support game competition (usually  by one to three teams playing five or six games a season), plus a few practices held on the field to allow the team to become accustomed to the surroundings. Game fields are also meant to be as aesthetically pleasing as possible, since football is the leading outdoor spectator sport at most high schools, colleges, and universities.

Practice fields, on the other hand, are designed to be safe, durable, and economical to maintain. Under such circumstances, flat sloped designs may frequently prove to be a better choice than crowned facilities, and the natural slope is normally more economical than a crowned field with catch basins or other drainage structures in place. As with a game field, the degree of slope should be between 1% and 1.75%.

Ideally, of course, practice fields should be laid out and lined on the same dimensions as a game field, to allow players and coaches the advantage of practicing under the most realistic possible conditions.

#### *Safety Issues*

The violent, high-speed collisions characteristic of adult football raise several important safety concerns. First of all, because of the popularity of the sport with spectators, many fields have traditionally been built with some form of barrier between the playing area and the grandstands. If such barriers are necessary, they should be placed well back from the sidelines, at least 20 to 25 feet away. Even at that distance, athletes running across the sidelines at top speed on wet turf may be unable to stop before reaching the barrier, so player safety should be a major concern in barrier design.

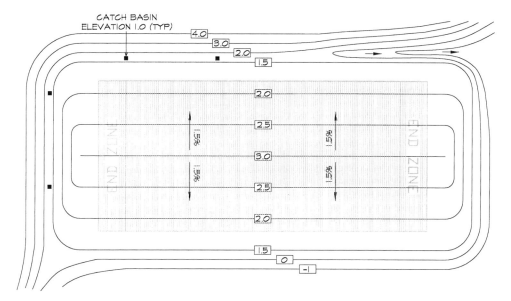

*Figure 12.1. Crowned field with level sidelines—elevations noted in feet.*

Player momentum can also be a concern at the end of the field, commonly referred to as the "back of the end zone." Particularly on passing plays, a receiver may be moving at top speed when he crosses out of the field of play, so allowance must be made for stopping room in that direction.

## 12.2c  Field Designs with Preferred Contours

Generally, field designs for surface drainage fall into one of two categories: a *crowned field* with level sidelines (see Figure 12.1), or a flat field sloped *side to side* (see Figure 12.2).

(Flat and level fields, which are designed to drain internally, are discussed in Chapter 24, Sand and Sand-based Fields.)

Probably the most common type of field is a *crowned* field with level sidelines. While this is a relatively easy design to build, and one which drains fairly efficiently away from the center third of the playing area, it has a couple of limitations. First of all, the area where the crowned field meets the level sideline can turn into a wet spot. That creates a hazardous area in exactly the spot where players may be trying to execute maneuvers that require good footing—like catching passes while keeping feet inbounds, or stopping quickly to avoid contact with players and coaches.

The second problem with the level sidelines arises from the increasing popularity of soccer as a high school and college sport. Many schools use one game field, and extend the width of the football field for soccer. Unless there is consistent slope through the sideline area—which tends to get badly torn up by foot traffic at the football field bench area—the outer edges of the soccer field can become a quagmire (Figure 12.3).

Figure 12.1 shows a contour plan for a crowned football field. (Note that this plan shows a field that is built by cutting at the top of the diagram and filling at the bottom, as when a field is built on terrain that originally sloped top-to-bottom. This design shows a swale at the top draining to right, with catch basins at the left and upper left.

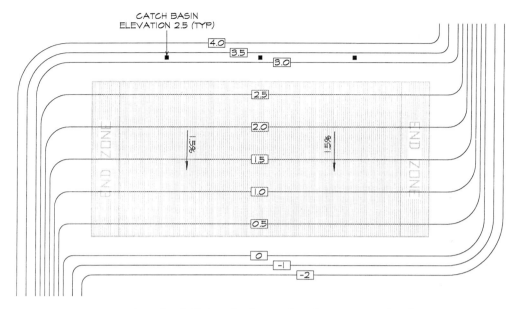

*Figure 12.2. Flat field sloped side-to-side—elevations noted in feet.*

The field could be built with either swales or catch basins around the entire upper side of the field.)

For a contour plan designed for a football field surrounded by a track, see Chapter 16, Figure 16.1.

*Side-to-side* sloped fields tend to be built that way because of the demands placed on the field by the surrounding terrain. If it's impractical or too costly to build a crowned facility, the flat, sloped design can work very well. When this design is chosen, internal drainage should be installed, at least in the lower half of the field to prevent that lower portion of the field from becoming too wet.

Figure 12.2 shows a contour plan for a side-to-side sloped field. Like Figure 12.1, this plan assumes original terrain sloping from top to bottom of the drawing. (Note the use of catch basins outside the upper edge of the field to prevent runoff entering the field of play.)

Fields that are sloped end-to-end should be avoided, for much the same reason. The lower end of the field almost invariably becomes muddy as the water flows across the field to the lower end. Furthermore, the end-to-end slope tends to create the impression in players that they are running uphill in one direction and downward in the other.

### 12.2d  Multiple Field Layouts

When laying out a complex that will have more than one football field, it's wise to leave 60 to 80 feet between fields that are laid out side-by-side, and 30 to 40 feet between fields laid out end-to-end. If there are grandstands between the fields, the distance should obviously be increased by the width of the grandstand structures.

Each field should be treated as an individual drainage unit, and should not be expected to perform acceptably with water running across it from adjacent fields. In laying out such fields, make sure to leave enough room outside the playing areas for cuts and fills, catch basins and swales.

*Figure 12.3. Fields that are used for soccer as well as football frequently have badly compacted areas where the football team stands outside the football field of play. These areas are often on the soccer field of play, and can be muddy and uneven, negatively affecting soccer ball response. Maintaining a consistent slope all the way to the soccer sidelines can minimize this problem.*

## 12.2e  Turfgrass Selection

Experience has shown that for most football fields in the **warm season zone,** bermudagrass is the turfgrass of choice. Bermudagrass can provide a fast, dependable surface, and tolerates close mowing favored by fast teams.

In the **transitional zone,** there is no such thing as a "best" turf choice for a football field. Bermudagrass, tall fescue, and Kentucky bluegrass can all be used, but each has obvious limitations.

The primary problems with bermudagrass are its winter dormancy period and the potential for winter-kill. If the turf is to be used for football only, then a cold-tolerant cultivar of bermudagrass can be used (see Chapter 1 for discussion of bermudagrass cultivars.) A bermudagrass field should maintain acceptable color in most parts of the transition zone at least through mid-October, and in some years there will be acceptable color into November. Field color can be further maintained through the use of turf paint or overseeding.

If the field is not overseeded, this will result in playing up to ⅓ of the schedule on dormant bermudagrass. The playing quality of dormant bermudagrass is fine, as long as the field has not received excessive wear prior to the onset of dormancy. To promote winter hardiness, mowing height should be raised to at least 1½″ prior to the first killing frost.

Bermudagrass fields overseeded with perennial ryegrass will maintain a green, actively growing  playing surface throughout the season. To overseed a bermudagrass field in the transition zone, apply seed in early to mid-September, preferably during a break in the schedule when the field is not going to be used because of an off-week. If there is no off-week on the field, seed right after a game and irrigate lightly and frequently to encourage rapid germination. Keep players off the field during germination (if possible), and be prepared to apply more seed the following week, particularly in the middle of the field. (Obviously, successful overseeding of transition zone bermudagrass fields requires special attention and a certain amount of good fortune regarding weather and field use.) For these reasons, overseeding is of questionable value in many situations, but if a football field will be used for spring soccer, overseeding might be the only way to have turf, rather than mud, to play on.

Tall fescue is also a popular choice for transitional zone fields, particularly in the northern sections of this region. The primary limitations of tall fescue are its bunch-type growth habit and the fact that it must be mowed at a height of at least 2″. Tall fescue has a deep root system that allows it to come through periods of moisture stress during the summer months, but it requires supplemental irrigation to achieve its highest quality for the early season games. Tall fescue has acceptable wear tolerance, but once it is damaged it has virtually no recuperative potential and requires reseeding.

Kentucky bluegrass can also be used in the northern areas of the transitional zone. The biggest limitation of Kentucky bluegrass is its poor performance during the summer months. Supplemental irrigation is essential to maintain acceptable bluegrass turf for the early part of the football season. Kentucky bluegrass tolerates cutting heights as low as 1″, but normally needs to be maintained closer to 2″ in this area. The rhizomatous growth habit of Kentucky bluegrass results in good recuperative potential during the fall months, but reseeding will likely be needed each fall.

For all the difficulties in maintaining game fields in the transition zone, the problems are even greater for practice fields. The limitations of turfgrasses for the region and the great stress placed on practice fields result in even less likelihood of high turf density. Practices should be moved around the field, and the rotating use of a second practice field can spell the difference between practicing on grass or mud.

Maintain an aggressive N fertility program (one pound of N per 1,000 square feet per month) on bermudagrass practice fields up to the point of killing frost. Even so, heavy practice field use during bermudagrass dormancy can result in fields that are more mud than grass by the end of the season. Overseeding with perennial ryegrass can help, but it's hard to get the ryegrass established on a heavily-used field. Unless a second practice field is available to rotate practice onto during overseeding establishment, it is unlikely a dense stand of perennial ryegrass will ever be attained.

For cool season grasses like fescue and bluegrass, supplemental irrigation during the late summer and early fall is necessary to maintain adequate growth and development. Begin N applications in late August and continue them through the football season as long as temperatures are suitable for turfgrass growth to encourage turf recuperation and increase wear tolerance. Again, an additional field to use for some practices can make a big difference.

In the **cool season zone**, Kentucky bluegrass is the preferred choice for nearly all football fields. The aggressive character of bluegrass allows the turf to recuperate strongly after stresses, and the thick thatch layer provides valuable mechanical protection for both the field and the players. From the field standpoint, bluegrass thatch prevents excessive tearing at the root structure. For the players, the thick thatch cushions falls better than other turfgrasses. In rainy weather, bluegrass thatch keeps the players up out of the mud, and allows competition to go on in relative safety.

Some of the more aggressive (and therefore superior) varieties of bluegrass for football fields include Princeton-104, A-34, Touchdown, and Blacksburg.

In any part of the country, seeded fields should be allowed to establish themselves before being used for practice of football games. Despite its superior performance, bluegrass takes a year to mature. A good policy is to seed a field in the spring of the year for use in the fall of the following year. If this is not possible, it's important to allow at least one full year for the turf to establish itself before using the field.

Where budgets allow, of course, sodding is the best method of turfgrass installation in all parts of the country. Standard-cut sod (with ½" of soil), can be used six to eight weeks after installation; thick-cut sod (with 1½" or more of soil) can be used within a week, as long as the thickness of the product is uniform and the seams are tight. When choosing sod, specify a mature product that is held together by its own thatch layer, instead of by netting. Tall fescue sod usually needs netting to hold it together because tall fescue varieties don't produce lateral stems or a thatch layer substantial enough to hold the sod together on its own. When using tall fescue, look for the oldest, best established sod available, to ensure that the netting will be secured well into the soil.

Some sports turf managers in the northern zone routinely seed ryegrass into a 100% bluegrass turf before and during the football season. This practice is designed to reduce mechanical stresses on the bluegrass plants, and to take advantage of the rapid establishment rate of the ryegrass.

## 12.2f   Installed Irrigation Systems

When designing an irrigation system for a football field, three important considerations must be kept in mind: The *placement* of sprinkler heads, the *size* of the exposed surface of the head, and the *durability* of the exposed components.

*Placement* of the heads should take into consideration the portions of the field where the largest number of players line up. Many designs show a five row system for football fields, with a row of heads directly down the center of the field. This design is not recommended unless the facility has sufficient maintenance resources to allow inspection of the center row of heads after every game. Figure 12.4 shows a football field with a four row irrigation system, which is a better choice for fields with a limited maintenance staff. Since the area between the hash marks gets the most player traffic, the four-row design places the heads away from the heaviest foot traffic, which can damage them and create a safety hazard.

This design requires water pressure of 75 PSI at field edge and yields a pressure of 60 PSI at the base of the sprinkler heads. Average precipitation rate for this system will be .44 inches/hour for full circle heads, .88 inches/hour for half-circle heads, and 1.76 inches/hour for quarter circle heads. Running time for 1" watering will be 2 hours 16 minutes for full circle heads, one hour 8 minutes for half-circle heads, and 34 minutes for quarter circle heads.

Many fields, especially in the North, have been built with two-row systems, but it should be noted that these systems will almost always require additional hand-watering at the edge of the field during dry weather. Two-row systems also have the additional drawback of watering unevenly, with the center of the field irrigated more heavily than the sides. Where two-row systems are used, the turf should also be mowed no shorter than 2" to protect the turfgrass from excessive drying.

Figure 12.4 shows a four-row system, which the authors recommend to provide superior irrigation on the entire field anywhere in the country.

The *size* of the exposed surface of the heads is also an important consideration, and smaller is obviously better. With good grass cover around the head, players should be able to step right on the sprinkler head without noticing a difference in traction.

In terms of *durability*, the heads should be designed to withstand foot traffic, and

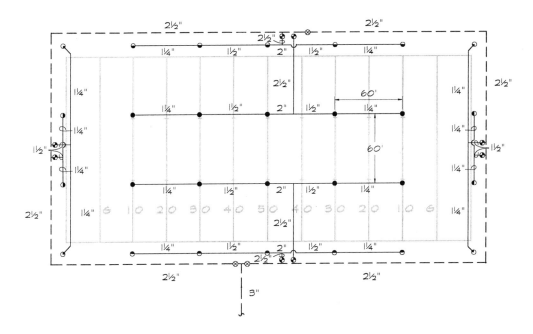

IRRIGATION LEGEND

| DESCRIPTION | PSI | GPM | RADIUS | ARC | UNITS |
|---|---|---|---|---|---|
| ● HUNTER I-40-36S-42 FULL CIRCLE | 60 | 15.5 | 59 FT. | 360° | 10 |
| ◒ HUNTER I-40-ADS-43 PART CIRCLE | 60 | 15.5 | 59 FT. | 180° | 14 |
| ◔ HUNTER I-40-ADS-43 PART CIRCLE | 60 | 15.5 | 59 FT. | 90° | 4 |
| ⊛ 2" HUNTER ICV 201G REMOTE CONTROL VALVE (SIDELINES) | | | | | 4 |
| ⊛ 1½" HUNTER ICV 151G REMOTE CONTROL VALVE (END LINES) | | | | | 4 |
| ⊗ 2½" GATE VALVE FOR MAINLINE ISOLATION | | | | | 3 |

—— NON-PRESSURE PIPE (PVC CLASS 160 RECOMMENDED)

– – PRESSURE PIPE (PVC CLASS 200 RECOMMENDED)

NOTES:
THE FOUR HEADS IN OPPOSITE END ZONES ARE ON ONE STATION
THE FOUR 90° CORNER HEADS ARE ON ONE STATION

NOT SHOWN:
BACKFLOW PREVENTION DEVICE
(AS REQUIRED PER CODE AND/OR ORDINANCE - AND FOR SAFETY)                1

HUNTER ICC IRRIGATION CONTROLLER (8 STATIONS)
LOCATION AS NEEDED                                                       1

DESIGN PROVIDED BY HUNTER INDUSTRIES

*Figure 12.4. Four row football field irrigation system.*

should be rated by the manufacturer as suitable for football. Heads used for football should always have a rubber cover.

Inspect the heads regularly (and especially those near the middle of the field) to check for damage and make sure they are seated properly.

## 12.2g  Installed Drain Systems and Catch Basins

Most turf managers would probably agree that improved drainage would contribute more to the quality of their fields than any other factor. More than any other type of sports field, a heavily used football field with no installed drain system can quickly turn into a "mud bowl" during rainy weather.

Surface drainage is seldom adequate to quickly shed heavy rains. A field with a 1.5% crown takes four hours to move water from the center of the field across the sidelines. So, a driving rainstorm results in standing water—even on the crown itself.

### Pipe Drains

The traditional type of drainage system for a football field is the pipe drain. In the past, this type of system was constructed of foot-long sections of clay tile pipe, either covered with felt paper or packed with coarse sand to prevent the system from filling up with silt and clay. The trenches in which the pipe drains are laid (usually 2 to 3 feet deep) are then filled in with gravel to a level about 6″ beneath the surface.

Pipe drain systems with the greatest longevity seem to be the ones with a heavy layer of sand (typically 12″ to 18″) around the sides and top of the pipe. However, pipe drain systems have some inherent drawbacks that persuade the authors that they are not the ideal type for sports fields.

As mentioned in Chapter 8, unless they are filled to the surface with sand or gravel, pipe drain systems remove water from the subsoil at a slow, consistent rate, and may have little effect in draining the topsoil of a field. Pipe drains also have the disadvantage that soil above the gravel can become saturated before water begins to percolate into the gravel, creating a false (or "perched") water table on top of the subsoil. Pipe drains also can dry out the soil immediately above the drain pipes in drought conditions. Because of the width of pipe drain trenches, filling them to the surface with sand would help drain the topsoil, but would adversely impact turf growth and traction.

Pipe drain systems installed today make use of more modern and more economical types of thermoplastic pipe, but work in about the same way (see Figure 12.5, traditional [pipe drain] football field drainage system.)

In planning and installing these drainage systems, two main problems need to be avoided: a heavily compacted sub-base that prevents water from getting to the system, and the destruction of the pipe by crushing when heavy equipment is being moved across the surface.

Although these problems are created by the excavating contractor, they most frequently result from faulty specifications provided by the field designer. For example, many plans and specifications call for a "compacted sub-base." To the excavator, this means that a sheepsfoot roller or vibrating roller should be used. When this sort of equipment is used, the sub-base becomes impervious to water, which passes through the topsoil but stops at the sub-base. The uncompacted topsoil will become fully saturated during a heavy rain, because the sub-base is so compacted there's nowhere for the water to go.

Actually, the solution to this problem is very simple. Adding the instructions, "Avoid overcompaction of the sub-base" and "scarify sub-base before installing topsoil" will alert the excavator to the drainage dynamics at work in the field system, and prevent nearly all of these problems.

### Strip Drains

Modern technology is also providing some new solutions to the challenge of properly draining football fields. One of these new solutions is called strip drains. These are cloth-wrapped plastic or fiber structures about an inch wide and 4″ to 6″ deep. Strip drains are installed in the top 12″ of the soil and require only a 3″ to 4″ wide trench. The strip drain is placed in the bottom of the trench and extends halfway to the surface. The trench is then filled with sand right up to surface level.

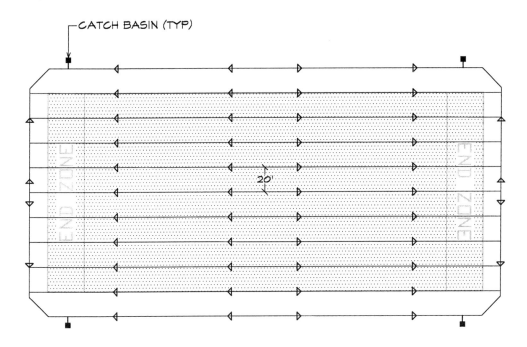

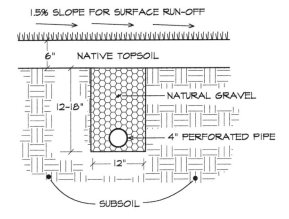

*Figure 12.5. Traditional [pipe drain] football field drainage system.*

Strip drains intercept and remove some of the surface water as it moves across the field. The best designs have strip drains at a 45 degree angle to the direction of the surface runoff. However, in order for strip drains to work as they are meant to, it's essential that the topsoil not be overcompacted. (And, of course, the system works better if the sub-base is not overcompacted either.)

An additional advantage of strip drain systems that are installed at a 45 degree angle to surface runoff is that the drains can be laid out at a consistent one-foot depth from the field surface. Pipe drains (as illustrated in Figure-12.5, where the pipe drain is installed along the long axis of the field that is level) must be laid out with a transit to ensure consistent downward slope, and will vary in depth from the field surface.

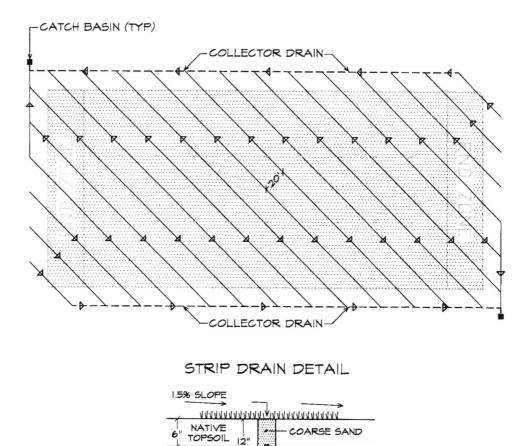

*Figure 12.6. A crowned football field strip drain system.*

(Figure 12.6 shows a design for a crowned football field drainage system using strip drains. Figure 12.7 shows a strip drain system for a side-to-side sloped football field. Note that the only difference in the two designs is the location of collector drains.)

### Catch basins

Catch basins on the sidelines are another common drainage structure used for football fields. At least 20 feet of sideline clearance should be allowed when using catch basins, to avoid dangerous falls. For the majority of fields, four catch basins are sufficient to assist prompt drainage—one outside the end zone sideline at each corner of the field. Catch basins are the "junction boxes" of many installed drain systems, and generally are equally valuable in connecting laterals and drain lines as they are in removing surface water.

One common drainage system design (often used in a crowned field with level sidelines) uses a number of catch basins around the field, with swales from basin-to-basin to assist surface runoff. This approach has two drawbacks: it creates an awkward appearance of hills and valleys along the field edge, and the swales tend to stay wet for ex-

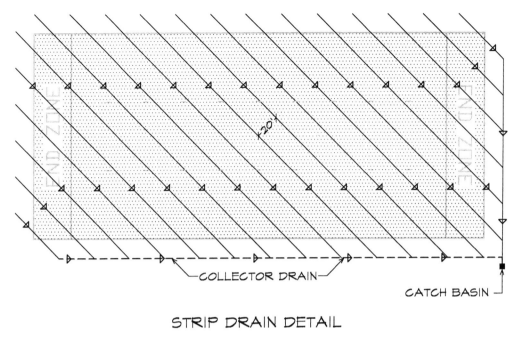

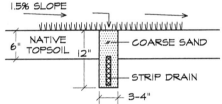

*Figure 12.7. A side-to-side sloped football field strip drain system.*

tended periods during wet conditions. When these two problems occur together the results can be a mess—muddy spots on the sideline which standing players then turn into mudholes.

When drainage from level sidelines is a concern, a good option combines both pipe drains and strip drains to avoid creating swales. For instance, lay out a trench 15″ deep, sloping away from the 50-yard line, parallel to and 20 feet outside the sidelines, running to catch basins outside the end zones. Lay a ½″ bed of pea gravel in the trench, then a 4″ perforated pipe. Then fill pea gravel to within 6″ of the surface, top with coarse sand and seed or install washed sod. The best sand has less than 5% passing a 100-sieve screen.

(A variation on this type of system can be found in Chapter 16, Track and Field Facilities [Figure 16.4]. This variation, called a "Trackside Sand Drain," works very well for the many fields that are crowned with level sidelines, and with a 400-meter running track around them. If the sand drain is placed next to the track, it will serve as an open catch basin draining water away from both field and track, and eliminating the annoying swales to catch basins.)

## 12.3   CONSTRUCTION AND RECONSTRUCTION

### Construction

Having surveyed the field carefully, and with grading plan in hand, construction begins. It's important to have an even grade from contour line to contour line, so grade stakes and spot elevation checks are vital. (Another option, of course, is to use laser grading.) Otherwise, the field will end up with puddles.

Since overcompacting the sub-base inhibits internal drainage, avoid any road-building equipment (see 12.2g, Installed Drain Systems). Bulldozer tracks and normal rainfall usually provide all the compaction a field needs. It's even a good idea to keep dozers and other heavy equipment off the field any time it's wet.

There are several other construction techniques that will help prevent drainage problems later. Grade the subsoil to match the final grade. Before applying topsoil, scarify or otherwise loosen the subsoil. Then, as soil is brought in to raise the grade, keep scarifying throughout the  process. This practice eliminates the layering that can restrict the movement of water and roots deep into the soil profile.

On a project that calls for lowering the grade, it's important to apply this same principle. Loosen the subsoil before spreading any topsoil, so the layers are intermixed.

### Reconstruction

In approaching the reconstruction of a football field, begin by surveying and setting proposed elevations. Then remove the existing sod and begin regrading. When filling low spots, scarify first to avoid layering. When making cuts, check to ensure that the excavated areas end up with as much topsoil as the fills. Don't leave some spots with 2″ of growing medium and other spots with 10″. If necessary, don't be afraid to remove all the topsoil, adjust the subsoil, and replace the topsoil.

When adding soil, match soil character with the existing soil at the site. When the final grade is achieved, it's a good time to add conditioners like calcined diatomaceous earth additives. Mix these products thoroughly into the soil.

Some fields have been built with sand added to the soil, but that's a temptation that should be resisted—unless the plan is to have 65 to 75% total sand content. Adding too little sand to a clay-based topsoil can actually inhibit field performance. Remember, if the field ends up with 50% total sand content, that is close to the formula for making clay bricks. The field could end up with soil so tight that roots and water can't penetrate.

If it seems like a great deal of attention is being given to the problem of overcompaction, that's because the result can be a maintenance nightmare that's next to impossible to fix. For example, if the process makes fills of three feet and compacts it in 6″ layers, the soil will remain compacted forever—or at least until someone gives up on the field and sells it for pasture. The deepest aeration the field is likely to get would be 12″, so two-thirds of the fill is like rock. Every time the field gets 1″ or more of rain, the loosened soil will quickly reach saturation and become a mud hole. So watch out for overcompaction.

## 12.4   RENOVATION

Renovating a football field is the process of repairing the damage of a competitive season, and assisting the recuperation process to prepare it for the next season. Typical renovation steps include aggressive aeration, filling in low spots, and planting by seeding,

*Figure 12.8. Topdressing the field provides a good opportunity to level the turf, using a level bar.*

sprigging, plugging, or sodding. Since the middle third of a field and the bench areas get the most abuse during the season, renovation efforts are normally concentrated there.

In the **North**, it's possible to perform overseeding in the late fall, provided heavy precipitation doesn't keep equipment off the field. Seeding at this time of year is considered "dormant seeding," since seed will not germinate until the weather breaks in the spring (see section 1.6c for more on dormant seeding). The advantage of seeding in the fall as opposed to the spring is that wet springtime conditions can delay planting, and cause the new growth to miss two or three weeks of prime growing conditions. If the field is to be in top condition by the start of the season, it needs every week of establishment time it can get—and that's particularly true of practice fields, which see heavy traffic for weeks before the first game. (In the South and the transitional zone, however, bermudagrass seeding should wait until the spring, because fall planting can lead to subsequent winter kill in the seedling bermudagrass.)

On northern fields, if worn areas have at least 75% turf cover and a good stand of bluegrass, seed 100% Kentucky bluegrass at 2 lb./1,000 sq ft. If the coverage is less that 75%, use a mixture of 2 pounds of Kentucky bluegrass to 5 pounds of perennial ryegrass. Completely bare areas should get an additional 5 pounds of perennial ryegrass.

Before applying seed to worn areas, aerate aggressively to loosen compacted soil. (The areas most likely to be worn are also those most densely compacted by competitive play, and turf recuperation is almost impossible where extreme compaction occurs.) Fill in low spots and divots, using similar soil to bring them up to grade. Then use a slit-seeder to slice the soil and improve seed:soil contact.

If the field is uneven or bumpy, consider topdressing before seeding (Figure 12.8).

*Figure 12.9. Solid tine aerating helps to relieve compaction in the middle of a field, loosening the soil with minimal disturbance to the turf.*

Begin by aerating, then spread a thin layer (¼″ to ½″) of similar soil, using a leveling bar to smooth the surface, then slit-seed. (Topdressing a regulation football field ⅜″ deep from goal line to goal line and sideline to sideline takes 80 cubic yards of material.)

During the renovation process, it's worth considering whether a field needs to be recrowned. If field performance suggests that recrowning is necessary, start with a survey to confirm two important matters: first of all, that the field actually has a crown, and second, that complete regrading of the field is not necessary. (If the grade is so far off that total regrading is necessary, follow the steps outline in section 12.3, Construction and Reconstruction.)

Many crowned fields gradually become worn in the center, creating a dished appearance and leading to the presence of wet and muddy areas down the middle of the field. This problem can often be corrected without removing the existing sod. Start by aerating the existing soil in the affected area, aerating as deeply as possible to avoid creating a layering effect that will inhibit drainage. Some field equipment manufacturers are now producing aerators that are designed to loosen compacted soil with minimal disturbance to the existing turfgrass. These are usually solid tine aerators with a vibrating and fracturing function, and they are ideal for applications like the center strip of a football field (Figure 12.9).

Aerate the affected area two or three times, until the soil is loose enough that it will crumble in your hands. If the soil is so badly compacted that it can't be loosened this much, strip off the existing turfgrass and go over the area with a scarifier before applying new soil. As always, be careful to apply soil that's as close as possible to the existing soil to prevent layering. With grade stakes in place, use a pulverizer, power rake, and level bar (or equivalent equipment) to regrade, then seed and mulch the area.

Another option that's coming into use for the center portion of football fields (as well as for bench areas) is sodding those areas only. For instance, we have installed Kentucky bluegrass sod in a 25 feet wide band down the middle of a practice field, where mechanical stress had worn through to the soil. (The area had been slit-seeded annually for years, and had always reverted to its "mud bowl" character by the end of the season.)

By season's end, after more than 100 practices on the field, we found the thatch layer intact and still keeping players up out of the mud. However, experience shows that the new sod will last only one season before soil becomes so thoroughly mixed into the thatch layer that muddy conditions reappear. Although this is not an inexpensive technique, strip-sodding can provide a solid playing surface with outstanding ability to deal with a season's worth of weather and competitive stress.

Making an informed decision on seeding or sodding the center section of a football field requires careful consideration of the amount of use the field will get, as well as the time, energy, and resources that can be spent on maintenance of the field. Seeding is cheaper but requires more work and care, and it takes longer before the field can be used. Sodding allows the field to be used within weeks, but costs more. Look at the whole picture before making a choice.

## 12.5 MAINTENANCE AND MANAGEMENT PROCEDURES

A professional turf management program begins with the process of field inspection, because any really effective management program requires that the manager know what he or she is working with. Of course, it's always wise to begin with a soil test.

We recommend that every field get some sort of quick inspection at least every other week year-round—even during the off-season. At first blush, that might seem like a lot of work, but it doesn't have to take more than five minutes, and it can save hours of work once the season rolls around. During the season, each field should be inspected once or twice a week.

During the growing season, one of the first things to look for is mowing problems. Lots of field problems occur because the grass is allowed to grow too high, and then cut too short. That creates a couple of different problems. That kind of cutting spreads so many clippings on the turf that it literally kills the grass. And it also cuts off too much of each plant. Cutting off more than one-third of the plant weakens the grass and makes it less resistant to stress.

In addition to mowing height, look for clean shearing, because dull blades tear the grass and make it susceptible to disease. If the grass has a whitish cast after mowing, that's a sign of dull blades. A close examination of the grass will reveal that the ends of the blades are probably shredded instead of cut cleanly. (Of course, make sure the maintenance staff follows the manufacturer's directions for safely sharpening mower blades.)

Inspections should also include a quick look at the moisture of the field. If it's too wet or too dry, or if there is water standing on the field, it's better to deal with those problems during the off-season, so more gradual processes can be applied.

During wet weather, visual inspection shows how the turf is dealing with precipitation. During dry weather, push a screwdriver into the soil until some resistance is felt. Under normal conditions, the screwdriver should easily penetrate 4″ to 6″ into the soil. If not, the field probably needs watering.

A useful tool for inspections of this kind is the "soil probe" or "soil profiler." These

Table 12.1. Sample Field Inspection Report

## Inspection Report

### Football

Field: —————————————

| | Overall Appearance | Clippings | Height of Cut | Sharpen Mower Blade | Soil Moisture | Other: Color, Density, Thatch, Compaction, Weeds, Catch Basins, Sprinkler Heads, etc. |
|---|---|---|---|---|---|---|
| Date: | | | | | | |
| Date: | | | | | | |
| Date: | | | | | | |
| Date: | | | | | | |
| Date: | | | | | | |
| Date: | | | | | | |
| Date: | | | | | | |
| Date: | | | | | | |

tools allow removal of a small core sample 4″ to 6″ deep, which can then be checked for compaction, thatch accumulation, and root development, in addition to soil moisture.

Look for the appearance of weeds in high-traffic areas of the field, especially in the center and bench areas. In the North, knotweed frequently appears in these areas, and is usually a sign of overcompaction. Relieving that compaction will allow the turfgrass to crowd out the knotweed.

If the entire field is rock hard, even away from the center and benches, arrange for aeration to relieve the problem and foster healthy turf culture.

When performing an inspection, it's helpful to have a form for recording findings. (See Table 12.1, Sample Field Inspection Report.) Using a form of this type helps to make sure the inspection has checked all the field conditions, and it also allows the manager to develop a record of how the field responds to various conditions year-round.

### 12.5a Warm Season Maintenance

Table 12.2 is a sample maintenance program that can be tailored to fit the needs of any football field in the warm season zone. It's important to remember that this is only a sample of one maintenance program that is being used successfully on a particular field. In planning a fertilization program, the field manager is advised to consult the more detailed information found in Chapter 3, Fertility and Fertilizers.

### Fertilization

The maintenance schedule detailed in Table 12.2 is used on the practice football field #1 at Mississippi State University. Like most collegiate practice facilities, this bermudagrass field receives heavy use during spring practice and the fall season. The field gets aggressive nitrogen fertilization from May through August to maximize the growth and recovery of the bermudagrass during its primary growing season. Water-soluble ammonium nitrate is the primary N source, and 21-2-20 and 8-24-24 are applied in mid- to late

**Table 12.2. Warm Season Maintenance Program**

## Sample Maintenance Schedule
### (Warm Season)

| | | | | |
|---|---|---|---|---|
| Field Name: | MSU #1 | Address: | Mississippi State |
| Type of Field: | Football Practice Field | | Mississippi |

| | | | | |
|---|---|---|---|---|
| Condition: | good | Compaction: | limited |
| Type of Grass: | Tifway bermudagrass | Drainage: | surface drainage—good |
| Type of Mower: | 5 gang reel | Irrigation: | installed automatic system |
| Type of Soil: | native clay | Thatch: | ¼″ to ½″ |

Notes: primary wear between hash marks and blocking sled at NE corner

| | | | |
|---|---|---|---|
| Soil Test Year: | 1997 | Phosphorus: | 65 |
| pH: | 6.7 | Potassium: | 300 |

| Time of Year | Fertilization | Aeration | Topdress | Overseed | ⅓ Rule Mowing Ht | 1″ Week Watering | Weed Control |
|---|---|---|---|---|---|---|---|
| May | 13-13-13 1 lb N | 12″ solid tine | ¼″ and drag | | ⅞″ | | 2.4-D plus MSMA spot treat |
| June | 34-0-0 1¾ lb N | 12″ hollow tine | ¼″ and drag | | ⅞″ | as needed | 2.4-D plus MSMA spot treat |
| July | 34-0-0 1¾ lb N | dethatch if needed | ¼″ and drag | | ⅞″ | 30 min. every day | |
| August | 21-2-20 1 lb N | | | | ⅞″ | 30 min. every day | |
| September | 8-24-24 ½ lb N | | ¼″ and drag after overseed | 20 lb perennial rye | ⅞″ | as needed for overseeding | |
| October | 34-0-0 1 lb N | | | spot seed | ⅞″ | as needed | |
| November | | | | | ⅞″ | as needed | |
| December | | | | | 1½″ every 2–3 weeks | | |
| January | | | | | 1½″ every 2–3 weeks | | |
| February | | | | | 1½″ every 2–3 weeks | | |
| March | | | | | ⅞″ | | |
| April | | | | | ⅞″ | | |

summer to prepare the turf for winter. The N application in September is limited to 0.5 pounds per 1,000 square feet to minimize bermudagrass competition with the newly seeded perennial ryegrass. A final pound of N is applied with ammonium nitrate in October to meet the needs of the newly established rperennial ryegrass.

### Aeration and Topdressing

The program outlined in Table 12.2 includes deep tine aeration with 12″ long, 1″ diameter solid tines in May, with a double pass over the middle of the field. The field is then topdressed with ¼ ″ of sand and is dragged with a chain link mat to work the sand into the turf. In June, the field is aerated again, this time with 12″ long, 1″ diameter hollow tine equipment, then topdressed and dragged once more. These cultivation events are performed when the turf is actively growing, and recovery is enhanced with the application of fertilizer with high nitrogen rates. The field is dethatched in July if the thatch layer exceeds ½″ depth. After dethatching, topdressing and dragging are performed as before. Under this regimen, the turf will have approximately 1 month for full recovery before fall practice begins.

### Overseeding

Overseeding is performed in mid-September. To prepare for overseeding the field is mowed at ½″, then a three-way perennial ryegrass blend is applied with a rotary spreader. The overseeded field is topdressed and dragged; the topdressing promotes seed-to-soil contact and improves seed germination. The seeding rate is 20 pounds per 1,000 square feet, a typical overseeding rate for a high-use field, and thinner areas are spot-seeded in October to improve density.

### Mowing

Bermudagrass sports fields are typically mowed at heights ranging from ¾″ to 1½″. (This particular field is cut year-round at ⅞″ at the request of the coaches. If acceptable to the coaches using the facility, the cutting height should be raised to 1½″ in the fall to promote winter hardiness in the bermudagrass.) Be sure to cut the turf as often as required to keep the ⅓ rule in effect. The MSU practice field is mowed 2–3 times per week throughout the active growing seasons of the bermudagrass and perennial ryegrass— even when the field is not in use during the summer. It is a common mistake by many sports field managers to neglect the field during the off-season, only to have the first practice or game date sneak up on them before the field is ready. The perennial ryegrass is mowed once every 2–3 weeks during the winter months, until more rapid growth resumes in March.

### Watering

Bermudagrass will typically need 1″ to 1½″ of water per week during the summer months to maintain active growth. Application rates are reduced during the overseeding months as temperatures cool and watering requirements diminish. The watering program delivers deep and infrequent irrigation, except following overseeding, when the turf is watered lightly and frequently in order to enhance seed germination.

### Weed Control

A preemergence (PRE) herbicide can be used in the early spring for the control of summer annual weeds. However, most PRE herbicides also delay reestablishment of bermudagrass turf thinned by heavy fall and winter use. With this in mind, a popular strategy for PRE herbicides has been to apply the lowest labeled rate of the product in the early spring for initial weed control when the turf is still thin, then to promote turf density with a balanced but aggressive fertility program when the grass resumes active growth.

If the field has received little or no use during the winter and has high density, many southern football field managers do not apply PRE herbicides, instead controlling weeds by thickening the turf canopy through a balanced fertility program. Any weeds appearing in the turf can be controlled with postemergence (POE) chemicals such as MSMA and 2,4-D. (See Chapter 9, Turfgrass Stresses and Remedies, for more on PRE and POE herbicides.) If weed pressure has been low in the past, only spot applications of POE are recommended.

If PRE herbicides are used, time summer applications well in advance of any planned overseeding events. Otherwise, the perennial ryegrass itself will unintentionally be controlled by the PRE herbicide.

## 12.5b  Transitional Zone Maintenance
In establishing a maintenance program for fields in the Transitional Zone, use the program appropriate for the type of turfgrass being used on the field. Maintain warm season varieties according to the warm season program, and cool season varieties according to the typical northern program.

## 12.5c  Cool Season Maintenance
Cool season turfgrasses run through an annual cycle of strong active growth in the spring and early summer, with dormancy in the hottest part of the year, followed by another strong growing season in the late summer and fall. Many of the maintenance practices of cool season fields give consideration to this annual cycle. Table 12.3 is a sample of a maintenance program that can be tailored to fit the needs of any football facility in the North. For a sample maintenance program with cutting heights less than 2″, see Chapter 13, Soccer, Lacrosse, and Field Hockey, Table 13.2.

### Fertilization
As a general rule, cool season fields should get less than 30% of their annual nitrogen needs in the spring, with the remainder applied in the fall. Restricting N application at this time of year helps to prevent excessive shoot growth, which often comes at the expense of needed root growth. The first fertilization of the spring is a good time to apply a starter fertilizer such as 18-24-12, since the actively growing turfgrass plants will benefit from the additional P and K at this point in the year. The starter fertilizer also helps the process of getting new seedlings established.

During the summer, one application of ½ pound N and a full pound of K helps preserve plant health during the heat of the summer, and enhances the turf's ability to resist disease.

Applying the largest portion of the N in the fall contributes to strong root growth, and helps the turf recover from the stresses placed upon it by the competitive season. The very best time to apply N is right after the last mowing of the season, when the grass is still green. During this period, shoot growth slows to a stop, but root growth continues. The extra N is absorbed and stored by the root system, and results in an early spring greenup, and a further enhancement of the turf's ability to withstand summer stresses.

**Table 12.3. Cool Season Maintenance Program**

## Sample Maintenance Schedule
(Cool Season)

| | | | |
|---|---|---|---|
| Field Name: | Hubbard Stadium Field | Address: | 350 Hall Ave. |
| Type of Field: | Football Game Field | | Hubbard, Ohio |

| | | | |
|---|---|---|---|
| Condition: | good | Compaction: | yes—middle & bench |
| Type of Grass: | blue/rye | Drainage: | installed pipe drain system |
| Type of Mower: | 60" rotary | Irrigation: | installed automatic system |
| Type of Soil: | clay/loam | Thatch: | ½" sides—0" middle |
| Soil Test: | | Notes: | knotweek (middle & bench area) |
| Year: | 1996   Phosphorus: 85 | | some clover—crabgrass (N. end) |
| pH: | 6.5   Potassium:   350 | | check sprinkler head elevations |

| Time of Year | Fertilization | Aeration | Topdress | Overseed | ⅓ Rule Mowing Ht | 1" Week Watering | Weed Control |
|---|---|---|---|---|---|---|---|
| April | 18-24-12 ½ lb N 50% SRN | core entire field | for surface leveling | bluegrass middle & bench areas | 2" | | |
| May | 24-5-11 ¾ lb N 50% SRN | 12" solid tine aeration | | blue/rye touchup spots | 2¼" | light frequent intervals | |
| June | | core 50' each side | | | 2½" | deeper less frequent | |
| July | 16-0-31 ½ lb N 25% SRN | | | | 2¾" | deeply | spot treatment |
| August | | slice middle | | primed ryegrass middle | 2" | deeply | |
| September | 32-5-7 1 lb N 50% SRN | | | | 2" | cautiously | |
| October | 20-5-10 ¾ lb N 50% SRN | | | | 2" | cautiously | |
| November | 1 lb N after last mowing | core entire field | for surface leveling | now or April | 2" | | |

### Aeration

Aerating frequently, and varying the equipment, helps to make the turf stronger. In June, core the sides of the field only, staying off the middle and any other newly seeded areas where the grass plants are not yet mature enough to withstand the stresses of aeration. Later in the season, solid tine aeration loosens the soil without littering the field with cores.

### Topdressing and Slit-Seeding

Performing these two processes together substantially magnifies the benefits to the turf, and provides the additional benefit of helping to level the surface. If the fall weather stays fairly dry, consider dormant seeding in late November or early December to give the turf a fast start in the spring. A wet fall may delay overseeding until the weather breaks the next year. (See Section 12-4 for more information on slit-seeding, or "overseeding.")

### Mowing

The perennial ryegrass starts growing first in the spring, so keep mowing height at about 2″ to let sunlight reach the Kentucky bluegrass base. When the bluegrass starts growing in May, raise the height by ¼″, and raise it another ¼″ in June to help the turf prepare for the summer's heat. In July, the grass should be higher than at any other time of year.

Three to four weeks before the first game, begin lowering the height to game height, remembering to reduce the height gradually by taking off no more than ⅓ of the grass plants at any one mowing. This gradual reduction in advance of the season will allow the turf to recover from the lower cutting height and be fully ready for play.

Keep mowing after the season until growth has completely stopped. If the grass is left too long, the risk of snow mold increases. However, scalping in the fall can expose the plant crowns during the winter, weakening the grass.

### Watering

In the spring, water in light amounts at frequent intervals, to help establish any newly seeded turf. Gradually reduce the frequency and increase the amount applied at one time.

If the fall is dry, water with an eye on the weather forecast. It's usually better to let the turf be a little dry than too wet in the fall, since sudden rains before or during a game can lead to a quagmire.

### Weed Control

As a general rule, blanket weed treatment on a football field is not a good idea. Because of the mechanical stresses placed on the turf, most fields need to be reseeded annually, which make preemergent applications unwise. Even if seeding is performed in the fall, the seed will not germinate until the spring, and preemergents will stop grass germination. Postemergents should be avoided until the new grass is fully established.

When following a good cultural management program, weed infestation will probably be minimal anyway. A spot treatment a few weeks before the first game will usually do the trick. (If special circumstances indicate a blanket treatment, refer to Chapter 9 for more on weed control.)

## 12.5d  Program Variations (Practice Fields)

In the **South,** the program outlined in Table 12.2 should be followed on most native soil

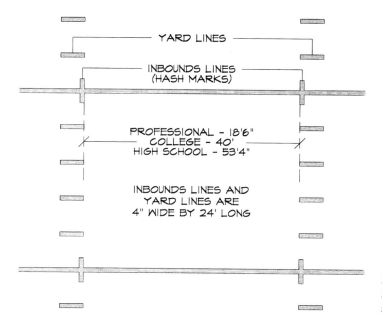

YARD LINES

INBOUNDS LINES
(HASH MARKS)

PROFESSIONAL - 18'6"
COLLEGE - 40'
HIGH SCHOOL - 53'4"

INBOUNDS LINES AND
YARD LINES ARE
4" WIDE BY 24' LONG

*Figure 12.10. Detail of inbounds lines (hash marks) and yard lines.*

fields, game fields, and practice facilities alike. If the stadium field is overseeded, many field managers choose to overseed the practice field as well, to closely simulate game conditions.

In the **North,** if the facility is fortunate enough to have more than one practice field, it will be possible to practice the program recommended in Table 12.3, moving practices off the field during recuperation periods. For most teams, with one practice field and 100 practices to hold during the season, the turf will be bare in the middle of the field by the end of the season. Obviously, there's little point in fertilizing and aerating bare soil. A better strategy would be to apply one pound N each month from April to July, before the field is being heavily used. In combination with careful mowing and watering practices, this aggressive fertilization program should allow the field to hold up much better to the demands of the season.

## 12.6   RULES AND REGULATIONS

### 12.6a   Common Points of Confusion

The painted lines representing the goal lines, sidelines, and end lines are *outside* the dimensions shown in Table 12.4, Football Field Dimensions. The yard lines are marked with the measured distance in the middle of the painted line. The dimensions given for the inbounds lines (hash marks) represent the distance between the closest points on the hash marks as shown in Figure 12.10.

The top of the goal post crossbar is to be 10 feet above the ground, (measured at the end of each upright) and the required width between the upright is measured from the inside of the uprights. The front edge of the crossbar is to be 30 feet behind the goal line for American football.

The flexible pylons placed at the intersection of the sideline and the goal line, and at the intersection of the sideline and the end line, are meant to be placed out-of-bounds. Any flags or pylons at the back of the end zone are also meant to be out-of-bounds.

Table 12.4. Football Field Dimensions

| | Football | | | | | | |
|---|---|---|---|---|---|---|---|
| Type of Field | Length of Playing Field | Length of Each End Zone | Total Length Including End Zones | Width | Distance Between Inbounds Lines | Distance Between Uprights | Height of Upright Above Ground |
| Professional | 300' | 30' | 360' | 160' | 18'6" | 18'6" | 30' |
| College—NCAA | 300' | 30' | 360' | 160' | 40' | 18'6" | 30' |
| High School[a]— | | | | | | | |
| NFSHSA | 300' | 30' | 360' | 160' | 53'4" | 23'4" | 20' |
| Canadian[b] | 330' | 75' | 480' | 195' | 51' | 18'6" | 20' |

[a]Pop Warner Little Scholars, Inc. recommends the same dimensions as High School Football (ages 7–15).
[b]For U.S. Football, the front edge of the goal post crossbar is 30' behind the goal line, but for Canadian Football it is on the goal line.

## 12.6b  Line and Boundary Dimensions

See Table 12.4.

## 12.6c  Governing and Sanctioning Bodies

*Professional:*
The National Football League
280 Park Avenue
New York, NY 10017
(212) 450-2000

*College:*
The National Collegiate Athletic Association
6201 College Boulevard
Overland Park, Kansas  66211
(913) 339-1906

*High School:*
National Federation of State High School Associations
11724 NW Plaza Circle, P. O. Box 20626
Kansas City, Missouri  64195
(816) 464-5400

*Canadian:*
The Canadian Football League
1200 Bay Street, 12th Floor
Toronto, Ontario, Canada    M5R 2A5
(416) 928-1200

*Pop Warner Football:*
Pop Warner Little Scholars, Inc.
586 Middletown Boulevard,  Suite C100
Langhorn, Pennsylvania  19047
(215) 752-2691

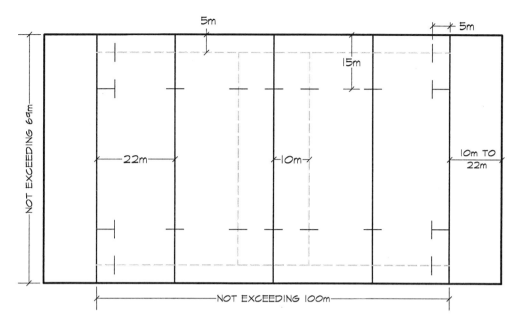

*Figure 12.11. Layout of a rugby field.*

## 12.7   RUGBY

The sport of rugby has been played in North American since the nineteenth century, and achieved an organized status with the formation of the Rugby Union in 1871. It grew slowly in the United States, with only 30 teams competing in 1950. But the 1960s saw an explosion of interest in the sport, and by 1980 there were more than a thousand rugby clubs in North America.

The fields used for rugby competition is generally the same as that used for football, and games are sometimes played on American football practice fields. The main difference between the fields used for the two sports is that, while football goalposts are installed at the back of the end zone, rugby goal posts are placed on the goal line itself. Because of the obvious hazard presented by a stationary object on the field, the home team is responsible for ensuring that padding at least 2″ thick is installed on the uprights of the goalposts from ground level to a height of 5 feet.

These goalposts have the same "H" shape characteristic of American football posts, and are to be 5.6 meters (18.37 feet) wide. The crossbar is to be 3 meters (9.84 feet) high, and the uprights are to be more than 3.4 meters (11.15 feet) high.

The playing area itself is a rectangle not to exceed 100 meters (328.08 feet) in length and 69 meters (226.38 feet) wide. (Figure 12.11 shows the layout of a rugby field.) As in American football, at each end of the field there is an end zone, but in the case of rugby this area can vary from a minimum of 10 meters (32.81 feet) to a maximum of 22 meters (72.18 feet).

A halfway line divides the field in half, and additional lines are drawn across the field 22 meters from the goal lines. Broken lines are to be marked 5 meters (16.40 feet) inside the touchlines and ten meters on either side of the halfway line. Hash marks intersect the goal lines, halfway lines, 22 meter lines, and 10 meter lines at a distance of 15 meters

(49.21 feet) from the touchlines. The hash marks at the goal lines are to extend 5 meters out onto the playing area.

The rugby field is to have a post at each corner of the playing area, where the touchlines intersect the goal line. These posts are to be at least 1.2 meters (3.94 feet) tall and topped with a flag. Posts with flags are also to be installed off the playing area to mark the halfway line and the 22 meter lines.

A sideline barrier is to be installed five meters outside the touchlines to prevent spectators from approaching the playing area.

## 12.8  RUGBY GOVERNING AND SANCTIONING BODIES

USA Rugby
3595 East Fountain Boulevard
Colorado Springs, Colorado   80910
(719) 637-1022

USA National Rugby Team (The Eagles)
Hudson Rugby Fieldhouse
Berkeley, California    94720
(510) 643-1971

# Chapter 13

# Soccer, Lacrosse, and Field Hockey Fields

## 13.1 INTRODUCTION

In many respects, the work of planning, constructing, and managing fields used for soccer, lacrosse, and field hockey is very similar to the corresponding processes for football fields. Of course, at many schools with both soccer and football programs, a single field serves as the game facility for both sports. Under these circumstances, the need for cooperation and coexistence between the two programs will dictate that turf management practices strike the best possible compromise between the needs of the two sports.

However, there are some important differences between the demands placed on turf by a football program and those presented by soccer, lacrosse, and field hockey. Wherever possible, these differences need to be recognized and accounted for in managing fields used for those sports.

Soccer players (and players in lacrosse and field hockey, as well) typically rely on rapid starts and stops and frequent changes in direction as a major tactical element of the game. These quick maneuvers place a good deal of localized mechanical stress on the turf, but without the concentrated gouging at the field typical of sports like football and rugby. Soccer shoes, or "boots," also feature shorter cleats which bite less deeply into the turf, and soccer players themselves tend to be smaller and lighter than football players.

However, although these factors would suggest that designing, building, or maintaining a soccer, lacrosse, or field hockey field would be substantially easier than a football field, there are other aspects of the games we are considering here that require more critical judgments.

In each of these three sports, ball response is of critical importance to the nature of competition. In order to pass and shoot the ball accurately, players in all three sports must be able to rely on even, stable turf that allows straight, consistent roll of the ball. Because ball response is so important, even minor turf damage can cause bad bounces and uneven roll that adversely affect the game.

Where ball response is a critical factor, shorter turfgrass is to be preferred, since shorter grass exerts less friction on the ball passing over it. Under these circumstances, the field manager must not only choose turfgrass species or cultivars that flourish under close mowing, but must also allow for the additional mowing time required of the maintenance staff. Because of the importance of cutting no more than one-third of the grass blade at a given mowing, fields for soccer, lacrosse, and field hockey must be mowed as much as three times a week during the competitive season. For cutting heights less that 2″, use a reel-type mower.

For field hockey, the height or cut is generally recommended to be from ¾″ to a maximum of 1½″, due to the effect of higher grass in dramatically slowing the roll of the field hockey ball.

Effective drainage is particularly important in these sports, because wet spots on the turf can literally stop the ball dead. Unlike football, in which a team can change strategies when the turf is wet (running the ball more and passing it less, for instance), the game of soccer is more severely restricted when the turf fails to drain effectively. What's more, each time a soccer player kicks the ball, he or she is by definition standing on one foot in a posture that requires good footing—so evenness of the surface becomes an increasingly important issue for the safety and performance of the athletes.

Wear and compaction patterns in soccer, lacrosse, and field hockey create some important demands on the management staff as well. Typically, the most troublesome spots are immediately in front of the goals, where the goalkeepers stand, and the areas about 18 yards out from the goals, where both defenders and attackers tend to congregate during play. Other trouble spots can include the four corners of the field, where corner kicks are taken, and sideline areas at the middle of the field.

An additional consideration with soccer is the fall season, which dictates that the season ends—and that important games and playoffs be held—after the natural growing season has ended in much of the country.

All of these factors, along with the need to coexist with football on many fields, make soccer field management (and management of the related lacrosse and field hockey fields) a special challenge.

## 13.2  DESIGN

### 13.2a  Survey and Layout

*Soccer*
Soccer fields vary in size, and field dimensions are typically stated in terms of ranges, rather than of absolute values. Perhaps the most common size for high school soccer fields in the United States is 120 yards long by 55 to 60 yards wide, because that is close to the size of American football fields which are adapted for soccer competition (frequently by extending the field beyond the football sidelines). The specifications for World Cup competition call for fields up to 150 yards long by 100 yards wide, but this size is probably impractical for most schools and public facilities. Children play on smaller fields, typically 60 to 80 yards long, but sometimes even smaller for the youngest players.

In planning the field, begin by determining that there is sufficient space for the facility. Ideally, 50 to 60 feet of free space should be left on all sides of the field. Survey the entire space to learn the contours of the terrain and the natural direction of runoff.

*Lacrosse*
A regulation lacrosse field is very similar in size and proportion to a soccer or football field. The field is meant to be 110 yards long and 60 yards wide.

*Field Hockey*
A regulation field hockey field is 100 yards long and 60 yards wide.

(Field layouts for all three sports are provided in this chapter as Figures 13.3 through 13.5.)

## 13.2b  Design Criteria for New Construction

Most fields are crowned down the longitudinal axis of the field to promote positive surface drainage, although flat fields sloping toward one touchline or sideline are not uncommon. A slope of 1.5% to 1.75% will normally provide adequate surface drainage, although some perfectly serviceable fields have as little as 1% slope, which is more desirable from a competitive standpoint. In most cases, however, slopes at 1% or less will need installed drain systems to keep the field fully playable during wet weather.

Probably the best overall design is a side-to-side sloped field with 1% slope and an installed drain system.

If the field being designed will also be used for football, several considerations need to be kept in mind. Since soccer players usually do not require the same large stopping area as football players, placing the touchlines outside the football sidelines usually does not present a safety concern. But extending the touchlines often means that the football bench areas become part of the playing surface of the soccer field. These areas are usually badly damaged by compaction and mechanical stress, and bad weather can turn them into slippery quagmires. In designing a field that will be used for both sports, it's important to keep an even slope through the football sideline area all the way to the soccer touchlines.

Some planners also forget that soccer players must leave the field of play to retrieve the ball when it crosses the touchlines, and throw it back in from outside the line. If the field is surrounded by an all-weather track, players may end up having to run across the track in cleated soccer boots, which many field managers try to avoid.

## 13.2c  Field Designs with Preferred Contours

As with football fields, soccer fields (and fields for related sports) are usually designed according to one of two general schemes: a crowned field with level touchlines (sidelines) as illustrated in Chapter 12, Figure 12.1, or a flat field sloped side-to-side, Figure 12.2.

The crowned field with level touchlines is relatively easy to design and build, and drains fairly efficiently away from the middle of the playing area. Remember, the area where the crowned field meets the level touchline can easily turn into a wet spot. That condition may cause the ball to slow or stop as it approaches the touchline, and may lead to unnecessary falls by players as they maneuver to keep the ball in bounds. What's more, unlike football, in soccer the ball is sometimes put into play from outside the touchline. So players executing throw-ins from outside the touchlines will place a substantial amount of mechanical stress on the turf at that point, and may aggravate the problem of sloppy footing.

In order to overcome this limitation, the slope of a soccer, lacrosse, or field hockey field should extend at least 10 to 15 feet outside the touchlines or sidelines, to provide an expanded area of solid footing.

Where the terrain permits, side-to-side sloped fields can work very well. Side-to-side fields should have a slope of 1.5% to 1.75% to provide adequate surface drainage. If an installed drain system can be provided, a flatter field with a 1% slope is preferred.

Sloping a field end-to-end should be avoided, because the lower end of the field almost always becomes sloppy.

## 13.2d  Multiple Field Layouts

Multiple field complexes for soccer are becoming widely used throughout North America as the sport increases in popularity. When designing such a complex, it's wise to leave at least 30 feet between fields that are laid out side-by-side, and 50 feet between fields laid out end-to-end. If there are grandstands between the fields, the distance should obviously be increased by the width of the grandstand structures.

In laying out multiple field installations, it's important to remember that each field must function as an individual drainage unit. It's virtually impossible to keep a field playable if it has water running across it from adjacent fields. If necessary, leave enough room outside the playing areas to allow for cuts and fills, catch basins and swales.

### 13.2e  Turfgrass Selection

Experience has shown that for most **warm season** soccer, lacrosse, and field hockey fields, bermudagrass is the turfgrass of choice. In addition to its durability, bermudagrass can be a fast, dependable surface, and tolerates the close mowing that improves ball response.

In the **transitional zone,** as in the warm season zone, the preferred turfgrass for soccer and related fields is bermudagrass. Bermudagrass fields need to be overseeded with perennial ryegrass fairly early in the competitive season, late August or early September. This combination of turfgrasses can tolerate both mechanical stress of competition and temperature variations, and the bermudagrass serves as a good base for traction.

In the **northern zone,** Kentucky bluegrass/perennial ryegrass mix is probably the ideal choice for soccer and related fields. The aggressive recuperation characteristic of Kentucky bluegrass helps the turf respond strongly to mechanical stress, and the Kentucky bluegrass thatch protects the root structure. In wet conditions, Kentucky bluegrass thatch keeps the players up out of the mud, preserving footing and allowing safe play. However, Kentucky bluegrass naturally produces more thatch than is ideal for these sports, and can slow the progress of the rolling ball. So the addition of perennial ryegrass varieties can improve the turf's performance as a platform for sports demanding good ball response.

Superior varieties of Kentucky bluegrass include Princeton-104, A-34, Touchdown, and Blacksburg. There are many good perennial ryegrass choices.

In any climatic zone, seeded fields need time (three to four months) to fully establish themselves before use for practice or games. Kentucky bluegrass needs even more time to mature; usually a full year. A good policy with any seeded turfgrass is to seed a field in the spring of one year for use in the fall of the next year.

If the budget allows for sodding, be sure to specify a mature product with a thatch layer thick enough to hold the sod together without netting.

The practice in the northern zone of seeding perennial ryegrass into a 100% Kentucky bluegrass turf before and during the competitive season was originally developed to reduce stresses on the Kentucky bluegrass plants. This practice can also help to eliminate the bare spots typically found in front of the goals in each of these three sports.

### 13.2f  Installed Irrigation Systems

Irrigation systems for fields in any of these sports must account for the traffic patterns of the players, as well as the placement, size, and durability of sprinkler heads.

Placement of the heads should take consideration of the portions of the field where the largest number of players line up. Since the goal area at each end is the portion of the field most subject to wear and tear, place the heads outside these areas to avoid mechanical damage or player hazards.

Smaller heads are obviously to be preferred, and they should be inspected at least monthly to ensure good grass cover and correct seating and to check for damage. The

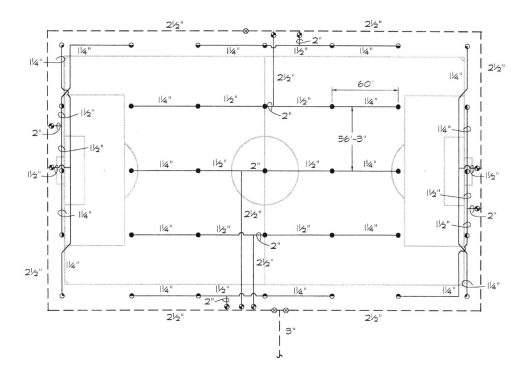

## IRRIGATION LEGEND

| | DESCRIPTION | PSI | GPM | RADIUS | ARC | UNITS |
|---|---|---|---|---|---|---|
| ● | HUNTER I-40-36S-43 FULL CIRCLE | 60 | 15.5 | 59 FT. | 360° | 15 |
| ◐ | HUNTER I-40-ADS-43 PART CIRCLE | 60 | 15.5 | 59 FT. | 180° | 16 |
| ◔ | HUNTER I-40-ADS-43 PART CIRCLE | 60 | 15.5 | 59 FT. | 90° | 4 |
| ⦶ | 2" HUNTER ICV 201G REMOTE CONTROL VALVE | | | | | 7 |
| ⦵ | 1½" HUNTER ICV 151G REMOTE CONTROL VALVE (CORNER HEADS) | | | | | 2 |
| ⊗ | 2½" GATE VALVE FOR MAINLINE ISOLATION | | | | | 3 |

—————— NON-PRESSURE PIPE (PVC CLASS 160 RECOMMENDED)

— — — PRESSURE PIPE (PVC CLASS 200 RECOMMENDED)

NOTE:
    THE FOUR 90° CORNER HEADS ARE ON ONE STATION

NOT SHOWN:
    BACKFLOW PREVENTION DEVICE
    (AS REQUIRED PER CODE AND/OR ORDINANCE - AND FOR SAFETY)        1
    HUNTER ICC IRRIGATION CONTROLLER (9 STATIONS)
    LOCATION AS NEEDED                                              1

DESIGN PROVIDED BY HUNTER INDUSTRIES

*Figure 13.1. A five-row irrigation system for large soccer fields.*

ball should be able to roll right over the heads without interruption of its motion. As always when selecting heads, choose a model that is rated by the manufacturer as suitable for the particular sport.

A four-row system suitable for soccer and related sports can be found in Chapter 12, Figure 12.4. Since the largest soccer fields can be substantially larger than football fields, a five-row system is included in this chapter as Figure 13.1. Unlike football, where play is concentrated at the middle of the field, soccer action is more widely distributed across the playing surface. For this reason, a five-row system with a row of heads in the middle of the field does not create safety or maintenance problems in soccer.

This design requires water pressure of 75 PSI at field edge and yields a pressure of 60 PSI at the base of the sprinkler heads. Average precipitation rate for this system will be .44 inches/hour for full circle heads, .88 inches/hour for half-circle heads, and 1.76 inches/hour for quarter circle heads. Running time for 1″ watering will be 2 hours 16 minutes for full circle heads, one hour 8 minutes for half-circle heads, and 34 minutes for quarter circle heads.

## 13.2g  Installed Drain Systems and Catch Basins

### Installed Drain Systems

For sports such as these, where ball response is critical, it's difficult to achieve sufficient surface drainage to efficiently remove heavy or sustained rains. It takes four hours for a field with a 1.5% crown to move water from the center of the field across the touch-lines/sidelines, so installed drain systems are often critical to acceptable field performance.

One common form of drainage system for sports fields is commonly referred to as a "French drain," but does not meet the strict definition of that type of system. Strictly speaking, a French drain does not include pipe, relying instead on carefully-constructed beds of gravel. But the common systems are constructed with pipe (originally tile pipe—leading to their common name: "drain tile"). Typically, the pipe was covered with felt paper or packed with coarse sand to prevent the pipe from becoming clogged with silt and clay. These "pipe drains" were usually laid in trenches 2 to 3 feet deep, and then filled with gravel to within 6″ of the surface.

Properly installed to prevent silt and clay intrusion, some of these pipe drain systems are still at work after 30 years. The most long-lasting systems have a thick layer of sand—normally 12″ to 18″ thick—packed around the pipe.

Pipe drains can be effective in helping to drain an area, because they lower the water table, removing water from the sub-soil, and eventually from the topsoil as well. However, their effect on the relative wetness of the topsoil is only gradual, and pipe drains cannot be relied upon for rapid removal of surface water if they are not filled to the surface with sand, a practice which negatively impacts turf growth and traction.

An additional concern with this type of drain system is that the layering of topsoil over the pea gravel in the drain trenches will create a perched water table, preventing water from reaching the pipes. Furthermore, in drought-like conditions, the topsoil above the pipe drains will create dry, brown stripes across the field. This effect occurs because, in dry conditions, the turfgrass root system will draw small amounts of water upward from the subsoil. However, the roots will not be able to draw water from the pea gravel, leading to the excessive drying of those portions of the field surface.

Two other problems plague pipe drain systems, especially with the conversion to modern plastic pipe. The first problem is crushing of the pipe by heavy construction equipment, and the second is overcompaction of the soil. Many contractors overcompact the subsoil because they are accustomed to the practice. Both problems compromise the effectiveness of the drainage systems, so contractors should be advised to avoid over-compaction of the subsoil, and to scarify the subsoil before installing topsoil. It's a good idea to add these instructions to the job specifications. (See Chapter 12, Figure 12.5 for a typical pipe drain system.)

A new type of field drainage are "strip drains," which provide a more effective choice

*Figure 13.2 A strip drain can be used to target problem areas on a soccer field, such as the area immediately in front of a goal.*

for surface water removal. Strip drains are cloth-wrapped plastic or fiber structures that are installed in a shallow trench 3″ to 4″ wide and about 12″ deep. The strip drain is placed in the bottom of the trench and extends halfway to the surface. The trench is then filled with sand right up to surface level.

See Chapter 12, Figure 12.6 for a strip-drain-based design for a crowned soccer, lacrosse, or field hockey field. See Figure 12.7 for a strip-drain-based drainage system for a side-to-side sloped field.

Strip drain systems at surface level remove some of the surface water from the field and shorten the distance the water has to flow (Figure 13.2). Of course, strip drains can also be compromised by overcompaction of the topsoil or subsoil.

### Catch Basins

Many fields have catch basins on the sideline as part of the drainage system. The primary value of catch basins is their function as "junction boxes" for pipe drains or strip drains. Catch basins should be at least 20 feet from the touchlines/sideline to avoid the risk of player injury. For most fields, four catch basins at the corners of the field are sufficient for prompt drainage.

The practice of using catch basins with swales from basin-to-basin to assist surface runoff is not generally an efficient way to provide drainage. It has a negative impact on field aesthetics, especially if the swales cause mowers to scalp or gouge the turf. The swales can also stay wet for extended periods. Given the problems with this approach, it is not recommended for most fields.

For draining level sideline areas, a combination of pipe drains and strip drains is usually more effective than swales. For instance, lay out a downward sloped trench 15″

deep parallel to the sidelines and 20 feet away, running to catch basins outside the end lines. Lay a ½″ bed of pea gravel in the trench, then a 4″ perforated pipe. Then fill pea gravel to within 6″ of the surface, top with coarse sand, and seed. The best sand has less than 5% passing the 100 sieve screen.

A "sand drain" system of this kind can be particularly effective for fields that have 400-meter running tracks around them. If the sand drain is installed near the track, it will drain both field and track more effectively than swales and catch basins. (This hybrid "trackside" system is illustrated in Chapter 16, Figure 16.4.)

## 13.3   CONSTRUCTION AND RECONSTRUCTION

(The construction and reconstruction processes are discussed in detail in the previous chapter—Chapter 12, Football and Rugby Fields. For information on such projects, see Section 12.3.)

## 13.4   RENOVATION

Renovation is the process of repairing the damage of a competitive season, and assisting the recuperation process to prepare the field for the next season. Typical renovation steps include aeration, leveling, and planting new turfgrass. Renovation must also give special attention to the parts of the field—such as in front of the goals—where compaction and stress are greatest.

Northern fields can be overseeded in the fall, if the weather allows maintenance vehicles onto the turf. Late fall seeding is considered "dormant seeding," since seed will not germinate until the spring. (See Chapter 1, Section 1.6c for more on dormant seeding.) Fall seeding allows new growth to get an earlier start in the spring, and prevents the kind of immature turf that can result from weather delays in spring seeding. Dormant seeding can be especially helpful on practice fields, which get extensive use weeks before the first game. (In the South and the transitional zone, however, bermudagrass seeding should wait until the spring, because fall planting can lead to premature germination and subsequent winter kill of the seedlings.)

On northern fields, if worn areas have at least 75% turf cover, seed 100% Kentucky bluegrass at 2 pounds/1,000 sq ft. If the coverage is less that 75%, use a mixture of 2 pounds of Kentucky bluegrass to 5 pounds of perennial ryegrass. Completely bare areas should get an additional 5 pounds of perennial ryegrass.

Before seeding worn areas, aerify aggressively to loosen compacted soil. (The areas most likely to be worn are also most likely to be densely compacted by play, and it's very difficult for the turf to recuperate in extremely compacted soil.) Level the field by filling in low spots and divots with a similar soil. A slit-seeder can help to improve seed:soil contact.

Uneven fields can be improved by topdressing before seeding. First aerate the turf, then spread a thin (¼″ to ½″) layer of soil, smooth the surface with a leveling bar, then slit-seed to encourage seed: soil contact. (Topdressing a typical soccer, lacrosse, or field hockey field to a ⅜″ depth takes 80 cubic yards of material.)

When renovating a field, consider whether adjusting the grade is necessary. If surface drainage has been inadequate during the season, perform a survey to determine the actual contours of the field and to determine whether a complete regrading is necessary. (If the grade is so far off that total regrading is necessary, follow the steps outlined in Section 12.3, Construction and Reconstruction.)

Many fields gradually become so worn and compacted in front of the goals or in other high-traffic areas that muddy spots become a problem. If the basic contours of the field are sound, these problem areas can often be treated without removing the existing sod. First, aerate the affected areas, aerating as deeply as possible to encourage drainage. Some aerators now on the market are designed to loosen compacted soil with minimal disturbance to the existing turfgrass. These are usually solid tine aerators with a vibrating and fracturing function, and they are ideal for applications like these heavily compacted spots.

Go over the affected area two or three times with the aerator, until the soil is loose enough that it will crumble. If the soil is so badly compacted that aerating won't loosen it to this consistency, it will probably be necessary to strip off the existing turfgrass, scarify the affected area, then apply new soil to the desired contours. Use new soil that's as close as possible to the existing soil to prevent layering. Place grade stakes to guide the recontouring process, then use a pulverizer, power rake, and level bar (or equivalent equipment) to regrade, before seeding or sodding the area.

One renovation technique for areas that are chronically compacted (such as those in front of the goals), is to install sod with at least ½″ of thatch in those areas only. Sodding will typically yield better results than seeding, because the thatch layer provides extra protection against wear.

## 13.5   MAINTENANCE AND MANAGEMENT PROCEDURES

A truly effective turf management program requires regular inspection of the fields, because that's the only way to make knowledgeable decisions about the best promotion of the turfgrass culture. At the beginning of a program of regular inspections, have a soil test performed to help understand the nutrient values of the soil.

Ideally, every field should get at least a quick inspection every other week all year long —even during the off-season. That might seem like a lot of unnecessary work, but even regular five-minute inspections can save hours of work once the season rolls around. During the season, each field should be inspected once or twice a week.

While the turfgrass is actively growing, watch carefully for signs of mowing problems. A thick layer of clippings on the turf means the field is being allowed to grow too high between cuttings, and then is being cut too short. That kind of cutting spreads so many clippings on the turf that it literally kills the grass. And cutting off more than one-third of the plant weakens the grass and makes it less resistant to stresses of all kinds.

In addition to checking mowing height, tear off a couple of blades and examine the cut ends for clean shear and no ragged edges; dull mower blades tear the grass blades and make the turf vulnerable to disease. If the field has a whitish cast after mowing, that's a sign of mower blades that are not sharp enough. A close look will show that the ends of the blades of grass are probably shredded instead of clean-cut. (Of course, make sure the maintenance staff follows the manufacturer's directions for safely sharpening mower blades.)

When performing an inspection, check the moisture of the field. If it's too wet or too dry, those problems are best solved during the off-season, when there's no looming game date. If the field has received substantial precipitation, visual inspection will show how effectively the turf is draining.

One quick way to check for soil moisture is to push a screwdriver into the soil until some resistance is encountered. The screwdriver should easily penetrate 4″ to 6″ into the soil. If the soil is too hard for that, the field probably needs to be watered. (Another tool, called a "soil probe" or "soil profiler," can help check soil compaction, thatch accumulation, and root structure as well as moisture.)

Look for the appearance of weeds in high-traffic areas of the field, especially in the most compacted areas. In the North, for instance, knotweed is usually a sign of over-compaction. Relieving that compaction will allow the turfgrass to crowd out the knotweed.

The previous chapter includes a sample field inspection report, which is very helpful for recording and comparing findings. (See Table 12.1, Sample Field Inspection Report.) Recording all observations in this way helps in remembering all the factors that should be checked, and allows the manager to understand how the field responds to various conditions year-round.

### 13.5a  Warm Season Maintenance

Table 13.1 shows a sample maintenance program that can be tailored to fit the needs of any soccer, lacrosse, or field hockey field in the warm season zone. Remember, this is only one maintenance program that is being used successfully on a particular field. In planning a fertilization program for any given field, the manager should consult the more detailed information found in Chapter 3, Fertility and Fertilizers.

*Fertilization*

The maintenance program outlined in Table 13.1 includes very aggressive fertilization, particularly in the spring, to promote the most rapid possible bermudagrass recovery from the competitive stress of the previous season. If the field is irrigated after fertilization, the heavy N applications can be performed all at once; otherwise, the fertilizer should be split into two applications two weeks apart.

A complete fertilizer (13-13-13) can be used in May to ensure P and K levels are adequate going into the summer months, while summer fertilization utilizes urea (45-0-0) for maintenance applications of one pound of N. Prior to overseeding in September, an application of 18-46-0 helps to promote seedling establishment. A supplemental application of K in October (after overseeding establishment) promotes winter hardiness of the turf, and the winter fertilization utilizes ammonium nitrate (34-0-0) to maintain sufficient ryegrass growth.

*Aeration and Topdressing*

For fields used by soccer programs throughout the year, the only periods of limited use during the growing season are the first of May and August. At these times, a spiker with 6″ curved blades is run over the turf in 2 directions. The field is then topdressed with sand to smooth the divots created by the spiker. An additional ¼″ of sand is applied after the field is overseeded in September to promote seed-to-soil contact.

*Overseeding*

It's a good idea to overseed the field with a three-way perennial ryegrass blend in late September at a rate of 15 pounds of pure live seed per 1,000 square feet. Poorly established areas can be spot-seeded in October. Overseeding is necessary wherever there is year-round use of the turf.

*Mowing*

Best results are achieved by mowing twice weekly at a 1″ height from May through September. Cutting at this height maximizes sod strength of the bermudagrass and encour-

**Table 13.1. Warm Season Maintenance Program**

## Sample Maintenance Schedule
### (Warm Season)

| | | | | |
|---|---|---|---|---|
| Field Name: | Starkville Youth Soccer | Address: | Airport Road | |
| Type of Field: | Game Field | | Starkville, MS 39759 | |

| | | | |
|---|---|---|---|
| Condition: | good | Compaction: | moderate |
| Type of Grass: | common bermudagrass | Drainage: | surface |
| Type of Mower: | 60″ flail mower | Irrigation: | traveling sprinkler |
| Type of Soil: | native clay | Thatch: | ¼″ |

| Soil Test | | | | Notes: | goal areas must be resodded |
|---|---|---|---|---|---|
| Year | 1997 | Phosphorus: | 85 | | in May |
| pH: | 6.4 | Potassium: | 360 | | |

| Time of Year | Fertilization | Aeration | Topdress | Overseed | ⅓ Rule Mowing Ht | 1″ Week Watering | Weed Control |
|---|---|---|---|---|---|---|---|
| May | 13-13-13 2 lb N | spiker two times | ¼″ sand | | 1″ two times a week | traveling sprinkler as needed | |
| June | 45-0-0 1½ lb N | | | | 1″ two times a week | traveling sprinkler every 3 days | 2,4-D plus MSMA spot treat |
| July | 45-0-0 1 lb N | | | | 1″ two times a week | traveling sprinkler every 3 days | 2,4-D plus MSMA spot treat |
| August | 45-0-0 1 lb N | spiker two times | ¼″ sand | | 1″ two times a week | traveling sprinkler every 3 days | |
| September | 18-46-0 1 lb N | | ¼″ sand after overseed | 15 lb perennial rye | 1″ two times a week | traveling sprinkler every 3 days | |
| October | 45-0-0 1 lb N 0-0-61 1½ lb K | | | spot overseed | 2″ one time a week | traveling sprinkler as needed | |
| November | 34-0-0 1 lb N | | | | 2″ one time a week | traveling sprinkler as needed | |
| December | 34-0-0 ½ lb N | | | | 2″ as needed | traveling sprinkler as needed | |
| January | | | | | 2″ as needed | | |
| February | 34-0-0 ½ lb N | | | | 2″ as needed | | |
| March | 45-0-0 ½ lb N | | | | 2″ as needed | | |
| April | 45-0-0 1 lb N | | | | 2″ as needed | | |

ages lateral spread. After overseeding, the cutting height is raised to 2″ to promote winter hardiness and maximize the wear tolerance of the bermudagrass during winter play.

### Watering

It's a good idea to water the field every 3 days (if needed) from June through September, and as needed during the rest of the year. The goal should be to deliver a minimum of 1″ of water per week to maximize turfgrass growth. Following overseeding, the turf is irrigated lightly and frequently to promote establishment of the ryegrass.

### Weed Control

A postemergence herbicide program utilizing MSMA and 2,4-D is helpful in spot-treatment of weed problems beginning in June, but herbicide treatment should be avoided during periods of environmental stress.

## 13.5b  Transitional Zone Maintenance

Maintenance programs in the transitional zone are determined largely by the varieties of turfgrass used. If the field has warm-season varieties such as bermudagrass, follow warm-season maintenance practices, but realize that the cooler weather will shorten the growing season on both ends. If the field has perennial ryegrass or other cool-season varieties, use northern practices but remember that growth will start earlier in the spring and extend later in the fall.

## 13.5c  Cool Season Maintenance

Cool season turfgrasses follow an annual cycle of strong active growth in the spring and early summer, dormancy in the hottest part of the year, and another strong growing season in the late summer and fall. Cool season maintenance practices need to account for this annual cycle. Table 13.2 shows a sample of a maintenance program that can be tailored to fit the needs of any soccer, lacrosse, or field hockey facility in the North.

### Fertilization

Cool season fields should get less than 30% of their annual nitrogen needs in the spring, and the remainder should be applied in the fall. Restricting nitrogen application in the spring of year helps to prevent excessive shoot growth, and encourages strong root growth, which is vital to the health of the turf. At the first fertilization of the spring, apply a starter fertilizer such as 18-24-12, since the actively growing turfgrass plants will benefit from the additional P and K at this point in the year. The starter fertilizer also helps get new plants established.

During the summer, one application of ½ pound nitrogen and a full pound of potassium helps protect plant health during the heat of the summer, and helps the turf to resist disease.

Applying the bulk of the nitrogen in the fall helps the turf recuperate from the stresses of the competitive season. The very best time to apply nitrogen is right after the last mowing of the season, when the grass is still green. During this period, shoot growth slows to a stop, but root growth continues. The extra nitrogen is stored by the root system, and contributes to an early spring greenup, as well as helping the turf withstand summer stresses.

**Table 13.2. Cool Season Maintenance Program**

## Sample Maintenance Schedule
### (Cool Season)

| | | | | | | | |
|---|---|---|---|---|---|---|---|
| Field Name: | Ohio Wesleyan Soccer Field | | | Address: | | Delaware, Ohio | |
| Type of Field: | Game Field | | | | | | |

| | | | | | |
|---|---|---|---|---|---|
| Condition: | good | | Compaction: | yes—goal and bench areas | |
| Type of Grass: | blue/rye | | Drainage: | installed drain system | |
| Type of Mower: | 60″ reel | | Irrigation: | installed automatic system | |
| Type of Soil: | clay/loam | | Thatch: | none | |
| Soil Test: | | | Notes: | some clover—scattered | |
| Year: | 1996 | Phosphorus: 95 | | knotweed—goal area | |
| pH: | 6.8 | Potassium: 450 | | check sprinkler head elevations | |

| Time of Year | Fertilization | Aeration | Topdress | Overseed | ⅓ Rule Mowing Ht | 1″ Week Watering | Weed Control |
|---|---|---|---|---|---|---|---|
| April | 18-24-12<br>¾ lb N<br>50% SRN | core entire field | for surface leveling | bluegrass entire field | 1¼″ | | |
| May | 24-5-11<br>¾ lb N<br>50% SRN | | | | 1½″ | light frequent intervals | |
| June | | solid tine aeration | | | 1½″ | deeper less frequent | |
| July | 16-0-31<br>½ lb N<br>25% SRN | | | | 1¾″ | deeply | |
| August | | | | | 1½″ | deeply | spot treatment |
| September | 32-5-7<br>1 lb N<br>50% SRN | solid tine aeration | | | 1¼″ | cautiously | |
| October | 20-5-10<br>¾ lb N<br>50% SRN | | | | 1¼″ | cautiously | |
| November | 1 lb N after last mowing | core entire field | | | 1½″ | | |

### Aeration

Aerating frequently, and varying equipment, helps to make the turf stronger. In April, core the entire field in preparation for topdressing and slit-seeding. Later in the season use solid tine aeration to loosen the soil without leaving the field strewn with cores. Core aerate the field again at the end of the competitive season.

## Topdressing and Slit-Seeding

Performing these two processes together substantially magnifies the benefits to the turf, and also helps to level the surface. (See Section 13.4 for more information on slit-seeding, or "overseeding.")

## Mowing

The ryegrass starts growing first in the spring, so keep mowing height at about 1¼″ to let sunlight reach the Kentucky bluegrass base. When the Kentucky bluegrass starts growing in May, raise the height by ¼″. In July, the grass height should be at its highest point of the year.

About a month before the first game, start gradually reducing the mowing height to reach the desired height for the first game, remembering to cut off no more than ⅓ of the grass plants at any one mowing. This gradual reduction in advance of the season will allow the turf to adjust to the lower cutting height in time for competitive play.

After the season, keep mowing until growth has completely stopped. If the grass is allowed to grow too long and left that way over the winter, the risk of snow mold increases. On the other hand, scalping in the fall can expose the plant crowns to winter weather, weakening the turfgrass.

A reel mower is recommended for cutting heights of less than 2″.

## Watering

In the spring, water lightly but frequently to help nurture new grass seedlings. Gradually decrease the frequency and increase the amount applied at one time.

If the fall is dry, water with an eye on the weather forecast. It's usually better to let the turf be a little dry than too wet during the season, since sudden rains before or during a game can severely compromise competition.

## Weed Control

The demands placed on sports turf dictate that, as a general rule, the use of blanket weed treatment should be avoided. In order to encourage full recuperation after the season, most fields should be reseeded annually, and that makes application of preemergents unwise, since they stop grass germination. Even postemergent applications should be delayed until the new plants are fully established.

When solid cultural management practices are being followed, weed infestation is usually fairly easy to control. One spot-treatment a few weeks before the season begins is usually adequate to control weeds until long after the last game. Where blanket treatment is necessary because of a particularly severe infestation, perform the application only if the turfgrass and the weeds are actively growing, and make sure the soil has at least normal moisture levels. Avoid weed control applications any time the turf is under drought stress.

## 13.5d  Program Variations (Practice Fields)

In cool season zones, the program outlined in Table 13.2 will support daily practices with minimal damage to the turf. (Of course, the ideal situation is to have more than one practice field to allow periods of recuperation, but that's impractical for most programs.) A team with one practice field usually holds about 100 practices on that turf in the course of a competitive season, resulting in several spots of bare soil by the time the last practice is held. Aerating and fertilizing these bare spots won't help much. A better strategy would be to apply one pound of nitrogen monthly from April to July, to strengthen the turf before the field is used. With careful mowing and watering, this kind of aggressive fertilization will help the field withstand the demands of the season.

## 13.6    RULES AND REGULATIONS

### 13.6a    Line and Boundary Dimensions

Before we look at the line and boundary dimensions for each of these three sports, it should be noted that lacrosse end lines and sidelines are outside the field of play (out-of-bounds), while corresponding lines for field hockey and soccer are considered within the field of play.

*Soccer*

The long sidelines of the field are called *touchlines*, while the shorter lines are referred to as *goal lines*. The *halfway line* divides the ends of the field. A *center circle* with a radius of 30 feet surrounds the *center spot*, from which the ball is put into play at the start of a half (or, for younger children, a quarter) or after a goal.

At each end of the field is a *goal area*, 60 feet wide and 18 feet deep, immediately in front of the goals. A larger area, the *penalty area*, is a rectangle 132 feet wide and 54 feet deep. Directly in front of the goal and 36 feet out is the *penalty spot*, from which point penalty kicks are taken. An arc extends from the outer edge of the penalty area, 30 feet away from the penalty spot, and is known as the *penalty arc*. At each corner of the field, an arc with a 3 foot radius marks the areas from which corner kicks are taken.

Team bench and coaching areas are located on the same side of the field. An officials' area occupies the 30 foot area at the middle of the field, and bench areas begin 15 feet from the officials' area. Each team's area is 60 feet long, and both bench and officials' areas are 10 feet back from the touchline.

(See Figure 13.3 for soccer field dimensions and lines. Table 13.3  shows minimum and maximum dimensions for high school and college.)

*Lacrosse*

A lacrosse field should be 330 feet long and 180 feet wide. Goals are positioned on the long axis of the field, 45 feet from the end line. A circle with a radius of 9 feet is marked around each goal.

A 4″ center line divides the halves of the field, and 2″ lines 60 feet away set off the center of the field from each team's "goal area." Thirty feet inside each sideline and parallel to it, a 60 foot line is marked with its center on the midfield line; these lines designate the "Wing Area." A broken line 30 feet from the sideline denotes the goal area.

As in soccer, team benches are on the same side of the field and 18 feet back from the sidelines. A timer's table sits 18 feet off the sideline at midfield, with a 30 foot wide clear space called the "table area" in front of it. Team benches are in a space from 30 foot to 60 feet away from midfield, and the space in front of the bench is designated as the "coaches' area." Finally, a "limit line" is marked 18 feet outside each sideline.

(See Figure 13.4 for lacrosse field dimensions and lines.)

*Field Hockey*

A regulation field hockey field is 300 feet long and 180 feet wide, with a midfield line and two 25 yard lines across the field. Goals are located on the goal lines, and an arc with a 48 foot radius from each upright is marked around each goal. Directly in front of the goals, a 12 foot long line connects the two arcs. Twenty-one feet from the goal in the center of

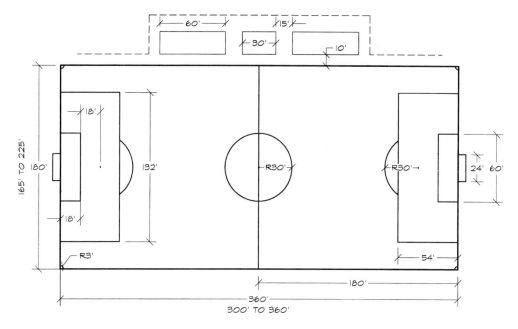

*Figure 13.3. Soccer field dimensions and lines.*

**Table 13.3. Minimum and Maximum Dimensions for High School and College Soccer Fields (in feet)**

| | SOCCER | | |
| | Minimum | Maximum | Recommended |
|---|---|---|---|
| **High School** - NFSHSA Rules | 165×300 | 225×360 | |
| High School | | | 195×330 |
| Junior High School | | | 165×300 |
| **College** - NCAA Rules | 195×330 | 240×360 | 225×360 |
| Post 9/95 construction | 210×345 | | |

the field, a 12″ "penalty stroke line" is marked. A circle with a 15 foot radius is marked around the exact center of the field.

At the boundaries of the field, and 15 feet from the sidelines, "alley lines" are indicated by marking hash marks across the midfield line, end lines, and 25-yard lines. Lines are also marked inward from the sidelines on each side of the field at 48 feet from the back line, to correspond to the top of the goal arc. Finally, small hash marks are made on the back lines 15 and 30 feet outside the goals themselves.

All lines must be at least 3″ wide.

Team benches are on the same side of the field, on either side of an officials' table and 15 feet back from the sideline. "Spectator lines" are marked 30 feet outside the sideline on the side where benches are located, and 15 feet outside the sideline on the other side.

(See Figure 13.5 for field hockey field dimensions and lines.)

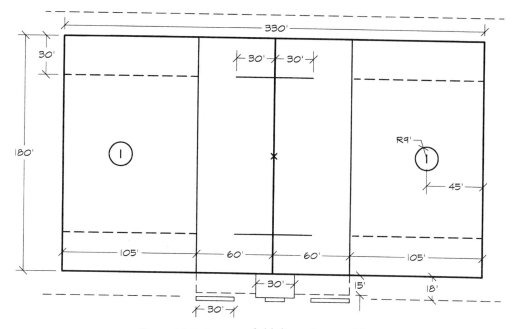

*Figure 13.4. Lacrosse field dimensions and lines.*

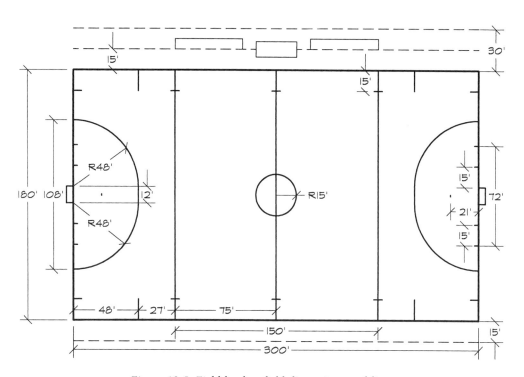

*Figure 13.5. Field hockey field dimensions and lines.*

## 13.6b Governing and Sanctioning Bodies

*Soccer:*

American Youth Soccer Organization
P. O. Box 5045
Hawthorne, California   90251-5045
(213) 643-6455

College:
The National Collegiate Athletic Association
6201 College Boulevard
Overland Park, Kansas  66211
(913) 339-1906

High School:
National Federation of State High School Associations
11724 NW Plaza Circle, P. O. Box 20626
Kansas City, Missouri  64195
(816) 464-5400

*Lacrosse:*

The Lacrosse Foundation
113 West University Parkway
Baltimore, Maryland  21210
(301) 235-6882     FAX (301) 366-6735

National Collegiate Athletic Association (NCAA)
National Federation of State High School Associations
(Addresses above)

*Field Hockey:*

Field Hockey Association of America
1750 East Boulder Street
Colorado Springs, Colarado   80909
(719) 578-4587

National Collegiate Athletic Association
National Federation of State High School Associations
(Addresses above)

# Chapter 14

# *Lawn Bowling Greens and Croquet Courts*

## 14.1 INTRODUCTION

From the perspective of the facilities on which they are played, lawn bowling and croquet have much in common. As the name implies, lawn bowling is a sport that is played on grass. For our purposes, we will consider croquet as a sport that is also played on grass, although it also can be played on hard surfaces such as fine granular or clay material (as discussed in Chapter 19, Bocce Courts). Both sports use similar size balls that must roll across the surface in a smooth and uniform fashion. For this reason, the height of the grass is very short, so maintenance considerations are critical for both sports. Both have flat and level surfaces, so design and construction techniques are much the same.

(In the related sport of "crown green bowls," played in Europe and some British Commonwealth countries, the green has a slight crown. In crowned greens, play can be in any direction, whereas with level greens, typical of North American play, competition is confined to designated areas called "rinks," 14 to 19 feet wide.)

Bowling greens and croquet courts also share a number of characteristics which set them apart from all other turf sports fields discussed in this book. The biggest difference is the list of turfgrass stresses which these facilities must tolerate. The number one turfgrass stress for bowling greens and croquet courts is the low mowing height used on their turf. Other stresses are caused by constant dethatching and limited irrigation; both necessary to keep the surface smooth and firm for good ball response. (In most other sports, the greatest stress is mechanical, caused by players' cleats ripping the turf and compacting the soil. Because of this tearing and compaction, some thatch is desirable to protect many other sports field surfaces.) The dethatching process is typically carried out during a period of active growth, and the turf is liberally watered to help in recuperation from the event. But bowling greens and croquet courts are at their best when firm and dry, so irrigation must be performed carefully and lightly.

Another important difference between other fields and bowling greens and croquet courts is that these facilities are meant to be flat and level. Because of the nature of the game and the importance of true roll (similar, in a sense, to the roll of a ball across a pool table), the surface needs to be flat, level, and smooth.

Golf and country clubs would seem to be the most promising places to build and maintain these facilities, because these clubs already have the equipment and the experienced personnel required to properly maintain such closely mowed turf. Not surprisingly, many lawn bowling and croquet facilities currently in operation are found at clubs of this kind.

Because the size of the courts are similar, some enthusiasts urge the construction of facilities used for both sports. However, some devotees insist that the traffic on dual-use facilities places additional stress on the facility, and compromises its quality. From a management standpoint, the critical issue is probably the amount of use the shared turf will support; lightly used facilities can withstand both sports, but heavily-used turf will not support competition well for either.

## 14.2   DESIGN

### 14.2a   Survey and Layout
The overall size of a court used for lawn bowling is 120 feet by 120 feet. For six wicket croquet, it is 84 feet by 105 feet, and for nine wicket croquet, 50 feet by 100 feet. (See drawings in Section 14.6a for detailed layouts.) As with any sports field, survey enough land to isolate the court against runoff from the surrounding terrain. The rule book does not recommend a north-south orientation for either sport.

### 14.2b   Design Criteria for New Construction
In designing facilities for these sports, the planner will need to follow different specifications for each sport. The American Lawn Bowls Association has published specifications calling for a 10″ layer of washed sand of fine-to-medium texture (.2 mm to .4 mm), with less than 1% silt and clay and no gravel layer underneath. (This specification calls for finer sand than United States Golf Association specifications, with the finer sand meant to provide a firmer surface.)

The published specifications produced in cooperation with the United States Croquet Association follow those issued by the USGA for golf putting greens. These specifications call for an amended medium sand over a gravel layer 4″ thick; the amended sand growing medium allows for the best possible percolation rates. (For more information on amended sand fields, see Chapter 24.)

### 14.2c   Turfgrass Selection
In the South, bermudagrass provides the best surface for both sports. The Lawn Bowls Association recommends Tifgreen™, while croquet authorities recommend that cultivar or Tifdwarf™. A new generation of bermudagrasses known as "ultradwarfs" are now available. These grasses require intensive management programs, including mowing heights of ⅛″ or less, frequent grooming and verticutting, and topdressing. They have become very popular as a putting green surface in the warm climates of this country, and it is likely they will be equally popular for lawn bowling greens and croquet courts. In the transitional zone, croquet recommends zoysiagrass grass (Meyer™ or Emerald™), bermudagrass, or creeping bentgrass (Penncross™), but lawn bowls recommends only bermudagrass or creeping bentgrass. In the North, both sports recommend creeping bentgrass. There are also new generations of zoysiagrass and creeping bentgrass that promise to provide playing surfaces superior to the standard cultivars listed here. These new grasses also have better tolerance to close cutting heights, but also require more intensive maintenance.

Bermudagrass greens for lawn bowling are regarded as faster; about 2 seconds faster than bentgrass. The speed of a lawn bowling green is judged by the number of seconds it takes for a bowl to come to rest 90 feet from its release point. The green is considered slow if the elapsed time is 9 seconds, acceptable at 11–13 seconds, and fast if the elapsed time is greater.

(This method of measuring the speed of the green may seem contradictory at first glance, since a green on which the ball takes a shorter time to travel the same distance is considered "slower." However, it's important to keep in mind that a lawn bowl is elliptical, which means that on a faster green, it will travel in a greater arc than on a slow green, where it will travel in a straighter line.)

Bentgrass is sometimes used in the South to overseed the bermudagrass base for winter play. The performance characteristics of rough bluegrass suggest that it may also be used for this purpose.

### 14.2d  Installed Irrigation Systems

To keep the surface firm and fast, the soil needs to be a little on the dry side. During dry conditions, irrigation start and run times should be adjusted manually each day on the controller rather than depending on the automatic feature. Constant monitoring of the soil by the maintenance staff is necessary to prevent a soggy surface.

The design in Figure 14.1 shows an installed irrigation system for a lawn bowling green. This design requires water pressure of 75 PSI at field edge and yields a pressure of 60 PSI at the base of the sprinkler heads. Average precipitation rate for this system will be .38 inches/hour for full circle heads, .76 inches/hour for half-circle heads, and 1.52 inches/hour for quarter-circle heads. Running time for 1″ watering will be 2 hours 38 minutes for full circle heads, 1 hour 19 minutes for half-circle heads, and 40 minutes per station for quarter-circle heads.

The design in Figure 14.2 shows an installed irrigation system for a six-wicket croquet court. This design shows a sprinkler head in the middle of the court. Offset this head a foot or so to avoid the stake that is directly in the center of the court.

This design requires water pressure of 75 PSI at field edge and yields a pressure of 60 PSI at the base of the sprinkler heads. Average precipitation rate for this system will be .37 inches/hour for full circle heads, .74 inches/hour for half-circle heads, and 1.48 inches/hour for quarter-circle heads. Running time for 1″ watering will be 2 hours 41 minutes for full circle heads, 1 hour 21 minutes for half-circle heads, and 40 minutes per station for quarter-circle heads.

The variety of croquet most familiar to Americans is considered nine-wicket croquet. The rules of this game have, in recent years, been added to the official rule book of the United States Croquet Association, and call for an area of 100 feet by 50 feet (as opposed to 104 feet by 85 feet) for the traditional six-wicket game. This smaller court area obviously requires a different irrigation system, and Figure 14.3 shows an irrigation system designed for this type of court.

This design for a nine-wicket court also requires water pressure of 75 PSI at field edge and yields a pressure of 60 PSI at the base of the sprinkler heads. Average precipitation rate for this system will be .72 inches/hour for half-circle heads and 1.44 inches/hour for quarter-circle heads. Running time for 1″ watering will be 1 hour 23 minutes for half-circle heads and 42 minutes per station for quarter-circle heads.

### 14.2e  Installed Drain Systems and Catch Basins

Lawn bowling authorities specify a somewhat different installed drain system than croquet organizations, who call for a slightly modified version of USGA specs.

Lawn bowling specifications call for dead-level 3″ drains 15″ below the surface and 5″ below the sub-base, with drain pipes to be 5 feet apart. This level system is tied into an

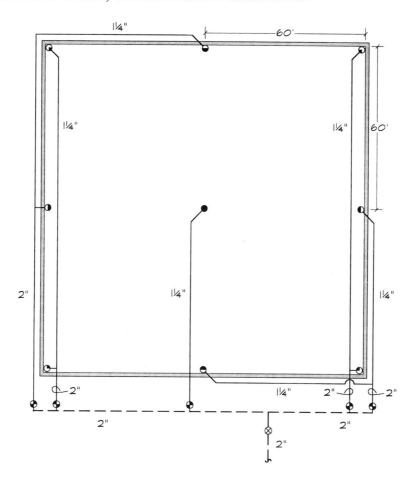

## IRRIGATION LEGEND

| | DESCRIPTION | PSI | GPM | RADIUS | ARC | UNIT |
|---|---|---|---|---|---|---|
| ● | HUNTER I-40-36S-43 FULL CIRCLE | 60 | 15.5 | 59 FT. | 360° | 1 |
| ◖ | HUNTER I-40-ADS-43 PART CIRCLE | 60 | 15.5 | 59 FT. | 180° | 4 |
| ◕ | HUNTER I-40-ADS-43 PART CIRCLE | 60 | 15.5 | 59 FT. | 90° | 4 |
| ◕ | 1½" HUNTER ICV 151G REMOTE CONTROL VALVE FOR PERIMETER HEADS | | | | | 4 |
| ◕ | 1" HUNTER ICV 101G REMOTE CONTROL VALVE FOR CENTER HEAD | | | | | 1 |
| ⊗ | 2" GATE VALVE FOR MAINLINE ISOLATION | | | | | 1 |
| —— | NON-PRESSURE PIPE (PVC CLASS 160 RECOMMENDED) | | | | | |
| - - - | PRESSURE PIPE (PVC CLASS 200 RECOMMENDED) | | | | | |

NOT SHOWN:
BACKFLOW PREVENTION DEVICE
(AS REQUIRED PER CODE AND/OR ORDINANCE - AND FOR SAFETY)      1
HUNTER ICC IRRIGATION CONTROLLER (5 STATIONS)
LOCATION AS NEEDED      1

### DESIGN PROVIDED BY HUNTER INDUSTRIES

*Figure 14.1. Lawn bowling green irrigation system design.*

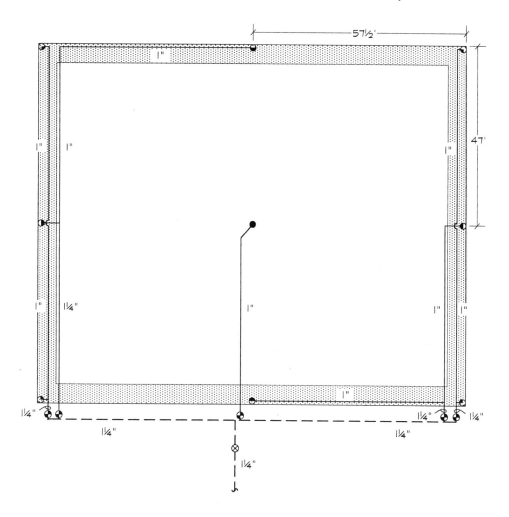

## IRRIGATION LEGEND

| | DESCRIPTION | PSI | GPM | RADIUS | ARC | UNITS |
|---|---|---|---|---|---|---|
| ● | HUNTER I-40-36S-40 FULL CIRCLE | 60 | 8.5 | 48 FT. | 360° | 1 |
| ◖ | HUNTER I-40-ADS-40 PART CIRCLE | 60 | 8.5 | 48 FT. | 180° | 4 |
| ◔ | HUNTER I-40-ADS-40 PART CIRCLE | 60 | 8.5 | 48 FT. | 90° | 4 |
| ◉ | I" HUNTER ICV IOIG REMOTE CONTROL VALVE | | | | | 5 |
| ⊗ | 1¼" GATE VALVE FOR MAINLINE ISOLATION | | | | | 1 |
| ——— | NON-PRESSURE PIPE (PVC CLASS 160 RECOMMENDED) | | | | | |
| — — | PRESSURE PIPE (PVC CLASS 200 RECOMMENDED) | | | | | |

NOT SHOWN:
BACKFLOW PREVENTION DEVICE
(AS REQUIRED PER CODE AND/OR ORDINANCE - AND FOR SAFETY)          1

HUNTER ICC IRRIGATION CONTROLLER (5 STATIONS)
LOCATION AS NEEDED                                              1

DESIGN PROVIDED BY HUNTER INDUSTRIES

*Figure 14.2. Six wicket croquet court irrigation system design.*

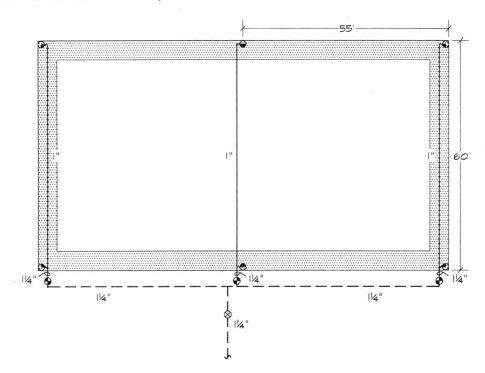

## IRRIGATION LEGEND

| | DESCRIPTION | PSI | GPM | RADIUS | ARC | UNITS |
|---|---|---|---|---|---|---|
| ◕ | HUNTER I-40-ADS-42 PART CIRCLE | 60 | 12.3 | 55 FT. | 180° | 2 |
| ◔ | HUNTER I-40-ADS-42 PART CIRCLE | 60 | 12.3 | 55 FT. | 90° | 4 |
| ⊕ | I" HUNTER ICV IOIG REMOTE CONTROL VALVE | | | | | 3 |
| ⊗ | 1¼" GATE VALVE FOR MAINLINE ISOLATION | | | | | 1 |
| —— | NON-PRESSURE PIPE (PVC CLASS 160 RECOMMENDED) | | | | | |
| — — | PRESSURE PIPE (PVC CLASS 200 RECOMMENDED) | | | | | |

NOT SHOWN:
  BACKFLOW PREVENTION DEVICE
  (AS REQUIRED PER CODE AND/OR ORDINANCE - AND FOR SAFETY)                    1
  HUNTER ICC IRRIGATION CONTROLLER (3 STATIONS)
  LOCATION AS NEEDED                                                          1

DESIGN PROVIDED BY HUNTER INDUSTRIES

*Figure 14.3. Nine wicket croquet court irrigation system design.*

area drain box, which can then be used as a tool to monitor the effectiveness of the system. This area box can also be capped to prevent drainage during construction to prevent drying. The entire sub-base, including the pipe drain ditches, is to be lined with plastic sheeting.

Croquet courts are to have sloped 4″ pipe drains, with pipes laid on 10 feet (minimum) centers. This varies somewhat from USGA specs, which call for the pipes to be 15 feet on center. The closer placement on the croquet court helps to accommodate the level playing surface. With no surface runoff, all the water that falls on the court must drain freely by gravity through the profile to the drains below.

Because of the flat surface, it's necessary to use catch basins or swales to isolate the court and keep runoff from reaching the playing area itself.

## 14.3 CONSTRUCTION AND RECONSTRUCTION

Contractors retained to build these facilities should be familiar with the methods of construction required for USGA putting greens. These methods are discussed in Chapter 24, and it's wise to read Chapter 24—Sand and Sand-Based Fields—in its entirety before planning or constructing a court based on USGA specifications.

In the context of lawn bowling or croquet, reconstruction is usually limited to the conversion of a native soil to American Lawn Bowls Association or United States Croquet Association specifications.

## 14.4 RENOVATION

The best renovation practice is to provide the turf a rest period, preferably during the growing season. Keeping players off the area for a week or two will allow the turf to recover from the mechanical stresses of close mowing and regular dethatching. Accomplishing this rest period during the growing season is obviously much easier for cool season turfgrass than for warm season turf, since the growing season for cool season grasses extends further into the fall than for warmer climates.

The best advice for bermudagrass groundskeepers is to raise the mowing height by at least ½″ in the fall and winter, when the court is not being used. The raised cutting height will help keep the bermudagrass from drying out in the winter. Also, protective covers can be placed over the bermudagrass turf to protect from winter temperature extremes. (See Chapter 26 for further information on covers.) Fortunately, bermudagrass thrives with a lower cutting height during the hottest part of the summer. (If the turf is overseeded, the mowing heights should be kept at or near their summertime levels.)

Core aeration and topdressing with significant amounts of sand (approximately ¼″ depth) are usually limited to the off-season because these two processes affect the roll of the ball. It is best to remove the cores and topdress with a sand that matches the soil profile. When topdressing, make sure the holes are filled all the way to the top to prevent little depressions from the settling of the holes. Topdressing also provides a good opportunity to fill in any low spots that have formed during the season.

## 14.5 MAINTENANCE AND MANAGEMENT PROCEDURES

In any part of the country, mowing and thatch management are the most demanding maintenance procedures, whereas irrigation and fertilization must be kept to a minimum. With a height of cut at ⅛″ to 5⁄32″, and following the ⅓ rule, the grass must be mowed on a daily schedule. Since thatch must be kept to a minimum, weekly, light vertical mowing is necessary during the growing season. The vertical mowing and grooming attachments available with most triplex or walk-behind reel mowers used on golf greens work well. Minimal applications of nitrogen (less than one pound per month) will help to keep thatch at a minimum. Also, as mentioned above, irrigation must be monitored very closely; provide the minimum required to keep the turf actively growing, since wet surfaces slow the roll of the ball.

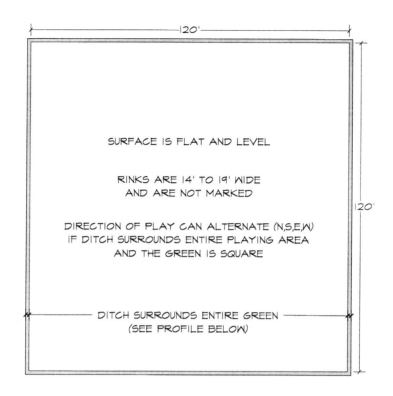

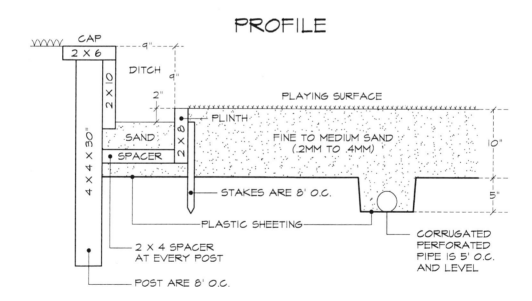

*Figure 14.4. Lawn bowling green layout.*

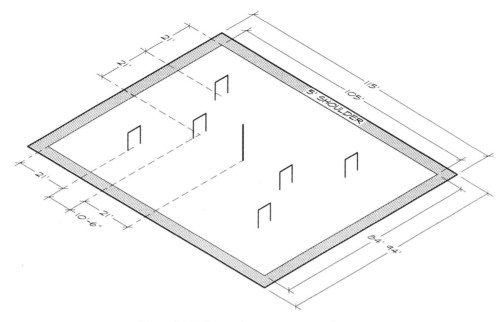

*Figure 14.5. Six wicket croquet court layout.*

Core aeration should be conducted three times a year when the turf is most actively growing. Unfortunately, for warm season courts, this is the time of year that the court gets the most use. If the court is closed for a rest period, as suggested above, the beginning of this rest period provides the best opportunity to perform core aeration. Water injection and/or solid tine aeration can be used for temporary relief of compaction during periods of heavy use without long-lasting surface disruption. Water injection in particular can be used frequently without an appreciable effect on the playing surface. (However, remember that these two cultivation techniques cannot replace the need for core aeration in a regular cultivation program.) For cool season courts, aerate once in the spring, at least two weeks before play begins, and twice in the fall after play ends.

There are fewer disease problems on lawn bowling greens and croquet courts than on golf greens, because of the reduced irrigation. By keeping irrigation at a minimum—a requirement for maintaining a firm surface—a secondary benefit is gained: less incidence of disease.

## 14.6   RULES AND REGULATIONS

### 14.6a  Line and Boundary Dimensions
See Figures 14.4 to 14.6.

### 14.6b  Governing and Sanctioning Bodies

*Lawn Bowling:*
American Lawn Bowls Association
17775 Main Street, Suite B
Irvine, California  92614
(714) 476-3133

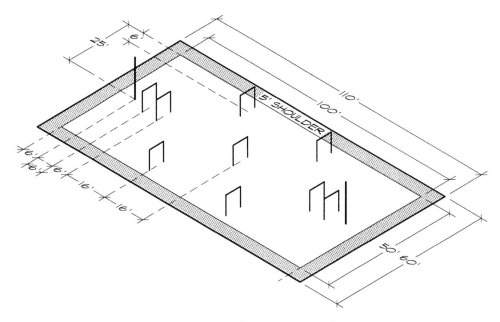

*Figure 14.6. Nine wicket croquet court layout.*

**Croquet:**
United States Croquet Association
511585-B Polo Club Road
Wellington, Florida  33414
(561) 753-9141

## REFERENCES

*Haley, E. R., The Construction of the Lawn Bowling Green.* American Lawn Bowls
    Association, Irvine, CA, 1990.
Maybee, C. H., *Recommendations for a Championship Croquet Court.* United States
    Croquet Association, Wellington, FL, 1992.

# PART III

# *Other Sports Surfaces*

Sports facilities often include a number of other surfaces for diversified sports and recreational activities—some with grass and some without. The people responsible for designing and maintaining these surfaces are usually the same people who are responsible for the rest of the fields.

Chapters 15 through 19 offer suggestions for designing, constructing, reconstructing, and renovating sports surfaces other than turf, which could be assigned to a designer or a facilities manager who is also responsible for fields. Among these surfaces are those used for tennis, track, volleyball, playgrounds, and bocce.

It should be noted that the terms (design, construction, reconstruction and renovation) have the same meanings for these surfaces as for turf sports fields, which are described in the chapters of Part II. These definitions can be found in the introduction to Part II.

These surfaces have much in common with turf fields. For example, they must be designed to protect the safety of the user, as well as to remain playable in a variety of temperature and weather conditions, and to provide uniform ball response. Drainage is another factor in common; in fact, many of these surfaces use the same type of installed drain systems as turf fields.

Likewise, the problems that arise with other sports surfaces are the same problems commonly found on turf fields: rain delays, standing water, and so on. Part III provides detailed information to assist the designer, the installer, and the manager to make the facility safer, easier to maintain, and more usable.

# Chapter 15

# *Tennis Courts*

## 15.  INTRODUCTION

In tennis court design, construction, and maintenance, the goals are the same as for any other sports facility: playability, safety, and the durability of the surface. A good design results in a tennis court which will remain usable for many years, eliminating the need for reconstruction a few years down the road, and reducing renovation and maintenance costs.

As with other sports facilities, construction errors are usually a result of incomplete or faulty designs. The most common error is to incorrectly contour the court and the surrounding area. For example, although the court is not to be perfectly level (a slight slope allows surface drainage), it needs to be flat so the height of the net will remain true. The court must also be isolated from the surrounding terrain so that outside surface water does not run onto the playing area. Properly designed tennis courts will shed water quickly, so they can be used soon after a rain.

Although there are a limited number of grass tennis courts in North America, these facilities are included in this chapter along with paved courts and clay courts, because the design criteria and contours for grass courts are the same as for the more common varieties.

Short courts, about one fourth the size of a regular tennis court, are becoming popular for backyard play. Short courts are also popular at retirement communities, apartment complexes, motels, and resorts, because "paddle tennis," which is played on short courts, is popular with players of all ages. Short courts can also be used for a variety of other sports, such as basketball, volleyball, and badminton. Short courts have the same kinds of surfaces as regulation courts; the only difference is the size of the court and the rules of the game. Short courts are also included in this chapter, since the design principles and the construction techniques are the same as regulation tennis courts.

## 15.2  DESIGN

Tennis courts are among the smallest playing surfaces discussed in this book, with only such facilities as bocce, nine-wicket croquet, and sand volleyball courts using less space. However, the construction cost per square foot of a tennis court is the highest of all sports fields in this book. For one thing, when the "clear playing area" around the court is added, the dimensions of the area commonly thought of as "the tennis court" are more than two and a half times the dimensions of the lined court itself. With the budget for necessary extras, such as high fences, windscreens, net posts, net, and even lighting, the cost per square foot of the court escalates rapidly.

### 15.2a  Survey and Layout

The standard tennis court, lined for both singles and doubles, is 36 feet × 78 feet. With 12 feet at each side and 21 feet at each end of the court for a clear playing area, the standard size court is 60 feet × 120 feet. (A court set up for singles only is 27 feet × 78 feet.) The standard size short court, including the clear playing area, is 30 feet × 60 feet. The design process begins with surveying enough land to determine the natural movement of surface water in and around the site to determine if catch basins, swales, or interceptor drains will be necessary.

Tennis courts need to be oriented a little differently in the northern U.S. than in the South, especially if the southern courts will be used year-round. In the North, tennis courts typically are used from May through September and a north-south orientation is used most often. In the South, it is better to orient the court 15°–25° off true north in a northwest-southeast direction, especially if players will use the court between 3:00 and 4:00 in the afternoon. This orientation prevents the players from looking directly into the sun during the winter months, when the sun is lower in the sky.

### 15.2b  Design Criteria for New Construction

The most critical issue to be dealt with in designing a tennis court is the height of the net, which is to be 36″ above the surface at the center of the court and 42″ above the surface at the post. Another critical issue is positive surface drainage, which is as important for tennis courts as it is for the skinned areas of baseball diamonds. If the court has a uniform slope with no deviations in the grade, the height of the net can be set correctly.

### 15.2c  Court Designs with Preferred Contours

The preferred tennis court contour is a flat surface that is sloped side-to-side. If the existing terrain is sloped in such a way that an end-to-end slope would work better, this contour would be the second choice. A third choice is to slope the surface from corner to corner. No matter what the contour of the existing land, *a tennis court surface should never be crowned in any direction.* Any crown at all affects the height of the net.

The recommended percentage of slope for a nonporous court (asphalt or concrete) is 1″ in 10 feet (.8%) to 1¼″ in 10 feet (1%). The percentage of slope for a porous court (grass or clay) is 1″ in 30 feet (.25%) to 1″ in 20 feet (.4%). The lowest percentage of slope (.25%) is recommended only for grass courts built with an amended sand growing medium, because water is expected to drain by gravity to an installed network of subsurface pipe drains to keep the court playable. Clay courts or fast-dry courts will dry faster when the percentage of slope is at .4%, because these courts must depend on surface drainage rather than internal drainage.

### 15.2d  Multiple-Court Layout

If there is sufficient space for multiple courts, there is a definite cost advantage in building them. The reason for a lower cost is that multiple courts (built side-by-side) share the clear playing area between the courts. For example, a court that is built alone needs a 12-foot clear playing area on both sides of the court. In the case of multiple courts, the 12 foot clear space is shared by two courts, eliminating an area that is 12 feet wide by 120 feet long. This saves about 20% of the cost of the second court.

For club play, the United States Tennis Association recommends limiting the shared clear space to three consecutive courts, with a 15-foot shared clear playing area on both sides of the middle court.

## 15.2e Tennis Court Surfaces

As mentioned above, surfaces for tennis can be divided into nonporous surfaces and porous surfaces.

### Nonporous Paved Courts

The most common nonporous surfaces for tennis courts are paved surfaces with a color coating. This color coating can take several forms, from paint to rubberized materials. In the North, asphalt is used more often than concrete. In the South, concrete is more common, because asphalt tends to melt as a result of prolonged high temperatures. Nonporous courts require the least maintenance, and when properly constructed, they need to be renovated only about every four to six years. Renovation is usually limited to color coating and line painting. (Follow local codes for proper base materials and surface installation.)

### Nonporous Sand-Filled Synthetic Turf Courts

A new type of tennis court playing surface that is increasing in popularity is sand-filled synthetic turf. This type of surface provides a durable playing surface that places reduced stress on players' feet and legs. Sand-filled synthetic turf also offers rapid drainage characteristics and limited maintenance (which consists primarily of applying, distributing, and smoothing the sand into and across the turf fibers). This type of surface has competitive characteristics that are a cross between those experienced on grass and clay courts. In using this type of surface, consult manufacturers' specifications regarding sand size and uniformity. The synthetic turf is installed over concrete or asphalt.

### Porous Clay Courts and Fast-Dry Courts

Fast-dry courts are sometimes referred to as "clay courts," but there is a difference between the two. The main difference is that what is called "clay" is actually a natural material consisting of a mixture of sand, silt, and clay (similar to the material used on the skinned area of a baseball diamond). Fast-dry material is manufactured from crushed stone or brick, mixed with a chemical binder. Fast-dry courts are more widely used than clay courts. In fact, most clay courts eventually are upgraded to fast-dry courts by adding a thin layer (⅜″) of fast-dry material on top of the clay.

Both clay courts and fast-dry courts require daily or weekly maintenance such as line painting, brushing and rolling the surface, and even daily irrigation to keep the surface playable in hot, dry weather. Annual renovation is necessary to renew the surface for another year's use. Fast-dry courts are popular at tennis clubs, which typically use them in combination with paved courts.

### Porous Grass Courts

There are not many grass courts in existence in North America, and most of those in use are found at golf or country clubs. The reason for their rarity is that grass courts need the attention of a professional groundskeeper to be maintained properly. (Country clubs already have such professionals on staff.)

Since grass tennis courts are designed with less slope than other tennis court surfaces, high water permeability rates are necessary to avoid a soggy surface. To achieve high permeability rates and less soil compaction, predominantly sand-based soils used in golf putting green construction are sometimes used. These systems (described in Chapter 24) typically contain 80% or more sand mixed thoroughly with an organic matter source. Installed correctly, these soil mixes deliver adequate water holding capacity, while still providing rapid drainage and reduced compaction. Amended sand as a growing medium can also provide another benefit for grass tennis courts: amendment with sand can help to minimize compaction tendency in concentrated traffic areas.

(It's important to remember, however, that predominantly sand-based soils also have high maintenance requirements, particularly in regard to fertility and irrigation management.)

A mid-1990s survey by the United States Tennis Association (USTA) indicated that most grass court tennis was not played on the typical sand-based soil systems used in golf putting green construction. The reason for this is that footing stability decreases as the grass wears. For this reason, many grass court facilities in this country simply manage their existing topsoil (if suitable), purchase and install a desirable topsoil such as a sandy loam, or if choosing to go with a sand-based system as described in Chapter 24, meet specifications that allow for the addition of some clay and silt-based material in the mix. These soils will obviously have very different physical and chemical properties and will have to be managed accordingly.

In the southern U.S., the type of grass used most often for grass tennis courts is bermudagrass. For instance, the Sonoran Clubhouse, near Scottsdale, Arizona, includes four Jack Nicklaus-designed golf courses, a grass tennis court, and a nine-wicket croquet lawn. The tennis and croquet courts were constructed to meet USGA putting green specifications. For irrigation, the Clubhouse uses a drip system 6″ below final grade with 12″ spacing, instead of the traditional pop-up rotors. A ½″ hot water pipe heating system was installed 2″ below the drip irrigation at 6″ on center to keep frost off the surface of the tennis court during the early morning winter hours. The grass is 'Tifgreen' bermudagrass and is mowed at ³⁄₁₆″. The tennis court is overseeded in the winter with perennial ryegrass.[1]

For cool season tennis courts, creeping bentgrass is usually the turfgrass of choice. At Wimbledon, however, the turfgrass is 70% 'Lorina' perennial ryegrass and 30% 'Barcrown' creeping red fescue.[2] The average height of cut during the playing season is 8 millimeters (approximately ⁵⁄₁₆″). There are 32 grass courts at Wimbledon, maintained by a crew of 14 full-time and 8 part-time employees. Needless to say, it is not an easy task to properly maintain top-quality grass tennis courts.

### 15.2f   Installed Irrigation Systems

The irrigation design shown in Figure 15.1 can be used for clay, fast-dry, and grass court surfaces. The only difference is that for clay and fast-dry courts, a faster-rotating sprinkler head is recommended to keep the surface from being saturated too quickly. The faster rotation allows for better control of the amount of water being applied at one time.

(The irrigation system in Figure 15.1 specifies Hunter's I-40 head. For clay and fast-dry surfaces, the I-42 head should be substituted; the I-42 rotates three times as fast, cutting rotation time from three minutes to one minute. However, to achieve the same throwing distance, substitute the next larger nozzle size. This large nozzle will increase

---

[1] Wimbledon Never Looked Like This!, *Sports Turf*, November/December, pp. 10–12, 1996.
[2] Getting Wimbledon Ready, *Dallas Morning News*, pp. 12 B, July 5, 1997.

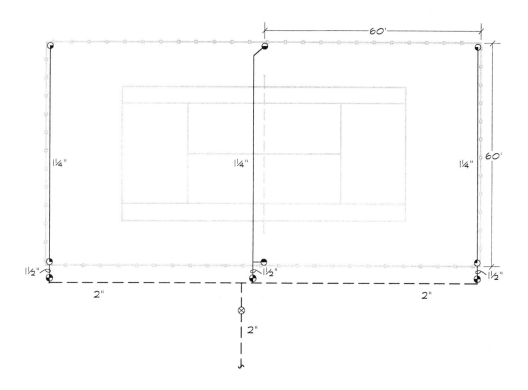

## IRRIGATION LEGEND

| | DESCRIPTION | PSI | GPM | RADIUS | ARC | UNITS |
|---|---|---|---|---|---|---|
| ◐ | HUNTER I-40-ADS-43 PART CIRCLE | 60 | 15.5 | 59 FT. | 180° | 2 |
| ◔ | HUNTER I-40-ADS-43 PART CIRCLE | 60 | 15.5 | 59 FT. | 90° | 4 |
| ◉ | 1½" HUNTER ICV 151G REMOTE CONTROL VALVE | | | | | 3 |
| ⊗ | 2" GATE VALVE FOR MAINLINE ISOLATION | | | | | 1 |
| —— | NON-PRESSURE PIPE (PVC CLASS 160 RECOMMENDED) | | | | | |
| — — | PRESSURE PIPE (PVC CLASS 200 RECOMMENDED) | | | | | |

NOT SHOWN:
BACKFLOW PREVENTION DEVICE
(AS REQUIRED PER CODE AND/OR ORDINANCE - AND FOR SAFETY)                    1

HUNTER ICC IRRIGATION CONTROLLER (3 STATIONS)
LOCATION AS NEEDED                                                          1

DESIGN PROVIDED BY HUNTER INDUSTRIES

*Figure 15.1. Irrigation system for porous tennis court surfaces.*

the gallons per minute applied, but the amount will still be less than half that applied by the I-40 head.)

This design requires water pressure of 75 PSI at field edge and yields a pressure of 60 PSI at the base of the sprinkler heads. Average precipitation rate for this system will be .83 inches/hour for half-circle heads and 1.66 inches/hour for quarter-circle heads. Running time for 1″ watering will be one hour 12 minutes for half-circle heads, 36 minutes for quarter-circle heads.

## 15.2g  Installed Drain Systems and Catch Basins

### Nonporous Surfaces

Under normal circumstances, nonporous tennis court surfaces will not need a subsurface drain system under the court. However, if they are constructed in a low-lying area, or an area known to have a high water table, a network of installed subsurface drains may be necessary to keep water from accumulating under the court. Underlying water will eventually degrade the paved surface and reconstruction will be necessary.

However, it may be necessary to intercept surface water as it runs off the court so it will not reach an adjoining facility. An interceptor drain placed at the low end of the court will serve this purpose. This type of drain has a perforated pipe with pea gravel all the way to the surface. (For more on interceptor drains, see Chapter 8, Section 8.4a)

Swales and/or catch basins are typically necessary around a court to stop surface water from reaching the court.

### Porous Surfaces

Porous tennis courts, especially those with grass surfaces, require an installed drain system. The type of subsurface drain system recommended for amended sand grass courts is discussed in Chapter 24. The only type of installed drain system recommended for a clay or fast-dry court is a traditional pipe drain system with 4″ pipes and pea gravel to within 4″ of the surface. However, it should be noted that this type of drainage system only helps in removing subsurface water. Water on the surface could be there for days, because the clay or fast-dry material is not porous enough to let water pass through quickly. Clay and fast-dry courts act much like a baseball field skinned area, so surface drainage is the most important factor in assuring a playable surface in wet weather.

Like nonporous surfaces, porous tennis courts need to be isolated from the surrounding terrain with swales and/or catch basins to stop surface water from reaching the court.

## 15.3   CONSTRUCTION AND RECONSTRUCTION

### Construction

With plans in hand, the construction process for any type of tennis court begins with the installation of grade stakes to achieve the proper grade. First, set the subgrade and install subsurface drainage structures and a granular layer, if specified. Then apply the surfacing material to achieve the finish grade.

For any type of court except grass, after finish grade is achieved, flood the area (or wait for a heavy rain) to check for low spots. If such low spots ("bird baths," large enough to cover a nickel) appear, raise the area with an appropriate fill material to correct the grade. If the standing water in the low spots does not cover a five-cent piece, these puddles should evaporate quickly, and are considered to be within the tolerance of good tennis court construction. After correcting the grade, reflood the area until no "bird baths" are present.

Net posts are usually installed after the final grade is achieved, so they do not obstruct grading equipment and so they will be at the right height above the surface. Then, for nonporous surfaces, apply the color finish system. For porous courts, install the irrigation system. Finally, apply the seed or sod for a grass court.

When painting lines on nonporous courts, make sure the paint is compatible with the color finish system. If it is not compatible, the lines will crack even when there is no

*Figure 15.2. Installation of asphalt surfacing material for a nonporous court. Note the sting line in the foreground to assure correct grade.*

cracking anywhere else on the court. Check with the supplier of the color finish system to ensure that the paint will perform as desired.

(For more information on the construction of sand courts, see Chapter 24.)

### Reconstruction

Tearing up an existing court and reconstructing it is necessary only when the sub-base was not prepared properly; most surface cracking is a sign of subsurface problems. For example, the wrong granular material (or not enough material) may not have been installed, the sub-soil may not have been sufficiently compacted, or drain systems required for proper drainage were not installed. Before constructing the new surface, it's important to identify existing subsurface problems and correct them, or the same surface problems will soon appear.

## 15.4  RENOVATION

Every tennis court eventually needs some type of renovation. The questions are how often and to what extent. Nonporous courts need the least, while porous courts need to be renovated yearly.

### Nonporous Courts

The color finish system on nonporous courts will need to be reapplied every 4 to 6 years, depending on how clean the court is kept and the amount of contrast desired between

*Figure 15.3. The application of the color finish on a nonporous surface is the last step before the painting of lines. These finishes are typically applied as a liquid, then a squeegee is used to ensure uniformity.*

the surface and the lines. Dirt can degrade the surface and sunlight can make the color fade. When this happens, the only solution is to recoat the surface and repaint the lines.

This is also a good time to fix any "bird-baths" that have appeared since the court was constructed or last renovated. Effective methods for eliminating these wet spots vary according to the surface material used in the construction of the court, and specific products have been developed for use with some of them. Court managers are advised to contact the manufacturer or distributor of the surfacing material for advice on correcting this problem.

Several other common tennis court problems can be fixed by simple renovation techniques, rather than total reconstruction. Spalling or raveling is the loss of material on an asphalt surface, a loss which is observed in small "chunks" rather than as a smooth wearing-away. This condition is usually caused by oxidation of unprotected asphalt. To correct raveling, overlay a thin coat (1″) of asphalt and then apply a sealer or product designed for this purpose.

Another common tennis court problem is rust spots on the surface. Rust spots are the result of asphalt which is contaminated with iron oxide at the mixing plant. This problem is sometimes observed as rusty trails leading from the contaminated point toward the low side of the court. This contamination cannot be removed once the iron oxide is introduced to the surface, but new coatings have been developed to stop the spread of rust.

Another common problem is cracking of the surface. Some cracks are caused by heaving or cracking of the subsurface, and these cannot be repaired by a renovation process;

they require reconstruction of the court. Smaller problems, such as hairline cracks, and "alligatoring" of the surface can be fixed with surface coatings. Moderate cracking, like networks of irregular shrinkage cracks, can be remedied by correspondingly moderate solutions, such as the application of a 1″ top coat of asphalt. Check with distributors of coatings for methods of application.

## Clay Courts and Fast-Dry Courts

At least once a year, a clay court should be loosened and leveled to fill in low spots. The United States Tennis Association recommends topdressing the surface with material that matches the existing surface. (Ten cubic yards are recommended for each court.)

A good process to follow is to start with a water-filled roller (30″ diameter with a 36″ width) to firm the surface. Next, scratch the surface with a nail drag 2″ deep to bring new clay to the surface. Then topdress, use a level bar to smooth the surface, drag the surface with a mat drag, and roll again. Finally, sprinkle a thin layer of clean sharp sand over the surface and roll again. The court is ready for marking.

Fast-dry courts should receive similar topdressing, but should not be scarified. These courts will require only about 10% (by weight) of the topdressing material used on clay courts. Fast-dry material can be spread with a fertilizer-type mechanical spreader.

As mentioned above, another common renovation process is to upgrade a clay court by adding a thin layer (⅜″) of fast-dry material without a chemical binder on top of the clay. This process takes approximately 5 tons of fast-dry material to resurface the entire area of 60 × 120 feet. First, scarify the clay at least ½″ and level the surface. Then, apply one ton of fast-dry material, mix it into the clay using rakes or a scarifying tool like a ½″ drag, and roll. Make five applications over the entire court until all the material is used.

## Grass Courts

After each competitive season, grass courts should be renovated to maintain the quality of play. To remedy low spots, remove the sod in a section at least 36″ square (most low spots will require the removal of a substantially larger sections) and scarify the soil. Then add soil that matches the existing medium, and seed or sod. Sodding is a better choice because seeding requires an extended establishment period (one year or more) for the turf to reach maturity to permit play. For routine surface leveling, even on courts with no low spots, topdress the entire surface with matching soil and drag or level. Before topdressing, core aerate if necessary to relieve compaction.

## 15.5   MAINTENANCE

One yearly maintenance practice for all tennis courts is to remove the net and wind screens at the end of the season, unless the court is used during the winter months. The removal of nets and screens will extend their life. Furthermore, in the colder sections of the country, if the net is left up through the winter, there is a good chance of cracking around the net post on nonporous courts. The tension of the net creates a constant pull on the post, which could result in cracks near the post due to surface expansion and contraction.

As with renovation, nonporous surfaces need the least maintenance and porous surfaces need the most.

## Nonporous Courts

The most important maintenance consideration for nonporous courts is to keep the surface clean; dirt ground into the surface by players' feet can degrade the court. Clean the surface regularly with a soft nylon broom. If rainfall is not sufficient to keep the court free of dirt, clean the surface monthly with a hose and broom to prevent the accumulation of debris. Stains can be removed with cold water, detergent and a soft scrub brush. A mixture of two parts water to one part household bleach can remove fungus that may grow as a result of food, soft drinks, or decaying matter on the surface.

## Clay Courts and Fast-Dry Courts

Besides keeping the lines visible, the most important daily maintenance process for clay and fast-dry courts is monitoring of surface moisture. Courts that are too wet or too dry, or that have standing water could delay use until conditions are more favorable. A properly working irrigation system, good surface leveling equipment and roller are the best tools to achieve this goal. Daily inspection for surface moisture is the best way to provide a playable clay or fast-dry court. Each day (or at least once or twice a week), the surface should be brushed, watered if needed, and rolled.

## Grass Courts

Not surprisingly, the daily maintenance requirements for grass courts are the highest of all tennis surfaces. During the growing season, daily mowing and monitoring of soil moisture are time-consuming (but necessary) maintenance practices. For turf that is cut this low (typically ⁵⁄₃₂″ to ⁵⁄₁₆″), a reel mower is a must, and to observe the one-third rule, the turf must be mowed every day. For cool season turfgrass, hand-watering (syringing) is often necessary in the afternoon during hot summer months to keep the surface cool. Of course, line repainting during the playing season is a regular maintenance requirement.

Along with carefully planned mowing, thatch management is critical on a grass tennis court. For most purposes, a thatch layer of ½″ or less is desirable in improving turf wear tolerance. The best thatch management is achieved through topdressing the surface with light and frequent applications of a soil material similar to the existing soil (typically ⅛″ depths when core aeration is performed). Also, regular light verticutting (blades set to penetrate no more than ⅛″ below the turf canopy) will minimize thatch development as well as the development of grain. The vertical mowing and grooming attachments used with triplex or walk-behind reel mowers on golf greens work well for tennis courts, as well. Being very efficient in fertility and irrigation management (neither too much nor too little) further reduces the chances of thatch accumulation.

Since core aeration disrupts the playing surface, water injection and/or solid tine aerifiers can be used for temporary relief of compaction during periods of heavy use. Water injection can be used frequently without an appreciable effect on the playing surface. (However, core aeration is still needed at some point during the year to maintain a healthy turfgrass culture. In cool season zones, this process can be performed before or after the playing season. The best practice is to aerate once in the spring, at least two weeks before play begins, and twice in the fall after play ends. In the South, where courts are used year-round, it will be necessary to close the courts to use for a few days to allow the turf to recuperate from aeration.)

Disease is typically less of a problem on tennis courts than on many turf surfaces, simply because irrigation is usually kept at a minimum to maintain firm footing; many diseases are promoted by prolonged leaf wetness that promotes fungal activity. Therefore, schedule irrigation events early in the morning (if possible) to minimize the duration of leaf wetness. Diseases on most grass courts can usually be managed by applying fungicides on a curative basis. However, a disease-prone grass such as creeping bentgrass

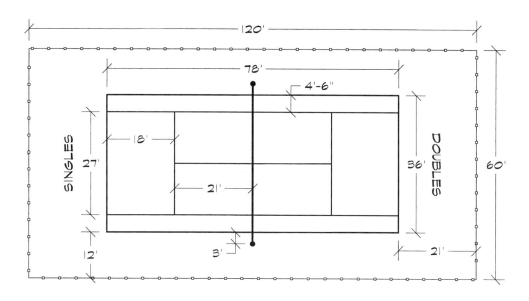

ALL LINES ARE 2" WIDE AND ARE
WITHIN THE DIMENSION SHOWN

*Figure 15.4. Tennis court layout.*

can sometimes require a preventive fungicide program at certain times of the year (see Chapter 9 for further information).

For more on maintenance requirements of sand-based tennis courts, see Chapter 24. Current USTA recommendations favor the United States Golf Association method of putting green construction with an amended sand growing medium. However, at this writing, ASTM standards for tennis courts are being developed with the input of the USTA, and therefore recommendations may change.

## 15.6   RULES AND REGULATIONS

### 15.6a  Line and Boundary Dimensions
Figure 15.4 shows how to lay out a tennis court for singles and doubles.

### 15.6b  Governing and Sanctioning Bodies
United States Tennis Association (USTA)
70 W. Red Oak Lane
White Plains, New Jersey 10604
(914) 696-7000

## REFERENCE:

*Tennis Courts.* United States Tennis Association 1990–1991.
This book provides further information on tennis court design and construction.

# Chapter 16

# *Track and Field Facilities*

## 16.1 INTRODUCTION

As most sports fields planners and managers are well aware, "track and field" represents a group of athletic events which use widely divergent facilities. Unlike other athletic teams, track and field squads consist of separate units that may never see each other compete. The "track" aspect is fairly cut and dried; teams compete in a series of running events on a single track. On the other hand, the "field" aspect includes a series of jumping and throwing events which place varying demands on the available facilities.

Theoretically, each field event requires only a flat space on which the competition can be held. The critical consideration, of course, is safety. Field events include throwing projectiles like the shot, discus, and javelin, each of which is perfectly capable of killing a spectator who is accidentally struck. (In fact, the number and seriousness of javelin accidents has led to the elimination of the event in many areas.) The rest of the field events are jumping events which require a safe landing area—especially the high jump and pole vault.

With these considerations in mind, it seems prudent to begin this chapter by agreeing on a couple of points of usage. In this chapter, when we talk about the "field," we will mean the grass area that is surrounded by the track itself. Because of the nature of the field events, the possibilities for laying out competition areas are exceptionally great. The high jump pit may be inside the track, 100 yards outside it, or across the street. But, for the sake of clarity, we will assume that the field inside the track is used for at least some of the field events, as well as other sports such as football, soccer, lacrosse, and field hockey.

As in baseball—which has separate but totally integrated parts (the infield, the skinned area, and the outfield)—the track and the field should be integrated to form one unit. The two areas support separate competitions, but interact in terms of such considerations as contour designs, installed drain systems, and irrigation. Ideally, these separate systems will work together harmoniously as a single facility.

A further complication is that, unlike most other sports fields, there are specialists in the design and construction of tracks, and there are specialists in the design and construction of fields. Unless the two are planned and constructed to work together, mistakes are bound to happen.

In this chapter we will look at a successful integration of the track and the field, as well as at some common construction problems that can occur when a track and a field are built simultaneously.

319

## 16.2  DESIGN

### 16.2a  Survey and Layout

The largest and most expensive sports field discussed in this book is a field with a surrounding 400-meter track. With a length of nearly 600 feet (between the outside edges of the track arcs) and a width of almost 270 feet (between the outside edges of the track straightaways), the total size of the playing surface is 162,000 square feet. (The next biggest field is a major league baseball field, which has approximately 120,000 square feet inside the fences.) Adding enough space around the track to provide for cuts and fills, catch basins and swales (typically at least 40 feet in each direction) increases the space requirement to 238,000 square feet or approximately 5.5 acres. Of course, the 40 foot minimum space around the outside of the track is not even enough room for grandstands. With spectator seating, the total space requirement could easily approach 7 acres.

The design process begins with laying out the outer boundaries of the track to determine whether there is sufficient space to build the facility. After verifying the space requirements, determine the exact location of the track by setting the center line and the two radius points 328.08 feet (100 meters) apart. A standard 400-meter track is divided into 4 segments—two straightaways and two radiuses—with each segment being 100 meters. (For more information on track dimensions, see Figure 16.6 in this chapter.)

The next step is to perform a topographic survey. Survey enough land outside the track to get a clear understanding of the contour of the surrounding terrain. That will help determine the need for cuts and fills, catch basins, and swales, and will also help in determining a finish grade of the track. (Like any other sports field, a track and field facility must be isolated from its surroundings, and expected to drain away only the water that falls on the facility itself.)

The most common way to perform a topographic survey is to lay out a 50-foot grid pattern and use those points to take elevation readings. When using a grid pattern, the planner uses those elevations to develop a contour plan that includes both existing and proposed contour lines. Spot elevations must also be included in the proposed grading plan, because a 50-foot grid will miss the most important elevations, such as the middle of the field and the edges of the track.

Another way to perform a topographic survey is to lay out the entire track and field and take predetermined spot elevations of the long axis of the field, the inside and outside edges of the track, and the area 40 to 50 feet outside the track. These readings will provide an immediate understanding of the existing topography as it relates to the facility to be constructed.

### 16.2b  Design Criteria for New Construction

The highest point of the field is the center line between the two radius points of the track. The field is crowned and sloped away from the center line in all directions at a consistent 1% to 1½% grade.

The maximum percentage of slope for tracks and runways in the lateral (side-to-side) direction for high school is 2%, for college it is 1%. It's wise to use a percentage of slope of 1%, even for high school tracks and runways, since that is sufficient for surface runoff. Both high school and college rules allow a maximum of .1% slope in the running direction except the high jump event. For high jump, the percentage of slope in the approach run is 1% for high school competition, .4% for college.

Plan to have a smooth transition between the track and field so athletes running off the field of play will not be disturbed by an uneven surface or by hazards like protruding or sunken catch basins.

Since the construction of a field is much different than the construction of a track, make sure all contractors understand that there are important differences in the methods to be employed. A track is constructed much like a road and needs to be compacted to 98%, but a field needs to be constantly scarified (the soil needs to be loosened) to prevent excessive compaction.

A common mistake, and one that is found in many specifications for building sports fields, is to include instructions to compact the field to 98%. This much compaction will stop internal drainage and inhibit root growth. The result will be thin turf and muddy conditions in rainy weather. The solution to this problem is very simple; just add the instructions, "Avoid overcompaction of the sub-base" and "scarify sub-base before installing topsoil" to the specifications to alert the excavator to the drainage dynamics at work in the field system.

## 16.2c  Facility Designs with Preferred Contours

As we have observed above, a track and the field it surrounds have something in common with a baseball diamond, because each is made up of separate structures that must work together as one functional unit. The main difference between the two facilities is that a baseball field has many possible combinations of contours that can work well together, while a track and the enclosed field can practically be designed in just one way, making the job easier for the designer.

From a practical standpoint, the only way to grade a track is with the entire inside edge level and 1% lower than the outside edge, so that water runs off toward the infield. Since the inside of the track is level, the field enclosed by the track has to be crowned. (The only other possibility would be to slope the entire field *inward* toward catch basins at the center, and this would make the field useless for most sports.)

If a track is being constructed around an existing field that slopes from end to end, it may be desirable to have one end of the track lower than the other. The rule book allows a maximum of .1% slope in the running direction, so one end of the track can be as much as eight inches lower than the other. Since this grade change is allowed by the rule book, the "sloped" track may fit into an existing site much better than a "level" track would.

In designing the field contours, a consistent percentage of slope is the best way to avoid wet spots. If the percentage of slope is inconsistent, the designer will be faced with one of two problems: either there will be large wet areas where the slope is less than a 1% slope, or there will be unsightly hills and valleys (with a percentage of slope much higher than 1%) to prevent swampy conditions. In most cases, these problem areas occur at the circular ends of the field and at the straightaways next to the track.

The only way to achieve a consistent percentage of slope and avoid these problems is shown in Figure 16.1. In this illustration, both the track and the enclosed field have a consistent 1% slope. No other contour plan will provide this consistency.

## 16.2d  Track Surfacing Materials

The selection of materials for the track begins with the choice of the sub-base material, or aggregates. In order to maintain a firm base of support for the track itself, and make the surface stand up to competitive stress and weather conditions, the sub-base must be the type of aggregates that are commonly used for construction of roads or walks in a particular area. For all-weather tracks (the most common type for new construction today), the type of sub-base aggregate depends on whether asphalt or concrete will be used as the paving material beneath the all-weather surface. In the South, concrete is

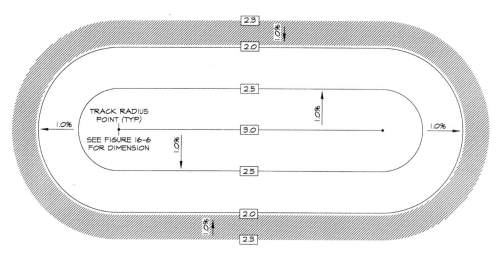

*Figure 16.1. Contour plan for a field with a surrounding 400-meter track—elevations noted in feet.*

most often used, because asphalt melts in the heat of the summer. In the North, asphalt is usually the material of choice.

### All-Weather Tracks

An all-weather track is one that is topped with a coating of rubber chips that are bonded together with a cementing agent. These rubber coatings are installed to a depth of ⅜″ to ½″ over an asphalt or concrete base to provide a soft running surface.

The preferred method of installing a rubber track is to spread the bonding agent over the track surface, and then spread the rubber chips. This method places a thick layer of rubber between the runner's foot and the paving material below the track, and results in a strong but resilient surface. A less expensive rubber coating is one that is sprayed on with multiple coats of tar. This system does not provide the same depth and softness as poured surfaces.

The most popular choices of rubberized coatings are latex or polyurethane, and generally latex is the less expensive of the two. On the other hand, the most expensive rubber coating is one that is orange in color. The reason for the added expense is transportation cost and not superior performance qualities; most orange rubber comes from Europe.

Another type of track surface, which is not actually considered a coating or even an all-weather surface, is rubberized asphalt. The rubber is mixed into the asphalt at the plant and installed in a one-step paving process. Some experimental roads are being paved with rubberized asphalt, but for running tracks it is considered the hardest surface in use. Since the rubber is mixed into the asphalt, only a small portion is near the surface to cushion the impact of the runners' feet.

### Cinder Tracks

All-weather tracks got their name in order to distinguish them from traditional cinder tracks, because the cinder facilities are usually degraded by adverse weather conditions. Despite the fact that cinder tracks can be very soft and comfortable to use, few new cinder tracks are being built today because of the additional maintenance and weather headaches that go with them. It's probably also true that many cinder tracks are being converted to all-weather because boosters and athletic directors see all-weather tracks at neighboring schools, and want to "keep up with the Joneses."

Where budgets do not allow the construction of all-weather tracks, many schools have been choosing to install a granular material (instead of cinders) that can be used to support concrete or asphalt at a later date. (If cinders are chosen, they will need to be removed and replaced with a granular material.) The granular materials will support competition until, for instance, local boosters can raise funds to finance the new track.

### 16.2e  Enclosed Field Turfgrass Selection

Turfgrass selection depends on the type of sports that will be played on the field. For school applications, most tracks surround football or football/soccer fields, which may also be used for some field events. (See chapters on different sports for the best turfgrass choices for each.) If the field will be used for throwing events such as discus and shot put, a heavy thatch layer is desirable. The thatch layer helps to protect the turf from divoting when a discus or shot put hits the ground.

For field events for warm season fields, bermudagrass is the best choice. For cool season fields, a combination of Kentucky bluegrass and perennial ryegrass is a serviceable choice, but a 100% bluegrass field provides the best thatch layer.

### 16.2f  Installed Irrigation Systems

Figure 16.2 shows an installed irrigation system for a field that is surrounded by a 400-meter track. This system is designed to irrigate the entire area inside the track. (It may be necessary to make adjustments to this plan, depending on the layout of field event structures such as the high jump and the long jump areas.)

This design requires water pressure of 75 PSI at field edge and yields a pressure of 60 PSI at the base of the sprinkler heads. Average precipitation rate for this system will be .45 inches/hour for full circle heads and .9 inches/hour for half-circle heads. Running time for 1″ watering will be 2 hours 15 minutes for full circle heads, one hour 8 minutes for half-circle heads.

### 16.2g  Installed Drain Systems and Catch Basins

To complete a successful integration of the track and field, installed drain systems and catch basins are just as important as proper surface grading. Typically, the biggest problem for track drainage is the removal of surface water at the inside edge of the track. Since the outside edge of the track is higher than the inside edge, surface water collects at the lowest point (the inside edge), and may wind up standing on the inner lane itself. Of course, the field contributes to the problem; since the field is higher in the center, surface water flows off the field and toward the inside edge of the track. Installed drain systems and catch basins used in combination are probably the best way to remove surface water from both track and field.

Sometimes catch basins are used as the only structures to intercept surface water at the inside edge of the track. In this scheme, as many as 12 catch basins 5 feet from the track and 115 feet apart with 6″ deep swales from catch basin to catch basin are necessary. In designing such a system, it's important to avoid installing catch basins with the tops so low that they create an unsafe condition for players or an unsightly appearance of hills and valleys (Figure 16.3). (Fewer catch basins require deeper swales in order to provide adequate surface runoff. This type of drainage plan can lead to some extreme solutions; we've seen catch basins 5 feet away from the track as deep as 24″.)

The catch basins must have a network of solid pipes (typically 8″ to 10″ in diameter) that connect them all together, and at least one main outlet pipe is required to service all the catch basins inside the track. The main outlet pipe, which carries the water away

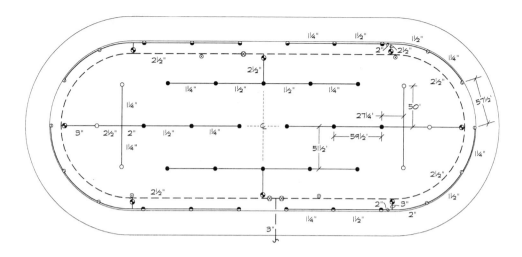

IRRIGATION LEGEND

| | DESCRIPTION | PSI | GPM | RADIUS | ARC | UNITS |
|---|---|---|---|---|---|---|
| ● | HUNTER I-25-36S-15 FULL CIRCLE | 60 | 14.3 | 59 FT. | 360° | 16 |
| ○ | HUNTER I-25-36S-13 FULL CIRCLE | 60 | 12.3 | 56 FT. | 360° | 6 |
| ◐ | HUNTER I-25-ADS-15 PART CIRCLE | 60 | 14.3 | 59 FT. | 180° | 12 |
| ◑ | HUNTER I-25-ADS-13 PART CIRCLE | 60 | 12.3 | 56 FT. | 150° | 10 |
| ⬤ | 2" HUNTER ICV 2016 REMOTE CONTROL VALVE | | | | | 8 |
| ⊙ | I" QUICK COUPLER VALVE - (OPTIONAL) | | | | | 4 |
| ⊗ | 2½" GATE VALVE FOR MAINLINE ISOLATION | | | | | 3 |
| ——— | NON-PRESSURE PIPE (PVC CLASS 160 RECOMMENDED) | | | | | |
| - - - | PRESSURE PIPE (PVC CLASS 200 RECOMMENDED) | | | | | |
| | NOT SHOWN: | | | | | |
| | BACKFLOW PREVENTION DEVICE (AS REQUIRED PER CODE AND/OR ORDINANCE - AND FOR SAFETY) | | | | | 1 |
| | HUNTER ICC IRRIGATION CONTROLLER (8 STATIONS) LOCATION AS NEEDED | | | | | 1 |

DESIGN PROVIDED BY HUNTER INDUSTRIES

*Figure 16.2. Track and field irrigation system design.*

from the facility, is usually a large pipe (typically 12″ diameter) that connects to an approved (by local code) storm sewer drainage system.

In some parts of the country, it is necessary to install perforated pipe drains beside the track to remove water from the base of the track and prevent surface cracking caused by freezing and thawing. In this case, the catch basins are used as junction boxes for the drain pipes, to collect the water that is removed from the subsurface of the track.

### Trackside Sand Drains

Another way to solve the problem of standing water at the inside edge of the track is to install a system of sand drains tied together by catch basins. Only four catch basins are required for this kind of system, since their purpose is not to collect surface runoff but to serve as junction boxes. The main advantages of using this system are improved drainage of the inner lane and the elimination of the annoying hills and valleys required by swale-and-catch-basin systems. The field can then be graded at an even percentage of slope all the way to the inside edge of the track.

*Figure 16.3. Using too few catch basins on a facility can lead to unsightly hills and valleys next to the track.*

These sand drains begin with the placement of perforated pipe in a cloth-lined trench, followed by pea gravel to within 4″–6″ of the surface. The pea gravel is then topped with coarse sand and seeded or sodded with a washed sod. Once these sand drains are in place, surface water is intercepted (at the low point of the facility) by the coarse sand and allowed to filter down through the sand and pea gravel into the pipe drains below. Figure 16.4 shows a design for a trackside sand drain system.

(If the perforated pipe is installed so that its highest point is below the subsurface of the track, this installed drain system can serve two purposes: removing subsurface water as well as surface runoff from the track.)

If an installed drain system is required for the field, consider a strip drain system that helps to collect some of the surface water as well as subsurface water. The collector pipe for this system can be the same pipe that is used for the trackside sand drain system described above. Under these circumstances, the trackside drain system serves a third purpose, as a collector drain for the field's strip drain system. (Figure 16.5 shows a design for a strip drain system.)

## 16.3   TRACK CONSTRUCTION AND RECONSTRUCTION

### Construction

One of the most valuable tools for track construction is the laser level. Since the track is meant to be level on the inside and outside edges, this instrument provides an accurate reading all the way around the track. The laser generation unit itself should be placed in a central location, such as the center of the field, and the rod with a "level eye" can be moved about the track edges to determine that the grade is correct. (The level eye can also be placed on a piece of grading equipment to assist the operator in leveling.)

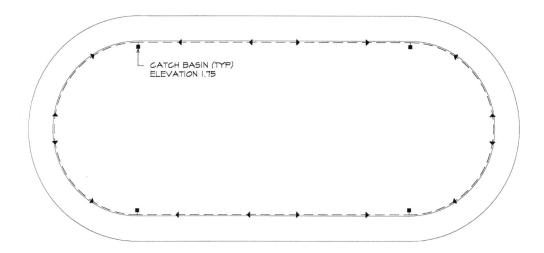

TRACK DRAIN DETAIL

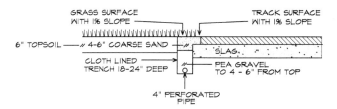

*Figure 16.4. Trackside sand drain system.*

Obviously, a laser level will not work if the track will slope end-to-end. Under these circumstances, placing grade stakes at 50 foot spacing with a .05 foot (approximately ⅝″) change in elevation between stakes will allow the grading crew to establish a consistent 1% slope between the inside and the outside edge of the track. That makes the job a little harder than using a laser level.

If a track and a field are being built simultaneously, it's a good idea to keep heavy equipment used for the track off the field to prevent overcompaction. The plans and specifications may require the contractor to compact the field to avoid excessive settling, but remember that each time the soil is compacted, it needs to be scarified to improve its performance as a growing medium.

### Reconstruction

As we said above, probably the most common reason to reconstruct a track is to convert a cinder facility to an all-weather track. This process begins with removal of all cinder material and the installation of the proper sub-base. When excavating the cinders, look for an old pipe drain down the middle of the track; many cinder tracks were built with these center drains in place. If such a drain is found, tear it out, because they generally do more harm than good. (As a rule of thumb, a poorly installed drainage system is worse than no drainage system at all.)

Reconstruction of an existing asphalt track involves the removal of the asphalt and the sub-base. As with sports facilities of all types, the real problem could be well below

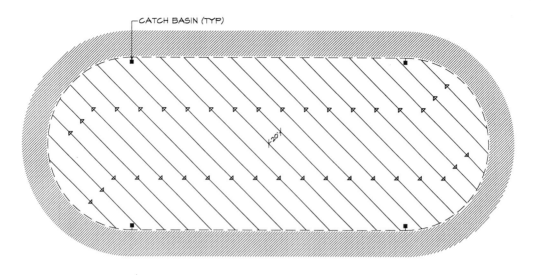

STRIP DRAIN DETAIL

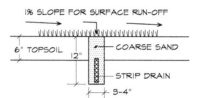

*Figure 16.5. Strip drain system.*

the surface. For example, the wrong granular material or not enough material may not have been used in the sub-base, the subsoil may not have been compacted or may not drain properly. Before constructing the new surface, identify existing problems and make provisions for correction.

In reconstructing a track, be sure to plan for proper surface runoff as well as subsurface water removal. Follow the steps for new construction in Section 16.2g, Installed Drain Systems and Catch Basins. Remember to isolate the track with interceptor drains, swales, or catch basins to collect surface water from the surrounding terrain before it reaches the track.

## 16.4 TRACK RENOVATION

Every 4 to 7 years, several renovation processes must be performed to counteract the effects of normal "wear and tear" on the all-weather track. These processes include cleaning the surface, repairing damaged or worn areas, resurfacing, and line striping. Lanes 1 and 2 will probably need repair first, since these lanes are used most often. Because of the complexity of these processes, it's wise to hire contractors who specialize in repairing all-weather tracks.

Cinder tracks need yearly renovation, primarily the adding of new cinders to reestablish the proper grade.

## 16.5    TRACK MAINTENANCE

All-weather tracks do not require regular maintenance by the staff. However, the best way to extend the life of an all-weather track is to protect it. Cover the track with out-door carpet or other protection when traffic, including vehicles, athletic teams, and even the marching band, are crossing. It's a good idea to use multiple layers of plywood to support the weight of heavy vehicles. Place carpet underneath the plywood to prevent cuts or indents from the plywood. Keep the surface clean by using air-blowers to remove debris, especially leaves. Another way to extend the life of an all-weather track is to make sure that runners' spikes do not exceed ⅛″.

Cinder tracks, however, do require regular maintenance. The maintenance staff will need to level the surface and paint the lane lines for each track event. This process is very labor-intensive, and is another good reason to replace cinder tracks with all-weather tracks.

## 16.6    RULES AND REGULATIONS

### 16.6a    Common Points of Confusion

The term "measure line" is commonly mistaken by some designers as a primary dimen-sion for building a track. But the measure line is an invisible line used to determine the distance that a runner will travel. It is taken from a point 8″ outside the inner line of a given lane. Sometimes the measure line is the only dimension given, and the contractor must find the proper dimensions for building a track. In laying out a track, the impor-tant dimensions are the distance between the two radius points and the distance from the radius point to the inside and outside edge of the track. Figure 16.6 shows the most im-portant dimensions for designing and building a track.

### 16.6b Line and Boundary Dimensions

The following descriptions and illustrations are for high school and college track and field. International rules (such as those used for Olympic competition) are not covered in this section. For international rules, write to the International Amateur Athletic Federa-tion, whose address can be found at the end of this chapter.

*Track*
Figure 16.6 shows a layout for an equal quadrant track (the most common type) which has 100-meter curves and 100-meter straightaways. This equal quadrant layout will ac-commodate a field up to 195 feet by 360 feet inside the track. (Although it should be noted that a soccer field 195 feet wide inside the track will only have 5½ feet between the edge of the field and the inside edge of the track. With this limited space, trackside sand drains must be installed instead of catch basins, since there is insufficient space for swales and catch basins. See Figure 16.4.) For larger soccer fields (up to 225 feet wide by 360 feet long), a nonequal quadrant track is required. On such a track, the two curved ends are equal in length and the two straightaways are equal in length, but the straight-aways are shorter than the curves. (This design, featuring the "international broken-back curve," is the only design that will accommodate a 225 feet by 360 feet soccer field inside the track.)

The standard lane width is 42″ for high school and 42″ to 48″ for college. (For high school competition, lane widths may vary, depending on the size of the track and the number of lanes desired.) If a curb is installed at the inside lane, a permanent or movable

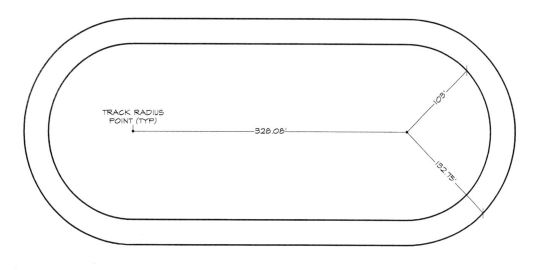

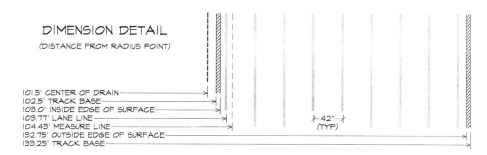

*Figure 16.6. Track layout.*

structure 2″ high by 2″ wide (with rounded edges) is recommended for both high school and college, but college rules also allow a 4″ wide curb. (NCAA records can only be set on a track with a curb.) When a curb is used, the measure line for the first lane is 11.81″ from the nearest edge of the curb instead of 7.87″ from the nearest edge of the 2″ painted line, making lane one 3.94″ wider than the rest of the lanes. The dimensions shown in Figure 16.6 will accommodate a 2″ wide curb if desired.

### High Jump

Figure 16.7 shows a high jump approach area traditionally used for high jump layout for high school and college competition. The disadvantage of this traditional design, according to many coaches and jumpers, is that it is too small. The athlete may have to run on grass when approaching the bar, and only one event can be held at a time. The traditional design is slowly being replaced by a larger, more modern design. For high school, coaches and jumpers prefer a 50 feet by 100 feet rectangle over the traditional semicircle, because the rectangular design allows more running space without leaving the all-weather surface. Also, the larger high jump area allows the running direction to be alternated depending on wind direction, and two events (such as men's and women's competition) can be held at one time.

HIGH SCHOOL

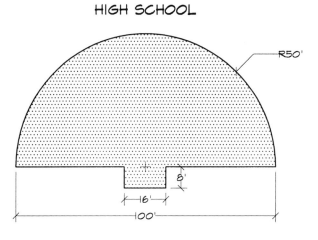

COLLEGE

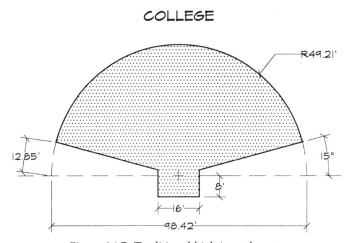

*Figure 16.7. Traditional high jump layout.*

Where budgets allow, some newer track and field facilities have an all-weather surface that covers most of the area inside the arc at one end of the track (or even at both ends of the track). With this much paved surface, the area can be used for multiple events. One end of the field can be used for multiple high jump events, and possibly even the long jump. The other end can be used for other events, such as the triple jump, the pole vault, and even the shot put.

### Long Jump and Triple Jump

Both high school and college rules allow for a great deal of flexibility in designing this type of facility. Figure 16.8 shows the critical dimensions of long jump and triple jump areas.

For high school, the runway should be at least 42″ wide and 130 feet to 147½ feet from the long jump scratch line (the edge of the takeoff board nearest the landing pit). The width of the takeoff board is a minimum of 8″ and a maximum of 24,″ and at least

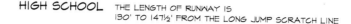

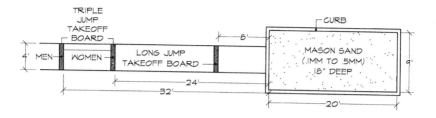

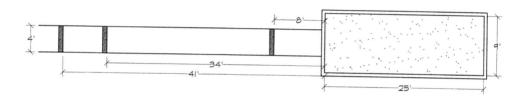

NOTE: THE SCRATCH LINE (HIGH SCHOOL) OR FOUL LINE (COLLEGE)
IS THE EDGE OF THE TAKEOFF BOARD NEAREST THE LANDING AREA

*Figure 16.8. Long jump/triple jump layout.*

48″ long. The takeoff board is made of wood or synthetic material which provides a firm base, and is installed to be level with the runway surface. (A painted line can replace the takeoff board.) The landing pit is the same level as the takeoff board and is a minimum of 9 feet wide and 15 feet long. The long jump scratch line is approximately 12 feet from the landing pit for boys and 8 feet for girls; the triple jump scratch line is 32 feet from the pit for boys and 24 feet for girls, but the position of the scratch line can be adjusted to accommodate different levels of competition.

For college, it is recommended that the runway be 48″ wide and 130 feet from each event's foul line (which corresponds to the high school "scratch line," the edge of the takeoff board nearest the landing pit). The width of the takeoff board is specified as 7.8″ to 8,″ and at least 48″ long. (For practical purposes, 7.8″ is 7 $^{13}$⁄₁₆″.) For the long jump, the distance between the nearest edge of the landing area and the foul line is a minimum of 3.28 feet and a maximum of 12 feet for both men and women. The distance from the long jump foul line to the farther edge of the landing area is at least 32.81 feet. For the triple jump, the distance between the nearest edge of the landing area and the foul line is a minimum of 36 feet for men (41 feet is recommended), and a minimum of 28 feet for women (34 feet is recommended).

Both landing areas shown in Figure 16.8 have a surrounding curb, 6″ wide by 18″ deep. The top of this curb is level with the runway and the landing area. There is a 4″ pipe drain in the center of the landing area, 30″ below the surface. The trench for the drain is 12″ wide and filled with natural gravel running the entire length of the area and sloping to an exit pipe. The landing pit is to be filled with mason sand 18″ deep.

## Pole Vault

The high school pole vault runway is a minimum of 130 feet in length, and where conditions permit, 147.5 feet is preferred. The width is to be 42″ whenever possible. For college, the runway is a minimum of 125 feet long, and a recommended width of 48″. The vaulting box should be painted white, and has the same dimensions for high school and college: it is 42.5″ long, 23.62″ wide at the open end, and 16.1″ wide at the closed end. The box must be firmly fixed into the ground, and the top is to be level with the surrounding surface. The authors recommend purchasing a manufactured box from a company that supplies landing pads and other track equipment.

## Water Jump

The water jump pit used in the NCAA steeplechase (Figure 16.9) is located on the inside (preferred) or outside of the running track, and is usually placed on the inside of the curve at one end of the track. A 23-foot straightaway before and after the water jump is recommended. The water jump pit is 12 feet wide by 12 feet long, and the hurdle is within the 12 feet by 12 feet measurement. The hurdle must be fixed firmly in place and be the same height (2.99 feet to 3.01 feet) as the other hurdles in the competition. The area between the vertical uprights of the hurdle should be made of a solid, rigid material to provide structural strength, and to aid the athletes with depth perception (since they typically step onto the hurdle in passing over it). The depth of the water at its deepest point (for any facility constructed after June 1991) should be 2.29 feet. The bottom of the water jump pit is to be lined with a nonskid, shock-absorbent matting.

## Throwing Circles

The throwing circles for high school and college have several things in common. For one thing, the sizes of the circles are the same, with a radius of 3′6″ for the shot (Figure 16.10) and 4′1¼″ for the discus (Figure 16.11). All circles are recessed ¾″ below the finish grade of the surrounding surface. The circumference is marked with a metal, wood, or plastic band that rises ¾″ above the level of the circle. In high school competition, if the circle is made of asphalt, concrete, or wood, a 2″ painted line can be substituted for the band. The inside edge of the painted line marks the circumference. There are meant to be 2″ lines outside the circle to divide it in half front-to-back. These lines are to start at the circumference of the circle. There are no painted lines inside the circle itself. The shot put circle has a stopboard in the shape of an arc. It is made of concrete, fiberglass, metal, or wood and is 4 feet in length along the inside edge and 4″ high by 4½″ wide. The inside edge of the stopboard abuts the circumference of the circle.

Because of the potential safety hazard if the thrower loses his or her grip on the projectile, an enclosure is required for the discus and hammer throwing events. (NCAA rules note that even this enclosure cannot guarantee the safety of spectators, competitors, or officials.)

In the landing area, the inside edges of the 2″ painted lines that designate the "throwing sector" (inside which the throw must land), start at the circumference of the circle.

There are also some basic differences between high school and college throwing facil-

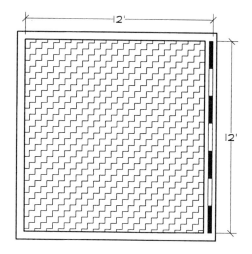

PROFILE

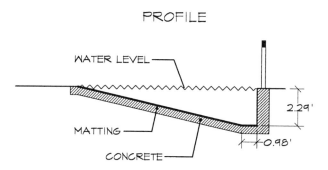

*Figure 16.9. Steeplechase water jump pit.*

ities' rules for construction. The percentage of slope from the throwing area to the landing area is a maximum of 1% for high school, while for college it is not more than .1%. In high school, the throwing sector for shot put is 65.5° and for discus it is 60°. College has a 40° throwing sector for all three throwing events. For the discus, the NCAA recommends a larger enclosure than the high school rule book. The NCAA rules require an entrance/exit at the rear of the enclosure. (The high school section of Figure 16.11 shows a typical layout for the discus enclosure with a recommended *minimum* clearance of 10 feet. The clearance can be increased to 11 feet, with a maximum front opening of 24 feet. College rules recommend only one size enclosure, as shown.)

For the collegiate hammer throw, the enclosure is basically the same as the discus enclosure. The only difference is that the hammer throw enclosure has movable panels at the front. These panels are a minimum of 13.78 feet and a maximum of 14.27 feet in length. To allow the fixed end of a movable panel to be 9.35 feet outside the sector line, the stationary front fence posts must be further apart than they are for the discus enclosure. For a right-handed thrower, the panel on the left is closed to 4.92 feet inside the left sector line and the panel on the right is opened parallel to the right sector line. This arrangement is reversed for left-handed throwers. The movable panels in Figure 16.12 are set up for a right-handed thrower.

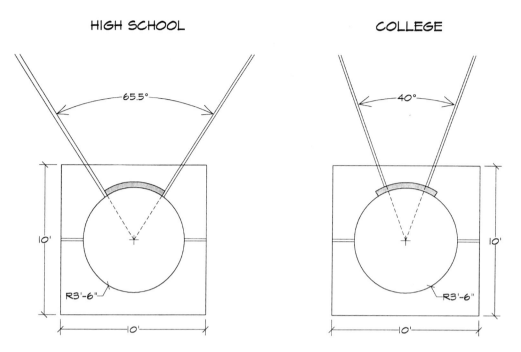

*Figure 16.10. Shot put pad layout.*

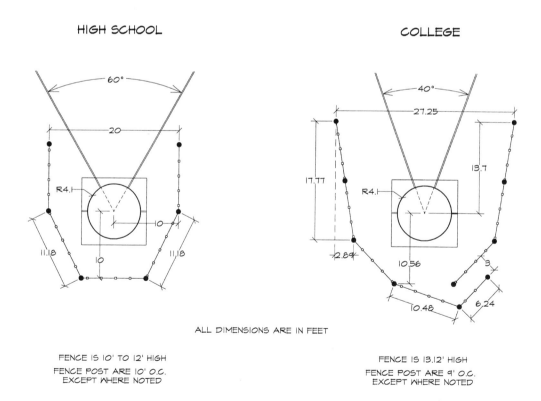

*Figure 16.11. Discus circle and cage layout.*

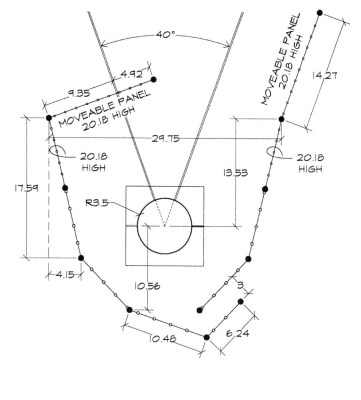

ALL DIMENSIONS ARE IN FEET

FENCE IS 16.4' HIGH
EXCEPT WHERE NOTED

FENCE POST ARE 9' O.C.
EXCEPT WHERE NOTED

*Figure 16.12. Hammer throw circle and cage layout (NCAA)*

## Javelin

The javelin runway for both high school and college competition is 120 feet long and 13.12 feet wide. The length is measured from the center of the foul line arc. For college, the first 70 feet of the runway is 4 feet wide (designated by a painted line) and then widens to 13.12 feet for the last 50 feet. NCAA specifications recommend that the runway be constructed with an artificial surface, such as asphalt or concrete. If an artificial surface is used, the runway should extend 3.28 feet past the foul line.

The foul line (high school "scratch line") is 2.76″ wide, painted white, and flush with the runway. High school recommends a metal, plastic, or wood band, while NCAA specifies a painted line.

The landing area is grass and its boundaries are determined by marking lines from a point at the center of the foul line arc which is 26.25 feet back from its circumference. These lines continue through the outside edge of the foul line and outward as far as required for the competitive level of the throwers. All painted lines are outside the dimensions shown in Figure 16.13.

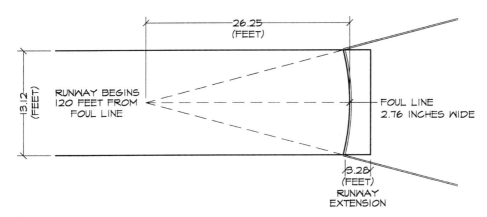

*Figure 16.13. Javelin runway, with artificial runway surface.*

## 16.6c  Governing and Sanctioning Bodies

*International:*
International Amateur Athletic Federation
17, Rue Princesse Florestine
MC 98000 Monaco
011-339-330-7070

*College:*
National Collegiate Athletic Association
6201 College Boulevard
Overland Park, Kansas 66211
(913) 399-1906

*High School:*
National Federation of State High School Associations
11724 Plaza Circle, Box 20626
Kansas City, Missouri 64195
(816) 464-5400

*United States:*
USA Track and Field
One Hoosier Dome, Suite 140
Indianapolis, Indiana 46225
(317) 261-0500

## REFERENCES:

*Track Construction Manual.* U.S. Tennis Court and Track Builders Association, Inc. 1996. Before designing or building a track, send for this book for more details on track design and construction. To receive a publication write or call:
U.S. Tennis Court and Track Builders Association
3525 Ellicott Mills Drive, Suite N
Ellicott City, Maryland 21043
(410) 418-4875

# Chapter 17

# *Sand Volleyball Courts*

## 17.1 INTRODUCTION

Over the last quarter of a century, few sports have enjoyed popularity comparable to that of volleyball. Once relegated to physical education classes and played seriously by only a handful of dedicated men and women, volleyball has grown into a widely played and even televised sport. And while the indoor version of the game has seen steady growth, interest in the outdoor variety played on beaches and on constructed sand facilities has exploded.

Of course, volleyball can be played on a grass court, and most "backyard" volleyball matches are played on existing topsoil. Grass volleyball courts can even be constructed on amended soils, or on amended sand (using the guidelines in Chapter 24). However, the most popular surface for outdoor volleyball in North America is sand.

There is obviously a great deal of difference between sand and turf, but the two surfaces also have a good deal in common. When it comes to constructing or maintaining a sand volleyball facility, many of the practices are exactly the same as in sports turf. The goals of safety, playability, and attractiveness remain the same, and drainage remains one of the principal problems to be solved.

One common mistake in the construction of sand volleyball courts is to have the surrounding terrain sloped toward the court, causing runoff to flow into the sand. If the court takes on water from the terrain, it may remain trapped in the sand for days unless the court has a porous sub-base or an installed subsurface drain system. As with any sports turf facility, proper drainage can eliminate many of the problems with sand volleyball courts.

## 17.2 SAND VOLLEYBALL COURT DESIGN

### 17.2a Survey and Layout

The regulation size for volleyball courts is 29'6" wide and 59 feet long, with a minimum 9'10" surrounding free zone which is actually part of the playing area.

Once the location and layout of the court has been determined, the next step is to survey the existing grade. Take elevations at the corners, the midpoints of each side and end, and the center of the net. It's a good idea to take elevations 25 feet to 50 feet outside the court to get a clear understanding of the contour of the surrounding terrain. That will help determine the need for cuts and fills, catch basins, and swales, and will also help in determining a finish grade for the court.

337

A thorough survey is also important for another reason: a sand volleyball court often needs an installed drain system, and the readings will help determine the direction of the collector drain for the system. Be sure to look around for existing catch basins and storm drains that the new drain system can be tied into. If these structures are in place, take a reading at the flow line. If there are no catch basins or storm drains to tie into, it will be necessary to run the collector pipe to daylight (that is, to a grade point lower than the downward sloping collector pipe).

## 17.2b  Design Criteria for New Construction

At some facilities, the presence of a newly-installed drain system may tempt the designer to allow the surrounding area to drain into the court. This temptation should be resisted. Like any sports field, a sand volleyball court should be treated as an individual drainage unit, and not be expected to serve as a drain for the grounds around it. The final grade for a sand volleyball court is level, which works fine as long as no outside water drains onto the court, the sand has the right particle-size distribution (see Table 17.1), and good drainage is in place underneath the sand.

When calculating the elevation of the subgrade, plan for 12″ of compacted sand. That translates to 14″ of installed sand, which will settle about 2″. USA Volleyball, the major sanctioning body of outdoor volleyball, requires that sand for competition be at least 12″ deep, so don't forget to allow for settling.

Net posts should be installed between 19½″ and 39″ outside each sideline. For safety's sake, posts must be rounded, smooth and, preferably, adjustable. The recommended height of the posts is 8′ 4″. If guy lines are used to support the posts, they are to be made of bright-colored material and marked with flags.

## 17.2c  Multiple Court Layout

In planning for multiple-court facilities, leave sufficient room for each court to have its own free zone, and do not expect two adjacent courts to share a free zone. That will mean a space of 20 feet between the sidelines of two adjacent courts.

## 17.2d  Sand Selection

At the mention of "sand volleyball," the mind naturally flashes images of beach volleyball by the ocean. However, it's important to remember that "beach sand" is not always loose and pliable like that seen on televised sand volleyball matches. Visitors to such heavily used beaches as Daytona Beach in Florida may remember that beaches are sometimes major thoroughfares for vehicular traffic. This particular sand is suitable as a roadbed, but is definitely not the best choice for sand volleyball courts.

In specifying sand for a volleyball court, it's very important to get only the desired grade of sand, with a minimum of gravel and fines (tiny particles of very fine sand, silt and clay). Sand with residual silt and clay mixed in is sometimes referred to as "dirty sand."

However, even specifying a sand without gravel or fines is not sufficient to guarantee acceptable performance on a volleyball court. For instance, Table 24.2 in Chapter 24 presents useful information on the relationships between sand size, the minimal depth for gravity drainage, and the resulting saturated hydraulic conductivity of the sand, all of which affect the drainage characteristics of the completed court. These guidelines can be used to determine appropriate depths of various sands to achieve adequate drainage.

For most purposes, a "medium-to-fine" (0.1 mm. to 0.5 mm diameter) sand will be best for a volleyball court, with less than 7% passing through a 100-sieve screen. (See

Table 17.1. Recommended Particle Size Distribution for Sand Volleyball Courts

| USDA System of Classification | | Sieve No. | Sieve Opening, (millimeters) | Appro. Opening, (inches) | Recommended |
|---|---|---|---|---|---|
| gravel >2mm | | 6 | 3.36 | ⅛″ | |
| | | 7 | 2.83 | | < 3% |
| | | 8 | 2.38 | | |
| S A N D | very coarse 1-2mm | 10 | 2.00 | ¹⁄₁₆″ | 10% max |
| | | 12 | 1.68 | | |
| | | 14 | 1.41 | | |
| | | 16 | 1.19 | | |
| | coarse .5-1mm | 18 | 1.00 | ¹⁄₃₂″ | 20% max |
| | | 20 | 0.84 | | |
| | | 25 | 0.71 | | |
| | | 30 | 0.59 | | |
| | medium .25-.5mm | 35 | 0.50 | ¹⁄₆₄″ | 35% min 60% ideal |
| | | 40 | 0.42 | | |
| | | 45 | 0.35 | | |
| | | 50 | 0.30 | | |
| | fine .1-.25mm | 60 | 0.25 | ¹⁄₁₂₈″ | 35% max |
| | | 70 | 0.21 | | |
| | | 80 | 0.177 | | |
| | | 100 | 0.149 | | |
| | very fine .05-.1mm | 120 | 0.125 | ¹⁄₂₅₆″ | < 5% |
| | | 140 | 0.105 | | |
| | | 170 | 0.088 | | |
| | | 200 | 0.074 | | |
| | | 230 | 0.062 | | |
| | | 270 | 0.053 | ¹⁄₅₁₂″ | |
| silt .002–.05mm clay <.002mm | | 325 | 0.044 | | < 2% |

Table 17.1 for recommended particle size distribution for sand volleyball courts.) Sand in this recommended range will provide the desirable firmness for footing, without being so firm as to discourage players diving for the ball. A 12″ depth of sand in this range will also allow for rapid drainage. A uniform "masonry sand" is usually suitable for volleyball courts, but "concrete sand," which contains fairly equal proportions of all gradations in size, is a poor choice, since it readily compacts and can be abrasive to players' skin.

## 17.2e  Installed Drain Systems and Catch Basins

### Installed Drain Systems

Where the subsoil does not permit adequate percolation to maintain a dry playing surface, an installed drain system should be constructed. Figure 17.1 shows a typical system that will prove effective in a wide variety of circumstances.

This system is based on a network of strip drains laid in trenches 4″ wide and 12″ deep in the sub-base. The trenches should be sloped ½% to 1% toward a collector drain, and should be placed at 10-foot intervals. The trenches which contain these strip drains

SAND VOLLEYBALL
DRAINAGE SYSTEM DESIGN

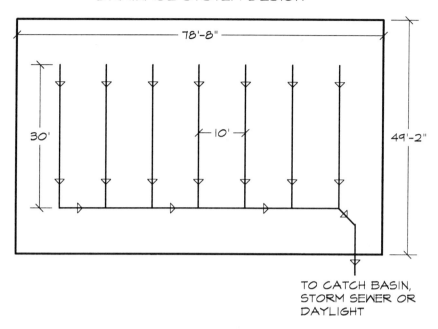

TO CATCH BASIN,
STORM SEWER OR
DAYLIGHT

DRAINAGE DETAIL

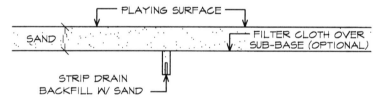

*Figure 17.1. Installed drain system for sand volleyball court.*

should be backfilled with sand matching that to be used for the court itself. (See Chapter 8 for more information on strip drains.)

It's tempting to avoid installing a drain system, instead relying on measures like sloping the sub-base to an exit pipe at one side or corner of the court to assist internal drainage. This step is usually taken with the expectation that water will drain through the sand to the sub-base, then follow the slope of the sub-base to the exit pipe. A court built on this design works fine until the sand is installed, then quickly runs into drainage problems.

The primary shortcoming of a court of this type is that all water must exit through one drain or an insufficient number of drains. All of the water next to the drain exits first, then the water right next to that, and so on through the sand. Water that falls on the portions of the court that are a long way from the drain must migrate all the way through the sand to the drain, and that can take hours or days.

The installed drain system we recommend removes water simultaneously from all

*Figure 17.2. A completed sand volleyball court. Note the small grid on top of the catch basin in the foreground.*

parts of the court, without forcing it to "wait in line." Water has to move only a maximum of 6 feet to reach a drain (1 foot down through the sand, 5 feet laterally to the drains). The whole process happens much more quickly than with a sloped sub-base, more efficiently restoring the playability of the court.

Even courts that are installed aboveground (with curbing to contain the sand) operate by the same drainage dynamics as those of in-ground facilities; installed drains are virtually a necessity for good sand volleyball courts.

### Catch Basins
Before finalizing the drainage system design, take a hard look at the surrounding terrain to make sure water can be effectively channeled away from the court. It may be necessary to install catch basins outside the sand area. (A minumum 20-foot clear space is needed.) Don't forget to install a small grid on top of the basin to provide pedestrian safety around the court (See Figure 17.2).

## 17.3   CONSTRUCTION AND RECONSTRUCTION

### Construction
As always, begin construction by transferring the design to the site using grade stakes, then excavating 12″ below final grade. The corner stakes can be used to support a line showing the limits of the excavated area and the final grade of the court. Measure down from the string lines and excavate.

After the subgrade is set, install the drain system as described above. Use a level and elevation rod to ensure a downward slope toward the collector drain.

Once the drain system is in place, install the net posts before filling the excavated area with sand. That way, all the soil from the postholes can be removed before sand is installed. If the budget allows, it's a good idea to line the entire excavated area with filter cloth. That keeps the sand and subsoil from mixing. Then fill the excavated area with sand, level and play.

## Reconstruction

Usually, someone embarks on a reconstruction project for one of two reasons: either the wrong sand was used, or no drain system was installed at construction. If sand was the problem, it could be replaced with a new sand of the correct particle size.

In either case, begin by removing the sand. Then carefully inspect the existing drain system. Some existing systems have poor slope or none at all. Some systems become clogged and can be cleaned out. Some are even installed without outlets.

Having analyzed the existing system, the planner can decide whether to try to improve the existing system or replace it. Under some circumstances (like systems with poor slope or too few drains), it may be much easier to install a new system than to fix an existing one. But frequently, an existing system can be upgraded to provide years of good service.

It's important to start reconstruction at exactly the same point as new construction described above: the grade. Set stakes and lines and rework the sub-base just as you would a new court.

## 17.4  RENOVATION

If there is grass around the edge of a volleyball court, the edge will need to be lowered every three to five years. The grass tends to collect sand around the edge of the court and form a mounded ridge. Cut sod to remove the ridge, lower the grade, and resod or seed. Remember that this process will remove part of the original sand along with the sod that is hauled away, so consider adding some sand.

## 17.5  MAINTENANCE AND MANAGEMENT PROCEDURES

Because it's not a horticultural system like turf, the sand in a volleyball court is obviously a lot easier to take care of. It does tend to collect cigarette butts, scraps of paper, and other litter thoughtlessly thrown into it. As one of the few sports surfaces typically used by barefoot players, the sand volleyball court requires some safety monitoring. Sand should be raked and policed regularly to maintain its quality and to remove any sharp objects that could be safety hazards.

The center of the court at the net tends to become lower than the rest of the court, as sand is progressively kicked out toward the boundaries. In order to maintain regulation net height, the sand will need to be pulled back toward the center. This task can obviously be performed with hand tools, but it's faster to use equipment like a tractor with a box scraper.

## 17.6  RULES AND REGULATIONS

### 17.6a  Line and Boundary Dimensions
The dimensions for sand volleyball courts for players of all ages are the same as those shown in Figure 17.3. Boundary lines are to be marked with $\frac{3}{16}''$ to $\frac{3}{8}''$ (.5 cm to 1 cm.)

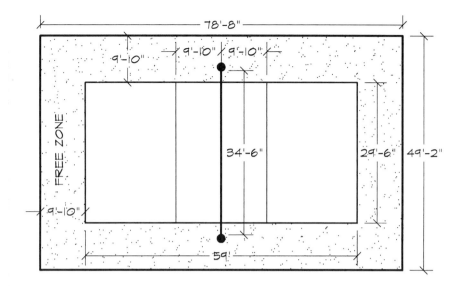

POST DETAIL

WITH MENS EYE HOOK
WOMENS ARE 7½" LOWER

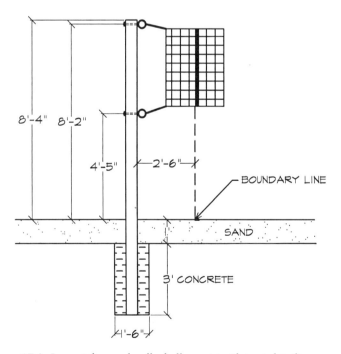

*Figure 17.3. Layout for sand volleyball court (with post detail).*

rope, or with 2″ to 3 ⅛″ (5 cm. to 8 cm.) tape or bands. Line markers are to be a color contrasting to the color of the sand.

The height of the net is 7′ 11⅝″ (2.43 m) for men and 7′ 4⅛″ (2.24 m) for women. In terms of court maintenance, the important point is that the net height is measured at the center. At the sidelines, the net may be no more that ¾″ above the regulation height.

This requires posts with sufficient strength and rigidity to hold a line taught. Select posts carefully, remembering that the cost of replacing a set that has failed in use will wipe out any savings realized by using cheaper, flimsier posts when the court is built. Remember that the post must be rounded for the safety of the players.

## 17.6b  Governing and Sanctioning Bodies

USA Volleyball
3595 East Fountain Boulevard, Suite 1-2
Colorado Springs, Colorado 80910
(719) 637-8300

# Chapter 18

# *Playgrounds*

## 18.1  INTRODUCTION

Playgrounds may well be the most common sports facility in the world; just about every elementary school, middle school, day-care center, public park, and private recreation area has one. While these facilities are not specifically designed to support athletic competition, they do support a wide range of play activities which place stresses on the surface that are similar to those caused by sports competition. Playgrounds are frequently managed by the same professionals who typically supervise the maintenance of sports fields, and their efforts are directed toward the same goals typical of sports fields themselves: playability in a wide range of weather circumstances, safety for users, and visual attractiveness.

Furthermore, the same principles of design, construction, and maintenance must be observed for playgrounds as for sports fields. Drainage remains the single greatest challenge in maintaining playable facilities.

However, playgrounds that are attached to schools and day-care facilities present some special challenges, due to their integration into the program of the school in general. If the playground doesn't drain properly, children wind up inside for recess, taxing the creativity (and patience) of teachers. Or they may be led to play on pavement, with attendant injuries. When the playground is marginally usable, kids track mud into the school, creating both safety and maintenance headaches.

So, in this chapter, we approach playgrounds as sports facilities.

## 18.2  DESIGN

### 18.2a  Space Requirements

Design of a playground differs from design of other recreational facilities in one very important respect: the first decisions which must be made are the types of equipment that will be installed. Until these decisions are reached, it is impossible to adequately determine how large the facility must be to permit safe use. If the available space is limited, then the playground planner is obviously limited in the type and size of equipment to be installed.

The minimum space which must be kept clear of hazards around a piece of equipment to allow for safe play is referred to by the U. S. Consumer Product Safety Commission (CPSC) as the "no encroachment zone." Because different kinds of playground equipment require different zones, the first step in laying out a playground is to determine

345

what equipment will be installed. After the equipment choices are made, a scaled layout should be prepared to provide for safe movement of pedestrian traffic around the equipment.

The best source of information on the necessary clearances between pieces of playground equipment is the CPSC "Handbook for Public Playground Safety." The authors recommend consulting this handbook before laying out any public playground facility.

It is also important to consult with manufacturers of playground equipment for their recommendations on minimum safe distances and other factors relating to playground safety.

## 18.2b Surfacing Materials

Playground surfacing material is meant to do three things:

1. To provide a barrier separating the feet of playground users from the soil layer beneath.
2. To allow surface water to drain easily through the profile and quickly reach an installed drain system or a naturally porous sub-base that will channel it away.
3. To safely absorb the shock of falls by kids using the facility.

Table 18.1 is based on a CPSC chart with recommended depths of surfacing material required to protect users falling onto the surface from variously-sized playground equipment. Understanding this chart requires the planner to determine the maximum height from which a user could fall in using each piece of equipment, then to find the depth in inches of material needed for proper shock absorption.

Almost all suppliers of surfacing material can provide information on how much each product will settle and/or compact in use. This information will help the planner make appropriate buying decisions regarding the amount of material required.

### Shredded Wood

The most common surface material used on playgrounds today is shredded wood. (For our purposes, we will referred to all of the wood products listed in Table 18.1, as "shredded wood.") The deeper the layer of shredded wood, the greater the ability of the surface to absorb the shock of falls (see Table 18.1).

With effective subsurface drainage under the material, wood loss through decomposition is minimal, but it will still be necessary to make occasional additions to the shredded wood layer. Frequently check the surface layer for both thickness and sogginess. If the bottom of the wood layer is usually waterlogged, it probably indicates that the drainage system is not adequate. Be aware that freezing temperatures reduce the cushioning ability of shredded wood surfaces.

### Sand

In some areas, sand is a popular alternative for playground surfacing. Sand has some attractive qualities as a playground surface material: sand is soft, it does not rot, and it cushions falls fairly effectively. However, wet sand sticks to shoes and clothes and tracks all over. Also, sand without fines (coarse sand) is unstable to walk or run across, and displaces easily out of the area. Check Table 18.1 for minimum sand thickness required.

Like shredded wood surfaces, sand loses its cushioning properties in the presence of moisture and freezing temperatures.

Table 18.1. Minimum Surface Depth for Various Falling Heights (from CPSC)

| Maximum Falling Height | Wood Mulch[a] | Double Shredded Bark Mulch[b] | Uniform Wood Chips[c] | Fine Sand[d] | Coarse Sand[e] | Fine Gravel[f] | Medium Gravel[g] |
|---|---|---|---|---|---|---|---|
| 6″ of Installed/Uncompacted Material | | | | | | | |
| 5′ | | | | x | x | | x |
| 6′ | | x | x | | | x | |
| 7′ | x | | | | | | |
| 9″ of Installed/Uncompacted Material | | | | | | | |
| 5′ | | | | x | x | | x |
| 7′ | | | x | | | x | |
| 10′ | x | x | | | | | |
| 12″ of Installed/Uncompacted Material | | | | | | | |
| 6′ | | | | | x | | x |
| 9′ | | | | x | | | |
| 10′ | | | | | | x | |
| 11′ | x | x | | | | | |
| <12′ | | | x | | | | |
| 9″ of Settled/Compacted Material | | | | | | | |
| 4′ | | | | | x | | |
| 5′ | | | | x | | | x |
| 6′ | | | x | | | x | |
| 7′ | | x | | | | | |
| 10′ | x | | | | | | |

[a] Random sized wood chips, twigs, and leaves collected from a wood chipper being fed tree limbs, branches, and brush.
[b] Similar to shredded mulch commonly used by homeowners to mulch shrub beds.
[c] Relatively uniform sized shredded wood fibers from hardwoods with no bark or leaves.
[d] Most of the particle sizes between .15 mm and .5 mm.
[e] Most of the particle sizes between 1 mm and 2 mm.
[f] Most of the particle sizes between ⅛″ and ¼″.
[g] Most of the particle sizes between ¼″ and ⅜″.

*Pea Gravel*

Pea gravel is another material sometimes used for playground surfacing. However, this material never stabilizes, which makes it difficult to walk or run across, and consequently less desirable as a playground material. Pea gravel is also somewhat abrasive, creating the safety concern of scrapes among playground users. Probably the best use of pea gravel for a playground would be to install a layer of it as a drainage material under a shredded wood surface layer, although some disagreement about this method remains (see Section 18.2c below.)

*Rubber Chips*

One of the new products of the recycling movement is rubber chips for playground surfacing. This material is soft and easy to work with, and it does not rot. The disadvantage of rubber chips is cost—at this writing, three to five times the cost of shredded wood. However, given the fact that the rubber does not rot, the cost of replacement material is eliminated. So if the price of rubber chips declines, the economics of using this material will look better and better.

Ask the manufacturer for the minimum depth of rubber chips to install for the maximum falling height of the equipment being used.

### Rubber Mats

Interconnecting rubber mats are also available for playgrounds. In addition to their advantages under swings and slides, these mats should also be considered for any areas that will be used by children with disabilities. Rubber mats are sometimes installed over asphalt beds, and are also used for indoor play areas, such as those becoming popular at fast-food restaurants.

As with rubber chips, ask the manufacturer for the maximum falling height, and for recommended drainage specifications.

## 18.2c  Planning for Effective Drainage

Whichever surfacing material is chosen for a playground, virtually all authorities agree that it is important to plan the facility to provide effective drainage. There is also general agreement that it is important to isolate the playground against runoff from adjacent areas by using swales and/or catch basins. However, there is substantial disagreement about how to achieve drainage underneath the surface material when it is placed over a nonporous sub-base.

For example, one common way to construct playgrounds with a shredded wood surface is to install pipe drains in cloth-lined trenches 12" deep in the subsurface. The pipe is covered with pea gravel to subsurface level, then filter cloth is laid over the entire playground. A layer of pea gravel is then installed with an additional layer of filter cloth on top of it. (The filter cloth keeps the materials from infiltrating each other.) Finally, the shredded wood is placed in a uniform layer on top of the gravel. Many playgrounds around the country have successfully used this design to achieve a dry and well-drained facility.

However, soil scientists point out that this layering of materials is a technique that is considered to result in a perched water table, which would hold water in the surface layer until it becomes fully saturated. To prevent this condition, these experts say that the only way to achieve effective drainage under the surface material is to contour the surface and the subsurface to allow positive runoff.

Those who construct the layered playgrounds, however, counter that relying on contouring alone has created conditions in which water lays in the surface materials, resulting in excessively wet areas and, in some cases, rotting of organic surface materials accompanied by an unpleasant odor.

If the planner is concerned about the possibility of a perched water table, one alternative method would be to omit the gravel layer, and to install strip drains in the sub-base, then to place the surfacing material directly on the sub-base. This method would also offer cost savings through the elimination of the pea gravel and through the substitution of less costly strip drains. If shredded wood is used as the surfacing material, the installer would need to backfill the strip drains with coarse sand. But if the surfacing material is inorganic (sand or gravel), that surfacing material itself can be used for the backfilling process. (See Chapter 8 for details on the use of strip drains.)

Whichever of these methods is used, the process of laying out a playground for effective drainage should begin with a topographic survey to solidify the planner's understanding of how water moves around the surface of the area. Then develop a set of proposed elevations to isolate the playground from that surrounding water movement. In most cases, playgrounds can be laid out on a fairly level plane, sloping 1% or less in any direction.

Where subsurface drain systems will be installed, pipe drains or strip drains on 20-foot centers will normally provide for adequate removal of surface water resulting from inclement weather.

Of course, one problem area on most playgrounds is mud puddles in the depressions under each swing or slide. An effective installed drain system will prevent this problem by draining away moisture before these mud puddles can develop. Also, rubber mats can be installed to prevent the formation of these depressions.

It has become common in some areas to build playgrounds "aboveground"—to construct wooden or plastic forms around the perimeter of the playground and fill the enclosure with surfacing material. Many planners have ended up with soggy, poorly draining facilities because they assumed that an aboveground facility will by definition drain quickly and easily. The truth is that the forms can turn into a sort of artificial lake in wet weather unless the sub-base is porous, or some sort of installed drain system is provided.

A drain system should be laid out at the same time as the playground equipment, to make sure drains will adequately serve trouble spots like those under swing sets, slides, etc. Smaller "tributary" drain lines can be run to serve these areas.

As mentioned above, catch basins can be a valuable tool for keeping the playground playable by channeling away surface water from the surrounding terrain before it reaches the playground. Catch basins also serve as the junction boxes of installed drain systems. Aim to leave 15 to 20 feet between the edge of the playground and the catch basins. Use small grate openings to prevent tripping and bicycle tire damage.

## 18.3 CONSTRUCTION AND RECONSTRUCTION

### Construction

The construction of a new playground, as with an athletic field, begins with the excavation of the area to achieve the subgrade required to match the surface contour indicated on the design. (This, of course, assumes that a survey has been taken and a contour plan developed.) Once the subgrade is set, the next step is to install the playground equipment. In installing the equipment, it is vitally important to follow manufacturer's specifications, especially for anchoring. This is a critical factor in assuring the safety of the children who will use the facility. Subsurface drains can then be laid as dictated by the position of the equipment and the overall design plan for the playground.

If the plan calls for a layer of pea gravel under a shredded wood surface, install the pea gravel in a uniform layer (with filter cloth layers above and below). Finally, install the surfacing material, taking care once again to achieve uniform surface depth (Figure 18.1).

### Reconstruction

In performing reconstruction, the first question that must be asked is whether or not the playground equipment will be removed and repositioned, or left in place. In most cases, reconstruction processes take place just as in new construction, with the additional complication of working around existing equipment (if it's left in place). This factor complicates the task of achieving adequate subgrade contours.

## 18.4 RENOVATION

A well-designed playground doesn't take much renovation. An additional layer of surfacing material may need to be added every two to three years (if shredded wood is

*Figure 18.1. A completed playground with a shredded wood surface.*

used), but well-drained facilities will need less because less rot will take place underneath.

If installing more shredded wood surface material, take time first to relieve the compaction of the existing material—scarifying works well in these circumstances. This step will help to achieve a softer, better-draining surface when the new material is installed.

## 18.5   MAINTENANCE AND MANAGEMENT PROCEDURES

Areas under swing sets and slides will need to be refilled and leveled with matching material from time to time to prevent larger holes. Remember that rubber mats can be used to prevent the formation of these holes.

Otherwise, use hand rakes to return surface material kicked out of the depressed areas by users' feet.

## 18.6   RULES AND REGULATIONS (SANCTIONING BODIES)

For more information on the design, construction, and maintenance of playgrounds, send for a free copy of "Handbook for Public Playground Safety," Publication Number 325, published by:

U.S. Consumer Product Safety Commission
Office of Information and Public Affairs
Washington, D.C. 20207
(800) 638-8270

The American Society for Testing and Materials also has a publication on playground safety called "ASTM Standard Consumer Safety Specification for Playground Equipment for Public Use," ASTM F1487.

ASTM
100 Barr Harbor Drive
West Conshohocken, PA 19428-2959
(610) 832-9500

# Chapter 19

# *Bocce Courts*

## 19.1  INTRODUCTION

Bocce, which dates back to the Roman Empire, is a popular backyard sport played by many amateurs. Unlike lawn bowling, which is played on grass, bocce is meant to be played on a specifically designed and built bocce court, constructed with wooden backstops and sides and a hard surface of compacted stone dust or clay.

## 19.2  DESIGN

### 19.2a  Survey and Layout

The length and width of a bocce court can vary from 8 to 14 feet wide and 60 to 90 feet long. Ten by sixty feet is a good size for a backyard court. For tournament play, courts are larger; 12 feet wide by 76 feet long, or even 13 feet wide by 90 feet long. Figure 19.1 shows a typical layout of a bocce court.

At each end of the court, foul lines are marked on the sideboards, and players are required to remain behind these lines while shooting.

A bocce court is meant to be flat and level to provide for straight, true roll of the ball. When laying out a court, it's important to make sure the area around the court drains properly, so the court will not take on water. As with any sports surface, a bocce court should be an isolated drainage unit, designed to drain away only the water that falls directly on it.

Once the location has been chosen for the facility, lay out the court and survey the grade. Take elevations at each corner of the court and midway down the sides. Survey enough land around the court to determine whether swales or catch basins are necessary to keep water away from the court.

### 19.2b  Design Criteria for New Construction

In designing a bocce court, it's important to consider how to move water off the surface. Since the surface is level, and is made of stone dust or clay, water movement (percolation) through the profile is very slow—essentially nonexistent. To make matters worse, the court is surrounded with wooden boards which can trap water on the surface. All of these factors make it more of a challenge to get water off the surface after a heavy rain. Unlike most other sports playing areas, which are either grass or hard surfaces contoured to promote drainage, a bocce court is hard and level.

In addition to the matter of drainage, the designer must consider the "backstop" at

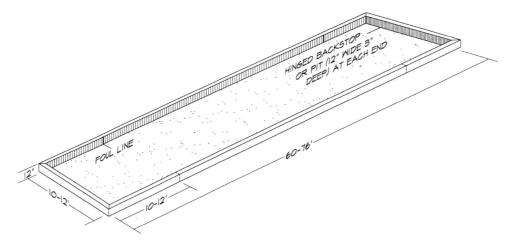

*Figure 19.1. Bocce court dimensions.*

each end of the court. In bocce, some rule books state that any ball hitting the backstop is to be taken out of play. If that ball strikes another ball after it bounces off the backstop, the ball that is struck is replaced in its original position and the ball that bounced off the backstop is taken out of play. Consider using a backstop hinged at the top to deaden the roll of the ball and prevent disturbing balls still in play (see Figure 19.2).

*Figure 19.2. A hinged backstop such as this one prevents the ball from rebounding onto the court, and is sometimes used when local rules prohibit playing the ball off the backstop.*

However, if rules followed by local custom allow bank shots, the hinged backstop may be inappropriate, since it deadens the rebound of the ball.

### 19.2c  Surfacing Materials
The most common surface material for a bocce court is stone dust. In choosing this type of material, make sure that most of the stone dust is predominantly fines. Too much gravel will prevent the surface from firming up (probably the most common reason for the failure of a bocce court), and lead to a bumpy playing surface. The type of clay used on baseball skinned areas can also be used to construct a smooth, firm surface, and represents an acceptable alternative where stone dust is unavailable. If the surface is firm, the ball rolls freely, but if the surface is too loose or contains too much coarse material, friction will slow the ball to an unacceptable degree. A loose surface will also cause the ball to roll erratically, because it's hard to keep a loose surface level and smooth. Every contact with the surface causes a depression: footprints, ball marks, even marks from grooming the surface. Grooming a loose surface becomes a never-ending challenge.

### 19.2d  Installed Drain System
Some provision must be made for drainage, since the court will be level with wood boards around it. Subsurface drains below the court itself are a waste of money, since water percolates too slowly through the surface to allow them to work properly. An installed drain system surrounding the court may be the only effective type of subsurface drainage. This type of drain system should be installed just outside the perimeter of the court, as close as possible without disturbing the playing surface.

Where courts are installed below ground level, it's nearly always necessary to install perimeter drains to prevent the court from becoming a pond in rainy weather. Even where the court is constructed above ground level, the boards can serve as a dam to hold water, so some provision will be necessary to allow water to drain from the surface. One simple method is to drill holes in the boards four to six feet apart and just above the surface of the court, providing exit points for water that lands on the surface. When the court is below ground level, these holes allow the water to drain into the subsurface perimeter drains. If the court is constructed above ground level, no installed drain system is necessary; these holes allow water to drain away from the court, typically providing sufficient drainage to keep the court playable. To work effectively, these holes should be ½″ to ¾″ in diameter. (For more on drainage, see Chapter 8.)

## 19.3   CONSTRUCTION AND RECONSTRUCTION

### Construction
Ideally, in order to achieve effective drainage, the court should be about 3″ above ground level, and the surrounding boards should extend another 6″ above the playing surface. Begin construction by setting the grade stakes according to the survey plan, then use string lines to assist in excavating the area about 3″ deep. (The subgrade should mirror the finish grade to allow for a consistent 6″ layer of surface material.) Install the end sideboards using treated lumber with the bottom at the subgrade and the top extending 6″ above the level of the planned playing surface. Then install the 6″ of surface material and compact it with a tamper. See Figure 19.3 for a below ground level court view.

*Figure 19.3. This newly constructed bocce court was built below ground level. Using "2X" lumber for side rails can make it easier to drill drainage holes and enhance removal of water from the playing surface.*

### Reconstruction

As with any sports surface which is not performing appropriately, the first step in reconstruction is to identify the cause of the failure. Otherwise, the reconstruction process will just repeat past mistakes. Probably the most common reason for failure of a bocce court is that the wrong material was used to build the surface. For example, in an attempt to promote good drainage, some courts traditionally have been built with a 3″ to 4″ layer of large gravel (over ¼″) over the sub-base with three to four inches of fines over the gravel. The problems with this design are that the fines eventually wash into the coarser material below, thinning the layer of fines at the surface, and that this method creates a perched water table, even when the fines do not wash into the coarse material.

To reconstruct a bocce court, begin by removing all of the surface material, including the gravel underneath. Then install 6″ of a fine aggregate, like stone dust, that will bind together properly and provide the firmness and stability that the sport requires.

### 19.4   MAINTENANCE

For a bocce court, the most important maintenance practices include leveling to provide an even surface for competition and removing surface debris that could interfere with the rolling of the ball. Court markings may need to be painted on the sideboards once or twice a year. Make sure the foul lines are clearly visible for each event.

## 19.5   GOVERNING AND SANCTIONING BODIES

World Bocce Association
1098 W. Irving Rd.
Bensenville, Illinois 60106
(630) 860-2623

International Bocce Association
187 Proctor Blvd.
Utica, New York 13501
(315) 733-9611

United States Bocce Federation
920 Harbor Drive
Martinez, California 94553
(510) 229-2157

# PART IV

# *Quality, Evaluation and Safety of Sports Facilities*

In sports fields as in many aspects of life, "quality" is largely in the eye of the beholder. Fans usually judge the quality of a sports field by appearance. Players and coaches evaluate the turf according to traction and ball control criteria. But even there, standards vary; a slower team about to play a fast one may pray for rain to soften the footing and neutralize the opponent's advantage.

Of course, in the real world, the variety of viewpoints on quality is even greater. The field manager's judgment includes factors like the hours of maintenance required to keep the field playable. The school board or parks department administrator factors cost into his or her evaluation of quality. And the insurance company regards the facility as a quality field if it has all the required safety equipment and clearances.

In our discussion of field evaluation, we'll consider some of the equipment and methods used to study the performance in relation to the two major field characteristics: traction and field hardness. We'll also look at some testing that has been done for each of these characteristics.

In Part IV, we will consider the critical issue of safety, and look at some of the judgments which must be made to allow players to compete without distracting worry about field conditions. Of course, spectator safety must also be addressed when designing, building, or maintaining any sports facility that will be used as a venue for public competition, so we will also review some of the issues affecting spectator safety.

# Chapter 20

# *Sports Field Evaluation Equipment*

## 20.1 INTRODUCTION

On any sports field, the interaction between the players and the surface is affected by two critical field characteristics: **hardness** and **traction**. Most casual observers would readily agree on a general evaluation of a field in regard to hardness and traction; either it's hard or soft, either the traction is good or not. But researchers have developed specialized equipment to allow for more precise and scientific measurement of these characteristics of turf surfaces.

From a scientific standpoint, **hardness** is the measure of the ability of a surface to absorb energy imparted by an object colliding with it—in other words, its shock-absorbing properties. During play, the object may be a ball, or the foot or body of a player. To measure hardness, weighted "missiles" are dropped on the turf to simulate a player falling or running on the surface. By dropping missiles onto different surfaces from a constant height and weight, variations in surface hardness can be measured and compared.

**Traction** is scientifically defined as "adhesive friction"—that is, the ability of a wheel, foot, hoof, etc. to remain securely in one place without slipping while force is applied to it. In the case of sports turf, of course, this adhesive friction defines the relationship between a player's foot and the surface. Traction is generally evaluated using equipment that simulates the action of cleats pressed into the ground.

In this chapter we'll look at some of the equipment and methods used to evaluate the hardness and traction of sports fields.

## 20.2 HARDNESS EVALUATION EQUIPMENT

### Clegg Impact Tester

The most commonly used device for testing field hardness is the Clegg hammer, also known as the "Clegg Impact Tester," or "CIT," originally developed by Baden Clegg in Western Australia for testing dirt road base surfaces. The Clegg hammer and corresponding computer equipment calculates the hardness of the surface based on its reaction to the impact of the missile. Unlike the bulky and cumbersome equipment used previously for these measurements, the CIT is lightweight and portable. It can be transported easily to the field for testing, and then returned to the lab for analysis of the results. In the CIT, an accelerometer is mounted on a 4.5 kg missile and several lighter missiles, which are then dropped from a predetermined height through a guide tube.

*Figure 20.1. The Clegg Impact Tester (or Clegg Hammer) measures surface hardness based on reaction to the impact of a missile dropped through a guide tube.*

Use of equipment of this type in sports field management is still in its infancy: a study was conducted by Penn State in 1986 and 1987 on 12 game and practice football fields to analyze this method of testing, but the results were largely inconclusive. The researchers did agree that there is a need to standardize both equipment and methodology for the scientific measurement of turf hardness. (The above information was reported in ASTM Publication 1073-1990. For results of this test see Chapter 21.3.)

## 20.3  TRACTION EVALUATION EQUIPMENT

"Traction," in its scientific definition as "adhesive friction," represents the ability of the turf or other surface to remain firm as force is applied on it by the foot of an athlete. From the standpoint of a sports turf manager, the goal in traction evaluation is to find a level of traction that allows the player to start, stop, and change direction without causing excessive stress to joints and ligaments. A number of devices have been developed to allow accurate and consistent measurement of traction.

### 20.3a Shear Vane

The shear vane is an instrument used to measure traction on natural turfgrass. Researchers J. N. Rogers III and D. V. Waddington used such a device in their 1987 study of 12 Pennsylvania high school fields, and Andrew S. McNitt, Robert O. Middour, and Waddington conducted a 1992 study comparing the shear vane to another device, called "PENNFOOT."

The shear vane consists of 12 fins welded at right angles to a cutting head. It is pressed into the surface using foot pressure. The foot is removed and torque is applied manually by turning the opposite handles in the same direction. The maximum torque is read from the calibrated gauge on top of the apparatus. A measurement is taken when shearing of the turf or soil occurs.

### 20.3b PENNFOOT

PENNFOOT was developed by Robert O. Middour and Andrew S. McNitt at Penn State University and was used by McNitt, Middour, and Waddington in September 1991. This device has the advantage of measuring traction both rotationally and linearly, whereas the shear vane measures rotational traction only. The PENNFOOT also accommodates various types of athletic footwear, and uses loading weights similar to those actually exerted by athletes.

*Figure 20.2. The PENNFOOT, developed at Penn State University, measures rotational and linear traction exerted through actual athletic footwear.*

The 1992 test described above was a direct comparison between the PENNFOOT and the shear vane used by Rogers and Waddington in their 1987 study of high school fields. The study also compared the PENNFOOT with the device developed by the research team of Canaway and Bell (Apparatus A). The details of this study have been published in a report entitled "Development and Evaluation of a Method to Measure Traction on Turfgrass Surfaces," published by the American Society for Testing and Materials, *Journal of Testing and Evaluation*, JTEVA, 25, (1) pp. 99–107, 1997.

To summarize the results of this study, the research team concluded that the other traction measuring devices were not measuring the same variables as the PENNFOOT. For example, the shear vane seems to measure primarily the shear resistance of the soil and belowground vegetation, probably because the user forces the fins of the apparatus through the turf and into the soil prior to taking a measurement. The PENNFOOT, however, rests on the turf surface. Depth of penetration becomes a function of soil moisture, turf density, shoe sole properties, and loading weight—the very factors that directly affect players' traction on a turf surface.

The comparison also indicated that these machines were differentially affected by turf under the conditions of this experiment. Neither Apparatus A nor PENNFOOT correlated well with the shear vane.

Comparisons of PENNFOOT to these traction-testing machines on different species, cutting heights, and different turf densities also resulted in low correlations. The researchers suggested that the other traction-measuring devices did not measure the same traction characteristics as the PENNFOOT. The team also concluded that the PENNFOOT probably does a better job of measuring the turf characteristics that affect traction as experienced by a player.

# Chapter 21

# *Field Quality and Evaluation*

## 21.1 INTRODUCTION

The "quality" of a field is largely defined by the effect of that field on player safety and performance, and on ball response.

In evaluating the safety of a field, hardness is an obvious consideration, and moderation is a most desirable feature. Fields that are too hard can increase the severity of falls by players, while soft, spongy fields create early fatigue in the leg muscles of a player, and may lead to pulls and cramping.

In considering ball response, uniformity is probably the critical characteristic. Bumpy, uneven playing surfaces can cause the ball bounce and roll to be erratic and unpredictable, and can also adversely affect footing. Player trips and falls degrade the quality of player performance as well as creating a safety hazard. On turf, of course, the presence of a continuous stand of turfgrass is crucial to the uniformity of the playing surface.

In this chapter, we will consider some of the testing and research that have been performed by universities and other turfgrass experts on field hardness, traction, and other important factors that influence the quality of a sports field.

## 21.2   AESTHETIC APPEAL AND QUALITY

As just about any sports field manager will tell you, fans generally rate a field by the way it looks. And that simple criterion is generally indicative of the other, less obvious aspects of turfgrass culture. Although other factors must be considered, it's generally true that a field that looks good is of better quality than one that looks bad. For example, a football field that's worn or muddy in the middle is obviously not as good as one with a full, thick grass cover. A baseball or softball skinned area that looks like a swamp does not have a consistent grade, and is therefore uneven. A soccer field that looks like a torn-up mess is probably poorly maintained and hard to play well on.

One aesthetic factor not overlooked by professional fields managers is the effect of mowing practices. The most attractive fields are those that reflect some forethought about the appearance of the facility after mowing is complete. Professional baseball probably sets the standard for careful mowing that will lead to an attractive striping pattern that enhances the perception of a quality field.

Since the primary controlling factor of the color variations is the direction in which the mower passes over the grass, the operator should be directed to give attention to this matter while mowing. Many football fields are mowed with all swathes in a given five-

*Figure 21.1. Mowing in alternating directions causes a striking color contrast that enhances the aesthetic appeal of the field.*

yard section going in the same direction, but other sports tend to favor back-and-forth alternating stripes.

The distinction between stripes is created by lightly rolling the turf (with a roller the same width as the mower) as it is being mowed. This effect can also be achieved by applying iron to every other five-yard section of a football field (see Figure 21.1).

## 21.3   EARLY TESTING

Work has been going on for at least 30 years to develop methods to evaluate the hardness of turf surfaces. Among the earliest studies involving hardness testing of turf surfaces were those of J. Gramckow in 1968. He found that there is a difference in the hardness of turf made up of different turfgrass varieties. For instance, bermudagrass absorbed more energy than either tall fescue or Kentucky bluegrass.

Gramckow's research also demonstrated that there is a marked difference in the hardness of different soils. Sand mixed with 50% sawdust (by volume) was the least hard, while loam soils were the hardest. Not surprisingly, increasing the moisture of the soil reduces its overall hardness. (More information on this research can be found in ASTM publication 1073-1990 "Portable Apparatus for Assessing Impact Characteristics of Athletic Field Surfaces," by John N. Rogers III and Donald V. Waddington. This publication also reports on a 1974 study by K. D. Bowers, Jr. and R. B. Martin comparing synthetic and natural surfaces. Their research showed that Kentucky bluegrass has superior impact-absorbing qualities, followed closely by new synthetic turf. Five-year-old artificial turf was found to have much poorer shock-absorbing characteristics than either new synthetic turf or bluegrass.)

The first reported research in the United States into hardness and traction on athletic fields was performed by Penn State University in 1986 and 1987 on 12 high school game and practice football fields in Central Pennsylvania. The purpose of this study was to assess the relationship of vegetation, soil properties, and maintenance practices, and to develop specific recommendations for turf managers on ways to improve field conditions. The conclusions of this "groundbreaking" study are widely regarded as the basis for good sports turf management practice, and are still followed today.

Hardness was measured with the Clegg Hammer and the 2515 portable vibration analyzer, and traction was measured using a Type IB shear vane apparatus.

The study found that good management practices and healthy turfgrass culture were generally associated with a less hard turf. Harder surfaces occurred when the soil was dryer, had greater bulk densities, and when the turf cover was thinner or less uniform. Aerated fields were found to have lower bulk densities, and consequently were less hard. Not surprisingly, fields were harder inside the hash marks, because the soil was more compact and the turf cover was reduced in those areas. Practice fields, which received little or no maintenance other than mowing, were generally found to be harder than game fields, which were more carefully managed.

The study found that traction is primarily a factor of differences in the turfgrass itself. Better turfgrass cover provides the best traction, and that means that traction is typically better on game fields and outside the hash marks. Superior turf cover corresponds with greater rooting, resulting in an increased resistance to shear and better traction.

The advice given to fields managers as a result of this study was a precursor to our contemporary theory of Integrated Cultural Management: turfgrass managers can improve traction and reduce hardness by selecting and using management practices that maintain adequate soil moisture, reduce compaction, and thicken turfgrass cover. The primary beneficial practices, then, are proper mowing, irrigation, adequate fertilization, and regular aerification.

The researchers also concluded that practice fields, which are typically neglected, should get more attention so they will provide playing conditions that are more typical of game fields, and to reduce impact injuries by reducing hardness. In football field maintenance and renovation, the center of the field needs more attention than the sides.

## 21.4 RECENT TESTING

In 1992, more traction testing was done at Penn State University by Andrew McNitt, Donald Waddington, and Robert Middour (reported by ASTM—Publication 1305, "Traction Measurement on Natural Turf," *Safety in American Football*, pp. 145-155, 1996.) The device used for this study was the PENNFOOT apparatus (see Chapter 20, Sports Field Evaluation Equipment).

The 1992 study showed that tall fescue and Kentucky bluegrass provided the best traction values, and that perennial ryegrass and creeping red fescue offered the worst.

The recent study also demonstrated that better traction occurred with lower cutting heights. Logic would indicate that, if the grass is twice as high, there would be twice as much unstable foliage between the sole of the foot and the more stable thatch and soil layers. To optimize traction, the field manager can take pains to ensure that the field is mowed frequently during the season and preseason, so that a lower height can be maintained without removing more than a third of the blade at each mowing.

(By the way, the 1992 study also looked at the effect of the traction that can be expected with various types of athletic shoe. A studded shoe gave the wearer better "linear traction" than a molded shoe, but the molded shoe provided higher "rotational traction." The results probably confirm what most coaches would suspect: put studded shoes on bruising linemen and fullbacks who spend most of their time going straight ahead, but molded cleats on the elusive halfbacks and wide receivers who need to change directions quickly.)

At this writing, another study on hardness and traction is being conducted at Penn State University by Andrew McNitt, who is testing the effects of soil amendments for sports fields. He prepared a sand-based turf area with an installed drain system, a layer of pea gravel, choker sand, and a 4″ root zone mix.

On top of the 4″ layer of root zone mix, McNitt installed an additional 6″ layer of sand amended with inorganic amendments designed to improve turf performance. These amendments include Netlon™ interlocking mesh elements, TURFGRIDS™ fibers, Dupont™ Shredded Carpet, Sportgrass™, and Nike™ "ground-up sneakers" (one plot with mostly uppers and one with mostly soles). McNitt is using the traction and surface hardness devices developed at Penn State to evaluate the performance characteristics of these amended soils.

# Chapter 22

# *Safety*

## 22.1 INTRODUCTION

The safety of players and spectators is a critical consideration in the design, construction, and maintenance of any sports facility. Because athletes are moving at high speed on and around the playing area, safety factors like clear stopping distance and slight irregularities in the turf can be much more important on a sports field than on a residential lawn. And for sports like baseball and softball, where the ball leaves the playing area at high speed, the potential for injury to spectators is well documented.

In this chapter we will consider some of the major factors affecting the overall safety of sports fields and related facilities, and we'll look into some common hazards to be avoided in designing, constructing, and maintaining a quality facility.

## 22.2 PLAYER SAFETY AND PERFORMANCE

In discussing issues of safety, a good starting point is the idea that a field designed to enhance performance is also likely to be a safer field. Along with considerations like hardness and traction (which were discussed in Chapters 20 and 21), player safety is directly affected by the levelness and uniformity of the surface, the consistent thickness of the turf cover, and the ability of the field to accommodate precipitation. For example, a properly designed baseball field is a safer field in wet weather than a poorly-designed field; the better field will shed water more effectively, allowing more solid footing and preventing slips and falls. An overcompacted football field, with thin turf or bare ground, forces players to compete in a cloud of dust, dirt, and stones on a rock-hard surface that prevents good traction (or, in wet weather, on a field of mud).

On many athletic fields, the greatest impediments to safety are stationary objects that are installed on or near the playing field itself. Scoreboards, fences, and even drainage structures like catch basins can cause serious or even fatal injuries if they are placed where athletes can crash into them. In the chapters of this book on specific types of sports fields, recommended clearances are shown for the guidance of field designers. These recommendations, it should be noted, are *minimum* safe clearances, and allowing more room increases safety correspondingly.

Designing a safe field requires the planner to consider safety at each stage of the process—and that means the details that are sometimes overlooked. For instance, is there easy access to the playing area for emergency vehicles in case of an accident? Is the backstop sufficient to ensure the safety of the spectators? Are fans at the concession

369

*Figure 22.1. Soil settling has left this catch basin protruding above the field surface, presenting a safety hazard. This situation should be repaired as soon as possible.*

stand exposed to foul balls? All of these concerns need to be addressed in the design of the field.

It's also important to be sure that field equipment has been installed in accordance with the manufacturer's instructions. Many of us tend to consult the directions only if all else fails; if we put it together and it seems right, we consider it done and go on to the next job. But the manufacturer may have included safety features in a product that will be missed if the installation instructions are discarded or ignored. Improperly installing equipment may lead to injuries, and may also cause the voiding of warranties and insurance protection. Worse still, it may lead to charges of criminal negligence if an injury occurs as a result. It's wise to consider equipment instructions to be just as important as those of chemical agents.

Another step in enhancing safety is to make sure that all required safety equipment is properly installed. Many youth baseball and softball leagues now require a fence in front of the dugouts to protect players from foul balls. On football fields, pads on goalposts are a wise precaution; it may look funny on the sports bloopers when a player runs into the post, but the resulting injuries can be anything but funny.

Remember, too, that the players must safely enter and leave the field, and be sure to provide for safe access. Smooth concrete or tile surfaces can be as slippery as ice in wet weather, so make sure the athletes have dry, secure footing before and after the game. If teams must approach the field up or down a pronounced grade, stabilize the path with fine stone dust or other self-binding materials to prevent slipping.

## 22.2a  Drainage and Irrigation Structures

In designing drainage structures, place catch basins well off the field and use a small grid on top. Inspect these structures before each competitive season, to make sure that the earth has not settled around a catch basin and left it protruding from the soil in a dangerous fashion. If it has, carefully fill all low spots to make the structure flush with the surrounding soil.

Swales can also represent a hazard, particularly if the change in grade is too sharp. An unsuspecting player can suddenly find himself or herself running through thin air. If the field's drainage system includes swales, the manager should jog across them personally to make sure they don't present a preventable danger.

Irrigation systems can also represent a safety hazard if improperly installed. Sprinkler heads or quick couplers should have rubber covers. Sprinkler heads should be selected in consideration of their intended use; some heads are specifically designed for use on football fields, for instance, and using other heads can lead to player injuries. As a general rule, heads installed in the playing area should cover a large area, so that fewer of them need to be installed, and should have a small exposed surface area. Like the drainage system, irrigation equipment should be inspected at the beginning of each season and throughout the season, and damaged or worn-out fittings replaced.

### 22.2b  Maintenance Practices

Another good way to increase the safety of a field is to aerate, topdress, and level the field at the end of each season. This regimen relieves compaction that can lead to turf loss and corresponding loss of traction. The leveling step also eliminates the bumps and low spots that erode player performance as well as cause unnecessary falls.

Good mowing practices can also help to enhance the safety of players. Cutting the turf too high, or cutting too infrequently, can lead to excess clippings on the field and contribute to trips and falls.

### 22.3  SPECTATOR SAFETY

Like player safety, spectator safety is dependent on the proper design, construction, and maintenance of a facility. When designing a facility, place yourself in the position of a spectator. Avoid unnecessary hazards that can trip people, such as catch basins or small steps. Remember that areas that seem safe and free of obstructions in broad daylight may be dimly lit and hazardous by the end of a night football game. Warnings such as "watch your step" can be provided when there is a small step off a bleacher to the pavement or ground level.

Obviously, the safety of spectators is largely dependent on the safety of the bleachers or grandstands provided for their seating, and it is not within the purview of this volume to address the intricacies of bleacher design and construction. However, two considerations in field design have a direct effect on spectator safety: clearance provided for player stopping and protection against balls flying out of the playing area.

Perhaps the most common situation in which players run off of the field and into groups of spectators is in soccer. In recent years, the exploding popularity of the sport has led to the construction of many multiple-field complexes, some of them with only a few feet between fields—virtually no clearance at all. This has created hazards as spectators are crowded into small areas along the field—often with half the spectators facing each way. As players cross out of the playing area at high speed, they may crash into spectators, or may injure themselves trying to avoid such a collision.

Although this danger is most often observed in soccer, youth football, lacrosse, and other popular sports also pose a similar hazard where multiple-field layouts are used.

In order to prevent this type of hazardous environment, field planners should try to reserve the small areas between fields for players and coaches, and restrict spectators to sidelines that are not squeezed between fields whenever possible. (This practice is formalized in regulations of many youth soccer organizations, which do not allow

*Figure 22.2. Excessive clippings left on the turf may erode the health of the turfgrass culture, and can even lead to player trips and falls.*

parents and other spectators on the same side of the field as the teams.) A restraining line ten feet or more from the edge of the field, behind which all spectators must stand, is another good practice that gives players more room to stop or change course to avoid a collision.

Spectator injuries from a ball leaving the playing field are most commonly a problem in baseball and softball. The single best strategy for preventing these occurrences is to place a fence or screen in front of the spectator areas (including, of course, the dugouts). Bleachers and grandstands should also be positioned as close as possible to home plate, and not down the baselines, where the hardest line drives typically land.

Perhaps the next greatest hazard of stray ball injuries occurs at the end lines of the soccer field, where missed shots may be moving at high speed when they leave the playing area. While the soccer ball is larger and softer than a baseball or softball, its extra mass can provide enough force to inflict injuries to inattentive fans, and especially to children. Pushing paths and walkways away from the end line can provide a real boost to safety.

In fact, it may be true in general that providing screens and fences to protect spectators along walkways, while standing at concession stands and other off-field areas is one of the best ways to enhance safety. While spectators in the stands have their attention fixed on the game, and are thus able to get out of the way if a ball approaches, those walking to the rest rooms or waiting to buy a hot dog may have no awareness at all of the progress of the game on the field, and are thus more vulnerable to injury.

## 22.4   CONCLUSION

The greatest tool of safety is forethought—anticipating a hazard and preventing it. In designing or building a field, always think ahead to the actual environment when a game or practice is in progress. How many people will be there? What will they be doing? What will the light level be? The sound level? The more factors that can be correctly anticipated, the safer the field will be.

# PART V

# *Ancillary Information*

While the development and maintenance of a healthy turfgrass culture is obviously the primary concern for any turfgrass manager, several related topics must be kept in mind to allow the professional to provide a complete sports facility to the players and coaches who will use it. In Part V, we will consider several of these matters in the context of effective Integrated Cultural Management.

Chapter 23 reviews the principles of effective surveying, a critical process in the establishment of field contours that will allow the facility to promptly shed rainfall and allow competition to be carried out. Although it is not the goal of this chapter to make the reader an expert surveyor, the explanation of the fundamentals of surveying should allow the sports fields manager to conduct routine surveying tasks required to keep fields in optimum condition.

In Chapter 24, we consider the design and construction of amended sand fields, which are occasionally installed in high-profile facilities. Amended sand can be an ideal growing medium for turfgrass, because of the porosity of sand and the ability of such fields to drain quickly. This chapter looks at the most commonly used type of amended sand fields, and considers some of the recent developments and refinements by designers and researchers.

Chapter 25 looks at stadiums, and the interaction between the grandstands and the playing surface as interconnected systems. Although most fields managers have little control over the design or construction of stadiums, an understanding of the relationship between field and stands can provide a useful framework for many management decisions.

Chapter 26 looks at the various types of paints which are used to apply field markings or decorative artwork to sports fields (or to achieve uniform color), as well as at the equipment used to make such applications. In this chapter we will also consider the three common types of turfgrass covers used to protect the field from weather or other stresses.

Chapter 27, the final chapter of this volume, considers the history and current state of sports field science, and speculates on some of the developments sports field professionals are likely to observe as the industry moves forward into the twenty-first century.

# Chapter 23

# *Surveying*

## 23.1 INTRODUCTION

For our purposes here, we will define surveying as the determination of the boundaries and elevations of existing or proposed sports fields by means of measuring angles, distances, and elevations using specific equipment designed for that purpose.

Surveying is a vital part of all aspects of sports field management. Every sports field professional should have the knowledge and the tools for surveying to make informed decisions regarding field design, construction, reconstruction, renovation, and even maintenance (Figure 23.1). A good construction or reconstruction design project starts with a complete survey including dimensions and elevations at specific points on and around the field. The best plans consider the way the field will actually be constructed, detailing dimensions and elevations at critical points; leaving no room for errors in the construction phase.

Even field managers need to use tape measures and levels on occasion to perform minor renovation and maintenance tasks, such as surface leveling and installing drainage systems. For example, routine water problems on the skinned areas of diamonds are impossible to solve unless the direction of water movement is known. Installed drain systems work properly only if they are constructed with a downward slope toward the outlet. Having knowledge of surveying procedures and having the equipment to do the job will help solve many problems that otherwise would be a guessing game.

For those who have not used surveying equipment in the past we'll start by looking at some basic tools of the trade and describe how they work. Then, we'll look at some surveying procedures. Finally, we'll go over some practical considerations to follow when performing sports field design, construction, and renovation surveys.

## 23.2 EQUIPMENT

Basic surveying equipment for sports fields can be broken down into either levels or transits. With either piece of equipment, the surveyor will also need some sort of measuring device, such as a measuring tape for distances and an elevation rod for grades.

### 23.2a Level
The level is used in combination with an elevation rod to read differences in grades. There are many different types of levels to choose from, so we'll start with the least expensive and end with the most expensive.

*Figure 23.1. Surveying for a sports field project.*

The least expensive level is the simple "builder's level" which needs to be adjusted manually across four legs that rest on the platform at the top of the tripod (see Figure 23.2). To set up this type of level, position the scope across two of the four legs and adjust it until the bubble is in the center. Then turn the scope 90° across the other two legs and adjust it level. Keep turning the scope 90°, making adjustments until both positions are level. Unless this instrument is in perfect calibration, (usually done by professionals where the instrument was purchased) there is a good chance that when the scope is turned 180°, it will be slightly out of level. With this type of level, it's best to set up the instrument at a location on the site where a 90° turn of the scope is the maximum turning angle to get all the elevations needed. This type of level cost about $250.00 to $500.00 with tripod and elevation rod.

One of the best choices for surveying sports fields is the "automatic level" (Figure 23.3). To set up the instrument, the operator centers a bubble within a circle. When the instrument is turned to any angle (from 1° to 360°) it will automatically relevel itself. These levels are more accurate, and typically cost about $500.00 to $1,500.00 with tripod and elevation rod.

Both the simple builder's level and the automatic level require two people to perform elevation readings—one to look through the scope and one to hold the rod. However, there is one type of level that requires only one person to operate, and that is the "laser level." A laser level comes with an instrument that shoots an invisible beam, and a rod with a "level eye." The unit that shoots the beam should be placed in a central location. In moving around the site, the level eye can be moved up or down the rod until a beeping sound becomes constant. The constant sound wave can be adjusted to be accurate to a tenth or a hundredth of a foot, depending on the degree of accuracy desired.

*Figure 23.2. A simple builder's level.*

*Figure 23.3. An automatic level.*

This instrument works well when constructing sports fields that are meant to be level, such as sand volleyball courts, 400-meter tracks and football fields with crowns and sidelines that are level down the long axis. It's important to remember that this instrument will only read level, and the differences in elevations must be calculated manually by subtracting the existing elevation from the proposed elevation. Carrying the proposed elevation plan and a calculator is a must when trying to set elevations alone. The cost is $1,100.00 and up.

A more expensive laser level is the "digitally adjustable laser level." The advantage of this type of level is that the beam can be adjusted digitally downward or upward to a constant percentage of slope. This works well when building fields or installing drain pipe that require a percentage of slope with no deviation in grade. The cost is $5,000.00 and up.

Another use for this type of level is "laser grading." The instrument that shoots the beam is set at a central location and the instrument that receives the beam is on a piece of equipment that's doing the grading. The beeping sound changes to a constant beep, letting the operator know when the grade is right on. The advantage of this type of equipment is the operator can be more accurate without the help of an additional crew reading the grade manually and then relaying to the operator to either cut or fill.

## 23.2b  Transit

A transit can be used in two ways: to set a straight line and an angle to that line for the boundaries of sports fields, or to set a percentage of slope especially for installed drain systems. In both cases, measure tapes (or a prism, discussed later under "total station" instruments) are needed to define the distance of a straight line that marks the boundaries of the field, or the length of an installed drain line used to calculate the amount of fall (determined by a percentage) in that distance. The advantage of a transit is that it can also be used as a level when budgets are limited and will not allow the purchase of an automatic level or laser level.

In setting straight lines and angles with transits, two people are required to do the work; one to look through the scope and determine the angles and the other to set the desired points at the proper distance.

As with levels, transits can range from relatively inexpensive to very expensive. So we'll start with the least expensive and end with the most expensive.

The least expensive transit is the "manual transit-level" (Figure 23.4). This type of instrument has to be adjusted by eye to turn angles. First, set the instrument and manually turn the dial on the base of the instrument to 0°. Then adjust the scope of the instrument until the dial shows the desired angle. The problem with the manual adjusting transit is that the lines marking the degrees are so close that the eye can play tricks on you. Everyone has a strong eye and a weak eye, and depending on which eye is used, the dial may look like it needs to be turned one way or another. In a distance of  300 feet, a small fraction of a turn of the scope will result in a much larger variation that far away (as much as 4″ to 8″ one way or the other). For this reason, it's a good idea for one person to read the transit because another person may think it needs to be turned a little. The cost is $500.00 to $2,000.00.

A better choice, if affordable, is the "digital transit-level." This device is operated in the same manner as the manual type, but the digital display results in a more precise turn of the scope. This transit can also be digitally adjusted up or down to allow accurate setting of drain line slope and related tasks. The cost of digital transit-levels ranges from $2,000.00 to $5,000.00.

*Figure 23.4. A manual transit level.*

The most costly instrument, and one that is used mainly by professional surveyors, is known as a "total station." This laser device is all digital, and does everything from shooting distances to turning angles and calculating elevations. One person reads the instrument while the other has a prism attached to a rod. A total station can be a very confusing device for a novice to use, and even professional surveyors rely on other instruments (such as automatic levels) for shooting elevations, because they are much easier to operate and just as accurate. The cost of a total station runs from $5,000.00 to $10,000.00.

### 23.2c Elevation Rod

An elevation rod is used to measure differences in elevations by comparing one elevation with another. Rods are calibrated either in feet and inches or in feet and tenths. The most useful readings are in feet and tenths, because there is less math involved in calculating differences in elevations. These differences are often used to figure the percentage of slope between one elevation reading and another (see Section 23.4b). If a survey is performed using a "feet and inches" elevation rod, all readings will have to be converted to feet and tenths to calculate the percentage of slope.

At first glance, feet and tenths may seem harder to work with than feet and inches, but in fact, "feet and tenths" is an easier system to use. (Figure 23.5 shows how to interpret a "feet and tenths" rod. The right-hand column shows how the rod is calibrated in tenths of a foot. The center of the illustration shows a magnified section of the rod. The left-hand column shows how to read the rod in tenths and hundredths of an foot.)

Table 23.1 shows how inches compare to tenths of a foot. Remember, the only differ-

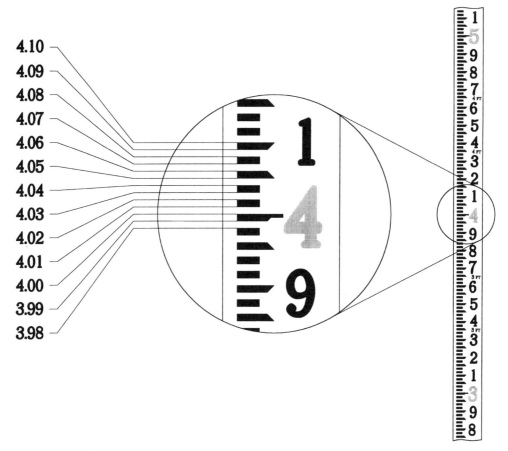

*Figure 23.5. Elevation rod in feet and tenths.*

ence between "feet and tenths" and "feet and inches" is the number of units into which one foot is divided, either into 12 units (feet and inches) or 10 units (feet and tenths).

To convert inches into tenths, *divide* the number of inches by 12. To convert tenths into inches, *multiply* the number of tenths by 12. It's important to remember that although the result will be in inches, it will also include *decimal* parts of an inch, rather than the more commonly used fractions such as ⅛″ or ¹⁄₁₆″.

An easy rough calculation that is frequently used by professional surveyors begins with the understanding that .01 foot is nearly equal to ⅛″. So a decimal reading of .51 foot is nearly equal to 6⅛″. By fixing in mind that 6″ is .5 foot, 3″ is .25 foot, and so on, the surveyor can quickly express decimal readings in inches and fractions.

**Table 23.1. Comparing Inches to Tenths**

| Inches | Tenths |
|--------|--------|
| 1 | .08 |
| 2 | .17 |
| 3 | .25 |
| 4 | .33 |
| 5 | .42 |
| 6 | .50 |
| 7 | .58 |
| 8 | .67 |
| 9 | .75 |
| 10 | .83 |
| 11 | .92 |

## 23.3 LAYOUT

The first step in surveying a sports field is to lay it out. (In laying out a sports field, it's wise to consult the latest rule book from the sanctioning body under which games will be played.) Using a transit, lay out the boundary lines of the field according to the rule book. Use the transit to set perpendicular lines or other angles that are appropriate for the sports field being surveyed.

Control points like field sidelines, baseball bases, etc., are most often set with a measuring tape, although a total station instrument can also do the job. Professional surveyors drive a 2″ × 2″ stake (referred to as a "hub") into the ground, then use a plumb bob to find the exact point to within one hundredth of a foot, and mark the point with a tack in the hub, although this degree of accuracy may be overkill for most amateur sports fields. The most useful measuring tapes are 100, 200, and 300 feet in length. Tapes are typically made of fiberglass (good), nylon-coated steel (better), and the best tapes are steel.

## 23.4 ELEVATIONS

It's important to understand that elevations are just about always stated as comparisons. One elevation reading alone will not provide meaningful information until it is compared to another elevation. The reason for comparing elevations is to determine the difference in grade between points on the field—otherwise known as the field contours.

### 23.4a Benchmark

A benchmark is a fixed reference point, such as a catch basin lid or an existing curb or similar stationary structure, which is used to make the elevations consistent. Once a benchmark has been established, the instrument can be moved to another location or removed and reset on another day. The height of the instrument will change, but the benchmark provides a way to compare each point on the field to a single fixed elevation. It's absolutely essential to make sure a benchmark location is chosen and the benchmark elevation is taken the first time the instrument is set up.

### 23.4b Rod Readings

The elevation rod is marked with numbers, expressed in either feet and inches or feet and tenths. Rod readings are comparative elevations (expressed in numbers) taken using a level and the rod. Remember that the key word in elevations is "comparative." One rod reading alone means nothing until there is another to compare it to. By comparing two or more readings (subtracting one rod reading from another), a determination can be made whether one point is higher than the other. The difference between the two readings is the amount of change in grade from one elevation and another.

In taking or interpreting rod readings, it's important to remember that a lower reading means that the grade is higher and vice versa. (As the land goes down, the rod gets lower, so the level will read a higher number.)

The most useful comparison for sports fields is the difference between two elevations as expressed in a percentage. To arrive at a percentage, divide the difference in the two elevations by the distance between them.

The percentage slope for hard surfaces (like skinned areas of baseball fields and clay tennis courts) should range between .25% and 1%, and grass areas should slope be-

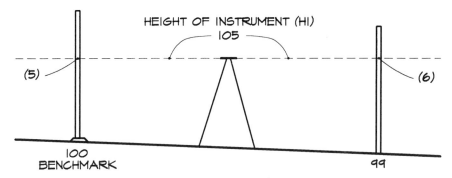

*Figure 23.6. Establishing elevations from a benchmark.*

tween .50% and 1.75%. In the construction phase, the minimum percentages of slope require string line grading to get the consistency required to prevent water puddles.

### 23.4c  Contour Plan Readings

Contour plan readings are specified elevations for the field to be constructed, and they are based on rod readings taken during the original survey. Like rod readings, they mean nothing unless they are compared to one another. Often these readings represent elevation above sea level.

The biggest difference between contour plan readings and rod readings is that on a contour plan, lower numbers represent lower points on the field. At first glance, this seems to make more sense than rod readings, where the opposite is true. However, rod readings are literally "read" off the rod, whereas calculating contour plan readings requires a good deal more mathematical computation.

The first step is to assign an elevation to the benchmark the first time the surveying instrument is set up. In many areas, previous surveying has established elevations above sea level for nearby points (such as a catch basin on the property), which can then be used as the benchmark for the field. (This information can often be found from old plans on file in the area.) First, set up and level the instrument somewhere near the center of the area to be surveyed, and place the elevation rod on the benchmark. Take a reading, and add the rod reading to the benchmark. The sum of the two is the height of the instrument, or "HI." Then subtract each subsequent reading from the HI to obtain the elevation at that point.

Figure 23.6 shows an example. In this example, the benchmark is 100. If the reading at the benchmark is 5 feet, adding this reading to the benchmark would yield a HI of 105. Then move the elevation rod to the first point to be surveyed. If the reading at that point is 6 feet, subtracting that reading from the HI would yield an elevation of 99 (105 − 6 = 99), meaning that the elevation at that point is 1 foot lower than the benchmark.

Each day that surveying is conducted on the same site, or whenever the instrument is moved, find the HI for that instrument location. Then continue subtracting readings from the HI to yield elevations.

If the terrain is so sloped that the instrument winds up being below the bottom of the rod for a particular point to be surveyed, the surveyor will see the ground through the scope when trying to take a reading (see Figure 23.7). In such a case, install a hub at a point where a reading *can* be taken. (This point is known to surveyors as a "turning

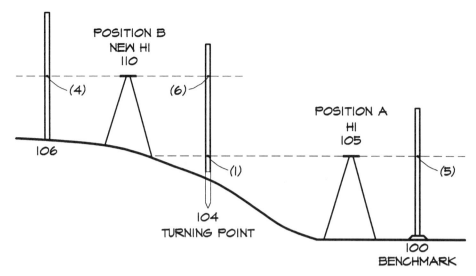

*Figure 23.7. Using a turning point to move the instrument.*

point.") Take a reading at the turning point and subtract the reading from the HI. Then move the instrument, leaving the elevation rod on the hub, and take a new reading with the instrument at the new (higher) location. Add the new reading to the elevation of the hub to determine the HI at the new, uphill location. Then continue to take readings and calculate elevations as described above.

## 23.5   PLACEMENT OF GRADE STAKES

Grade stakes are usually wooden stakes that are secured into the ground and have a marking on them to assist in contouring an area of land. The markings on the stake will instruct the contractor to cut or fill at that particular location.

A grid pattern (50-foot grid patterns are typical) is easy to lay out and install, and grids are generally the accepted practice in surveying. However, grid patterns have some limitations in surveying sports fields. For one thing, at the boundaries of fields where swales are typically installed to enhance drainage, a break in the grid pattern would be necessary to accommodate swales with their lower contours. A grid pattern would also be inadequate for a complicated contour plan that has high points and low points that do not fall on the grid pattern. For example, a baseball or softball field may have a crown through center field. In this case, the grade stakes would have to be set on the high point, and consequently the grid pattern would be disrupted. A much better stake pattern would be based on the contour design itself.

## 23.6   PRACTICAL CONSIDERATIONS FOR SPORTS FIELDS

Sports fields should be surveyed with the field and its free zones or out-of-bounds areas as if they were a floor plan of a building with various elevations. Every change in elevation needs to have grade stakes to reflect that change. Remember that grid patterns don't work, because the gridlines seldom fall at the point of the change in elevation. Center lines, end lines, and sidelines are important points that need grade stakes, and grid patterns will miss these points. Out-of-bounds areas, fences, and other structures also need grade stakes, and grid patterns will miss these points, too. Incomplete surveys lead to bad designs and consequently, to poorly constructed fields.

The most common reason for failure of baseball and softball fields is improper surveying. Since these fields have the most complex contours of all sports fields discussed in this book, let's look at how a diamond should be correctly surveyed. Lay out the field according to the rule book. Using home plate as the starting point, lay out the foul lines to the outside edge of the foul pole. Then, lay out the bases. Set the pitcher's plate and the outfield arc. Use string lines on straight lines and use paint on arcs. Take elevation readings at each of these points because they are the most common places to have breaks in elevations.

For the outfield, set up center field, and right and left center. Take an elevation reading at each of these points. Then shoot elevations at the fence lines around the entire field. Sometimes it's necessary to go beyond the fences for elevation readings because these grades may channel water onto the field. (More information on how to survey a baseball field can be found in Chapter 11, Section 11.2a. Figure 11.22 shows a survey worksheet for a baseball diamond.)

This example can be adapted to surveying and layout of other types of sports fields. Grid patterns are useful for determining the topography of a site, but designing and especially constructing a field requires elevations based on the field itself.

# Chapter 24

# *Sand and Sand-Based Fields*

## 24.1 INTRODUCTION

Sand is defined as fine particles of disintegrated rock between .05 mm and 2 mm in diameter. From a practical standpoint, most material sold as "sand" has varying amounts of other material mixed into it; coarser sand has large particles that are considered "gravel," while fine sand has smaller particles of silt and clay called "fines." Concrete (or "construction") sand may contain both gravel and fines. Certain grades of highly processed sand are available with very uniform particle size.

For our purposes, sand-based fields have a growing medium (or "rootzone") that consists of sand as the primary soil material. Sand-based rootzones may include one or more amendments intended to improve their performance as a growing medium or as a playing surface.

Today, amended sand fields are coming into more common use, and when properly designed and installed, they can offer dramatically improved playability. Methods of design and construction for sand fields vary widely, and there is no single set of sand field specifications that can be considered applicable to all sports, geographic locations, or intensity of use.

However, sand-based sports fields have a long and somewhat controversial history. In the United States, one of the first published techniques for using sand as a soil material for sports turf was the California Method of Sand Putting Green Construction, first outlined in the mid-1950s. The United States Golf Association (USGA) specifications for putting greens were first published in 1960. Prescription Athletic Turf (PAT) specifications were patented in 1969. In initial installations, various unanticipated pitfalls in the design, construction, and maintenance of sand-based rootzones caused many field failures. These historic problems are the background causes of the continuing suspicion of sand as a soil material for sports fields.

Sand-based athletic fields became popular in the early 1960s, as players, spectators, and owners demanded new and better fields. In most cases, the existing native soil fields (or at least those with proper slope and drainage) had provided adequate playing surfaces. However, as intensity of use and the financial stakes in professional games increased, sand-based fields were installed in hopes of improving playability.

It's important to note that a sand-based rootzone is not the answer for all fields and should be used only when circumstances justify it. Justifications for this type of field might include high profile use, availability of substantial funds for both construction and maintenance, player and owner expectations that the field would remain playable in a wide range of weather conditions, and intensity (frequency) of use. In the absence of these justifications, the properly designed and installed native soil field is still the most practical choice.

The sand field offers several key advantages that cannot be provided by a native soil field. Primary among these advantages of a sand-based rootzone is its high water permeability, which allows for rapid surface water removal by internal drainage. This rapid water removal advantage will seldom be needed, typically in a worst-case rainfall scenario of heavy downpours (3 to 5 inches per hour) just prior to or during a game, or when heavy rain continues for several days prior to competition. Although the probability of such a worst-case rainfall may be low, the necessity of assuring playability may justify the decision to install a sand-based field.

A second (and equally important) advantage is that a properly designed and installed sand-based rootzone will protect against a field's worst enemy: compaction. A correctly specified and tested sand will not compact to levels that significantly limit its internal drainage properties (i.e., macropore space—pores large enough to allow water to be drawn downward by gravity). This type of growing medium also provides an excellent environment for the soil and atmospheric gas exchange necessary for vigorous plant growth.

## 24.2   CRITICAL CONSIDERATIONS IN SAND-BASED GROWING MEDIA

Although sand-based rootzones provide rapid surface water removal and a noncompacting growing medium, the nature of sand as a soil material carries the possibility of many hidden pitfalls that makes its selection and management complex and demanding. Just about everyone is familiar with sand as it occurs on the beach, but few people (even sports field managers) have a good understanding of sand in terms of its size range distribution, chemical composition, and physical properties. This section will discuss the many critical considerations associated with sand as it is used in sports field construction.

### 24.2a  Size Range Distribution
Sand particles range in size from 0.05 mm to 2 mm. This range of sizes is extremely wide and represents one potential problem with the use of sand. The largest sand particles occur in "very coarse" sand (1 to 2 mm), and are up to 40 times larger than the particles of sand labeled "very fine" (0.05 to 0.1 mm).

### *Wide Size Range*
A wide size range distribution (widely varying particle sizes within a particular sample of sand) can be a problem in sand used to construct a sports field. Sand with a wide size range is usually sold as "concrete" or "construction" type. If sand with a wide range of sand sizes includes a high proportion of fine gravel or very coarse sand, then rootzones constructed from that sand may be prone to drought and difficult to irrigate properly. If a wide size range is equally balanced between coarse and fine sand, interpacking (compaction) of the sand may occur over time, causing reduced water permeability. A sand with a high proportion of very fine or fine sand is susceptible to compaction and reduced water permeability with only slight contamination by silt and clay particles.

This contamination of silt and clay can occur over time from windblown dust, silt, or clay, contaminated sod, or silt or clay contaminated topdressing mixtures. Sand can also be contaminated due to improper screening or washing at the pit, during construction (by dragging silt or clay from the surrounding area onto the field), or when the sand is purchased (if, for instance, a loader scrapes up silt and clay from the ground under the sand stockpile).

Table 24.1 shows recommendations for particle size distribution from a number of institutions and organizations. These recommendations have obvious differences as well as some underlying similarities. One of the obvious differences is the recommended amount of silt and clay, which varies from 3% to 15%. This wide range in recommended silt and clay percentage results from the differences in geography and climate under which the underlying research was conducted, as well as in the sport for which the recommendation was developed. For example, a sand-based field in Oregon, where local rainfall is high, will need greater permeability than another field located in Nebraska, where local rainfall is lower. Also, a field designed with a sloped or crowned center for surface runoff will typically require less permeability than a flat, level field. Surfaces for some sports, such as football, require enhanced surface strength, so more fines would be desirable. Sand used to build a field which will see only limited use can have some fines in the mix, while the same percentage of fines on a heavily-used field would create compaction problems.

## 24.2b  Sand Particle Stability

Sand particle stability refers to the relative resistance of sand to weathering or fracturing. Natural or manufactured sand is derived from weathered or crushed rock, and consists of quartz, feldspar, mica, and/or calcite. Quartz is a hard and durable mineral that is inert in its chemical composition and represents the majority of sand particles. Feldspar, mica, and calcite are softer minerals, and are not as chemically inert as quartz. Sand from nonquartz rock may have accelerated weathering (i.e., breakdown) or a tendency to fracture under the pressure of traffic and cultivation. Over time, these particles may change (decrease) in size or add chemical ions to the soil. The time required for significant weathering and fracturing of these softer minerals is not well-defined, but there is evidence that this weathering process does occur after field installation, and that weathering is enhanced by cultural practices such as fertilization, aeration, and irrigation, and especially by heavy field traffic.

The release of ions into the soil may change its chemical properties. For example, as a result of the release of ions, calcite sand (calcium carbonate composition) will tend to raise the pH of the soil as it weathers. This increase in pH will result in a more alkaline soil, reducing the availability of certain nutrients and causing nutrient deficiencies. Higher pH can also promote the occurrence of some turf diseases that strike an alkaline soil, such as take-all patch.

The physical stability of sand should be tested during the selection process. A quartz sand is most desirable because it will provide good stability. However, in some areas, quartz sand may be hard to find. Ideally, sand rootzones should have no more than 0.5% calcium carbonate.

## 24.2c  Sand Selection

When purchasing sand for a sports field, it's important not to simply specify "sand," but rather to specify the desired sand size classes, particle size distribution, and mineral composition. In addition, physical properties tests should also be conducted on the proposed sand and amendments. These tests allow the manager to predict field performance before the field is installed, and are based on laboratory analyses that include total porosity, air-filled porosity, capillary porosity, and saturated hydraulic conductivity measure-

**Table 24.1. Recommended Particle Size Distributions for Sports Fields**

| Name | Fine Gravel >2 mm | Very Coarse 1–2 mm | Coarse .5–1 mm | Medium .25–.5 mm | Fine .1–.25 mm | Very Fine .05–.1 mm | Silt .002–.05 mm | Clay <.002 mm |
|---|---|---|---|---|---|---|---|---|
| Penn State[a] | | | 95%* | | | | | |
| Penn State[b] | <10% | <10% | 50–75% | | <25% | <10% | <15% | |
| Univ. Minn.[c] | 3% max | | 60% min | | | 3% max | | |
| USGA[d] | 3% max | 7% max | 60% min | | 20% max | 5% max** | 5% max** | 3% max** |
| Univ. Calif.[e] | <10% | | 82% min | | | | 8% max | |
| Pac. NW[f] | | 30% max | 70% min | | 15% max | 10% max | 5% max | |
| Miss. State[g] | | 15% max | >60% | | 25% max | | 12% max | |
| PAT[h] | 3% max | 10% max | 60–80% | | 5–20% | 5–10% | 6% max | 6% max |

* 60% should be in the medium range (.25 to .5 mm)

** Total particles in these ranges shall not exceed 10%.

[a] Athletic Field: Specification Outline, Construction and Maintenance. Pennsylvania State University, Agriculture Extension Service Bulletin, 1982.

[b] The New Pennsylvania Design. Personal communications, Andrew McNitt. Pennsylvania State University, 1997. (McNitt based his design on USGA specifications, which classify very fine sand as .05 mm to .15 mm.)

[c] Athletic Field Construction and Maintenance. University of Minnesota, Minnesota Extension Service. Bulletin no. AG–BU 3105, 1987.

[d] USGA Recommendations for a Method of Putting Green Construction. 1993. USGA Green Section Record. March/April 1993 Issue. (USGA specifications classify very fine sand as .05 mm to .15 mm.)

[e] The Sand Putting Green: Construction and Management. Cooperative Extension, University of California, Division of Agriculture and Natural Resources. Publication no. 21448, 1990.

[f] Construction and Maintenance of Natural Grass Athletic Fields. A Pacific Northwest Cooperative Extension Publication. Bulletin no. PHW0240, 1983.

[g] Mississippi State University Sand Size Specifications for Sports Fields. Personal Communication, M. Goatley, J. Krans & D. Nagel, Mississippi State University, 1997.

[h] Prescription Athletic Turf. Sand Size Specification. Motz Group Technical Information, Cincinnati, OH, 1969.

ments in inches per hour. Testing of sand rootzone mixes should be performed by a laboratory that uses standard methods of analysis adapted from those published by the American Society of Agronomy (ASA) or American Society for Testing and Materials (ASTM). Furthermore, laboratories used for this testing should follow established guidelines for quality assurance, and should be subject to independent monitoring by an outside agency for accuracy and precision.

## 24.2d Depth of Sand Rootzones

All single-size sand classes have sufficient saturated hydraulic conductivity (water permeability) rates to allow their successful use on sports fields (see Table 24.2). However, an important consideration affecting a sand's hydraulic conductivity rate is the depth of the sand layer required to obtain this rate. For example, all sand classes listed in Table 24.2 have saturated hydraulic conductivity rates that would meet the minimum water permeability of most fields. Yet, when a rootzone is constructed using a highly uniform sand, a minimum depth of the sand layer is required to attain its stated permeability. The depth of a coarse or medium sand layer required to achieve these stated permeabilities is within dimensions practical for sports field construction (approximately 5″ to 9″). However, if the rootzone is composed primarily of fine or very fine sand, the required depth would be outside the practical range for sports field construction (16″ to 35″). The properties affecting minimum required sand depth are the cohesion and adhesion forces of water and sand. These forces cause water to be held in the sand layer against the force of gravity (under tension). The depth of the sand layer determines the amount of water which must be held in the sand before gravity breaks this tension and allows water to drain through.

## 24.2e Sand from Natural Deposits

Most sand used in sports field construction comes from mined deposits laid down by the forces of nature. These natural deposits vary, based on their geographical location and pit geology. Some areas lack a local natural sand supply acceptable for a sports field rootzone. Under these circumstances, the common temptations are to "cheat" on the sand size specification or not to conduct performance tests. These temptations arise out

**Table 24.2. Saturated Hydraulic Conductivity of Sand Classes and Minimum Depth Required for Gravity Drainage**

| Class and Particle Size Range (mm) | Minimum Depth of Sand for Gravity Drainage (inches) | Saturated Hydraulic Conductivity at Minimum Depth (inches/hr) |
|---|---|---|
| Coarse sand (0.5–1.0) | 4.7 | 216.5 |
| Medium sand (0.25–0.5) | 8.7 | 59.1 |
| Fine sand (0.10–0.25) | 15.7 | 17.7 |
| Very fine sand (0.05–0.10) | 35.4 | 5.1 |

Adapted from Adams and Gibbs, Soil Constituents and Properties in Turfgrass Systems, In *Natural Turf for Sport and Amenity: Science and Practice*, CAB International, Wallingford, UK, p.19.

of the desire to reduce the cost of the project. However, these attempts to cut budgetary corners may prove counterproductive over the long run if chronic field performance problems develop, requiring expensive remediation. Even where appropriate local sand is available, it's important to remember that sand pit geology can vary (and sand size composition can change) within just a few feet. Particle size analysis must be performed repeatedly during the mining process if the sand is coming from a pit, rather than from a stockpile. Otherwise, consistent particle size distribution cannot be assured.

### 24.2f   Surface Firmness (Strength)

Surface firmness or strength refers to the ability of a sand layer to resist surface forces, such as foot and equipment traffic, which could disturb the uniformity of the sand matrix. Sand layers constructed from any size particles tend to lack firmness, and this can be a special problem when the turf cover becomes thin or nonexistent. From a field standpoint, footing and traction can quickly deteriorate under these conditions. Sand rootzones lack firmness because of the rounded shape of the particles, the lack of particle cohesion, and the low moisture holding capacity of the sand layer. (Layers constructed from angular shaped sand particles have enhanced stability because of the particles' ability to interlock, but this characteristic is rare because natural weathering quickly rounds off their edges. Because of the rarity of sharp sand, most suppliers do not even think to test for this characteristic.)

Surface strength of sand can be enhanced by maintaining a minimum moisture level in the sand profile, by the addition of silt or clay particles (fines) to improve cohesiveness and improve moisture retention, and by the addition of a polypropylene amendment (see Section 24.3b below). However, enhancing the strength of a sand layer by adding fines must be balanced against the disadvantage of reducing the sand's permeability. The use of polypropylene amendments has been shown to improve the strength of sand layers without reducing permeability, but these products are costly.

### 24.2g   Nutrient and Moisture Retention Capacity of Sand

Nutrient and moisture retention by sand is a critical consideration for good health and vigor of the turfgrass culture. Sports fields with a sand rootzone are sometimes erroneously considered "low maintenance," a phrase which suggests that all management problems are solved by such construction methods. A wise field manager will beware of such claims, because some important management problems remain. It's true that sand fields offer improved water permeability and resist compaction, but these rootzones create other management challenges. Sand lacks water holding capacity and (because it lacks cation exchange capacity), the ability to retain nutrients. Various inorganic and organic amendments are routinely added to sand to address these deficiencies. But even with the addition of amendments, the sand rootzone remains a difficult system to manage in terms of nutrients, water, pH, microbial populations, and pesticide applications. Controlled-release fertilizers, careful water management, precise applications of pesticides, and close attention to pH, fertility, and disease infestations, are all required to properly manage a sand rootzone.

## 24.3   SAND FIELD AMENDMENTS

Amendments are materials added to the sand in order to increase the water and nutrient retention of the growing medium and to increase field stability. Amendments include both organic and inorganic materials, and sometimes soil. The best amended sand fields

Table 24.3. Advantages and Disadvantages of Commonly-Used Sand Amendments

| Amendment | Advantage | Disadvantage |
|---|---|---|
| **Organic Matter** | | |
| Peat | Increases nutrient, water, and buffering capacity of sand | Inappropriate peat reduces water permeability |
| Compost | Increases nutrient, water, and buffering capacity of sand | Must be thoroughly composted; if not, poor growth and concerns with possible phytotoxicity are likely |
| **Inorganic Matter** | | |
| Calcined clay | Increases capillary porosity and moisture retention | Much of water held at tensions unavailable for turf use |
| Vermiculite | Increases available moisture and cation exchange capacity | Particles are compressible and decreases water permeability |
| Perlite | Increases available moisture and total porosity | Decreases water permeability and poor particle stability |
| Calcined diatomaceous earth | Slight increase in available moisture | Reduced air-filled porosity and poor particle stability |
| Zeolite | Increases cation exchange capacity and available water | Particle stability unknown |
| **Polyacrylamide Gel** | Increases available water | Conflicting results show both positive and negative responses |
| **Polypropylene** | | |
| Fibers | Enhances surface stability and shear strength | High cost |
| Mesh elements | Enhances surface stability and water permeability | High cost |
| **Soil** | Increases surface stability and cation exchange capacity | Decreases water permeability |

include both organic and inorganic amendments and soil, because each contributes unique performance characteristics (see Table 24.3 for a list of common amendments and their advantages and disadvantages.)

## 24.3a  Organic Amendments

Nearly all sand rootzone mixes are amended with some type of natural organic amendment, such as peat or compost. Many organic matter sources will work successfully as a sand amendment, but they differ significantly in physical and chemical properties. Furthermore, organic matter sources are usually not even 100% organic matter.

Peat is decomposing plant tissue that is mined from the earth, and is probably the most commonly used organic amendment. Peats can have soil contamination, excessive mineral content, or ultra fine humus particles that can alter the water permeability of the amended sand. An inappropriate peat, even when mixed with a well-specified sand, can result in rootzone failure. To avoid this problem, the wise manager will have the selected peat analyzed for minimum organic matter percentage and level of soil contamination. A suitable peat should contain a minimum of 85% organic matter (by volume). To ensure the correct proportion of peat to sand, the mix should be tested according to the previously stated physical performance categories. Fibrous peats are generally to be preferred over sedimentary peats, because sedimentary peats contain too much silt and clay.

Other organic amendments added to sand fields for water retention include rice hulls, finely ground bark, sawdust, and other organic waste products. Compost is sometimes used, but should be aged for at least one year. All of these organic amendments can work effectively in a sand field, but a testing laboratory should analyze the final mix to determine its overall performance characteristics.

## 24.3b  Inorganic Amendments

Although organic amendments historically have been the most widely used, inorganic amendments are becoming more popular. Examples of inorganic amendments include calcined clay and diatomaceous earth, vermiculite, perlite, and zeolite. Today, the field manager can also consider other amendments, such as polyacrylamide gels, various polypropylene fibers, and mesh elements. All of these materials have distinct advantages and disadvantages that should be considered carefully before any of them are incorporated into a sand rootzone.

### Calcined Materials

Calcined clay and calcined diatomaceous earth are sometimes added to sand sports fields. Diatomaceous earth (DE) is the skeletal remains of prehistoric microorganisms called "diatoms." Although DE is of organic origin, it is considered an inorganic amendment, in part because it does not change composition as organic amendments do.

In a recent study by Dr. Ed McCoy at Ohio State University, it was concluded that a calcined diatomaceous earth amendment (the product tested was Axis™) has the effect of increasing the availability of water to the roots of plants in an amended sand medium of 70% sand, 20% peat, and 10% diatomaceous earth. Prior to the publication of the OSU study, the accepted wisdom had been that calcined materials hold water within their particles, but that this water could not be extracted by the plants for their use. However, the Ohio State study concluded that the DE amendment actually increased available water, particularly in coarse sand mixtures with the described 70/20/10 blend. The material also increased permeability in fine sand mixtures, increased buffering of soil temperature, increased rooting and clipping yields, and enhanced evapotranspiration.

### Vermiculite and Perlite

Two materials which are commonly used as amendments in potting soil and other domestic soil mixtures are vermiculite and perlite. These amendments were tested as sand field amendments in some of the earliest research in the field, but are not widely used today for sports field construction.

### Zeolite

Zeolite is an inorganic amendment which offers some substantial advantages in sand field applications. Because it increases the cation exchange capacity (CEC) of the sand mix, zeolite can increase the nutrient retention of the rootzone.

### Polymer Amendments

A new group of materials being tested as amendments are made of polymers, which are a class of chemical compounds used in the manufacture of diverse products. These amendments typically take the form of polyacrylamide gel particles (typically ¹⁄₁₆″ to ⅛″

when dry) that expand to absorb moisture and contract as they dry. Initial testing at Kansas State University seems to support the manufacturers' claim that the expanding and contracting of the particles reduces compaction by constantly fracturing the root-zone mix. Polymer amendments absorb water during rainfall or irrigation and release it slowly into the profile for use by turfgrass roots. (The results of the initial tests also suggest that polymer amendments have the capability of making the soil softer because of their gel texture, thus reducing field hardness and related injuries.)[1]

### Interlocking Mesh Elements

Interlocking mesh amendments are approximately $2'' \times 4''$ polypropylene "geogrids" that are mixed into the sand (approximately 9 pounds of these elements per cubic yard of sand is recommended) to provide stability. When the recommended amount of this material is mixed into the sand profile, the sand firms up tremendously. These mesh elements were the first attempt to stabilize sand for football field use, and they show great promise for stabilizing sand fields. (Known manufacturers include Netlon™.)

The three-dimensional mesh elements have been used for rootzone stability on horse racing tracks and on golf tees where divoting is a common stress. In trials and on site performance tests, divoting has been reduced and turf recuperation has been enhanced. More recently, there is evidence that the addition of mesh elements to a sand rootzone can improve total and air-filled porosity and maintain high saturated hydraulic conductivity.

In demonstrations by distributors, a 2-gallon bucket is filled with pure sand and compacted. Another bucket is filled with sand with mesh elements mixed in and compacted. Both buckets are turned over and the buckets are removed. A volunteer from the audience is asked to stand on the samples. The one with no elements mixed in collapses immediately. The one with the mesh elements withstands the weight of the volunteer, and does not break apart.

(It should be noted that these synthetic products are most beneficial when the turf density is low or nonexistent.)

### Individual Synthetic Fibers

Individual synthetic fibers (typically $1\frac{1}{2}''$ long) have been mixed randomly into the top 4–6" of rootzone at a rate of approximately 6 pounds of fiber per ton of sand and evaluated as a reinforcing amendment to increase the firmness or strength of the surface.

These fibers have been shown to improve the shear strength of sand surfaces, both with and without turf. The addition of organic or synthetic fibers has been shown to affect soil physical properties and cultivation practices. Before using any synthetic amendment, the field manager is advised to check the latest research results.

Although all of these synthetic amendments can improve the surface strength of sand rootzones for sports fields (performing best where turf cover is low or nonexistent), it should be remembered that the turfgrass plant and its fibrous root system are the most effective, direct, and cost-effective means to enhance the surface stability of sand rootzones. (Known manufacturers include Fibersand, Synthetic Industries, and DePont.)

### 24.3c  Soil as a Sand Amendment

Soil is sometimes mixed with sand to add stability and water retention to the profile. The question is, how much soil can be added before permeability is lost? The answer

---

[1] J. Nus, Polymers: Triple Threat or Untested Rookie, Northern Turf Management, January 1992, p. 24.

is: "surprisingly little." As soon as fines are added to the sand, permeability slows down dramatically. The reason is fairly simple; as fines are added, the pore spaces through which water drains become filled with particles. The result could be a mix that works like a heavy clay soil (which drains about $\frac{1}{100}$ of an inch per hour). This could even happen to sand fields that are as much as 85% sand and 15% clay based soil.

Loam soil (preferably sandy loam) should be added at a rate of 5% to 20% of the mix (by volume). Don't forget to have the soil analyzed by a reputable lab to determine how it will affect the final mix.

## 24.4   PRACTICAL CONSIDERATIONS FOR SAND-BASED FIELDS

Over the past decade, several high-profile projects have included the construction of sand-based fields. In fact, for sports such as soccer, lawn bowling, or croquet, sand is the only medium that can be used to build a field that is level—as opposed to sloped—and still have a playable surface in wet weather. Level sand fields are designed to use gravity to remove the water from the surface, through the profile, and into an installed drain system. The importance of some of these projects, and the potential long-term value of this type of field design, suggest that we should invest some time to consider the practical aspects of this type of facility.

While superior drainage is usually the goal in building a sand field, there are a number of problems associated with this type of facility. The primary problem is stability, especially for sports such as football. Soil or another amendment has to be added to firm up the sand, or else the players' cleats will tear through the turf and into the loose sand base. (This is especially true of cool season turfgrasses, which are less tightly knit than the bermudagrass used in the South. The best quality bermudagrass cultivars, when maintained according to proper cultural practices, are sufficiently tight-knit to prevent players' cleats from penetrating past the plant material.)

Additional considerations to be made before building a sand field are:

- **Cost.** The cost of constructing a single sand field for football, soccer, or baseball, with all recommended extras like installed drain and irrigation systems, amendments, etc., could easily approach one-half million dollars, so most sand fields are high-profile fields.
- **Knowledge.** There is limited information on design, construction, and maintenance techniques for sand sports fields. Also, in most areas, there are few contractors with the expertise to build an effective sand field, and their unusual acumen may come at a high price.
- **Maintenance.** It's almost impossible for a general institutional groundskeeping crew to adequately maintain an amended sand field. In almost all cases, it will be necessary to hire a professional turfgrass manager, because maintaining sand fields is as much an art as a science.

Despite all these concerns, both the academic community and the sports turf industry remain committed to developing the techniques needed to design, construct, and maintain effective sand fields. In the remainder of this chapter, we'll look at some of the methods currently being used to produce better sand fields, as well as at some of the latest research in the field.

*Figure 24.1. This soil profile shows a common problem with soil-grown sod that is installed over a sand-based rootzone; the turfgrass roots have not penetrated effectively into the sand.*

## 24.5   DESIGN

Finding a qualified sand field designer is likely to prove a challenge; probably only a handful of people in North America really understand the process. Ask for references and make a point to visit similar fields the person has designed, and talk to those who maintain the facility. As part of the negotiations with a designer, specify that he or she will help with locating the sand and supervise the addition of amendments. (For one thing, it's almost impossible to develop an accurate cost estimate for the field until the sand source has been identified.) And since a qualified testing lab is necessary to monitor the mixing and amending process from start to finish, specify that the designer will help secure those arrangements. (An experienced planner will usually want to use a lab that has done sports field testing before.) Finally, negotiate the designer's assistance in establishing the turf and getting it ready for competition.

One design consideration that must be noted is that sod installed over a sand-based rootzone must be sod that is grown in a similar sand-based medium. Sod grown in soil and laid over amended sand will root poorly and have poor permeability due to a layering effect (see Figure 24.1).

## 24.6   METHODS OF CONSTRUCTION

It is possible for a sports field planner to develop his or her own method of constructing an amended sand field. While research is continuing to refine various techniques, four methods now in use in North America have been sufficiently tested to suggest that they can have effective application in sports field construction. We will consider each of these four methods.

### 24.6a  USGA Method

Many fields feature designs based on United States Golf Association (USGA) specifications for constructing a putting green to provide the optimum water removal *and retention* rates. The critical nature of greens in the sport of golf has led to a good deal of advancement in sand field construction, and these lessons are now being applied to other sports. Some recently constructed professional baseball fields, for instance, have been built according to USGA specifications.

These facilities typically have 12″ of rootzone mix (amended sand) over a 2″ to 4″ intermediate layer of very coarse sand and fine gravel (1 mm to 4 mm). Under the intermediate layer, there is a 4″ layer of ¼″ to ⅜″ (6 mm to 9 mm) pea gravel, with an installed system of pipe drains. (The intermediate layer can be eliminated if a finer grade of pea gravel—2 mm to 6 mm—is used for the bottom layer.)

The different textures (coarse on the bottom and fine on the top) create what is called a "perched water table." That is, water will not move through the rootzone mix until a point of near saturation is reached. When this point is reached, surface tension is overcome by gravity and the water begins to drain through the rootzone mix and into the gravel, and finally to the pipe drains. This perched water table is a desirable quality for sand fields, since it holds moisture in the rootzone, where it can be used by the plants.

Figure 24.2 shows a typical profile using USGA specifications with an intermediate layer.

Sand fields operate primarily by internal gravity drainage, which makes careful construction of the **installed drain system** a critical step. The drain system recommended by the USGA for amended sand construction consists of pipe drains, a minimum of 4″ in diameter, at 15-foot spacing, in trenches a minimum 6″ wide and 8″ deep. Corrugated or plastic pipe is preferred. (Strip drains are not recommended for USGA greens at this

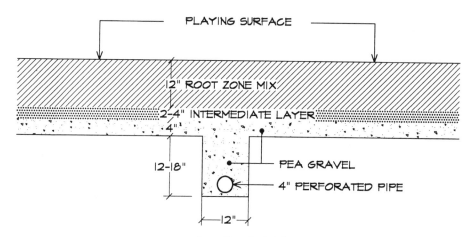

*Figure 24.2. Typical profile of a USGA putting green.*

time; techniques for their application have not yet proved their long-term effectiveness.) A filter cloth can be used to line the sides and bottom of the trench, but should not be placed around the pipe or on top of the trench.

A **gravel layer** (typically 4″ deep) is installed on top of the drain pipe and over the entire sub-base. Whether or not an intermediate layer is installed, the gravel layer (with particle sizes as described above) keeps the rootzone mix from infiltrating into the gravel. In either case, using materials with the proper particle size creates a "bridging effect," keeping openings in the gravel so that the drainage system works as intended. According to the USGA, the best way to encourage bridging is to make sure that the particle size in a lower layer is a maximum of five times larger than the layer above it.

The **rootzone mix** is the amended sand mixture which will serve as the growing medium for the turfgrass. Appropriate physical properties of the **rootzone mix** are: 35%–55% total porosity, 15%–30% air filled porosity, and 15%–25% capillary porosity. Water permeability in the normal range is 6″–12″ per hour and 12″–24″ per hour in the accelerated range. Organic matter should be 1%–5% by weight.

Table 24.4 shows the breakdown of particle sizes for a USGA rootzone mix.

If soil is used in the rootzone mix, it must have a minimum of 60% sand, and a maximum of 5% to 20% clay, and the final particle size distribution of the sand/soil/peat mix must meet the specifications shown in Table 24.4. Inorganic amendments are not recommended at this time.

For more details on design and construction, call or write the USGA and ask for their publication, "USGA Recommendations for Putting Green Construction" [USGA, Post Office Box 708, Far Hills, New Jersey 07931; (908) 234-2300].

## 24.6b New Pennsylvania Design

Over the past decade, sports field managers in the northeast have begun using a successful new design for amended sand football fields. This method was drafted into a set of suggested specifications by Penn State University faculty member Andrew McNitt. The New Pennsylvania Design has many points in common with the USGA specifications, but differs in one important respect: USGA specifies a maximum of 10% fines in the rootzone mix, and the Pennsylvania design allows up to 25% fines. (Fines are particles small enough to pass through a #100 sieve.)

The key to a successful field built according to the New Pennsylvania Design is to have the testing laboratory ensure that the rootzone mix will have 35% to 55% porosity, 15% to 30% air-filled porosity and the same amount of capillary porosity, 5″ to 10″ per hour of water permeability, and 1% to 4% organic matter content by weight. (The air-filled and capillary porosity should be about the same, varying by no more that 8%.)

See Table 24.5 for particle size distribution for New Pennsylvania Design rootzone mix.

## 24.6c Prescription Athletic Turf™ (PAT) System

In the 1980s, the Prescription Athletic Turf system became widely used for football by many professional teams and large universities. Invented in 1971 by the late Dr. William Daniels at Purdue University, a PAT field is designed to be flat and level with no surface runoff. The surface is meant to trap water which percolates through the sand-based mix to drains below. In heavy rains, an external pumping system is turned on to suction the water out of the profile (see Figure 24.3).

The biggest challenge for the PAT system has been stability, especially for cool season fields. In order to provide a stable surface for sports such as football, the turf cover has

**Table 24.4. Particle Size Distribution of USGA Rootzone Mix**

| USDA System of Classification | | Sieve No. | Sieve Opening (millimeters) | Appro. Opening (inches) | USGA Recommendations |
|---|---|---|---|---|---|
| Gravel >2 mm | | 6 | 3.36 | ⅛″ | |
| | | 7 | 2.83 | | 3% max |
| | | 8 | 2.38 | | |
| S A N D | Very coarse 1–2 mm | 10 | 2.00 | | |
| | | 12 | 1.68 | 1⁄16″ | 7% max |
| | | 14 | 1.41 | | |
| | | 16 | 1.19 | | |
| | Coarse .5–1 mm | 18 | 1.00 | | |
| | | 20 | 0.84 | 1⁄32″ | |
| | | 25 | 0.71 | | |
| | | 30 | 0.59 | | 60% min |
| | Medium .25–.5 mm | 35 | 0.50 | | |
| | | 40 | 0.42 | 1⁄64″ | |
| | | 45 | 0.35 | | |
| | | 50 | 0.30 | | |
| | Fine .1–.25 mm | 60 | 0.25 | | |
| | | 70 | 0.21 | 1⁄128″ | 20% max |
| | | 80 | 0.177 | | |
| | | 100 | 0.149 | | |
| | | 120 | 0.125 | | |
| | | 140 | 0.105 | 1⁄256″ | |
| | Very fine .05–.1 mm | 170 | 0.088 | | 5% max[a] |
| | | 200 | 0.074 | | |
| | | 230 | 0.062 | | |
| | | 270 | 0.053 | 1⁄512″ | |
| Silt .002–.05 mm | | 325 | 0.044 | | 5% max[a] |
| Clay <.002 mm | | | | | 3% max[a] |

[a]Total particles in these ranges shall not exceed 10%.

to be dense. A good thatch layer and a tightly knit sod prevent the players' cleats from "blowing out" the turf.

One of the earliest installations of the PAT system on a football field was at Mississippi State University in 1974. MSU's cultural maintenance practices contribute to a very dense bermudagrass turf, which seems to be the key in a successful application for football. As a result, the university's field has performed well throughout its life.

### 24.6d Synthetic Subsurface Mats

The blanket-type fabrics used as subsurface mats were first introduced in Europe in a variety of designs. One of the first European blanket-type fabrics was termed Grass Fleece™. In the United States, SportGrass™ carpet has been used to add strength and durability to the surface of a sports field. The SportGrass system consists of a flexible, porous polypropylene fabric with low density synthetic turf.

Table 24.5. Particle Size Distribution of New Pennsylvania Design Rootzone Mix

| USDA System of Classification | | Sieve No. | Sieve Opening (millimeters) | Appro. Opening (inches) | New Pennsylvania Design |
|---|---|---|---|---|---|
| Gravel >2 mm | | 6 | 3.36 | ⅛″ | |
| | | 7 | 2.83 | | < 10% |
| | | 8 | 2.38 | | |
| S A N D | Very coarse 1—2 mm | 10 | 2.00 | | |
| | | 12 | 1.68 | ⅟₁₆″ | < 10% |
| | | 14 | 1.41 | | |
| | | 16 | 1.19 | | |
| | Coarse .5–1 mm | 18 | 1.00 | | |
| | | 20 | 0.84 | ⅟₃₂″ | |
| | | 25 | 0.71 | | 50% min |
| | | 30 | 0.59 | | |
| | Medium .25–.5 mm | 35 | 0.50 | | 75% max |
| | | 40 | 0.42 | ⅟₆₄″ | |
| | | 45 | 0.35 | | |
| | | 50 | 0.30 | | |
| | Fine .1–.25 mm | 60 | 0.25 | | |
| | | 70 | 0.21 | ⅟₁₂₈″ | < 25% |
| | | 80 | 0.177 | | |
| | | 100 | 0.149 | | |
| | | 120 | 0.125 | | |
| | | 140 | 0.105 | ⅟₂₅₆″ | |
| | Very fine .05–.1 mm | 170 | 0.088 | | < 10% |
| | | 200 | 0.074 | | |
| | | 230 | 0.062 | | |
| | | 270 | 0.053 | ⅟₅₁₂″ | |
| Silt .002–.05 mm Clay <.002 mm | | 325 | 0.044 | | <15% |

SportGrass system construction starts with an installed drain system and then a heavy layer (6″ to 12″) of sand. Then the SportGrass carpet is laid over the sand, and an additional thin layer of sand (about 1″) is spread on top and is seeded or sprigged. During the establishing process, the roots penetrate the backing of the SportGrass carpet and reach down into the 6″ to 12″ layer of sand. It's next to impossible to blow out the sand surface, because the carpet keeps the cleats from reaching deeper than the backing of the carpet.

Sportgrass fields in use today include the University of Utah's football stadium field and the Baltimore Ravens professional football facility.

## 24.7   RECONSTRUCTION

How long will a sand field last? Is there a rated "life of the system?" Some sand field managers say "yes." After years of heavy usage, a sand field begins to show a dramatic

*Figure 24.3. PAT installations typically have a pumping system which helps to remove excess water from the rootzone. This system is installed at the Mississippi State University field.*

decrease in water permeability. A field may start with a perk rate of 10″ to 15″ per hour, but five years later may have a perk rate of 2″ to 3″ per hour. The reason, not surprisingly, is compaction from regular traffic on the surface.

Some experts suggest that the sand needs to be replaced after 8 to 10 years of use with new, uncompacted sand. That's another reason why this type of field is probably better suited to high profile facilities than to high school or park facilities.

Some installed drain systems in sand fields need to be cleaned out or replaced after 10 to 15 years, due to clogging of the pipes. This clogging is typically the result of fines from the sand and/or the soil settling into the pipe. The pipe eventually becomes filled with fines, slowing the removal of water and making the surface soggy. (This cleaning can be performed by digging up one portion of the drain system, then clearing the lines with high-pressure water hoses.)

## 24.8    MAINTENANCE

A well-designed and constructed field can quickly turn bad if it's not maintained properly. As we said above, maintenance techniques for sand fields are difficult, and may require the expertise of a trained professional. A maintenance supervisor needs to be on the field everyday to check for things like fertilization requirements, moisture retention, compaction, mowing, presence of pests, and other stresses.

Fertilization of sand fields should be done with controlled release fertilizer or by using the "spoon-feeding" method: applying small amounts of fertilizer at frequent intervals. On sand fields, the need for nutrients happens much faster, because the sandy soils have a low nutrient-holding capacity. More frequent soil testing is recommended for these fields, and it is quite common for a sand field to need nitrogen and potassium at 1:1 ratios throughout the growing season. (See Chapter 3 for more detailed information on fertility programs.)

For most turfgrasses, one inch of water per week during the growing season is adequate to support turf growth. But this amount will frequently prove insufficient for sand fields, which could need light watering daily during dry circumstances. Remember that exposed dry sand has poor soil strength and provides very poor traction and sod stability, but the same sand when moist has much better soil strength, traction and stability.

Aeration equipment that works on native soil fields may not work on sand-based fields. Try different pieces of equipment to see which one gives the best results. In some field trials, typical hollow-core aerators have proved to be too surface-disruptive for the sand fields, tearing the turf canopy instead of pulling clean cores. At this point, the best recommendation might be aerators with narrower, widely spaced tines.

Mowing a sand field almost always requires a reel mower and cutting every other day. (Remember that golf greens are usually cut every day.) Considering the initial investment in a sand field, it makes sense to have the best mowers available and to mow on a regular schedule.

In terms of pests, nematodes can be a particular problem in sand fields, because they prefer well-aerated, light textured soil. (See Chapter 9 for information on how to watch for and control nematodes.)

## 24.9    SAND FIELD TESTING

At this writing, sand football field testing is being done by Andrew S. McNitt at Penn State University. Hardness is being evaluated with the Clegg Impact Tester (CIT) and traction is being tested with the PENNFOOT device. The results are scheduled for publication in 1999.

A number of amendments have been added to the sand in this study to determine traction, hardness, and the general stability of the turfgrass surface. Among the additives being tested are Netlon interlocking mesh elements, TURFGRIDS fibers, ground-up Nike athletic shoes, and ground-up DuPont carpeting. The SportGrass system is also being evaluated in these tests.

# Chapter 25

# *Stadiums*

## 25.1  INTRODUCTION

A stadium is defined as "a large open structure for sports events with tiered seating for spectators." Stadiums are built for such sports as football, baseball, soccer, and even tennis. For professional sports in North America, there are hundreds of football and baseball stadiums, some designed for a combination of football and baseball. However, professional franchises are increasingly requesting a stadium designed exclusively for their own sport, often with a natural turf playing surface. There are also thousands of high school and college stadiums, with the most common type being high school football stadiums. However, with the increasing popularity of soccer, many high schools and colleges are now building separate stadiums for soccer.

In this chapter we'll look at design, construction, and maintenance considerations for both the stadium and the field, as well as at the interaction between the two. We'll also look at how nonathletic events such as concerts have an effect on field performance, since these events have become important income producers for professional stadiums.

This chapter will also consider the question of artificial vs. natural turf. In the past, artificial turf was the norm for domed stadiums, but today the natural turf domed stadium (with a retractable roof) is an alternative to open-air stadiums in areas where the weather is either too cold or too hot for spectator comfort. These new domed stadiums create special challenges for the turf manager: maintaining a healthy turfgrass culture under low light situations, controlling temperature, and assuring adequate air circulation. Finally, we'll look at the most recent techniques for converting an artificial turf field into a natural turf field—forms of the "modular system."

## 25.2  STADIUM/FIELD INTERACTION

A successful stadium is often the result of an architectural firm's ability to coordinate the efforts of many different design and construction specialists. The architectural firm is charged with the responsibility of choosing the right designers and contractors, supervising and coordinating their work, and overseeing the project until the complex is occupied and running smoothly. (A stadium is not complete until it's ready to be used by the general public, and a field is not complete until it is ready for competition.)

Another specialist, the field contractor, is responsible for performing all the steps required for getting the field ready to use.

During the planning stages of a professional stadium, the architect and the owner make provisions for continuing maintenance of the stadium and the field. This same planning process is necessary to ensure professional-quality performance for a high school or college stadium. Sufficient manpower and specialized equipment are typically necessary to keep the stadium/field complex running smoothly. One of the most important (and most often overlooked) considerations is planning for the maintenance processes necessary to keep the field in optimum playing condition.

## 25.2a Design

The design of a quality sports facility involves many different specialists. The process typically begins with the architect and the owner (which, in the case of a school or college, may be representatives of the administration) physically inspecting the site. Surveyors are usually the next professionals on the site, determining property lines, space required for related facilities like parking lots, and existing contours. Soil engineers are also brought into the project at this early stage; their responsibilities include taking samples to determine the stability and the drainage characteristics of the existing soil. The design of the building's foundation and the field's drainage systems (both surface and internal) are based on the engineers' findings.

With this information in hand, the architect begins the process of designing the complex. At this stage, he or she must consider a wide range of factors: spectator access and seating, access for vehicles and equipment, spectator and player safety, sufficient rest room and concession areas, adequate lighting and sound system, and the number and type of events that will be held in the stadium.

It's also important to carefully consider the soil selection, installed subsurface drainage system, and the appropriate turfgrass for the sport to be played in the stadium and location (warm season zone, transitional zone, or cool season zone) of the field. Specifications for all these elements should be prepared by the architect or other qualified specialist. There are many options available in each of these three areas, and an error in any of them will reduce the quality of the finished playing surface.

One problem that has been encountered, even in professional stadiums, is the need to isolate the field and the grandstands as drainage units. The field drainage system should not be expected to remove excess water draining out of the grandstands and onto the field. Provisions should be made for adequate drainage of the seating area through a separate and isolated system.

Planners must also make provisions for on-site storage of field maintenance materials and equipment. Some materials must be kept in dry areas, and chemical agents need to be stored in a secure, temperature controlled, well-ventilated area with appropriate curbing to control potential leaks or spills. Ideally, shop and locker areas for the maintenance staff will be provided.

## 25.2b Construction

Some of the problems which have plagued stadiums built in North American follow from the customary way the projects are constructed after the architect's work is complete. Frequently the general contractor for the building of the grandstands and related buildings is simply assigned to secure the services of excavators and others to build the field. In many cases, the excavator used for the field will be the same one who excavates the grandstands, parking lots, and foundations of the outbuildings. Although the general contractor may be highly competent and conscientious about supervising the work, the firm may have little or no experience in supervising the construction of sports fields, and so may not have the experience and expertise required to correctly direct the work of the excavation contractor. A number of problems result from this situation.

For example, a general contractor with little sports field experience may not understand the effect of overcompaction of the sub-base on the field area. With no special direction, the excavator will use the same methods considered appropriate for building roads and highways. As a result, the excavator uses heavy equipment on the field, leading to a situation in which water cannot drain adequately through the soil, and resulting in a field which holds water in rainy weather and becomes unplayable in a crucial situation.

This situation can be aggravated if the excavator brings heavy equipment onto the field during wet weather, when the sub-base is most susceptible to overcompaction.

The point of these observations is that the knowledge and experience most necessary for building grandstands may not be sufficient for building fields. The wisest course is to secure the services of a an experienced sports field specialist to help plan and supervise the construction of the playing surface itself.

### 25.2c  Maintenance

Sometimes the same maintenance personnel are involved in the maintenance of the stands as well as the field. That, in itself, is not bad. The problem which sometimes arises is that a maintenance supervisor is chosen primarily for his or her ability to maintain electrical systems, grandstand structures, plumbing systems, and the like. This expertise, while necessary for the efficient operation of the stadium, is not sufficient to properly maintain a healthy turfgrass culture.

In planning a stadium complex, it's important to remember that field maintenance is a specialty, and to make sure that qualified people will be in charge of that work.

### 25.3   LIGHTING

The popularity of outdoor sports, in combination with the time constraints associated with jobs, school, and other daytime activities, has resulted in the prevalence of lighted athletic fields to accommodate the growing level of sports participation. Recommendations for the lighting requirements of various sports have been established by sanctioning bodies, manufacturers, and others. These lighting requirements vary according to the size of the playing surface, the size and speed of the ball used, the number and locations of the players, and so on. However, some factors remain constant for all lighted sports facilities: the need for enough light to allow safe competition, the need for uniform diffusion of the light, and the need for lights to project adequate illumination from their installation points off the field of play.

Several lamp types are used for athletic field lighting, but the most common is metal halide. These energy-efficient lamps provide natural-colored light that can be readily concentrated or dispersed, according to the requirement of the particular sport. Metal halide lamps also improve the quality of videotapes of the games. Other types still in use include quartz and sodium (both of which emit a yellowish glow), mercury and halogen.

The field manager without substantial lighting system experience is well advised to consult with a professional when selecting and installing lighting equipment, due to the wide variety of considerations which need to be accounted for in the selection of poles, the planning of the electrical system, and the safe operation and maintenance of the lights.[1]

---

[1] Information on lighting systems provided by Musco Sports Lighting of Oskaloosa, Iowa.

## 25.4    CONCERTS AND NONATHLETIC EVENTS

Professional stadiums are more likely than school facilities to be used as the site of nonathletic events. Experienced field managers know that these events can subject the turf to just as much stress as sports events themselves. When concerts and other events are scheduled, it's important to protect the grass with covers and plywood. (For more information on covers, see Chapter 26.)

It's also important to be ready for emergency repair work before the next game. It's impossible to assess the damage from a concert or other event until the crowd has cleared and the field can be inspected. Typically, the worst damage can be caused under stage areas and at spots where heavy vehicles move on and off the field. This stress can easily leave the turf completely dead. Several years ago, when the Rock and Roll Hall of Fame held a large concert at Cleveland's Municipal Stadium, the stage and heavy vehicles had to be left on the field for 10 days at the end of August. In order to prepare the field for a Browns' game days later, large areas of the turf had to be replaced quickly with sections of thick-cut, big-roll sod.

While some stadium managers view these events with resentment, it's important to think of repairing the damage as a part of the job. Many professional facilities depend on these large events as a significant source of extra income.

Perhaps more in keeping with the demands placed in school or college fields, extra events like "band nights" and graduations can result in substantial damage to the field, and the wise fields manager plans for emergency repairs or such remediation efforts as solid tine aeration to help relieve the compaction from thousands of marching feet on the turfgrass. It may be necessary to roll the field before aeration if the event was held while the turf was wet, because the stress of the traffic may create unacceptably bumpy conditions.

## 25.5    ARTIFICIAL TURF

Due to the pressures associated with multiuse facilities, many sports fields have been (and continue to be) built with artificial turf. The artificial turf industry is a spin-off of the carpet manufacturing industry, and the first artificial sports field was installed in 1964 as a playing surface at an inner-city school in Providence, RI. The first widely recognized use of artificial turf was in 1965 at the Houston Astrodome. Billed as the "Eighth Wonder of the World," the Astrodome was originally a grass field with a transparent roof. The grass performed fairly well until the roof was darkened to cut down the glare from sunlight because players complained they couldn't see fly balls against the translucent ceiling. With less light, the grass eventually died and "AstroTurf" was installed.[2] The typical cross section of an artificial turf system is a compacted subgrade, overlayed with a gravel blanket (which may or may not have installed subsurface drainage), open graded asphalt, a perforated pad, and finally the artificial playing surface itself. There are numerous systems available, each similar to this basic cross-section, but having slight modifications that make the playing surface unique. If a subsurface drain system is not used, the field must be designed with a surface sufficiently sloped to channel water away quickly.

The turf surface is manufactured in one of three ways: tufted, knitted, or woven

[2] Morehouse, C. A., Artificial Turf, in *Turfgrass*, Agronomy Monograph #32. D.V. Waddington, R.N. Carrow, and R.C. Shearman, Eds.  ASA, CSSA, and SSSA, Inc., Publishers, Madison, WI, 1992,  pp. 89–127.

polypropylene fibers. The fibers are either inserted or knitted into a polypropylene backing using the same technology that produces carpeting. Knitted and woven turfs are the most expensive because they are more complicated to manufacture. However, these surfaces are stronger and more durable than tufted products. Fiber lengths are variable, and can be adjusted depending on the needs of the particular field.

The synthetic turf is glued to an underpad that functions primarily as a shock absorber. Underpads vary, not only in composition, but also in thickness. Make sure to install the appropriate underpad for the primary use of the field. For example, the typical underpad used on a football field is often inappropriate for a baseball field because the baseball will bounce inordinately high upon impact. (There are even professional sports facilities currently in use where improper underpad selection has caused problems in competition.)

The base of the field is asphalt that has been meticulously smoothed and leveled to the desired standards. This is poured over a base of crushed stone. Consult with the manufacturer or other qualified designer to determine what base materials (and thickness) are warranted by the local climate and the intended field uses.

There are numerous concerns with using artificial turf, many of which have been researched, while others are primarily perceived. One that is not perceived will be realized immediately: the cost of installation. While artificial fields are fairly "low maintenance," in the long-term, they do require substantial care to keep them playable. Furthermore, the initial cost can be staggering, and this cost largely recurs within five to seven years, when the synthetic turf (and the padding underneath) need replacement. In fact, calculations of the long-term cost show that a heavy-use natural turf field can be resodded yearly, and over a 20-year period will still cost less than a synthetic field.

However, a field that is going to host an intensive combination of baseball, football, concerts, rodeos, etc., can justify the initial cost of installation. Other factors to consider regarding artificial fields are the effects of the playing surface on ball response (bounce, roll, and speed), surface temperature (known to reach 125 degrees on sunny days in the South), and footing (particularly in regard to traction and appropriate shoe selection).

Of course, at the top of every list of considerations in regard to artificial turf is player safety. Most surveys of professional athletes indicate their desire is to play on natural grass fields due to concern for injury. Clearly, there have been (and continue to be) examples of artificial fields that are unsafe for use, many at high-profile facilities. In fact, major league baseball has committed to awarding no new franchises where the playing surface would be synthetic turf. However, the data on injuries are variable; American football shows a slight increase in injuries on artificial surfaces as compared to natural grass, but for soccer, statistics suggest the opposite. Abrasion injuries will be more common, and of course, "turf-toe" will always be associated with artificial turf. Confounding all of the data from injury studies are the differences in the type, quality, and uniformity of all the playing surfaces, but particularly of grass fields. This variation must be considered in future evaluations.

The 1990s has seen a shift by many facilities back to natural grass fields. Data continue to be collected regarding safety characteristics of both playing surfaces. While the authors believe that natural grass fields are generally the desirable playing surface, there are a limited number of situations where artificial turf is warranted as a better choice— almost exclusively in domed stadiums without a retractable roof. Under such circumstances, field managers should not necessarily consider artificial turf strictly as the "enemy," but should keep an open mind in regard to its use for certain situations where natural grass simply cannot succeed. (For a more extensive discussion of artificial turf, review the chapter by C.A. Morehouse entitled "Artificial Turf", in Agronomy Monograph No. 32, cited in Footnote 2 of this chapter.)

## 25.6   DOMED STADIUMS

The logical place for artificial turf is the domed stadium that hosts numerous sporting and commercial events. In recent years, as players have complained about the effects of the synthetic surface, efforts have been renewed toward developing ways of using natural turfgrass indoors.[3]

At this writing, the first retractable-roof domed stadium with a grass field is being used in Phoenix for the Arizona Diamondbacks professional baseball team. The roof is unique in that it can be programmed through the use of computers to physically move across the top of the stadium in a manner that concentrates light on the grass field, rather than in the stands where the heat load of the concrete and steel structure would be immense. The field, roof, and air conditioning system have been designed to work together in nurturing a healthy turfgrass culture. Only time will tell how successful this facility is, but other locations in the U.S. have pending plans for similar stadiums in the near future.

## 25.7   MODULAR GRASS FIELDS

One of the newest areas of development in turfgrass for stadium use is "modular" grass fields. This concept uses blocks of turf grown off-site and then laid over a synthetic surface to allow competition on natural grass where the turf cannot be kept alive over long periods of time. The first installation of a modular field was in Detroit at the Pontiac Silverdome for world cup soccer competition. The artificial turf was covered with plywood and the modular turf system was placed on top of the plywood sheeting.

Research directed at the development of modular systems has been maintained as professional players have continued to express their preference for natural turf fields. Specific cultivars, soil types, lighting and irrigation requirements, and the use of plant growth regulators to maximize turf performance are all being evaluated. At this writing, the most recent modular system is being tested and installed at Giants Stadium in New Jersey. The turf modules are being grown in containers of a sand-based growing medium, and then are removed from the pots at the time of installation.

The search for ways to replace synthetic turf with natural turfgrass has been given additional urgency with the expansion of free agency for professional athletes. Many players have expressed the view that regular play on synthetic turf may lead to career-shortening injuries, and have made signing decisions based in part on the surface used by a particular team.

The next generation of stadiums promises to be even more mind-boggling. As science and technology advance, what used to be considered impossible in terms of growing grass may well become commonplace.

---

[3] The Search for Indoor Turf, by Bob McCarthy; Baseball's Newest Team Looks to UC Riverside for Answers, *Turf Magazine*, November 1996, Page A6.

# Chapter 26

# *Paints and Covers*

## 26.1  INTRODUCTION

This chapter will deal with paints and covers, which can be considered as "finishing touches" in the development of a sports field, and which represent integral parts of the facility as a playing area for athletic competition.

Paints play an important role in the management of sports fields. Almost every sports field has some kind of painted lines to define the boundaries and divide the playing area. Because these lines affect team strategy and officiating decisions, straight lines, crisp edges, and minimal overspray are important goals for the application of lines. Paints are also used for decorative purposes, such as marking team logos at the 50-yard line or in the end zones of a football field. They can also be used to color an entire field, as in the case of dormant turf, or to achieve uniformity on a field that has different colors of green due to the presence of a variety of turfgrass cultivars.

Covers are used to protect the field from excessive rain, to enhance turfgrass growth, and to protect the turf from extreme traffic. Different covers are used for each situation.

We will limit our discussion to covers for the turf itself, although the materials used for the surface of fences, goalposts and other structures are also referred to as "covers." (These structural covers are typically meant to provide additional safety for players, or to allow for the painting of sponsors' signs or other artwork on outfield fences.)

## 26.2  PAINTS

### 26.2a  Painting Equipment

A wide variety of painting equipment is currently available in the marketplace. Although the lines on some fields are painted with standard 4″ rollers, the vast majority of paint applications are performed using spray equipment. This spray equipment usually takes the form of either compressor-driven or "airless" sprayers and can be either walk-behind units or riding equipment. Other options for painting and striping fields include hand-pumped pressure machines (which use a mechanism similar to that used by home gardeners for applying pesticides to trees and shrubs), and stripers which hold aerosol cans of paint. Applying paint through stencils to mark yard-line numbers or logos is usually performed using pressurized spray guns or aerosol cans.

To paint (or apply colorant to) an entire field, the most common type of application equipment is a boom-type sprayer like that used to apply chemical pesticides. The booms for these sprayers are typically 5 to 15 feet wide, and the pumps operate at 30 to 75 PSI.

Handheld lawn spray guns attached to tanks with pumps can also be used for large areas, and backpack sprayers can be used for touch-up.

## 26.2b  Turf Marking Paints

In selecting paints for marking lines and other artwork on sports turf, the best advice is to use a paint that is specifically formulated for these applications. These products are designed to be harmless to the turf, as well as to the players' skin and eyes, and are also formulated not to stain uniforms. Avoid making a trip to a paint store and buying a product the staff says "ought to work;" these paints cannot be counted on to have the benefits of real turf-marking paints.

Turf paints come in all types and forms. The most widely used paint on the market today is an environmentally friendly water-based acrylic paint. This type of product usually contains about three times the amount of pigment and whiteners of other paints, resulting in durable, long-lasting markings without harming the grass or the environment. These paints coat the grass blade totally without affecting its ability to "breathe." The stronger the paint, the more flexibility the user will have in adapting the paint to his or her particular needs (mixing/dilution ratios). This type paint also provides easy and safe cleanup with soap and water.

Athletic field paint should not contain calcium carbonate, which makes the paint look "powdery" when dried on the field and scuffs easily off the grass. Paint with calcium carbonate is also cost-prohibitive, because any leftover paint will harden like concrete if not used soon. Good field-marking paints also should not contain vinyl copolymers; vinyl-based paints will kill the grass. Paint for athletic fields should resist mold growth, livering, skinning, putrefaction, and hard setting of the pigment. Any settled pigment should be homogeneous paint, free from persistent foam.[1]

(In the past, some fields were marked with powdered lime, which was known to cause skin and eye irritation. Today, facilities that have no spraying equipment have largely switched to ground marble dust products, which are less likely to cause irritation. These dry products are used fairly widely for marking the skinned areas of baseball and softball fields. The authors recommend against the use of any lime-based products on sports fields.)

## 26.2c  Line, Boundary, and Stencil Painting

### Line and Boundary Marking

In painting lines that mark specific playing areas of the field or the out-of-bounds areas, it is important to know, not only where the lines should be painted, but also their exact width; individual sanctioning bodies typically specify the dimensions of critical boundary lines.

Perhaps the most common violation of line-painting principles occurs where a string line is used to designate the line location. Painting on one side of the string will yield slightly different dimensions than painting on the other. It's also critical to know whether the line will be in-bounds or out-of-bounds, and to paint on the appropriate side of the string. On a football field, for example, the sideline is out-of-bounds, and must be painted on the outside of the string. (For the exact dimensions and lining requirements of playing areas for individual sports, see the chapters on each sport.)

---

[1] Information supplied by Tra Dubois, World Class Athletic Surfaces, Leland, MS.

*Figure 26.1. Line painting on a football field must be performed carefully to avoid problems for players and officials. (Photo courtesy of James Thompson, Mississippi State University.)*

### Stencils

Stencils can be purchased or made in-house. They are used to paint numbers on a football field or logos in the end zone or middle of the field with minimal overspray. It's also possible to paint numbers and artwork without stencils; when using this method, keep the sprayer close to the turf surface to maintain crisp edges and mini-mize blurring drift (see Figure 26.2).

## 26.2d An Example of Field Marking Procedures

Bart Prather, Sports Field Manager at Mississippi State University, provides this sequence of field-marking procedures used for the football field at Razorback Stadium:

1. Establish the four outside corners of the field. (Unless the staff includes a skilled sur-veyor, it is best to have a local survey company perform this critical measurement.) Once the corners have been established, put some type of permanent, sunken marker beneath the grass (wood wedges make good markers and do not damage equipment as badly as something harder).
2. Take long nails with ¾" tape wrapped around the top and painted with a bright paint. This makes them easy to find and reduces the risk of leaving them on the field.
3. Using the nails as markers, measure off each yard line with a 360-foot tape. The long tape prevents having to pick the tape up and move it while measuring.
4. Stretch a long string or light rope to designate the two sidelines and two end lines.

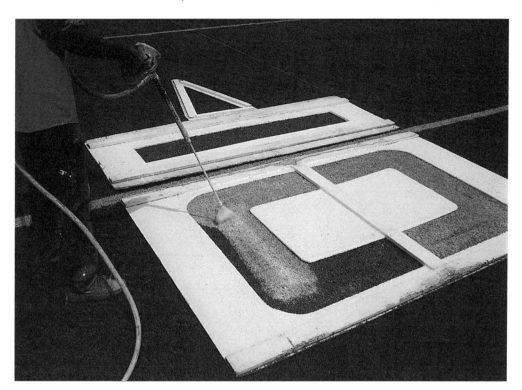

*Figure 26.2. Stencils provide a convenient way to paint crisp yard-line numbers on a field.*

Paint these lines, then give the rope some time to dry before moving it, to prevent unwanted paint marks between yard lines.

5. Then stretch the rope or string from sideline to sideline, lining up on the nail heads, and paint each yard line from one sideline to the other.
6. After completing the lines, begin marking the numbers. Spacing from yard line to yard line must be precise. Stencils make this job relatively simple.
7. When numbers are completed, mark the individual yard lines.
8. Paint the end zones and midfield logos last; that way, if weather interrupts the marking process, the teams can still play on a properly marked field. End zone letters and logo designs are laid out with stencils and then filled in freehand (see Figures 26.3 and 26.4).

Mr. Prather also passes along some other suggestions for successful field marking:

The paint should be mixed at 2:1 or 3:1 water:paint ratios by volume, and all mixing and paint machine filling is conducted off the field. Dilute the paint more (or less) depending upon the desired line color and the quality of the paint used.

The paint machine preferred by his crew is an airless sprayer run at maximum allowable pressure for better grass coverage.

The growth regulator trinexapac ethyl (Primo™) is frequently added to the paint mixture to extend the life of the field markings and the boundaries of the midfield logo and end zone borders. The Primo is added at a rate of 1 ounce of product per 1,000 square feet of application area. (In order to calculate the amount of growth regulator to add to the paint, it is necessary to first calculate the amount of paint required to cover 1,000 square feet.)

Figure 26.3. A pattern stencil (or template) allows the precise painting of school logos and other on-field artwork. This stencil has holes to allow applicators to mark the outline of the letters and borders. (Photo courtesy of Tra Dubois, World Class Athletic Surfaces.)

Figure 26.4. After the design of the logo has been transferred with the template, staff members can finish the design freehand. (Photo courtesy of James Thompson, Mississippi State University.)

## 26.2e  Turf Colorants

As fields begin to go dormant and turn brown before the competitive season ends in the fall (sometimes a problem with bermudagrass fields), many sports field managers choose to maintain the appearance of the turf by applying a "colorant" instead of overseeding the field with perennial ryegrass.

(In this case, the use of the term "colorant" refers to products specifically formulated to apply a permanent coloring to the turf, and not to the temporary dyes that are sometimes mixed with pesticides and other chemical agents to aid the staff in assuring an even application.)

Colorants can also be used to restore a uniform appearance to turfgrass after events such as concerts, which can cause areas of the turf to become yellowed where a stage or other equipment has been left in place for several days. Another potential application is for uniformity where resodding of problem areas has created an uneven appearance; this situation is sometimes observed on high-profile football fields, where midseason replacement of turf on the middle of the field results in a noticeable difference in color.

Permanent turfgrass colorants are specially formulated latex paints which restore an esthetically pleasing green color to the turf. In applying these products, a few prudent practices will help in achieving the best results. It's wise to raise the mowing height slightly before application, and to spread the colorant on damp, but not wet, grass. Test the colorant on a small area before making the general application to ensure the eventual color is as desired. Adjacent areas may need to be masked with cardboard to prevent coloring sidewalks or other surfaces. Some experts recommend thoroughly wetting areas where coloration is not wanted, then flushing off any overspray immediately after coloring. When using a boom sprayer, have the boom at the back of the riding equipment to avoid streaks. When using hand equipment, walk in front of the sprayer to avoid tracking the colorant. Of course, it's best to apply colorant on a calm day to prevent drift. (One additional advantage of colorants is that they may help turf greenup quickly in the spring, because their darker color absorbs sunlight and warms the soil slightly.) [2]

As with any sprayed product, carefully follow label directions.

## 26.3   COVERS

Covers are used for many reasons, and each purpose requires a different choice of covering material. It's also important to note that cultural management practices for covered turf vary according to the type of cover and the reason for using it.

## 26.3a  Rain Covers

Probably the best-known type of cover is a rain cover, which baseball fans see being spread on the infield when bad weather hits. Rain covers are meant to allow rainfall to drain off the field without soaking into the playing surface. However, it's important to remember that this runoff must still be channeled away from the field to prevent wet areas on, for instance the outfield or in foul territory of a baseball diamond. Some fields are build with systems of strip drains or small catch basins at the edge of the covered areas to assist in drainage. This practice can make a substantial improvement in the overall condition of a covered field, because it relieves the uncovered areas of the need to deal with the runoff from the covered area. (The authors recommend strip drains rather

---

[2] Harlow, S., Paint Your Grass, *Turf Magazine*, November 1993, pp. 4–5.

than catch basins for this purpose, because catch basins require much more maintenance to prevent their becoming a safety hazard or affecting ball response.)

Rain covers are made of weatherproof plastic, typically reinforced with nylon or other material for strength and durability. These covers are available in both light and dark colors. Dark covers absorb solar energy, and thus make the underlying soil warmer, while light covers reflect more sunlight and warm the turf less. Some covers are dark on one side and light on the other, allowing the turf manager to install the cover "dark side up" when the temperatures are cooler and "light side up" in hotter weather.

Although rain covers can be a big help in assuring the playability of turfgrass (as well as of baseball skinned areas), it's important to know how a particular field reacts to being covered. For example, some fields are slippery right after the cover is removed, due to the "greenhouse effect" of the enclosed environment underneath. In this situation, the covers obviously should be removed sufficiently in advance of each game to allow the field to dry adequately.

Rain covers should only be used to assure a playable surface for one game, and should not be left on the field more than one day at a time. Leaving the cover on for extended periods will increase the risk of certain diseases, particularly Pythium blight. Cool season turfgrasses, whether permanently established, as in the North, or used for temporary overseeding, as in the South, are especially susceptible to Pythium blight.

### 26.3b  Turf Enhancement Covers

The second type of cover is known as a "turf enhancement cover," and is designed to keep the soil warm in cold weather. They can also be used to stimulate seed germination or to protect the turf from winter injury, and offer the additional benefits of causing quicker greenup in the spring, preventing erosion, and keeping the turfgrass green longer in the fall.

Turf enhancement covers are very lightweight and transparent, and are typically made of spun synthetic fabric. These covers are designed to be porous and translucent so that air, water, and sunlight can pass through to the turf underneath. Because of their porosity, turf enhancement covers can be left in place for weeks or months at a time, or even over an entire winter. (However, it should be noted that Pythium blight can still occur under a porous cover, and therefore a preventive application of a fungicide specific to Pythium may be advised where the cover will be left in place for an extended period.)

The use of turf enhancement covers for winter protection of bermudagrass turf has been increasingly common in recent years. The cost of covering an entire field can be substantial, but the effects of extreme cold and subsequent turf degradation that is possible in the mid-South and transition zone can require remediation (including total replanting) that is more costly still.

### 26.3c  Turf Protection Covers

The third type of cover is a "turf protection cover." These covers are used to protect the turf in heavy traffic areas, such as the bench area of a football field, or the points at which teams enter and exit the facility. They can also be used to protect the turf during such events as graduations, religious gatherings, and concerts, when fans will stand or sit on the field. Turf protection covers are typically made from a porous, nonwoven synthetic fabric. They allow water, air, and limited sunlight to reach the turf, but protect it from the extreme compaction of heavy traffic, and particularly from cleated shoes.

Because of their porosity, turf protection covers can be left in place for a few days at a time, but because they restrict sunlight from reaching the turfgrass, they should not be left in place for extended periods.

Research has been conducted by Dr. Steven Cockerham[3] and colleagues at the University of California-Riverside to evaluate turfgrass durability and recovery to simulated traffic when protected by various types of covers. The "traffic" in their research trials was imposed by passing a 7-ton forklift 20 times a day for either 2 or 4 days over various field cover treatments designed to protect a perennial ryegrass base. After the simulated traffic period, the covers were removed, the field was slit aerified, and the turf was syringed. All plots received a thorough irrigation event at 4 hours after cover removal.

The effectiveness of the cover treatments was rated as follows: the most effective cover was ¾″ plywood over two layers of geotextile fabric. The next most effective cover was plywood over one layer of geotextile fabric. Plywood over geotextile plus Enkamat™ was less effective still, but more effective than plywood alone, and all tested options were better that no cover at all.

The study showed that syringing treatments were effective in enhancing turf recovery, particularly after the 4-day traffic trial. The researchers concluded that a combination of covers and syringing was necessary to promote optimum recovery of the turf.

[3] Cockerham, S.T., R.A. Khan, G.H. Pool, R. Van Gundy, and V.A. Gibeault. Events Traffic on Sports Fields: Protection and Recovery. *California Turfgrass Culture*, 44, (1 & 2), pp. 6–7, 1994.

# Chapter 27

# *Sports Fields:*
# *Past, Present, and Future*

## 27.1   INTRODUCTION

Having given attention to nearly all of the sports fields and related facilities in general use in North America today, it seems appropriate to spend a few minutes considering the history of the industry, as well as some of the trends which seem likely to shape its future.

## 27.2   THE PAST

Historically, many of the sports fields in use in North America were simply marked-off areas on school yards or public parks. And while these spaces served reasonably well for recreational competition, the changing circumstances of the twentieth century have required that more professional disciplines be applied to their design, construction, and maintenance.

Throughout the modern era, the growth of professional sports has played a role in improving the facilities used by public, scholastic, and collegiate athletes. As professional franchises have come to regard themselves more in terms of entertainment, they have consistently improved the aesthetic and performance characteristics of the fields on which their employees competed. Many of the developments which have found their way to school and park fields found their genesis on professional turf.

The costs associated with mounting athletic competition have steadily increased. Teams which once were driven to games in coaches' and parents' cars now travel in expensive-to-operate buses. Drivers must be secured and paid. Maintenance staff at the home school must be assigned to the task of preparing the field for competition. In the face of these expenses, a rain-out or delay because of an unplayable field can be excessively costly. In recent years, schools have recognized the need to minimize these problems, as well as the corresponding drain on dwindling budgets. These budgetary pressures have compelled authorities to ask how fields can be designed and built to allow for greater utility and reduced costs.

The recent past has also seen a rise in the number of liability lawsuits, and this is true of sports facilities as well as all aspects of life in modern America. The danger of litigation has created a greater awareness of the need for attention to the safety of all sports facilities. Many leagues and other sanctioning bodies, concerned for the increased likelihood of liability lawsuits, have demanded that fields be improved to reduce the possibility of injury.

All of these factors have served to create an environment in which the development and management of sports fields have become more professional.

Sadly, a simultaneous development has been the erosion of the quality of sports facilities in many of the nation's largest cities. As municipal budgets have been stretched ever thinner, many cities have been forced to slash their expenditures for the parks and recreational fields under their management. The sad irony of this development is that, in exactly the time when impoverished young people most need the constructive influence of healthy competition, this influence is being denied to them by the economic constraints under which their municipal officials must labor.

## 27.3   THE PRESENT

In a sense, this book is designed to be an extended consideration of the present state of sports field design, construction, and maintenance. The authors have endeavored throughout to present the best available academic and professional knowledge and experience from those engaged in the industry.

The field of sports turf management can be seen as an industry that is reaching a kind of "adolescent" stage—not fully mature, but beginning to apply some of the scientific management principles characteristic of a mature industry. With the proliferation of formal scientific research, today's sports field manager has access to a greater body of useful information than ever before.

Another important trend in today's industry is the growth of trade organizations, such as the Sports Turf Managers Association, which are bringing together leaders in both the academic community and the professional ranks. Through their programs of trade shows, seminars, and publications, these organizations are creating an environment that fosters the free exchange of knowledge and ideas among practitioners in the sports turf industry. Through their programs of continuing education and certification, these groups are also seeking to upgrade the level of professionalism throughout the industry.

## 27.4   THE FUTURE

Looking forward to the future, the authors would venture to predict that the following factors will play a substantial role in shaping the sports field industry. These factors are grouped into several general categories, although there is a great deal of overlap and interconnectedness among these trends.

### 27.4a  Demographic and Social Trends

*Aging Population*
Sociologists tell us that the population of North America is aging steadily, and this trend can be expected to have an effect on the development and management of sports facilities. Field managers should expect increased demand for the types of fields (soft, as softball) used for recreational sports by mature citizens.

*More Competition among Girls and Women*
It could be argued that the single most important development in sports over the last 25 years has been the rapid growth of sports participation by girls and women. Many of the

fields being constructed today are needed to relieve overcrowding which is a direct result of this trend. As more girls grow up watching and idolizing female sports figures, it must be expected that the trend toward increased sports activity among girls and women will continue to create demand for additional fields and related facilities.

### Recognition of Fields as Crime-Prevention Tools

For years, parks and sports facilities in the nation's cities have been allowed to deteriorate because they were regarded simply as amenities whose upkeep could no longer be afforded. However, studies have made it plain that providing opportunities for athletic competition has a positive effect on criminal activity in urban neighborhoods. Although some politicians have mocked such ideas as the "midnight basketball leagues," these unorthodox approaches have gained popularity because they work. This growing awareness of the role of sports in preventing crime can be expected to have an effect on the construction and maintenance of sports fields and related facilities in cities and towns throughout North America.

### Increasing Attention to Safety and Liability

With the explosion of personal injury lawsuits, organizing and sanctioning bodies have become more conscious than ever of the potential liability for player injuries. Insurance and other injury groups are currently at work on new standards for the safety of sports fields, and their work will continue to impact sports field management for decades to come. Managers who once saw uneven turf in terms of "bad bounces" now see it in terms of "lawsuits waiting to happen." As a result, fields of the future should be vastly safer than their counterparts of the past.

### Popularity of New Sports

The growth of such sports as lacrosse and soccer are having an obvious effect on the work of sports field managers. Soccer fields make up a substantial portion of the new fields under construction in North America today. The explosion of sports activities virtually unknown 25 years ago—from roller blading to snowboarding—suggests that the manager of the future may be required to understand the facilities used for sports that scarcely exist today.

## 27.4b  Scientific and Technical Trends

### New Turfgrass Varieties

One of the most productive areas of research today is the development of new turfgrass varieties. It seems beyond question that field managers of the future will have access to cultivars that require less maintenance, thrive in more extreme climatic conditions, and resist pests better. Any manager planning to plant turfgrass even today is well advised to check the latest literature before choosing a variety, and this trend will only accelerate in the future.

### Increasing Orientation Toward Integrated Cultural Management (ICM)

The coming of the age of Integrated Pest Management (IPM) was a great step forward in the responsible use of chemicals. But in educating the new generation of sports turf managers, the critical consideration will be to orient their thinking toward steps necessary to maintain the health and durability of the turf. A more useful conceptual framework for the future is what we have called "Integrated Cultural Management" (ICM), which will place increasing emphasis on the use of careful cultural practices to nurture a turfgrass culture requiring less and less use of pesticides and other chemical agents. As field managers come to a clearer understanding of the characteristics of turfgrass as a growing culture, they will be able to deal more effectively with the kinds of environmental, mechanical, and competitive stresses which weaken turfgrass and allow pests to become established.

### Greater Use of Amended Sand Fields

Amended sand fields have come into use in a number of high-profile facilities in recent years, especially in professional and major collegiate programs. The continuing advancement of this technique is making it more widely useful for a greater variety of facilities, and allowing its consideration on fields which do not enjoy the budgetary and maintenance advantages of the big-time programs.

### Transitional Zone Fields Research

As we have mentioned in several portions of this book, achieving a healthy and vigorous turfgrass culture has been especially difficult for many managers in the transitional zone, where climatic conditions are not ideal for either the southern or northern cultivars. Continuing research in coming years can be expected to yield new varieties which deal more successfully with the specialized conditions in the transitional zone, leading to improved fields throughout this region.

### Greater Use of European Soccer Technology

European field managers have spent decades developing cultural practices, contouring methods, and other management techniques that are specific to the sport of soccer. With the growing popularity of the sport in North America, more and more field managers are now addressing the challenges of maintaining facilities which provide the uniformity of ball response required for high-level soccer competition. In the coming years, it is reasonable to expect that many managers in North America will be studying the practices of their European counterparts to determine how best to provide fields that match the best "pitches" in the traditional homelands of the sport.

### More Overall Sports Turf Research

Although formal research in turfgrass science has been a growing area of academic and scientific study, many areas have not yet been the subject of rigorous study. For more than a century, governmental bodies have been supporting research into the specific needs of the golf industry, but corresponding support into research on other types of sports turf has not been forthcoming.

In recent years, academic and scientific programs have begun to scratch the surface of sports turf-related questions (for instance, on the appropriate levels and composition of thatch for various types of sports), but the coming decade can be expected to see increased attention to a wide variety of issues leading to turf that can better withstand the unique set of stresses characteristic of sports turf.

### Improvements in Equipment and Materials

Most of the equipment now in use by North American field managers was originally designed for maintenance of lawns around schools, colleges and universities, large industrial facilities, etc. Now, for the first time, equipment such as mowers, aerators, and skinned area grooming machines—specifically designed to meet the needs of sports field managers—is being brought to market. From this point forward, any manager contemplating the purchase of new equipment for his or her facilities will have access to a wide variety of new devices that promise to make the maintenance process easier and more efficient.

The same trend is occurring in materials used for sports field construction and maintenance. For example, new processed clay products are now on the market for the pitcher's mounds and batter's boxes of baseball and softball diamonds. The industry has also seen the introduction in recent years of diatomaceous earth skinned-area conditions, which provide improved performance characteristics when compared to the clay and organic materials which have been the staples of the industry in the past. In materials, as in equipment, manufacturers can be expected to develop and market new products that will provide improved value to those who manage sports fields.

## 27.4c  Trends in Sports Field Management Practices

### Replacement of Synthetic with Natural Turf

As mentioned above, synthetic surfaces have drawn increasing criticism from players and coaches, who have charged that these facilities lead to extra injuries and other problems. A recent survey of NFL players quoted in a major metropolitan newspaper listed the ten best and five worst playing surfaces in the NFL. All of the ten best were natural turf; all of the five worst were synthetic.[1]

The trend toward replacement of synthetic turf with natural grass can be expected to continue, reaching down to high schools and smaller colleges which have invested in the synthetic surfaces in the past. As these surfaces come up for regular replacement, school districts can be expected to replace the artificial material with natural turf.

### More Single-Use Professional Facilities

In the past decade, more and more professional stadiums have been committed only to a single sport. Cities that have long used a single facility for their NFL and major league franchises are choosing to construct separate stadiums devoted to the unique needs of each sport. This trend, which has already occurred in Baltimore and Cleveland, among other cities, is the subject of public debate and financing efforts in a variety of other cities.

On a high school level, soccer and football have long been forced to coexist on a single field in many school districts, but more and more schools are constructing separate fields to support competition in their fast-growing soccer programs.

### Improve Cooperation with Community Groups

The national trend toward taxpayer activism and the downsizing of government had forced facilities managers in many school districts and parks and recreation department to deal with the reality of smaller and more closely monitored budgets. In order to continue to provide players with quality facilities, many field managers are forming innovative partnerships with local boosters and other community groups who can help to raise funds for needed construction and renovation projects.

In the future, the ability to work successfully with members of the public in efforts of this kind will be one of the hallmarks of the most successful sports field programs. This trend will compel many managers to develop a whole new set of management skills, and turn them into spokesmen (if not cheerleaders) for their programs.

---

[1] *Dallas Morning News*, August 3, 1997.

### Attention to Cost, Not Price

The recent trend toward tighter budgets has led many managers to cut back on their expenditures for materials and services. But the results have often included increased remediation costs when important preventive practices were eliminated. In many other cases, construction shortcuts have saved hundreds of dollars, but required thousands of dollars a year to fix. In other words, by focusing on the *price* of proper management, these managers have actually increased the long-term *costs* of maintaining their facilities.

A new generation of field managers is now coming to recognize that decisions on the wise use of their resources must be made after considering the long-term costs associated with their facilities. This includes such "outside" costs as travel costs for teams who must make up games, and so forth. The most successful managers of the future will carefully plan the allocation of their budgets to prevent the kind of problems that require expensive remediation to correct.

### More Professional Training for Field Managers

Academic programs, such as that operated at Mississippi State University by two of the authors of this book, are now beginning to offer students the kind of formal scientific and management skills required to properly maintain the fields of the future. This trend can be expected to continue, leading to the development of a new generation of sports field managers who can successfully practice the tenets of Integrated Cultural Management to provide their athletes with safe, attractive fields on which they can nurture their sports skills.

Of course, this trend can be expected to be aided by the availability of more comprehensive and scientific instructional materials, such as this book.

# Glossary

**Acidic**   Having a pH of less than 7.0 (neutral)

**Active ingredient (AI)**   In a pesticide formulation, the material that actually destroys the target pest or performs the desired function

**Aeration**   The exchange of gases between the soil and the atmosphere, or the process of disturbing the soil by mechanical means to relieve compaction and maximize air, water, and nutrient availability to turfgrass

**Aeration, deep drill**   The creation of vertical channels in the soil using drill bits; the channel is typically 12″ deep and 1″ in diameter, and the aeration is often followed by the insertion of soil amendments

**Aeration, deep tine**   The creation of vertical channels in the soil to depths of 8″ to 12″ using either solid or hollow tines of various diameters

**Aeration, hollow tine**   The creation of vertical channels in the soil with a hollow cylinder that physically removes a core of turf and soil to a specified depth; also referred to as "core aeration"

**Aeration, solid tine**   The creation of vertical channels in the soil without physically removing a core

**Aeration, water-injection**   The use of fine sprays of high-pressure water to penetrate the turfgrass canopy

**Aggregate**   Soil structures made up of many soil particles held in a single mass, or mineral material of uniform fine size used in construction projects

**Alkaline**   Having a pH higher than 7.0 (neutral)

**Amendments, inorganic**   Soil additives such as sand or calcined clay that are not carbon-based, used to improve physical and chemical properties of soil including drainage and retention of water and nutrients

**Amendments, organic**   Carbon-based soil additives such as peat, rice hulls, sawdust or humus used to improve physical and chemical properties of soil including drainage and retention of water and nutrients

**Annual**   A plant that completes a life cycle within one growing season

**Apex, root**   The growing point at the end of a plant root

**Apex, stem**   The growing point at the end of a plant stem, and the location of apical buds which originate new stem and leaf tissue

**Application efficiency (EA)**   The measure of the amount of water applied during irrigation which is available to the effective root zone of the turfgrass plants (Sometimes referred to by the abbreviation "EA")

**Application logbook**  A book or binder used to record the particulars of all applications of pesticides on a particular site

**Application threshold**  The point at which the severity of a pest infestation becomes great enough to warrant application of a chemical agent

**Application, post-emergent (POE)**  The application of herbicides to control weeds that have already emerged from the soil

**Application, pre-emergent (PRE)**  The application of herbicides to prevent the germination of weeds that have not yet appeared

**As-built drawing**  A drawing showing the actual installed location of all elements of a construction project

**Asphalt, rubberized**  A track surface made of asphalt mixed with rubber

**ASTM**  The American Society for Testing and Materials, an association which establishes safety and performance standards for a wide variety of products, including those used in sports and recreation facility construction

**Astroturf**  The original synthetic turf product, named for one of its first installations, at the Astrodome in Houston

**Available water holding capacity (AWHC)**  The amount of water which can be held in the root zone between the wilting point of the plants and the field capacity

**Axillary buds**  Growth structures which appear at the axil, or internal fold of a leaf sheath

**Backflow prevention**  The process of preventing contaminated water from flowing backward into a potable water supply. Backflow prevention equipment is required between field irrigation systems and incoming water supplies in most areas.

**Bacteria**  Microscopic, single-cell organisms which live in a variety of forms throughout the biosphere; some perform useful functions in host organisms, while others cause disease

**Ball response**  The manner in which a thrown, struck or kicked ball contacts and rebounds from a playing surface. Ideal ball response is consistent in both direction and speed.

**Bench area**  The area adjacent to a playing field where coaches and reserves sit or stand while a game is in progress

**Benchmark**  A fixed reference point that is used in the surveying process to accurately measure elevations

**Biennial**  A plant that completes a life cycle in two growing seasons

**Blanket application**  Application of a material, especially a pesticide, by spreading it over an entire area, including portions of the area not showing symptoms of disease or infestation

**Bridging**  The mixing of soil particles in such a way that spaces are created between the particles to allow the passage of air, water and nutrients

**Buds, apical**  Buds located at the apex, or tip of a turfgrass stem

**Buds, axillary**  Buds located in the axil or internal fold of a leaf sheath

**Bunch-type**  One of four morphological types of turfgrass, growing in tightly knit clumps or bunches, such as perennial ryegrass

**Calcined clay** An inorganic soil amendment formed by expanding clay at high temperatures (calcining), and used to alter soil strength by affecting its ability to retain moisture

**Calcined diatomaceous earth** A product made by calcining diatomaceous earth, a material composed of the calcified remains of microscopic life-forms known as "diatoms," and used to condition soil by altering its ability to retain moisture

**Calcite sand** A material rich in calcium carbonate, which has the effect of raising the pH of soil as it weathers

**Calcium carbonate** A lime source used to raise soil pH, but rarely on established turf, because of its burn potential

**Calcium oxide** A lime source commonly used to raise soil pH

**Calibration** The process of adjusting equipment to allow for the desired rate of application of chemicals

**Canopy** The continuous layer formed by the leaves of a stand of turfgrass

**Catch basin** A common drainage structure which allows surface water to flow into an underground network of pipes, and which also serves as a "junction box" for installed drain systems

**Catchment test** A procedure used to measure the amount of water being applied to a field by irrigation, to determine whether the application is uniform

**Cation** A positively charged ion

**Cation exchange capacity (CEC)** In soil science, the sum total of exchangeable cations that a soil can adsorb; commonly used to describe a soil's nutrient holding capacity; soils with large amounts of clay and organic matter typically have higher cation exchange capacities than sandy soils low in organic matter

**Caution** In classification of chemical agents, the designation used for the least hazardous products. More hazardous substances are labeled "Warning" or "Danger."

**Center loading** Backfilling the center of a pipe trench of an irrigation system, leaving the fittings exposed so that a pressure test can be conducted

**Chelates** A chemical formulation in which a metal atom (very often a micronutrient such as iron) is bound with an organic component to improve the overall uptake of the micronutrient

**Chlorotic** In describing foliage, abnormally yellowed

**Clay** A soil material with particles of 0.002 mm diameter or less, noted for high moisture and nutrient holding capacity; also used to refer to a soil mixture containing more than 40% clay

**Clegg Impact Tester** The most commonly used device for testing field hardness, also known as the Clegg hammer or CIT

**Coated fertilizer** Granular fertilizer which has been coated with a material of known permeability to allow for the controlled release of nutrients into the soil

**Compaction, soil** The compression of the topsoil, primarily due to foot or vehicular traffic. Excessive compaction can prevent the passage of air, water and nutrients into the soil, and may require loosening of the soil through aeration.

**Conditioners**   Materials which are added to soil to improve its performance characteristics, often to correct a problem occurring in a small area of a field, such as the skinned area of a baseball diamond

**Contact pesticide**   A pesticide that acts only on the portion of the plant covered by the compound

**Continuous pressure main line**   Pipe between an irrigation system point of connection to the supply line and the system's zone control valves

**Contour plan**   A drawing which represents existing and/or proposed contours of a field or other designated area; changes in grade are illustrated in uniform one-foot or half-foot increments

**Controlled release fertilizer**   A product specifically engineered to release nutrients into the soil over a designated period of time

**Controller charts**   Charts showing the valves of a sprinkler system, and the zones they cover

**Cool season zone**   An area of North America, comprised of Canada and roughly the northern third of the continental United States, where climatic conditions support a specific group of turfgrass cultivars; cool season turfgrasses are adapted to maximum growth under temperatures of 60 to 75 degrees F during the growing season

**Court, clay**   A tennis court surface made from a mixture of sand, silt, and clay

**Court, fast-dry**   A tennis court surface manufactured from crushed stone or brick, mixed with a chemical binder

**Court, grass**   A tennis court constructed from extremely smooth and closely cropped turfgrass

**Court, nonporous**   A tennis court whose surface is asphalt or concrete

**Court, porous**   A tennis court whose surface is grass or clay

**Court, sand-filled synthetic turf**   A tennis court made by laying a loosely-woven synthetic turf material on asphalt or concrete, which is then overlaid with sand; the sand fills in the turf material, providing a cushioned playing surface

**Cover, rain**   A cover made of weatherproof plastic, designed to allow rain to drain off the field without soaking into the playing surface

**Cover, turf enhancement**   A cover made of spun synthetic fabric, designed to keep the soil warm in cold weather for winterkill protection or to enhance turf establishment

**Cover, turf protection**   A cover made from porous, non-woven synthetic fabric, designed to protect turf in heavy traffic areas

**CPSC**   The Consumer Product Safety Commission, a federal agency responsible for monitoring and certifying the safety of products sold on the open market

**Crop coefficient**   A mathematical method for expressing the difference in moisture needs among plants of various types

**Crown**   A collection of compressed stems located in a central core, also called a node cluster

**Crown**   The elevated center portion of a sports field, raised to promote the runoff of surface water

**Crowning**   Building a field so the center portion is elevated

**Cultivar**   A variety or subdivision of a plant species that, because of similar morphology and performance characteristics, can be distinguished from other plants within that species

**Cultivar, hybrid**   A cultivar created by crossing varieties of dissimilar genetic constitution

**Cultivator, agricultural**   Also called a "scarifier" or "earthcavator", used to loosen the soil before planting

**Curative application**   Application of pesticide after the outbreak of disease or infestation, as opposed to preventive application, which applies pesticide in advance of the outbreak

**Cuts**   In the construction of a field or other facility, areas where soil is removed to achieve the desired contours, as opposed to "fills," which are areas where soil is added

**Danger**   The designation used to label the most hazardous of chemical agents. Less hazardous agents are labeled "Caution" or "Warning."

**Daylight**   In an installed drain system, a grade point lower than the downward sloping collector pipe

**Defoliation**   The destruction of the foliage in a specific area, often through the application of herbicides

**Desiccation**   The withering of plant tissues due to the acute lack of moisture

**Design, sports field**   Includes surveying, layout, contour plans and specifications, drainage and irrigation systems

**Dethatching**   The process of mechanically removing or thinning the thatch layer between the surface of the soil and the turfgrass canopy

**Diatomaceous earth (DE)**   The skeletal remains of prehistoric microorganisms called "diatoms", often used as an inorganic soil amendment

**Dicots**   Plants that emerge from the seed with two cotyledons (seed leaves); most often broadleaf plants

**Diffusion**   A process occurring when substances in different concentrations are connected by permeable environments

**Disease**   The compromise of the normal function of a host organism through the intervention of another organism or abiotic entity inside or on the host

**Dispersible granules (DG)**   A form of chemical agent with pelletized carriers of the active ingredient; synonymous with "dry flowable (DF)" or "water dispersible (WD)"

**Distribution uniformity**   The evenness with which an installed irrigation system distributes water over a field

**Dolomitic limestone**   A lime source containing both calcium carbonate and magnesium carbonate that is commonly used to raise soil pH

**Dormant seeding**   The distribution of seeds during a period outside the normal growing season, so that the seeds will be in place and ready to germinate when conditions allow

**Dormant sodding**   The installation of turf in which the plants are in a dormant phase

**Drain, French**   Strictly speaking, drainage trench backfilled with stone or gravel, and containing no pipe, the term is also incorrectly used to refer to any pipe drain

**Drain, interceptor**   Pipe drain, filled to the surface with stone, gravel or coarse sand, and used to prevent the flow of water onto a field from an adjacent area; also used in swales and low-lying areas off the field

**Drain, pipe**   Any of a number of types of installed drain system, including subsoil pipe drains, interceptor drains and trackside sand drains

**Drain, sand-slit**   An installed drain system using perforated pipe in narrow trenches, with perpendicular sand filled trenches above to collect the water and channel it into the pipes

**Drain, strip**   Cloth-wrapped polyethylene structures about an inch wide and 4″ to 6″ deep, laid in shallow trenches to remove surface water

**Drain, subsoil pipe**   A system of perforated pipe laid in gravel-filled trenches beneath the topsoil

**Drain, trackside sand**   A pipe drain installed along the inner circumference of a running track to drain both the track surface and the enclosed field area; perforated pipe is laid in a trench and covered with gravel, then the trench is filled to the surface with 4″ to 6″ of coarse sand

**Drainage, internal**   The downward movement of water into, through, and out of the soil profile, which may be enhanced by means of an installed drain system

**Dry flowables (DF)**   A dry, granular pesticide formulation intended to be mixed with water for application; synonymous with "water dispersible (WD)" and "dispersible granule (DG)"

**Elevation rod**   A surveyor's tool that measures differences in elevations, calibrated either in feet and inches or feet and tenths

**Elevation, spot**   In surveying, the difference in grade between any point and an established benchmark

**Emulsifiable concentrate (EC)**   A pesticide formulation that contains one liquid suspended in another, usually an oil-based pesticide carrier suspended in water

**Endophyte-enhanced varieties**   Grasses whose seeds and tissues contain a fungal endophyte that is beneficial to the overall health of the turf

**Enkamat™**   A protective cover used to prevent turf damage in high-traffic areas

**Entomopathogenic nematodes**   Microscopic, eel-like worms that attack and kill certain insect pests

**Establishment**   All steps taken to promote a viable stand of turf after installing turfgrass seed, sprigs, plugs, or sod

**Ester**   A chemical formulation that is oil-soluble, and therefore is typically effective in penetrating waxy leaf surfaces; esters typically react poorly with "hard" water, and are generally more volatile than other formulations

**Evapotranspiration (ET)**   The loss of water from the soil through a combination of evaporation from the surface and transpiration through the plants, sometimes referred to by the abbreviation "ET"

**Extraction procedure**   A laboratory method for determining the proportion of various nutrients in a given soil sample

**Fertilizer analysis**   Percentage by weight of nitrogen, phosphate and potash in a fertilizer product

**Fertilizer, natural organic** A nutrient source of plant or animal origin, typically with low nutrient analysis and requiring soil microbial activity to convert nutrients to plant-available forms

**Fertilizer, synthetic organic** A chemically engineered carbon-based nutrient source, which may be either water soluble or water insoluble

**Field capacity** The upper limit of storable water in a field layer after the water has drained through due to gravity

**Field contour** In sports fields, the overall shape of the field surface, designed to facilitate the movement of surface water away from the playing area

**Field, crowned** A field having an elevated axis down the center and sloped to the sides

**Field, flat sloped** A flat sports field that slopes to one side or to one end

**Field, level** A playing surface which has no slope

**Fills** In the construction of a field or other facility, areas where additional soil is added to achieve the desired contours, in contrast to "cuts," which are areas where soil is removed

**Filter cloth** Loosely woven textile material that is installed between layers of a field or around pipe drain trenches to prevent infiltration of soil particles; sometimes pre-installed on drain pipe, where it is called a "sock"

**Fines** Microscopic particles of sand, silt and clay small enough to pass through a 100 sieve screen

**Finish grade** The process of finalizing the surface contours of a field in preparation for installation of turf

**Flow-by** Leakage from a sprinkler head due to a worn seal

**Foliar absorption** A method of nutrient uptake through the stomates and cracks in the leaf cuticle

**Foliar burn** Desiccation of leaves due to application of fertilizers or other materials in excessive concentrations

**Foliar feeding** The practice of introducing nutrients through the leaves

**Footprinting** Failure of turf to spring back quickly after foot or vehicular traffic during drought conditions

**French drain** See drain, French

**Fumigant** A pesticide which forms gases that are toxic to plants and animals when absorbed or inhaled

**Fungicide** A pesticide used to control fungi

**Fungicides, localized** A group of penetrant fungicides which enter the plant but undergo very little translocation, and therefore protect only a limited, or "localized" part of the plant

**Fungicides, penetrant** Fungicides that are absorbed into a plant. See Penetrants

**Germination** The initiation of growth in primary root and shoot systems from which a plant develops; requires the uptake of water by the seeds

**Gibberellic acid (GA)** A plant hormone used in seed priming to speed germination

**Gibberellin**   Plant hormone that influences cell elongation, photoperiod response, and chilling tolerance

**Grade**   A slope or gradual incline, or to achieve such a slope by use of earthmoving equipment

**Grade stakes**   Stakes driven into the ground at selected points around a field to indicate the desired elevations at each point

**Grass, modular**   Turf that is fixed in sections in rigid trays so that it can be quickly placed on a field, then removed after use

**Growing medium**   See medium, growing

**Growing points**   Also known as meristematic zones, the portions of a plant where new tissues form

**Hardness**   The ability of a surface to absorb energy imparted by an object colliding with it, or its shock-absorbing properties

**Hashmarks**   The short lines on a football field, perpendicular to the five-yard lines, which divide the field lengthwise into three sections

**Height of the instrument (HI)**   In surveying, the sum of the benchmark elevation and a rod reading at the benchmark, from which all subsequent readings are subtracted to establish elevations (The benchmark elevation may be established from older surveys, or may be arbitrarily assigned to provide a consistent basis for comparison.)

**Herbicide**   A pesticide used to control unwanted vegetation

**Herbicide, non-selective**   A herbicide that kills all plant tissues that it contacts

**Herbicide, post-emergent**   A herbicide that is applied to control weeds after their germination and emergence from the soil

**Herbicide, pre-emergent**   A herbicide that is applied to turf to control germinating weed seeds

**Herbicide, selective**   A herbicide that targets a specific weed or group of weeds with minimal effects on desirable plants

**Hub**   A 2″ by 2″ stake used by surveyors

**Hybrid**   A cultivar created by crossing two individuals with dissimilar genetic makeup

**Hybrid, interspecific**   A hybrid created by crossing two different species within the same genus; many bermudagrasses popular for sports turf use are interspecific hybrids of *Cynodon dactylon* and *C. transvaalensis*

**Hybrid, intraspecific**   A hybrid created by crossing two plants within the same species; many seeded bermudagrass cultivars are hybrids of *C. dactylon* varieties

**Hydrated Lime**   A lime source used to raise soil pH; characterized by high burn potential and rapid soil pH response

**Hydraulic conductivity**   Water permeability

**Hydrology**   The study of the behavior and characteristics of water on the surface of the earth

**Hydrophobic**   In turfgrass culture, a term used to describe soil that tends to repel water, instead of allowing it to pass through the surface into the rootzone; often a symptom of excessive thatch, or improper mixing of soil materials

**Infield** Strictly speaking, the area inside the bases of a baseball or softball diamond; in common usage, also refers to the adjacent skinned areas

**Infiltration** The downward entry of water into the soil

**Inoculum** A pathogen or part of a pathogen which can cause disease

**Insecticide** A pesticide used to control insects

**Installed drain system** A system of pipe drains or strip drains designed to collect and remove water from the surface or the soil profile

**Installed irrigation system** See irrigation system, installed

**Integrated cultural management (ICM)** The process of managing sports turf by considering and analyzing all environmental factors, pests, maintenance processes and player-applied stresses which affect the health of the turfgrass culture

**Interceptor drain** See Drain, interceptor

**Internal Drainage** See Drainage, internal

**Interpacking** In sand which contains particles in a variety of sizes, a process of compaction which can reduce the permeability of the sand

**Interspecific hybrid** See hybrid, interspecific

**Intraspecific hybrid** See hybrid, intraspecific

**Irrigation** The process of supplying water to a stand of turfgrass or other plant culture

**Irrigation system, installed** A network of underground pipes and pop-up sprinklers controlled by manual or automatic valves, which supplies water to a playing field or other designated area

**Irrigator, rain gun** A large stationary or movable impact-type sprinkler used to irrigate turf areas

**Irrigators, quick coupler** A series of underground pipes connected by quick couplers, with valves activated by a "quick coupler key," or by the attachment of a removable sprinkler

**Irrigators, traveling** A rotating sprinkler attached to a hose, which moves itself by gradually reeling in the extended hose, or by propelling itself along a wire (also referred to as a "reel irrigator")

**Laser grading** The use of laser devices to assist in the construction of fields with the desired contours

**Laser level** See level, laser

**Lateral lines** Non-pressure pipes that connect the control valves to sprinkler heads

**$LC_{50}$** Lethal concentration of a substance that kills half of the test organisms in an acute study

**$LD_{50}$** Lethal dosage of a substance that kills half of the test organisms in an acute study

**Level** In surveying, an instrument used in combination with an elevation rod to read differences in grade

**Level, automatic** A surveyor's level which the operator sets by centering a bubble within a circle; when turned, it automatically re-levels itself to allow quick and accurate readings

**Level, laser**   A level, which can be used by one person without assistance, and which uses a laser beam and special elevation rod to assure precise readings

**Liming agent**   A material applied to soil to increase its pH, making it less acidic

**Lip**   On a baseball or softball diamond, a slightly elevated ridge in the turfgrass adjacent to a sinned area, caused by the intrusion of skinned area soil into the turf, which can prevent proper drainage and inconsistent ball response; also referred to as a "mounded ridge"

**Loam**   A type of soil comprised of moderate amounts of sand, silt and clay

**Localized penetrant**   A fungicide which enters the plant but has little mobility within the plant, and therefore protects only a limited, or "localized" part of the plant

**Longitudinally**   Lengthwise

**Macronutrients**   Nine nutrients required by turf in large quantities: nitrogen, phosphorus, potassium, calcium, magnesium and sulfur are soil-derived; carbon, hydrogen and osygen are derived from carbon dioxide and water.

**Macropores**   Large pore sizes in soils that drain freely by gravity

**Magnesium carbonate**   A lime source commonly used to raise soil pH; characterized by low burn potential and slow soil pH response

**Management allowable depletion (MAD)**   The maximum acceptable depletion of water from a given turfgrass stand

**Material safety data sheet (MSDS)**   A federally mandated written description of the action of a product, with instructions on cleaning up spills and treating accidental exposure

**Measure line**   An invisible line on a running track, used to determine the distance that a runner will travel

**Mechanical stresses**   Stresses applied by the physical action of objects that transmit force onto a surface, such as the feet of players on a playing field

**Medium, growing**   The soil, sand or other material in which plants have their roots, and from which they are drawing water, air and nutrients

**Meristematic zones**   The growing points at stem or root apices

**Mesh elements**   A material made up of small sections of synthetic mesh which is added to soil to increase stability

**Micronutrients**   Seven nutrients required by plants in small quantities: manganese, iron, boron, zinc, copper, molybdenum, and chlorine

**Micropores**   Small pores that retain water and do not drain freely by gravity

**Monocots**   Plants that emerge from the seed with one cotyledon (seed leaf); grasses are monocots

**Monostand**   An area of turfgrass made up of one species of plant

**Mounded ridge**   See lip

**Mower, flail**   Mowers with pivoting blades or flails that spin at high speed around a horizontal axis

**Mower, reel**   A mower that shears the grass between a blade on a spinning reel and a bedknife at the base of the cutting unit

**Mower, rotary** A mower that cuts by the impact of a horizontal spinning blade

**Mower, tri-plex** A reel-type mower consisting of a set of three spinning reels with bed knives working in tandem to cut a wide swath

**Mowing, vertical** (Also known as verticutting) The use of a device with blades that cut vertically into the turf canopy to sever lateral stems, thin grass and dethatch

**Mycelia** Branching threadlike filaments forming the main growth structures of fungi

**National Turfgrass Evaluation Program (NTEP)** A program administered by the USDA (usually in cooperation with land grant universities) for analyzing the overall performance of various turfgrass cultivars in several locations

**Native soil** Unamended soil of the type normally found in a specified area

**Natural organic fertilizer** See fertilizer, natural organic

**Nematicide** A pesticide used to control nematodes

**Nematodes** Soil-borne, microscopic, worm-like animals, some of which attack the root systems of plants

**Nitrogen, water insoluble (WIN)** A form of fertilizer in which the nitrogen is not readily available for uptake by plants, and which provides sustained color and growth response, extended response duration and low foliar burn and leaching potential; WIN sources are typically more expensive per pound of nutrient than water soluble nitrogen (WSN) sources

**Nitrogen, water soluble (WSN)** A form of fertilizer in which the nitrogen is readily available for uptake by plants, and which provides quick color and growth response, limited response duration and high foliar burn and leaching potential; WSN sources are typically less expensive per pound of nutrient than water insoluble nitrogen (WIN) sources

**No encroachment zone** In playground design and construction, the necessary free space which must be left around a piece of equipment to allow its safe use

**No-till soil preparation** A process of preparing soil for planting without tilling; the goal of this method is to maintain soil structure

**One-third rule** A rule for mowing in such a way to encourage healthy turfgrass culture: cut off no more than one-third of the leaf blades at any one cutting

**Overseeding** The application of additional turfgrass seed to existing turf; in the warm season zone, fall overseeding of cool season turfgrasses into bermudagrass to provide an actively growing turf for winter and spring sports; in the cool season zone, turfgrasses are overseeded (usually with the same cultivar or species) to improve turf density, often in combination with slicing the turf to promote seed:soil contact

**Particle size distribution** In a soil or sand sample, the range and variety of particle sizes

**Pathogen** Any agent which causes disease

**Pea gravel** Uniformly sized washed gravel ranging in size from ⅛″ and ⅜″ and containing minimal amounts of sand, silt and clay

**Peat** A commonly-used organic amendment, consisting largely of undecomposed (or only slightly decomposed) organic matter which accumulates under conditions of excessive moisture

**Penetrant**    A class of pesticides which are absorbed into the plant; also known as "systemic" pesticides

**Penetrants, acropetal**    A class of fungicide that enters the plant and is translocated upward within the plant through the xylem by way of the transpiration stream

**Penetrants, localized**    Penetrant fungicides that move into the leaf tissues and remain near the point of entry

**PENNFOOT**    A device developed at Penn State University and used to measure rotational and linear traction on turfgrass

**Perched water table**    Layered soil conditions which retard the movement of water downward through the soil

**Percolation**    The downward movement of water through the soil

**Perennial**    A plant that can reproduce numerous times over several growing seasons

**Perlite**    An inorganic substance sometimes used as a soil amendment

**Permanent wilting point**    Percentage of water remaining in a soil when irreversible wilting occurs

**Permeability, water**    The movement of water into and through the soil as measured in inches per hour; also referred to as "hydraulic conductivity"

**Pest**    In turfgrass management, any living organism that competes with turfgrass plants for nutrients, light, water, air, and space to the degree that it adversely affects the performance of the turfgrass; examples include weeds, insects, fungi and nematodes

**Pesticide**    A general term for chemical agents used to destroy pests, control their activity, or prevent them from causing damage

**Pesticide resistance**    The gradually acquired ability of a particular group of pests to withstand the application of pesticides which would have effectively controlled other populations of the same organism

**Pesticides, general use**    Pesticides which may be legally used by the general public

**Pesticides, restricted use**    Pesticides which may be legally used only by licensed applicators

**Photodegradation**    Breakdown when exposed to sunlight

**Phytotoxicity**    The quality of being toxic to plants

**Pipe drain**    See drain, pipe

**Pitot tube**    A gauge used to measure operating pressure at the sprinkler head of an irrigation system

**Plant growth regulator (PGR)**    A chemical agent applied to plants to suppress their growth

**Plugging**    The process of installing turfgrass by planting rooted pieces or "plugs" of live turf, which will be encouraged to spread over a desired area

**Point of connection (POC)**    The point at which an irrigation system taps into the main water supply line

**Polyacrylamide gels**    A synthetic polymer sometimes used as a soil amendment because of its ability to hold water

**Polypropylene fibers**   Fibers of specially formulated plastic used as a soil amendment because of their ability to add stability to the soil

**Polystand**   An area of turfgrass made up of more than one species

**Portable vibration analyzer**   A device used for measuring the hardness of soil

**Post-emergent herbicide**   See herbicide, post-emergent

**Precipitation rate**   The rate, expressed in inches per hour, at which water is applied to the surface of a field

**Precipitation, matched**   A characteristic of a properly operating irrigation system which is providing the same amount of water to an entire field

**Pre-emergent herbicide**   See herbicide, pre-emergent

**Pregermination**   A method used to reduce seed germination time; seed is soaked or placed in a moist environment to encourage partial germination, then planted as soon as possible to prevent desiccation; addition of gibberellic acid to soaking water can enhance the process

**Preventive application**   The application of pesticides before the outbreak of disease or an infestation, usually on turf that has a history of such outbreaks or infestation

**Probe, soil**   A tool that removes a small core sample 4″ to 6″ deep

**Profiler, soil**   A tool used for removing an intact sample of the soil profile approximately 1″ × 4″ and 8″ deep to allow accurate assessment of the thatch and root zone

**PTO**   Power Take Off—a fitting on a tractor or other vehicle allowing the application of power from the engine to other tools and attachments

**Pure live seed (PLS) percentage**   Calculated by multiplying grass seeds' purity percentage by its germination percentage

**Rain gun**   See irrigator, rain gun

**Raveling**   The loss of material on an asphalt surface

**Reconstruction**   The process of destroying an existing facility and rebuilding it in a substantially improved fashion

**Reel irrigator**   See irrigator, traveling

**Renovation**   In sports fields, the process of restoring a field to its original condition after it has undergone the stresses of a competitive season

**Restricted use pesticides**   Pesticides whose application is limited to certified pesticide applicators or employees of a certified applicator

**Rhizomes**   An underground, horizontally growing plant stem which produces both upwardly growing shoots and new roots from nodes; distinguished from a root in that it has buds and nodes

**Rod reading**   In surveying, a comparative elevation taken using a level and elevation rod; a lower reading means the grade is higher at the point where the rod is placed and vice versa

**Roller, sheepsfoot**   An earth-tamping machine with distinctive knob-like protrusions on the surface giving it its name; widely used in road-building and similar construction, it causes too much compaction to be appropriate for sports field applications other than building running tracks

**Roller, vibrating**    An earth-compacting implement with combines vibration with weight to increase the compaction of the soil; widely used in road-building and similar construction, it causes too much compaction to be appropriate for sports field applications other than building running tracks

**Rootzone**    The layer of soil in which the roots of the turfgrass plants are found, and from which they must draw air, water and nutrients

**Rubber**    The pitcher's plate in baseball, located on top of the pitcher's mound

**Rubber chips**    A loose material of virgin or recycled rubber which is used as a surfacing material for playgrounds; a more finely ground version is used to install all-weather tracks

**Sand particle stability**    The relative resistance of sand to weathering or fracturing

**Sand, calcite**    See calcite sand

**Sand, concrete**    A sand made up of particles having a variety of sizes

**Sand, masonry**    A sand with most of its particles in the medium to fine grades (.1 mm to .5 mm)

**Scarify**    The process of loosening the surface of the ground in preparation for seeding, sprigging or sodding; sometimes performed on subsoil before the installation of topsoil to promote the drainage of water downward between layers; term is also used to describe the chemical or mechanical scratching of the seed coat (typical of zoysiagrass) to improve germination

**Seeding, dormant**    See dormant seeding

**Seeding, slit**    See slit seeding

**Shear vane**    An instrument used to measure traction on natural turfgrass

**Sheepsfoot roller**    See roller, sheepsfoot

**Sieve screen**    A screen used to strain soil and related materials; materials are sometimes classified according to the fineness of screen they can pass through

**Silt**    A soil material made up primarily of microscopic soil particles ranging in size between .002 mm and .05 mm

**Skinned area**    The portion of a baseball diamond which is kept intentionally free of vegetation to promote uniformity of ball response

**Skinned area soil**    A planned mixture of sand, silt and clay used on baseball and softball skinned areas which allows for firm footing, uniform ball response and efficient runoff

**Slicing, soil**    The process of cutting vertically into the soil to cut horizontal stems and promote aeration; slicing equipment is used in the process of slit-seeding

**Slip fix**    A PVC telescoping repair part, designed to replace a section of existing irrigation pipe

**Slit seeding**    The process of spreading seed over established turf, and making slits in the turf canopy with a soil slicer to promote seed:soil contact

**Sodding**    The process of installing mature turf in rolls or sections, as opposed to spreading seed or sprigs over a prepared area of bare soil

**Sodding, dormant**    See dormant sodding

**Soil aggregates**   Soil consolidated by natural forces to form larger particles of mixed composition

**Soil porosity**   The characteristic of having air-filled spaces between the particles of soil, expressed as a percentage of the volume of soil not occupied by solid particles

**Soil profile**   A vertical section of the soil through all its layers and extending into its growing medium; term is also used to refer to the corresponding layer of a baseball field skinned area

**Soil reaction**   The degree of acidity or alkalinity of soil expressed as a pH value; low pH indicates acidic soil, high pH indicates alkaline soil

**Soil solution**   The liquid phase of the soil containing the ionic forms of elements that are released from the soil components or other soluble materials

**Soil stability**   The ability of soil to deal with mechanical stresses and moisture without losing its soil structure and turning into mud

**Soil strength**   The ability of soil to resist displacement by an external force such as cleats or tires

**Soil structure**   The combination or arrangement of soil particles into aggregates

**Soil textural triangle**   A triangle diagram illustrating the range of particle sizes for the twelve textural classes of soil

**Soil texture**   The relative coarseness or fineness of a soil, determined by the relative proportions of sand, silt, and clay particles

**Spalling**   The loss of material on an asphalt surface

**Spiking, soil**   The process of using equipment with blade-like protrusions to puncture vertically into the soil, cutting horizontal stems and promoting aeration; differs from slicing in that spiking punctures are not continuous openings in the soil like the slices created by slicing equipment

**Spot application**   Application of a pesticide only to those portions of an area which show evidence of infestation

**Spot elevation**   See elevation, spot

**Spreader, centrifugal**   Also called a rotary spreader, a device used to apply seed, fertilizer and other granular materials

**Spreader, drop**   An agricultural implement used to spread granular material over an area by allowing it to fall through openings of a specific size

**Sprigging**   The process of vegetatively establishing turfgrass by spreading rhizomes or stolons over a prepared seed bed and pressing them into the soil to promote sprig:soil contact; primarily used in warm season zones

**Stolons**   Creeping, above-ground stems which take root at the nodes to form new plants

**Stresses, turfgrass**   Any force that tends to strain or damage the turfgrass culture; examples include drought, extreme temperatures, pests, and the mechanics of player traffic

**Strip drains**   See drains, strip

**Striping**   Creating an esthetically pleasing striped pattern on a field by mowing, rolling, or the application of iron in alternating stripes

**Sub-base**   Layer of soil beneath the topsoil of a sports field, or under a running track, bocce court or other surface; sometimes referred to as "subsoil"

**Subgrade**   The set of contours established by arranging the subsoil to allow the installation of a layer of topsoil, aggregates, asphalt, sand or other material to achieve the desired finish grade of a project

**Subsoil pipe drain**   See drain, subsoil pipe

**Subsoiler**   A piece of equipment used to loosen the subsoil

**Surface firmness**   The ability of a sports field surface to support competition or maintenance processes without being compromised

**Surfactant**   A chemical additive that improves the spreading, dispersing and/or wetting properties of pesticide mixtures

**Surveying**   The determination of the boundaries and elevations of a specified piece of land by means of measuring angles, distances, and elevations

**Suspension**   A dispersion of solid particles in a liquid, differing from a true solution; in spraying, a suspension must be agitated to keep the particles uniformly dispersed during application

**Swale**   A valley-like excavation, wider than it is deep, designed to conduct surface water away from a facility, toward a catch basin or low-lying area; differs from a ditch, which is deeper than it is wide

**Synthetic organic fertilizer**   See fertilizer, synthetic organic

**Syringing**   The process of lightly watering turf, mainly to cool the turf canopy

**Testing, tissue**   See tissue testing

**Thatch**   An intermingled layer of living and dead grass stems, roots, and other organic matter, found between the soil surface and the grass blades

**Thrust blocks**   Poured-in-place concrete blocks that protect an irrigation system's pipe connections

**Tissue testing**   The chemical analysis of plant leaves to determine the level of nutrients present in the plants

**Topdressing**   The addition of sand or soil to the surface of the turf to level the turf surface and promote thatch decomposition

**Total station**   A digital laser surveying instrument used by professional surveyors

**Touchline**   Sideline of a soccer field

**Track, all-weather**   A running track with an asphalt or concrete base that is topped with a coating of rubber chips that are bonded together with a cementing agent

**Track, cinder**   A track constructed by spreading fine cinder or other fine aggregate material over a sub-base

**Trackside sand drain**   See drain, trackside sand

**Traction**   Adhesive friction, or the ability of a foot to remain securely in one place without slipping, while force is applied to it

**Traction, linear**   Traction as experienced when force is applied in a straight line

**Traction, rotational**   Traction as experienced when force is applied by pivoting

**Transit**   A surveying instrument used to set a straight line and an angle to that line

**Transitional zone**    A turfgrass climatic zone comprising roughly the central third of the United States, in which both northern and southern turfgrass varieties can be successfully cultivated

**Transit-level, digital**    An electronic surveying instrument that serves as both a transit and a level

**Transit-level, manual**    A manual surveying instrument that serves as both a transit and a level

**Turf, artificial**    Synthetic turf made from either tufted, knitted, or woven polypropylene fibers

**Turning point**    In surveying, a hub used on hilly terrain to allow the surveyor's instrument to be moved to another location, where a new height of the instrument (HI) can be established to allow surveying to continue

**Vegetative planting**    Installation of turfgrass by distributing live plant material, such as sprigging, plugging and sodding

**Vermiculite**    A clay mineral sometimes used as an amendment for sand-based soils which is noted for its high nutrient holding capacity and low shrink/swell capacity

**Vertical mowing**    See mowing, vertical

**Viruses**    Disease-causing sub-microscopic organisms

**Volatilization, chemical**    Conversion from a liquid to a gas

**Warm season zone**    A climatic area, roughly corresponding to the southern third of the United States, with its own set of turfgrass varieties; warm season turfgrasses are adapted to maximum growth under temperatures of 80 to 95 degrees F during the growing season

**Warning track**    An area inside the fence of a baseball or softball diamond surfaced with some material other than turfgrass, so that players running onto it will know without looking that they are approaching the fence

**Water hammer**    The violent shaking of an irrigation piping system when it is turned on or off

**Water, available**    The water that can be extracted from the soil by the roots of plants

**Water, unavailable**    Also called non-extractable, water that is present in soil but can't be taken up by plants' roots because it is so tightly adsorbed to soil particles

**Wettable powder (WP)**    A form of chemical agent which is meant to be suspended in water and applied by spraying; small particle size makes them hard to handle and keep suspended in water

**Yardlines**    The short lines on a football field, perpendicular to the sidelines and parallel to the five yard lines, which break the field into 100 (US) or 110 (Canada) even increments

**Zeolite**    A mined soil mineral sometimes added as an inorganic amendment to sand-based soils to improve water and nutrient holding capacity

# *Index*